POSTCOLONIAL GEOGRAPHIES

WRITING PAST COLONIALISM

Series Editor: Phillip Darby, University of Melbourne

The *leitmotif* of the series is the idea of difference – differences between culture and politics, as well as differences in ways of seeing and the sources that can be drawn upon. In this sense, the series is postcolonial. Yet the space the series opens up is one resistant to new orthodoxies, one that allows for alternative and contesting formulations. Though grounded in studies relating to the formerly colonized world, the series will also extend contemporary global analysis.

Books in the series:

The Fiction of Imperialism
Phillip Darby

Settler Colonialism and the Transformation of Anthropology
Patrick Wolfe

POSTCOLONIAL GEOGRAPHIES

EDITED BY
ALISON BLUNT AND
CHERYL McEWAN

BLOOMSBURY
NEW DELHI • LONDON • OXFORD • NEW YORK • SYDNEY

BLOOMSBURY INDIA
Bloomsbury Publishing India Pvt. Ltd
Second Floor, LSC Building No. 4, DDA Complex, Pocket C–6&7,
Vasant Kunj, New Delhi 110070

BLOOMSBURY, BLOOMSBURY ACADEMIC INDIA and the Diana logo are
trademarks of Bloomsbury Publishing Plc

First published in India 2024
First published 2002

This edition published with permission from Bloomsbury Publishing Plc,
50 Bedford Square, London, WC1B3DP, UK

British Library Cataloguing-in-Publication Data
A catalogue record for this book is available from the British Library

Library of Congress Cataloging-in-Publication Data
A catalog record for this book is available from the Library of Congress

ISBN: 978-93-54358-28-9

Typeset by Aarontype Limited, Easton, Bristol
Printed at Manipal Technologies Limited, Manipal

To find out more about our authors and books
visit www.bloomsbury.com and sign up for our newsletters

CONTENTS

LIST OF ILLUSTRATIONS

INTRODUCTION

Alison Blunt and Cheryl McEwan

Writing about his early life in Jerusalem, Cairo, Lebanon and the USA in his memoir *Out of Place*, Edward Said explains that, 'Along with language, it is geography – especially in the displaced form of departures, arrivals, farewells, exile, nostalgia, homesickness, belonging, and travel itself – that is at the core of my memories' (1999: xvi). The story that Said tells of his early life is a spatial story, weaving together memories of place and displacement, dislocation and dispossession, exclusion and exile. While he has explored elsewhere the imaginative geographies of Orientalism, the contrapuntal geographies of culture and imperialism, and the politics of place in the Palestinian struggle, Said's memoir is a deeply personal geography that traces the inescapable, and often fraught, interplay between a sense of place and a sense of self. But, as Said shows, senses of place and self are neither fixed nor bounded, and while both are located at local and individual scales, they also exceed these immediate limits. By writing that 'just as none of us is outside or beyond geography, none of us is completely free from the struggle over geography' (Said, 1993: 7; also see Gregory, 1995), Said points to the intensely political nature of place and to the complex intersections of both place and politics with identity. *Postcolonial Geographies* addresses the ongoing struggle over geography as both discourse and discipline and investigates the intersections of place, politics and identity in colonial and postcolonial contexts. Each chapter seeks not only to decolonize the geographical constitution and articulation of colonial discourses in both the past and present, but also to decolonize the production of geographical knowledge both in and beyond the academy.

Postcolonialism and geography are intimately linked. Their intersections provide many challenging opportunities to explore the spatiality of colonial discourse, the spatial politics of representation, and the material effects of colonialism in different places. As Ashcroft *et al.* put it, 'Every colonial encounter or "contact zone" is different, and each "post-colonial" occasion needs … to be precisely located and analysed for its specific interplay' (1998: 10), so geography should clearly lie at the heart of postcolonial critiques. While postcolonial studies have inspired new ideas, a new language, and a new theoretical inflection for a wide range of teaching and research in human geography, geographical ideas about space, place, landscape and location have helped to articulate different experiences of colonialism both in the past and present and both 'here' and 'there'. And yet, although an increasing range of geographical teaching and research is located within a broadly postcolonial context, there have been few sustained discussions about what might constitute a postcolonial geography (although see Blunt and Wills, 2000; Clayton, forthcoming). At the same time, although spatial images such as location, mobility, borderlands and exile abound in postcolonial writings, more material geographies have often been overlooked. Reflecting and extending the productive connections between postcolonial and geographical thought, this book investigates the geographies of postcolonialism and charts the contours of a postcolonial geography.

Although postcolonial studies have always been intrinsically geographical, it is only in recent years, and particularly over the last decade, that geographers have begun to develop a critical engagement with their theoretical and substantive challenges. As Jonathan Crush explains, the aims of a postcolonial geography are diverse and encompass:

> the unveiling of geographical complicity in colonial dominion over space; the character of geographical representation in colonial discourse; the de-linking of local geographical enterprise from metropolitan theory and its totalizing systems of representation; and the recovery of those hidden spaces occupied, and invested with their own meaning, by the colonial underclass. (1994: 336–7)

Despite early studies of colonialism and imperialism as part of a broader Marxist critique of the capitalist world economy (Blaut, 1975; Hudson, 1977), and despite more recent geographical work that investigates and critiques postcolonial geographies of globalization and development (Corbridge, 1993; Crush, 1995; and see McEwan, 2002, for an overview), most postcolonial geographical research remains largely cultural and/or historical in focus. This focus is, to a large extent, reflected in *Postcolonial Geographies*, although the chapters by Morag Bell and James Sidaway address wider concerns including poverty and philanthropy in a globalizing world. Postcolonial geographical research to date has concentrated on a number of intersecting themes, including: the imperial production of geographical knowledge through, for example, school textbooks, exploration and fieldwork; geographies of encounter, conquest and colonization; geographies of colonial representation, particularly in travel writing, photography, maps and exhibitions; the production of space in colonial and postcolonial cities; the gendered, sexualized and racialized spaces of colonialism, colonial discourse and postcoloniality; and geographies of diaspora and transnationality through the movement of people, capital and commodities. Each chapter in *Postcolonial Geographies* engages with at least one, but usually more, of these themes. So, for example, Claire Dwyer explores the ways in which diasporic geographies of home are gendered in particular ways for young British Asian women, while Richard Phillips shows how the regulation of sexuality across the British Empire was closely tied to the exercise of British imperial rule and the networks of knowledge on which it relied. Through his focus on the Antarctic expeditions of Amundsen and Scott, John Wylie shows how it is possible to write very different histories and geographies of exploration that attend both to an embodied mobility and to the landscape itself. By combining an imaginary narrative alongside other intertextual sources about the Empire Exhibition in Johannesburg in 1936, Jenny Robinson addresses not only the visual spaces of the exhibition in its colonial urban setting, but also considers the racialized politics of representation, history, and identity.

The book as a whole, and each chapter within it, are thus located on a number of thresholds between postcolonialism and geography. The notion of a threshold is particularly apt in representing not only the connections and flows within and between postcolonial and geographical thought, but also in articulating a politics of location within such movement and interchange (and, for an exploration of similar thresholds between geography and feminist theory, see Jones *et al.*, 1997). An emphasis on the spatiality of postcolonial thought can help to move beyond the impasse of thinking primarily in temporal terms. The 'post' of 'postcolonialism' has two meanings, referring to a temporal aftermath – a period of time *after* colonialism – and a critical aftermath – cultures, discourses and critiques that lie *beyond*, but remain closely influenced by, colonialism. These two meanings do not necessarily coincide, and it is, in part, their problematic interaction that has made 'postcolonialism' such a contested term. Focusing on the temporal difference between a colonial past and postcolonial present not only obscures colonial and neocolonial inequalities that persist today, but can also obscure the power relations between colonizer and colonized. Moreover, defining the world purely in terms of western expansion, and studying people and places purely because they have been colonized, means that 'colonialism returns at the moment of its disappearance' (McClintock, 1995: 11). As Ania Loomba suggests, 'it is more helpful to think of postcolonialism not just as coming literally after colonialism and signifying its demise, but more flexibly as the *contestation* of colonial domination and the legacies of colonialism' (1998: 12, emphasis added). In a similar way, Jane Jacobs writes, 'Postcolonialism may be better conceptualised as an historically dispersed set of formations which negotiate the ideological, social and material structures of power established under colonialism' (1996: 25). As the chapters in this book all show, postcolonialism should also be understood as a *geographically* dispersed contestation of colonial power and knowledge.

While it is important to challenge a temporal binary between a colonial past and postcolonial present, it is also important to challenge a spatial binary between colonial centres and postcolonial margins. The effects of colonialism were, and are, not just one-way, transported from metropolis to colony. Rather, as Loomba writes:

> Postcolonial studies have shown that both the 'metropolis' and the 'colony' were deeply altered by the colonial process. *Both* of them are, accordingly, also restructured by decolonisation. This of course does not mean that both are postcolonial *in the same way*. Postcoloniality, like patriarchy, is articulated alongside other economic, social, cultural and historical factors, and therefore, in practice, it works quite differently in various parts of the world. (1998: 19)

Loomba suggests that thinking about difference in spatial rather than temporal terms can help to represent postcoloniality in more effective ways. As she puts it:

> imperialism, colonialism and the differences between them are defined differently depending on their historical mutations. One useful way of

> distinguishing between them might be to not separate them in temporal but in spatial terms and to think of imperialism or neo-imperialism as the *phenomenon that originates in the metropolis, the process* which leads to domination or control. Its result, or what happens in the colonies as a consequence of imperial domination is colonialism or neo-colonialism. (ibid.: 6)

But this vision of a postcolonial geography reinscribes a binary distinction between metropolis and colony that risks obscuring complex internal colonialisms as well as the multidirectional effects of colonial power. In contrast, the chapters in this book explore internal as well as external colonialisms (particularly the chapter by Karen Morin, who considers the postcolonial geographies of the American West) and the spatial dynamics of colonial power both within and between metropolis and colony. Two central concerns of the book include the ways in which geographical knowledges and networks have been closely tied to the exercise and imaginings of colonial power and the mobile locations of colonial and postcolonial subjects in domestic, urban, national and diasporic spaces. These concerns resonate not only with the structure and organisation of the book, but also with the locations of its contributors. While not all of the contributors are British and not all live in Britain, the majority work in British universities. Many of the chapters were first presented as papers at a conference on Postcolonial Geographies held at the University of Southampton in 1998, which was organized by the editors and supported by the History and Philosophy of Geography Research Group of the Royal Geographical Society (with the Institute of British Geographers). Unlike many other edited volumes and readers on postcolonialism, this book is unusual in its metropolitan focus, written from a former heart of empire. But this location is clearly neither fixed nor bounded. With contributors based in England, Scotland, and Northern Ireland, the volume includes chapters written from different parts of an increasingly devolved UK. At the same time, the chapters span South Africa, India, Australia, the USA, Portugal, Antarctica, and Britain itself, reflecting the transnational extent of postcolonial geographies. Crucially, many contributors explore how geographical knowledges and imaginations produced in Britain and its empire were mutually constituted, and how the mobile locations of both colonial and postcolonial subjects transcend a spatial binary between home and away.

One of the major dilemmas for postcolonialism is the charge that it has become institutionalized, representing the interests of a Western-based intellectual élite who speak the language of the contemporary Western academy, perpetuating the exclusion of the colonized and oppressed. Perhaps this is a charge that might be levelled at this collection from some quarters. While all of the contributors are located within the Western academy, this location should prompt questions about the nature and geographies of academic production and how these relate to power/knowledge. Moreover, this situatedness does not preclude attempts to produce critical work exploring these relationships. As James Sidaway (this volume) argues, postcolonial geographies themselves might be problematic and even ironic, but they do hold out possibilities of allowing a critical reflection on knowledge production and how to confront difference. These concerns are at the core of this book. *Postcolonial Geographies* traces the critical interfaces between postcolonial and geographical thought, exploring the diverse geographies of colonial power and discourse by interrogating the colonial production of space, destabilizing imaginative geographies of empire, and disrupting the hierarchy of colonial centres and margins.

Postcolonial Geographies is organized into three parts: postcolonial knowledge and networks; urban order, citizenship and spectacle; and home, nation and identity. Each part combines theoretical and empirical analysis in chapters that are both historical and contemporary in focus. *Postcolonial Geographies* thus differs from two recent and important books on postcolonialism that are notable, in part, for their geographical organization. In *Postcolonial Discourses*, Gregory Castle explains that he has adopted a 'regional approach', reflected by the titles of five of the six main parts of the book: 'Indian nations', 'African identities', 'Caribbean encounters', 'Rump Commonwealth', and 'The case of Ireland' (Castle, 2001). At the same time, Robert Young's important historical introduction to postcolonialism is also structured geographically, with chapters entitled 'Latin America' I–II, 'Africa' I–IV, and 'India' I–III (Young, 2001). Complementing these two books, *Postcolonial Geographies* is organized thematically rather than regionally. One reason for this organization is to show that, while postcolonial geographical work might lead to a revitalized and critical regional geography, its implications for understanding the spatial dynamics of power, identity, and knowledge extend far beyond any regional limits. Another reason for its thematic rather than regional organization is to reflect the common concerns that cut across different postcolonial geographies and thereby to reveal both continuities and differences over space and time. Each part therefore ensures a wide geographical scope that ranges over metropolitan powers (Britain, Portugal and the USA), settler colonies (both South Africa and Australia), other imperial spaces and territories (including British India and Antarctica), and diasporic homes (particularly Britain, the USA, and Australia). The focus and main themes of each part of the book are introduced more fully in three separate introductions.

CONCLUSION

In many ways, *Postcolonial Geographies* is a response to the criticism that greater theoretical sophistication has created greater obfuscation, and that postcolonialism is too theoretical and not rooted enough in material contexts (Ahmad, 1992; Dirlik, 1994). Critics suggest that an emphasis on discourse detracts from an assessment of material ways in which colonial power relations persist. As the chapters in this volume attest, discourse itself is intensely material, as shown by examples ranging from the ordering of imperial and postcolonial urban spaces, to the material realities of travel and emigration, to concerns with embodiment, identities, cultural politics and reconciliation. Of course, *Postcolonial Geographies* is intended only as a beginning. There are absences here just as there are absences in postcolonial studies more widely, and two are of particular note.

First, although one of the key aims of the book is to locate postcolonial geographies on material rather than solely textual or abstract terrains, these terrains themselves remain largely, but not exclusively, limited to European imperialism in the nineteenth and early twentieth centuries and its legacy today. Much work needs to be done that investigates not only the geographies of pre-modern colonialisms, but also studies the exercise of colonial power by other empires located within Asia and Latin America (Jones and Phillips, 2001). Second, although *Postcolonial Geographies* reflects the particular importance of cultural and/or historical research to date, there is much scope for economic and development geographies to consider the relationships and tensions between postcolonialism and global capitalism.

This book represents some of the key debates taking place in postcolonial studies at present and how these debates are informing and, in turn, being informed by geography. The breadth and scope of *Postcolonial Geographies* reflect the vitality not only of postcolonial work in the discipline of geography, but also the spatiality of postcolonial studies in disciplines beyond geography. The chapters reflect the diversity of postcolonial geographies and the critical importance of postcolonial perspectives in analysing space, power, identity and resistance. Although postcolonialism might not have had much impact on the power imbalances between North and South, the diverse body of approaches identified as postcolonial are a significant advancement and offer a great deal to the possibilities of a meaningfully decolonized geography. Postcolonial approaches demonstrate how the production of western knowledge is inseparable from the exercise of Western power. They also attempt to loosen the power of Western knowledge and reassert the value of alternative experiences and ways of knowing. They articulate clearly some difficult questions about writing the histories of geography, about imperialist representations and discourses, and about the institutional practices of geography itself. Postcolonialism has an expansive understanding of the potentialities of agency, sharing a social optimism with other discourses, such as those surrounding gender and sexuality in Western countries (and we should not forget that rethinking here has helped generate substantial changes in political practice). Therefore, despite the seeming impossibility of transforming North–South relations by a politics of difference and agency alone, the chapters in this volume demonstrate that postcolonialism is a much-needed corrective to the Eurocentrism of some geographical writing.

PART I

POSTCOLONIAL KNOWLEDGE AND NETWORKS

INTRODUCTION TO PART I

Geography is a part of those dominant discourses of imperial Europe that postcolonial critiques seek to destabilize because they are unconsciously ethnocentric, rooted in European cultures and reflective of a dominant Western worldview. A key feature of postcolonial approaches is the attempt to problematize the very ways in which the world is known, challenging the unacknowledged and unexamined assumptions at the heart of European and American disciplines that are 'profoundly insensitive to the meanings, values and practices of other cultures' (Gregory, 1994). A fundamental aspect of postcolonialism is challenging the experiences of speaking and writing by which dominant discourses come into being and understanding the spatiality of power and knowledge. Spivak (1990) has shown that practices of speaking and writing are not innocent, but are part of the process of 'worlding', or discursively setting apart certain parts of the world from others. Knowledge is a form of power and, by implication, violence; it gives authority to the possessor of knowledge (Said, 1978). Knowledge has been, and to a large extent still is, controlled and produced in the West; the power to name, represent and theorize is still located here. These issues inform many of the chapters in this book but are the explicit concern of the chapters in Part I.

These theoretical concerns and the challenges posed to geography by postcolonial studies are at the heart of James Sidaway's chapter, which also reflects on the importance and difficulties of writing postcolonial geographies. Sidaway expands upon some of the debates about the 'postcolonial' that were raised in the introduction, exploring its various and contested meanings and the ways in which the term has been deployed within geography and social theory more broadly. Mindful of this diversity of meaning, Sidaway presents a speculative geography of the varied and complicated senses (and non-senses) of the conditions and approaches purported to be described by the term postcolonialism. He draws on Chakrabarty's (1992a) contentions to argue that the location and development of geography, like history, inescapably mark it (both philosophically and institutionally) as a Western-colonial science. Thus, calls for a postcolonial geography are perhaps both ironic and impossible. However, as Sidaway argues, the paradoxes of geographical encounters with the 'postcolonial' also hold out promising possibilities, in particular, being aware of what it means to confront difference and reflecting again on how geographical knowledges are constructed.

Imperial and geographical discourses are also the focus of Alan Lester's chapter, which examines the importance of analysing the flows of capital, material, information and ideas that connected the British metropole with the wider colonial world. The implication in a great deal of postcolonial theory is that colonial discourse emanated from the metropole alone. Lester seeks to challenge this assumption and argues for a more spatialized and grounded postcolonial understanding through a focus on the circuits of knowledge traversing the imperial terrain. He draws on a specific case study of the Cape Colony in South Africa and its connections with Britain to explore how social boundaries were progressively reformulated and discourses of citizenship adjusted in both metropolitan and colonial sites. A 'knowledge' of immutable class, race and gender difference, elaborated mutually by the bourgeoisie in the metropole and settlers at the colonial peripheries during the era of mass industrialism, came to constitute colonial discourse. Thus, Lester demonstrates that scientific racism and eugenics became discursively entrenched not primarily as the result of metropolitan imaginings, but from material and discursive exchange between metropolitan and colonial sites.

Lester's focus on the scripting of imperial knowledges is developed further in Richard Phillips' chapter on imperialism, sexuality and space. Through his focus on purity movements in the British Empire, Phillips explores the imperial regulation of sexuality and the uneven geographies of knowledge, control, and resistance. The study of imperial sexualities is more advanced in history and post-colonial studies than in geography, and Phillips offers a timely analysis of the spatiality of sexual regulations on embodied, national and imperial scales. He does so by exploring both formal and informal networks of knowledge and the multiple, and often ambivalent, locations of sexual subjection and resistance in British India and settler colonies such as Australia.

Debates about knowledge and spatiality are also explored in Morag Bell's discussion of twentieth-century discourses of international philanthropy and her examination of the possibilities of postcolonial theorizations of social and political sciences (including geography). Bell argues that these discourses are part of a broader discourse of 'useful' knowledge, central to the public power of which is the immediacy, urgency and moral authority that they have assumed through an emphasis on philanthropic concern and governability. By reference to the Second Carnegie Inquiry and the production of 'useful' knowledge about poverty in South Africa and the USA, the chapter examines how, at particular moments during the twentieth century, scientific beliefs and cultural technologies have been deployed to extend the meaning of quality of life beyond a concern for the body to questions of citizenship both within and beyond the state. In exploring these links between normative science and relational ethics, Bell highlights the complexities of international humanitarian impulses within the North, the anxieties and uncertainties underlying these impulses and raises questions about postcoloniality and alternative formulations of time. As with Sidaway's chapter, the concern here is to critically examine the ways in which knowledge and power are conceptualized and to revisit North–South encounters through a postcolonial framework.

1

POSTCOLONIAL GEOGRAPHIES

SURVEY-EXPLORE-REVIEW

James D. Sidaway

'Postcolonialism' or 'the postcolonial' has figured as a significant marker of geopolitical and cultural debate and difference in the last few decades of the twentieth century. In human geography in the 1990s, the term 'postcolonial' has cropped up in many different texts that seem to use it to signify rather different things. The presence or absence of a hyphen is one point of difference, for some would emphasize the break between colonialism and a postcolonial condition or stance, while others might chose to focus on the continuity (postcolonialism). In the context of such an array of postcolonialisms, what follows offers a tentative, partial and speculative geography of the varied and complicated senses (and non-senses) of postcolonial geographies.

Some of the tentativeness originates in the important sense in which any 'mapping' of the 'postcolonial' is a problematic or contradictory project. This arises from the impulse within postcolonial approaches to invert, expose, transcend or deconstruct knowledges and practices associated with colonialism, of which objectification, classification and the impulse to chart or map have been prominent. The prospect of 'exploring' or 'surveying' postcolonial geographies that is promised in the title is intentionally contradictory and ironic. Like calls for a postcolonial history (Chakrabarty, 1992a), any postcolonial geography 'must realise within itself its own impossibility', given that geography is inescapably marked (both philosophically and institutionally) by its location and development as a western-colonial science. It may be the case that Western geography bears the traces of other knowledges (Sidaway, 1997) but the convoluted course of geography, its norms, definitions, inclusions, exclusions and structure cannot be disassociated from certain European philosophical concepts of presence, order and intelligibility. Feminist and poststructuralist critiques have sometimes undermined these from within, but can never credibly claim to be *straightforwardly* outside or beyond those institutions and assumptions that have rooted geography amongst the advance-guard of a wider 'Western' epistemology, deeply implicated in colonial-imperial power.

I begin with some reconsideration of different and diverse demarcations of the postcolonial. The focus on diversity necessarily leads to critical consideration of how societies may be described as postcolonial (in the sense of formal independence) but experience or exercise continued neocolonial or imperial power and/or contain their own internal colonies. The initial mapping of the varied and complicated senses of postcolonialism thus becomes a review of neocolonialism, internal colonialism and imperialism. While this is a selective and inevitably limited tour through overwhelmingly English-language academic sources, the last section returns briefly to the (im)possibility and promise of some other postcolonial geographies.

(RE)DEMARCATIONS OF THE POSTCOLONIAL

For Arif Dirlik (1994: 329), the term 'postcolonial' is: 'the most recent entrant to achieve prominent visibility in the ranks of those "post" marked words (seminal among them, postmodernism) that serve as signposts in(to) contemporary cultural criticism'. Already something of an intellectual and publishing phenomenon, it has come to be deployed in a variety of ways. As Ashcroft *et al.* (1995: 2) point out, 'the increasingly unfocused use of the term "post-colonial" over the last ten years to describe an astonishing variety of cultural, economic and political practices has meant that there is a danger of it losing effective meaning altogether.' But rather than fearing excess or loss, perhaps we should celebrate the open constellation of meanings associated with a term that crops up in academic writings, journalism and literature. A few examples follow.

In a review of a novel by the (UK-based) Zanzibari writer Abdulrazak Gurnah, Maya Jaggi (1996: 11) notes how 'The novel's outrage at the "petty hardships" of African shortages and blocked toilets, and its satire on obscenely self-serving leaders, is uncompromising. Yet Gurnah is acutely aware of the hazards of raging against post-colonial Africa.' Similarly, in a newspaper article about conflict in Northern Ireland, Robert Fisk (1994: 7) refers to the formation in the 1970s of 'a power-sharing "executive" in Belfast endorsed by London and Dublin which proved to be as fragile as those other post-colonial power-sharing governments in Cyprus and Lebanon'.

Northern Ireland may be a particularly ambiguous case, but in the references to Cyprus, Lebanon and Africa, Fisk and Jaggi are using the term 'post-colonial' to signify a particular form of state or society, one that is a *successor* to (yet derives some of its parameters from) colonialism. Sometimes too this is broadened to refer, in a related fashion, to the 'post-colonizers'. For example, when Anna Marie Smith (1994: 14) refers to the fact that

> When [the racist British politician Enoch] Powell campaigned against black immigration in the late 1960s and early 1970s, and when Thatcher successfully translated an unnecessary and distant military skirmish [in the Falklands/Malvinas] into legitimation for her domestic policies, both figures were addressing Britain's postcolonial condition.

Elsewhere, however, the term postcolonial is being granted a rather different (though related) application. For Stephen Sleman:

> Definitions of the post-colonial, of course, vary widely, but for me the concept proves most useful when it is not used synonymously with a post-independence historical period in once-colonised nations, but rather when it locates a specifically anti- or *post-* colonial *discursive* purchase in culture, one which begins in the moment that the colonising power inscribes itself onto the body and space of its Others and which continues as an often occluded tradition into the modern theatre of neocolonialist international relations. (1991: 3)

Yet until recently, 'postcolonial' has usually been used to describe a condition, referring to peoples, states and societies that have been through a process of formal decolonization. This is what Fisk or Jaggi denote in the quotations above, or roughly what Alavi (1972) was seeking to describe in an agenda-setting essay on 'the state in post-colonial societies'. Until the later part of the 1980s these were the most frequent uses of the term, and they endure as a mark of geopolitical status (Mbembe, 2001). However, the quotation from Sleman provides an example of the way that postcolonial is also used to signify aesthetic, political and theoretical perspectives (which have mostly been elaborated in literary and cultural theory). In these senses, postcolonial approaches are committed to critique, expose, deconstruct, counter and (in some claims) to transcend the cultural and broader ideological legacies and presences of imperialism. In literary criticism this has meant re-reading 'canonical' texts to reveal how the backdrop of colonial power and its social and 'racial' relations are variously diffused through, structure and frame them, even those that may appear on the surface to have nothing to do with issues of empire or colonialism. More specifically, however, it is also about the possibility and methods of hearing or recovering the experiences of the colonized (in literary terms, to broaden the range of texts that are studied to include more contributions representing the experiences of colonized peoples).

This later set of meanings (though with significant precedents in earlier anti-colonial politics and writings) are arguably the most challenging and potentially significant for the content and nature of cultural and academic production, as recent surveys such as Williams and Chrisman (1993), Pieterse and Parekh (1995), Hall (1996), Rattansi (1997), Loomba (1998), Mignolo (2000) and Ashcroft (2001) have argued. However, such challenges will be conducted against a set of longer-established issues, topics and political debates about an historical–geographical condition of postcolonialism. The latter, more 'traditional' senses of postcolonialism deserve a re-airing and reassessment, particularly in the context of a widely shared sense of a shifting world order.

The relative amnesia regarding the 'old' debates about postcolonial states and politics in the 1970s has been noted by Aijaz Ahmad (1995: 1), who expresses 'a peculiar sense of *déjà vu*, even a degree of fatigue', on coming across the current discussions of postcolonialism in the domain of *literary* theory in so much as the 'term resurfaces in literary theory, without even a trace of memory' of earlier debates about the conditions of postcolonial states. Ahmad perhaps overstates the amnesia, for many writing literary theory are all too well aware of those prior (and continuing) discussions. However, at times the two sets of uses of the term do appear to follow separate tracks. This chapter insists on linking (or at least juxtaposing) them and recognizes that:

> It is not that one conceptual frame is 'wrong' and the other 'right', but rather that each frame only partly illuminates the issues. We can use them as part of a more mobile set of grids, a more flexible set of disciplinary and cross-cultural lenses adequate to the complex politics of contemporary location, while maintaining openings for agency and resistance. (Shohat and Stam, 1994: 41)

Given the breadth and complexity of such an agenda, what follows can do no more than serve as a selective review, and as set of suggestions and pointers. I am acutely aware that a whole series of issues (for example, that of diasporic geographies) remain either underspecified or are barely touched upon here (see Cohen, 1995 and Ong, 1999 and Dwyer, this volume). Nor are gendered differences in the experiences of and literature about postcolonialism given systematic consideration here (see Yuval-Davis, 1997 and McClintock, 1995). There can be no simple or singular format for the kind of exercises this chapter conducts. Therefore, the resulting contrasts between different treatments of the 'postcolonial', both within this chapter and between its presentations and those of other texts, should be seen as a potential source of analytical departures, debates and reconceptualizations.

POSTCOLONIAL GEOGRAPHIES: MAPPING POSTCOLONIALISMS

In an abundantly suggestive essay, Anne McClintock (1995) insists on the need to be careful not to use the term postcolonial as though it described a single condition. This plea is echoed by Loomba, who describes how:

> imperialism, colonialism and the differences between them are defined differently depending on their historical mutations. One useful way of distinguishing between them might be to not separate them in temporal but in spatial terms and to think of imperialism or neo-imperialism as the phenomenon that originates in the metropolis, the process which leads to domination or control. Its result, or what happens in the colonies as a consequence of imperial domination is colonialism or neocolonialism. (1998: 6)

I draw upon some of these arguments as departure points, taking up a number of the issues they raise about the multiplicity of postcolonial conditions. In this respect McClintock (1992: 87) describes postcolonialism as 'unevenly developed' globally. In her terms:

> Argentina, formally independent of imperial Spain for over a century and a half, is not 'postcolonial' in the same way as Hong Kong (destined to be

independent of Britain only in 1997). Nor is Brazil 'post-colonial' in the same way as Zimbabwe.

Furthermore, she draws attention to complications presented by those societies which were subject to imperial power, but not *formal* colonies. This is true for much of China (though to add to the complexity it was divided into quasi-colonial spheres of influence and fell into the domain of the Japanese empire). Certainly, places such as Anatolia and Persia, Ethiopia, the interior of Arabia, Afghanistan, Thailand and Tibet, disrupt any conception of the south as essentially postcolonial. It should be added that the colonial epoch is not by any means *the* defining feature of other societies with longer historical trajectories. The dynasties of India and China spring first to mind, but the point is valid much more widely. In this respect, writing about the treatment of South American histories, Harris (1995: 20) points out that one of consequences of the increased recognition in the social sciences and humanities of the importance of colonialism has been 'to reinforce the self-importance of Europeans'. What she means is that other histories which do not see the coming of the Europeans as an historical axis on which 'pre' and 'post' colonial periods can be constructed are further marginalized. This paradox leads Harris to conclude that:

> My argument is not that we should dismiss the coming of the whites in historical analysis, but recognise that usually this moment is treated not as a historical fact with consequences that must be investigated inductively, but as a transcendental event upon whose axis history is created, a rupture from which fundamental categories of periodisation and identity are derived. (1995: 20)

The status of the post-Soviet and post-Yugoslav republics and, for that matter, European states that have succeeded empire in the twentieth century (such as Albania or Ireland) raises some further problematics. Stephen Howe's (2000) extensive survey of academic and political debates about Ireland and empire has indicated just how tangled and contested these can be. I should also mention here, in passing, that much of Europe has, at one time or another, been subject to imperial rule (Hapsburg, Ottoman, English, French and, briefly, Italian Fascism and German Nazism). More widely, Robert Bartlett's (1994: 3) account of conquest, colonization and cultural change in medieval Europe contains an analysis of 'English colonialism in the Celtic world, the movement of Germans into Eastern Europe, the Spanish Reconquest and the activities of crusaders and colonists in the eastern Mediterranean'.

Bartlett claims to demonstrate:

> Conquest, colonization, Christianization: the techniques of settling in a new land, the ability to maintain cultural identity through legal forms and nurtured attitudes, the institutions and outlook required to confront the strange or abhorrent, to repress it and live with it, the law and religion as well as the guns and ships. The European Christians who sailed to the coasts of the Americas, Asia and Africa in the fifteenth and sixteenth

> centuries came from a society that was already a colonizing society. Europe, the initiator of one of the world's major processes of conquest, colonization and cultural transformation, was also the product of one. (ibid.: 313–14)

Such legacies reverberate throughout the textures (and themes) of 'Europe' (see Halperin, 1997). Yet, Gibraltar and Northern Ireland aside, imperialism and colonialism in Europe have recently been most obvious or evident in the contemporary 'Balkan wars'. Writing of former Yugoslavia, Neil Smith (1994: 492) notes how:

> Yugoslavia presents an interesting entrée in any discussion of geography and empire. First it resides in Europe, generally accepted to be the font of imperial ambition in recent centuries, yet it finds itself a casualty of empire. Secondly it lies on the edge of European and Asian imperia, its original nationhood resulting as much from the defeat of the Ottoman as from the Hapsburg empire. More recently, the genocidal implosion of Yugoslavia was precipitated by the collapse of the Soviet empire. And further, the ethnic cleansing of Sarajevo and Gorazade is in large part about the nostalgic reassertion of a nineteenth-century Serbian empire.

An influential strain of debate has stressed the way that the political and ecclesiastical fractures from the days of the Roman imperia coincide with significant lines of fragmentation in the contemporary Balkans. Thus it is with some reluctance (but a certain relief), given the limited problematic of this essay, that I leave aside more direct consideration of premodern empires. Some connecting threads do inevitably emerge, to the extent they also figure in our times – in all kinds of spectres, 'revivals' and invented 'traditions' that make quasi-mythical uses of 'the past'.

Returning, however, to the comparative themes raised by Russian-Soviet 'imperial' strategy, it can be argued that the Soviet successor states are symptomatic of postcolonial states more widely. Of course it is notable that it has long been amongst the *raisons d'être* of Western 'Sovietology' to demonstrate that the USSR was merely the latest form of great-Russian imperialism. Two 'classic' examples by British commentators are Seton-Watson (1961) and Conquest (1962). Both these impassioned polemics against Soviet/Russian imperialism register (or attempt) a certain *displacement* of a North–South geopolitics of decolonization onto an East–West Cold War axis. The script is roughly as follows: Britain and other West Europeans are now good decolonizers, Russia cynically backs Third World liberation while continuing to exercise its own imperialism. Russian colonialism is therefore the real imperial force in the 1960s: not the West. Such claims are made just a few years after the British–French–Israeli intervention at Suez (and while Britain was still an imperial force to be reckoned with in the 'Middle East') and at a moment when the US intervention in Vietnam was gearing up. A variation of this script was also produced by commentators in other European powers in the 1960s and 1970s, notably in France during the Algerian War and in fascist-colonial Portugal (see Sidaway, 1999a). Yet, like many Cold War clichés, these charges of 'Soviet imperialism' reflected (albeit in a distorted and one-dimensional manner) something of the experiences of Soviet governance. In more recent times, Roman Szporluk (1994) is one of a number of observers to consider the imperial, postimperial or postcolonial elements of the Soviet successor states. He prudently argues that the new postcolonial or postimperial status does not define politics in the former USSR, for the much debated 'transition' from state socialism combined with (formal) 'democratization' are registered as more significant elements of the current conjuncture. However, for Szporluk (1994: 27), the peoples of the former USSR are: 'facing the dual task of coming to terms with the legacy of the communist "counterparadigm of modernity" and their imperial legacy. These issues are not easily separated, although the difference is clear enough.'

There is no scope here for further consideration of the relevant historical trajectories and literature concerning them. However, a feature that is particularly evident in the non-Russian territories of the former USSR, but which is also paradigmatic (though to enormously variable degrees) for other postcolonial states, deserves further comment. This concerns the way that the (imperial) processes of the USSR were *constitutive* of nationalities and of those broader apparatuses of governance which were destined to become the post-Soviet states. In the USSR this took a particular format, through the 'Leninist' nationalities policy and Stalin's highly arbitrary application of it. The Soviet Union was not simply a project of imperial Russification (even though this was always significant) nor simply an alternative (non-capitalist) modernity. The USSR certainly embodied these things. But, critically, it was also a system for managing multiple ethnicities and the inheritance of a dynastic realm. This procedure included the granting of titular nationality to its non-Russians and a formal federal structure. Once Soviet power weakened, these provided the units that became the new states.

It is true many of these units date back, in very loose terms, to before the establishment of the Russian empire. But their particular configuration was overdetermined by the imperial and Soviet experiences (and reactions to them). 'Postcolonial' Tajikistan or Armenia, and other Soviet successor states, thereby share a key feature with those longer-established 'postcolonial' states of South and South-East Asia, Africa and Latin America. This concerns the extent to which basic 'structures' (including formal boundaries) and a good deal in their political configuration have emerged out of the colonial experiences, while not being simply reducible to outcomes of colonialism.

Having said this, proper recognition of the enormously complex relations between resistances to and complicities with the colonial is also essential. In this context, Said (1993) insists that colonial discourses frequently overlook resistances and rebellions that accompany colonialism. Homi Bhabha (1990) has shown the coupling or co-presence of 'colonial' and 'anti-colonial' discourses, confronting the combined 'ambivalence, mimicry and hybridity' of 'anti-colonial' subjectivities (and movements). Therefore, even if, 'as he enacts what he describes, at times Bhabha's discourse becomes as incalculable and difficult to place as the colonial subject itself' (Young, 1990: 156), Bhabha's works serve to move beyond some of the earlier *oversimplifications* that tended to characterize a previous generation of critical psychoanalytical and political studies of colonial situations and anti-colonial movements.

Adding to such messy complexities is the necessity for any critical 'mapping' of postcolonialisms to take into account a variety of contemporary internal colonialisms and colonial occupations. In McClintock's polemical words:

> Currently, China keeps its colonial grip on Tibet's throat, as does Indonesia on East Timor, Israel on the Occupied Territories and the West Bank, and Britain on Northern Ireland. Since 1915, South Africa has kept its colonial boot on Namibia's soil . . . Israel remains in partial occupation of Lebanon and Syria, as does Turkey of Cyprus. [Therefore] None of these countries can, with justice, be called 'post-colonial'. (1992: 88)

Indeed, 'internal colonialisms' are virtually a characteristic of state formation and as such have generated a substantial literature beyond Latin America where commentators first drew systematic attention to the appearance of this form of colonial relation (Kay, 1989). In addition to the deployment of the concept to refer to the structural position of African Americans (Carmichael and Hamilton, 1967) and Native Americans (Garrity, 1980; Churchill and LaDuke, 1992), works such as Michael Hechter's (1975) *Internal Colonialism: The Celtic Fringe in British National Development, 1536–1966* have developed and reapplied the analytical category of the 'internal colony'. Hechter's book did not pass unnoticed by geographers (Williams, 1977; Rogerson, 1980; Drakakis-Smith and Williams, 1983, for example) and it has also influenced later critical political studies of the UK such as Tom Nairn's (1977) brilliant study of the morphology of the British state. Thinking about internal colonialisms also requires consideration of the ways that colonial categories and discourses are reimported into the wider politics of the metropolitan powers, where they then crop up in racist discourses and practices as well as disseminating into other images of, for example, the unruly classes (or the nonwhite 'inner city'; see McGuinness, this volume) as some kind of 'uncivilized', 'dark' forces beyond some imagined 'urban frontier'.

More specifically, however, the words of the Kurdish writer Ismet Sheriff Vanly poignantly express the (multiple) tragedies of many 'internal colonialisms':

> Within the artificial frontiers inherited from imperialism, many Third World states practise a 'poor people's colonialism'. It is directed against often sizeable minorities, and is both more ferocious and more harmful than the classical type. The effects of economic exploitation are aggravated by an almost total absence of local development and by a level of national oppression fuelled by chauvinism and unrestrained by the democratic traditions which in the past usually limited the more extreme forms of injustice under the old colonialism. (1993: 189)

One might reasonably question Vanly's notion that these internal colonialisms are really 'more ferocious' or 'unrestrained' than, for example, French counter-insurgency in Algeria, Japanese military imperialism in Asia or German settler-colonialism in Namibia. Nor are such internal colonialisms unrelated to the 'machinations' of, for example, US strategy, which has aided some such occupations as part of its wider system of alliances (for example, in the cases of Indonesia in East Timor; Israel in Gaza, the West Bank and southern Lebanon; and Turkey in northern Cyprus). More will be said below of this US role.

At this point, I will simply reiterate the striking way that internal colonialism has evolved in a number of avowedly 'postcolonial' states. In the more severe cases, 'postcolonial' states have, almost at their 'founding moments' (a moment that cannot be contained, nor separated from that which precedes it and which is always being re-enacted by independence days, constitutional amendments and the like as well as the presence of signs and signatures of independence, flags, seals, anthems, and so on), felt it necessary to deny the existence of minorities or to expel or murder large numbers of them, and subject their lands, culture and society to the enduring mode of internal colonialism of the kind that Vanly denounces.

Although China's 'minority areas' of Tibet, Xinjiang and Inner Mongolia might also constitute examples of long-established 'internal colonies' (Sautman, 2000), the Turkish case deserves special comment, if only for reasons of its historical primacy. Turkey was never formally colonized by outside powers, but as the Ottoman empire terminally weakened, Anatolia was about to be dismembered by the European powers. At this moment and under the *Ittihat ye Teraki Cemiyeti* (Committee of Union and Progress) the decaying empire sought to convert itself into a simulacra of a modern state, committing perhaps the first large-scale twentieth-century genocide (in 1915–16) against its Armenian minority and expounding *Türkçülük* (pan-Turkism) (see Landau, 1995). After 1923, under the 'bonapartist' Mustafa Kemal Atatürk, some of the area cleared of Armenians thenceforth became a *de facto* internal colony of the new Turkish 'national state' with a subject Kurdish population. Lest this be misinterpreted as some kind of singling out of Turkey, I will add that this early example of 'ethnic cleansing' has since become one of the first examples of what turns out to be a much more universal phenomenon, a model not only for the Holocaust, but also (on a smaller and less total scale of course) especially pronounced in other 'national states' that succeeded the multinational Ottoman empire.

Many contemporary internal colonialisms are associated with the settler colonization which prevails in breakaway settler colonies (see Gooder and Jacobs, this volume). These are distinguished by their formal independence from the founding metropolitan country, thus *displacing* 'colonial' control from the metropolis to the colony itself. For McClintock (1992: 89): 'The United States, South Africa, Australia, Canada and New Zealand remain ... break away settler colonies that have not undergone decolonization, nor with the exception of South Africa, are they likely to in the near future.'

The historical achievement of the Zionist movement is also a special case of this. Israel therefore shares some key features of other colonial-settler states, notably a frontier/pioneer mentality and dispossession of an indigenous population, while not being simply reducible to such a category (see Rodinson, 1973; Piterberg, 2001). As Edward Said notes:

> In many instances ..., there is an unmistakable coincidence between the experiences of Arab Palestinians at the hands of Zionism and the

> experiences of those black, yellow, and brown people who were described as inferior and subhuman by nineteenth-century imperialists. For although it coincided with an era of the most virulent Western anti-Semitism, Zionism also coincided with the period of unparalleled European territorial acquisition in Africa and Asia, and it was as part of this general movement of acquisition and occupation that Zionism was launched initially by Theodor Herzl. (1979: 68–9)

In Zionist discourse, the Palestinian Arab therefore occupies an analogous place to the 'native' in other colonial discourses:

> The Arabs were seen as synonymous with everything degraded, fearsome, irrational, and brutal. Institutions whose humanistic and social (even socialist) inspiration were manifest for Jews – the Kibbutz, the Law of Return, various facilities for the acculturation of immigrants – were precisely, determinedly inhuman for the Arabs. In his [*sic*] body and being, and in the putative emotions and psychology assigned to him, the Arab expressed whatever by definition stood *outside, beyond* Zionism. (ibid., 88)

However, it is the USA that is probably the most striking example of a breakaway colonial settler society, given its rise to the position of a hegemonic power in the twentieth century, long after the original breakaway colonies had themselves annexed a continent, parts of the Caribbean and Central America and a swathe of the Pacific. The status of the USA and its relationship to postcolonialism are much debated (see Morin, this volume). For some it is the USA as a postcolonial society that is most evident (rather than its persistent internal colonies or contemporary imperial power). This view is perhaps most explicit in Ashcroft *et al.* (1989), which has done much to promote a claim for the analytic utility of the term postcolonial in literary and cultural studies. In their vision:

> Perhaps because of its current position of power, and the neocolonizing role it has played, its postcolonial nature has not been generally recognized. But its relationship with the metropolitan centre as it evolved over the last two centuries has been paradigmatic for postcolonial literatures everywhere. What each of these literatures have in common beyond their special and distinctive regional characteristics is that they emerged in their present form out of the experience of colonization and asserted themselves by foregrounding the tension with the imperial power, and by emphasizing their differences from the assumptions of the imperial centre. It is this which makes them distinctively post-colonial. (Ashcroft *et al.*, 1989: 2)

This may be so. However, for an alternative reading, see Kaplan and Pease (1993), which indicates how things become rather complex, given that the USA itself becomes an imperial centre on a scale the world has never before seen.

Across the Canadian border, Moore-Gilbert (1997: 10) argues that:

> The example of Canada serves to suggest just how tangled and multi-faceted the term 'postcolonial' has now become in terms of its temporal, spatial,

> political and socio-cultural meanings. Here there are at least five distinct but often overlapping contexts, to which the term might be applied.

These contexts are: (1) the legacy of the dependent relationship with Britain; (2) the relative (cultural, strategic and economic) US domination of North America; (3) the issue of Québec; (4) the relationship of the indigenous inhabitants to the various white (Québecois and Anglo) settler colonialisms; and (5) the arrival, role and status of migrants from Asia.

More will be said concerning the US case later, where I concentrate on the analysis of imperialisms. However, at this point it is vital to note that, beyond the USA and Canada, the other states of the Americas also represent evolutions of settler colonies, not least in terms of the political hegemony exercised in a number of Latin American states by predominantly white elites. There is an enormous variation between the southern cone countries (Argentina, Chile, Uruguay) that may be characterized as (largely white) breakaway settler colonies, where the indigenous population has been largely exterminated, and those countries where the majority indigenous populations (Peru, Bolivia, Paraguay and Guatemala, for example) are governed by white-dominated and highly militarized states. Moreover, a closer look at the class and racial hierarchies within different Latin American societies indicates a very considerable variation in extent and formats of exclusion, domination, hegemony, 'mixing' (*mestizaje*) and specificity, which defies simple generalization.

Perhaps the sharpest case of such domination, and therefore a good one to focus on, is the recent trajectory of 'postcolonial' Guatemala, where over 150,000 people have died in political violence (mostly victims of state and quasi-state powers) in the past 40 years. The violent format of Guatemala's recent history is understandable only through reference to the interactions of local reaction and wider neocolonial relations that exist between Guatemala and the USA. The result of this sinister mix is (as elsewhere in Meso-America) captured well in the words of Victor Perera (1992), who refers to an *Unfinished Conquest.* Perera's argument is that the conquest of the Maya peoples of Meso-America is not a singular event that happened 500 years ago. Rather than being a distant (if not forgotten) historical event, 'conquest' is an ongoing process (see also Chomsky, 1993). Perera's account might be seen as exaggerated by those unfamiliar with modern Guatemalan politics. But this thesis bears reading against some passages in James Dunkerley's *Power in the Isthmus: A Political History of Modern Central America.* Dunkerley has noted that:

> From the autumn of 1966, when the campaign was first fully implemented the people of Guatemala were subjected to a policy of systematic state violence. This has certainly evidenced fluctuations, acquiring particular ferocity in 1966–68, 1970–73 and 1978–84, but it has been far more prolonged than in either El Salvador or Nicaragua and cannot simply be treated as the reaction of a regime in extremis. It is estimated that since 1954 no less than 100,000 people have died as a result of political violence, and whilst perhaps half of this number have been killed since 1978, the political culture of assassination and massacre was established much earlier ...,

> the great majority of those killed were not caucasian, middle-class and European in culture; they were 'Indian', indigenous Americans who if they speak Spanish at all do so only as a second or third language, adhere resolutely to their autochonous culture and appear both physically and in their tangible 'otherness' to be oriental. (1988: 430–1)

All this flowed logically from the US-supported counter-insurgency regimes since the (US-directed) overthrow of the leftist-nationalist Arbenez government in 1954. The coordinator of a 3,400-page UN-directed investigation, which was commissioned following 1997 Guatemalan peace accords and formation of a 'Government of National Unity', commented that:

> In no other Latin American country have there been registered as many cases of violations of human rights as here – the report documents 150 000 deaths, 45 000 disappeared and over one million displaced, with over 90% of the killing perpetrated by the armed forces. According to the statistics, Guatemala heads the list. (cited in Rico, 1999: 3, my translation)

The Guatemalan counter-revolution provided 'a model for US destabilization and intervention in the region, being followed by other instances – the Bay of Pigs (1961); invasion of the Dominican Republic (1965); Chile (1973); Grenada (1983); and the campaign against Sandinista Nicaragua – which made it part of a larger and wider pattern' (Dunkerley, 1988: 429). This also gives Guatemala a singular place in the history of contemporary US imperial power in the Americas. Thus, as Walter Mignolo (1996: 685, my translation) has noted, the Latin American experience of 'postcolonialism' has been 'characterized by the tension between the loosening of a decadent colonialism [originating in Iberia] and the emergence of a new type of imperial colonialism emerging from the first independence movement in the Americas [i.e., the USA]'.

The case of US power in the rest of the Americas, or for that matter the roles of Australia in the Pacific or of South Africa in Namibia, also serves to indicate how breakaway settler colonies (in one sense 'postcolonial') themselves may become various imperial or 'subimperial' powers (see Marini, 1972; Simon, 1991; Zirker, 1994). It is above all the various forms of such contemporary neocolonialisms, imperialisms and subimperialisms that allow McClintock to stress that:

> Since the 1940s, the United States' imperialism-without-colonies has taken a number of distinct forms (military, political, economic and cultural), some concealed, some half-concealed . . . It is precisely the greater subtlety, innovation and variety of these forms of imperialism that makes the historical rupture implied by the term 'postcolonial' especially unwarranted. (1992: 89)

Others have made similar criticisms. Miyoshi (1993: 750), for example, argues that: 'Ours is not an age of postcolonialism but of intensified colonialism, even though it is under an unfamiliar guise.' Yet such lamentations of the limits to postcolonialism tend to leave the theorization of (contemporary) imperialism relatively under-developed, usually invoking it simply as a limiting factor that renders incredible and untenable the straightforward assertion that today's is a postcolonial world. The complex social relations and ideologies of contemporary imperialism, therefore, deserve further critical reflection.

CONTEMPORARY IMPERIALISMS

Something of contemporary Western imperialism is evident in some of the international events of the last two decades, most notably the Gulf War and the US interventions in Grenada, Panama, Afghanistan, Somalia and Haiti. Whatever the manifold complexities (let alone the rights and wrongs) of these engagements, from one vantage point, that is in terms of the asymmetry of the technological level of forces pitted against each other, these new Western interventions bear considerable resemblance to classic nineteenth-century colonial wars.

Reflecting on this, some observers (e.g., Callinicos *et al.*, 1994; Furedi, 1994) speak of a 'revived' or 'new' *ideology of imperialism.* Furedi sees 'the emergence of a new more overt Western imperial rhetoric' in the 1990s as:

> the product of three separate but mutually reinforcing causes ... the failure of what has been called Third Worldism (specifically the crisis of a number of postcolonial states, itself a complex affair very much tied to imperial legacies and cold-war weapons flows) ... the emergence of a conservative intellectual climate, which is the product of the decline of other social experiments ... [and] the end of the Cold War, which has removed one of the major restraints on Western intervention. (ibid.: 99)

Furedi's argument is focused on what he sees as the renewal and reinvigoration of cultures of imperialism among the European powers. However, it also echoes many of the themes in Chomsky's (1991) earlier account of post-Cold-War US foreign policy. Even allowing for a degree of polemic in such arguments, there is an undeniable sense in which the combination of such facts as the end of the peculiar 'stability' of the Cold War, the weakening of some Third-Worldist nationalisms and the violent trajectory of some 'postcolonial' societies (perhaps epitomized by Lebanon in the 1980s and by Angola, Afghanistan, Liberia, Sierra Leone, Somalia and Rwanda in the 1990s) provided the frame for a certain rehabilitation of what may be termed 'imperial temperament'. Traces of this temperament can also be found in many social science representations of the 'Third World', particularly of Africa, be they political science and international relations texts (see Doty, 1996) or basic geography textbooks (see Myers, 2001). In such representations, 'Third World' states are frequently seen to lack the putative presence and self-identity of Western statehood. In a schema that has deep colonial lineages, the South is read through a Western lens and seen as suffering from *lack* of the vigour and conduct which originates in and finds its full development only in the West. Doty comments on the perpetuation of this discourse as:

> a sort of cultural unconscious that always comes back to the presumption, generally unstated, especially in more recent texts, of different kinds of human beings with different capacities and perhaps different worth and value. 'We' of the West are not inefficient, corrupt, or dependent on a benevolent international society for our existence. 'We' are the unquestioned upholders of human rights. 'We' attained positions of privilege and authority as a result of our capacities. 'We' of the West are different from 'them.' 'Their' fate could not befall us.' 'They' can succeed only if 'they' become more like 'us.' These intertexts begin with the presupposition of a clear and unambiguous boundary between 'us' and 'them,' between the North and the South, between 'real states' and 'quasi states.' They thus disallow the possibility that rather than being independent and autonomous entities, these oppositions are mutually constitutive of each other. (1996: 162)

In other words, that the apparent violence or 'failure' or 'weakness' of select 'Third World' states is inseparable from the historical and contemporary role and reproduction of the West is thereby obscured (Power, 1998; Sidaway, 2002).

Yet it should be added that recognizing ongoing imperial motives/motifs or practices is not in itself the end of the analytical problems, as any serious engagement with debates about imperialism will reveal. There is, of course, a long history of polemics about the causes, forms and consequences of imperialism (see Brewe, 1980, and, for a geographical reading, Blaut, 1975). Within the Marxist tradition alone, the disagreement is such that Arrighi (1978: 17) could claim that the Marxian theory of imperialism had become 'a Tower of Babel'. Such debates deserve some reconsideration in contemporary circumstances.

Within radical theorizations of imperialism, the main lines of difference have long been between what became known as 'Leninist' arguments that inter-imperialist conflict was an inevitable part of the logic of twentieth-century capitalism and those of Kautsky (1970, originally 1914), who saw the prospects for an ultra-imperialism which involved 'cartelization of foreign policy' whereby leading powers jointly and co-operatively govern the periphery. The inter-imperialist conflicts of 1914–18 and 1939–45, and the elevation of Lenin's polemics to the status of quasi-sacred gospel in the USSR and the international communist movement, meant that Kautsky's ideas were marginalized. However, the growth of multinational capital in the 1960s and 1970s led a number of Marxists to return to Kautsky (for example, Sklar, 1976). At the same time, others claimed to detect a new phase of inter-imperialist rivalry in the rise of Japan, the EEC and the eclipse of US hegemony (Mandel, 1975; Rowthorn, 1975; Kaldor, 1978). More recently, a valuable survey which considers these issues in the new context of a post-Cold-War world has been presented in articles and debates contained in a special issue of *Radical History Review* (1993, Volume 23) under the title of 'imperialism: a useful category of analysis?' In these articles a variety of commentators revisit the concepts of ultra-imperialism first formulated by Kautsky. As has been noted, the notion of ultra-imperialism holds that co-ordination between states and multinational capital will produce a global ultra-imperial system that will displace inter-imperialist contest and by the 1970s, some had argued that since 1945, the role of multinational companies combined with the balance of power produced via the International Monetary Fund (IMF) and World Bank made for just such an ultra-imperialism.

While Haynes (1993) and others writing in *Radical History Review* wish to rehabilitate and rework Kautsky's ideas, they also indicate that the evolution of the global polity during the past 30 years has extended a system of governance and international financial regulation that can neither be captured by versions of the classical Leninist theory of imperialism, nor by theories of ultra-imperialism. As Lipietz (1987: 48) writes, both these sets of theorizations were 'developed in a context of a specific historical reality: predominantly extensive accumulation and competitive regulation in the first countries undertaking capitalist industrial revolution'.

Lipietz suggests a way forward through the critical study of transnational (capitalist) regulation. It is notable that Aglietta (1979) in his original formulation of regulation theory was not systematically able to consider the significance of imperialism, which he referred to as: 'An ambiguous notion not studied in this work' (1979: 29). Subsequently (and despite Lipietz, 1987) imperial and colonial relations have tended to remain relative blind spots within the otherwise vibrant literatures on capitalist regulation. Yet work influenced by regulation theories has indicated how the contemporary system of transnational power might be thought of as manifesting itself as a kind of *phantom state* (Thrift and Leyshon, 1994) of global governance constituted out of the nexus between powers of multinational companies and international finance and the core formal regulatory structures, notably the IMF and the World Bank. There is another echo here of Kautsky.

The IMF and World Bank have become the subject of an already prodigious critical literature on the framework for and impact of so-called 'structural adjustment' (see Mosley *et al.* 1991; George and Sabelli, 1994; Mohan *et al.* 2000). However, they are just one aspect (though perhaps a particularly important one) of what Graham Smith (1994: 63) termed: 'the specific non-national character [of today's imperialisms], associated in particular with the growth of transnational and supranational institutions'. Not only is this irreducible to a single story (see Gibson-Graham, 1998; Kayatekin and Ruccio, 1998), but the geographies of such transnational powers (by the very nature of their highly dynamic and multiform natures) are perhaps rather more difficult to specify than that of classical imperial systems. Referring to a 'new hegemony of transnational liberalism', Agnew and Corbridge (1995: 205) describe a system that is: 'both polycentric and expansionist, and possibly unstable (in some respects)'.

Hardt and Negri (2000, back cover) have argued that:

> Imperialism as we knew it may be no more, but Empire is alive and well ... the new political order of globalization should be seen in line with our historical understanding of Empire as a universal order that accepts no boundaries.

As they explain:

> Our basic hypothesis is that sovereignty has taken a new form, composed of a series of national and supranational organisms united under a single

> logic of rule. This new global form of sovereignty is what we call Empire. (ibid.: xii)

However, when this account is contrasted with other contemporary Marxist texts on the world order (such as Gowan, 1999), the theme of Kautsky's argument with Lenin is being reiterated. One way forward is to examine how the most transnational financial modes of capital may themselves (in their promotional rhetoric and marketing strategies, for example) be read as a contemporary reformulation of colonial idioms. Thus the discourse of 'emerging markets', which has been promoted by Western-led investment funds (in tandem with the World Bank, financial media and elites in certain of the states receiving inflows of speculative investment) is replete with colonial-style images and unreflexive languages of discovery and exploration (Sidaway and Pryke, 2000).

POSTCOLONIAL GEOGRAPHIES: NOT ON ANY MAP

Postcolonial theories have been described as 'an attempt to transcend in rhetoric what has not been transcended in substance' (Ryan, 1994: 82). Despite the kinds of substantial limits specified above, such rejection concedes too much. For a start, 'rhetoric' and 'substance' are too closely mixed up, as has been shown in a wide range of poststructuralist literatures, to which in turn, most versions of postcolonial theory subscribe. Among the insights of these, and of postcolonial theory in particular, is to see knowledge and understanding of, say, (post)colonialism or imperialism, as limited and partial, and thereby to point out the requirement of such 'knowledge' to be sensitive to its limits, its absences and to the possibility of its displacement. With this in mind it seems appropriate here to cite the words of Carole Boyce Davis, who also rejects the term 'postcolonial' as altogether spurious:

> post-coloniality represents a misnaming of current realities, it is too premature a formulation, it is too totalizing, it erroneously contains decolonizing discourses, it re-males and recenters resistant discourses by women and attempts to submerge a host of uprising textualities, it has to be historicized and placed in the context of a variety of historical resistances to colonialism, it reveals the malaise of some Western intellectuals caught behind the posts and unable to move to new and/or more promising re-/articulations. (1994: 81)

In this she joins many commentators, including those cited above (such as McClintock, Miyoshi and Ryan) and others, such as Goss (1996), Parry (1987), Jeyifo (1990), Mukherjee (1990), who are in some way uneasy with or wary of the term 'postcolonial'. Yet for Boyce Davis:

> Each use of a term must be used provisionally, each must be subject to new analyses, new questions and new understandings if we are to unlock some of the narrow terms of the discourses in which we are inscribed. In other

> words, at each arrival at a definition, we begin a new analysis, a new departure, a new interrogation of meaning, new contradictions. (1994: 5)

Her demands for provisional use of terms and concepts, for caution and for a kind of reflexivity are relevant to the challenge of deconstructing Western (imperialist) forms of knowledge (within which, as has been noted, geography has been prominent). There is in this an indication too that seeking the 'whole truth' or a straightforward project or formula for a 'postcolonial geography' reproduces something of the epistemological drive of the colonial project itself. Indeed, creating and completing rational, universal knowledge about the world (earth-writing) was among the quests of colonialism. One cannot simply reject all this and declare victory, any more than we can we simply erase exploration from what is geography (see Wylie, this volume). It is not so easy to get outside something that has arisen as a certain kind of 'world-picturing' (Mitchell, 1988; Costantinou, 1996; Gregory, 1994; 1998).

The term 'world-picture' (*Weltbild*) (attributed to Martin Heidegger) stresses what is common to a good deal of Western representations, which condense, essentialize, summarize and presume to be offering *the* essential 'truth' about their object of scrutiny. Yet, at their best and most radical, postcolonial geographies will not only be alert to the continued fact of imperialism, but also be thoroughly uncontainable in terms of disturbing and disrupting established assumptions, frames and methods. Between the encouragement to rethink, rework and recontextualize (or, as some might prefer, to 'deconstruct') 'our' geographies and the recognition of the impossibility of such reworked geographies entirely or simply escaping their ('Western') genealogies and delivering us to some postcolonial promised land, are the spaces for forms and directions that will at the very least *relocate* (and perhaps sometimes radically dislocate) familiar and often taken-for-granted geographical narratives.

While one starting point for postcolonial critiques is an interrogation of Western geography as sovereign-universal-global truth, it is important to restate here that postcolonial critiques do not offer a simple or straightforward way out of complex theoretical and practical issues and questions. Instead they open layers of questions about what underpins and is taken for granted in Western geographical narratives and how they have been inextricably entangled with the world they seek to analyse and mistaken for self-contained, universal and eternal truths. More poetically, the multiple paradoxes of geographical 'encounters' with and 'explorations' of the postcolonial (in all its guises) can help us, in the words of Lucy Stone McNeece (1995: 47), writing about postcolonial approaches to the works of the greatest of contemporary Maghrebi authors, Tahah Ben Jelloun: 'to become aware of what it means to confront difference, to look again at what we think we know.'

ACKNOWLEDGEMENTS

This is a shortened and updated version of an essay first published as 'Postcolonial geographies: an exploratory essay' in *Progress in Human Geography*

2000, 24:591–612, reproduced with permission from Arnold Publishers. Cheryl McEwan made valuable suggestions on how it could best be reworked for publication here. I have taken the opportunity to correct a number of errors, but I am responsible for any that might remain.

2

CONSTRUCTING COLONIAL DISCOURSE

BRITAIN, SOUTH AFRICA AND THE EMPIRE IN THE NINETEENTH CENTURY

Alan Lester

This chapter argues that an uneven, trans-imperial network of discursive connections was critical to patterns of race and class subordination and domination in Britain, the Cape Colony and other colonial sites during the nineteenth century. As well as suggesting that impersonal colonial discourses were constructed through multidirectional flows of knowledge and representation, the chapter also aims to highlight the agency that individuals – largely middle-class men – exercised in facilitating these flows and in constructing the networks along which they moved.

The main assertion of the chapter is that metropolitan notions of class were inflected by colonial representations of race, as well as vice versa. However, the underlying message is that if one is to comprehend the construction of metropolitan and colonial forms of oppression and discrimination in general, then the binary and hierarchical division between metropolitan and colonial spaces, discourses and practices, which is so often reproduced in accounts of the colonial and postcolonial world, has to be upset. Colony and metropole, periphery and centre, were, and are, co-constituted.

A number of postcolonial scholars have argued that modern metropolitan practices and discourses of race, class and gender domination, rather than being preformed and then projected into and modified by colonial spaces, have been fashioned from the start through their relations with those spaces (Viswanathan, 1989, 1998; Hall, 1992; Said, 1993; Sinha, 1995; Chakrabarty, 2000; see also Bell and Phillips, this volume). Thus, neither former colonies nor former imperial 'centres' such as Britain can be understood as self-contained vehicles of their own history (Burton, 2000). Each place within the imperial and post-imperial frame is 'less an origin than a meeting point ... less a centre than a crossroads' (Driver and Gilbert, 1999: 5).

If the 'metropole' as well as the 'colony' is 'always already a product of wider contacts' (Massey, 1995: 183), then it is only by thinking about power and knowledge within extensive, trans-national or trans-imperial, frames – by thinking about the interconnected historical geographies of the sites studied – that the embedded connections that underpin contemporary power relations can be revealed (Gilroy, 1993a; Stoler and Cooper, 1997; C. Hall, 1994, 1996). While this insight has been widely accepted, it remains to develop a more detailed and materially 'grounded' understanding of the intricately fabricated imperial networks that actually linked colony and metropole together (see Comaroff and Comaroff, 1991; Hall, 1992, 1994, 2000). As Thomas (1994) and Stoler and Cooper (1997) argue, it also remains to identify the nature and extent of the tensions that destabilized colonial power and precluded any homogeneity among colonizers and the projects that they pursued. These tensions were expressed in multiple, contested colonial discourses, each of which travelled through imperial discursive networks via different routes and nodes.

In an attempt to contribute to the agendas of charting discursive circuits and identifying the contested discourses that flowed along them, this chapter examines some of the ways in which British colonial discourses were constructed through the circulation of conflicting representations. It argues that British humanitarians, on the one hand, and settler capitalists and planters, on the other, came to constitute themselves around different 'ensemble[s] of regulated practices' during the first half of the nineteenth century, and thus to generate particular discourses (Foucault, 1991: 69). These discourses were created and recreated out of incompatible projects, to be carried out in a variety of colonial spaces (Thomas, 1994). They were continually refashioned in relation to each other and to the contested politics of the metropole. But they were not produced and reproduced in an impersonal and mechanistic manner. Rather, they were products of a vehemently contested colonial and metropolitan politics in which identifiable bourgeois men, and to a much lesser extent, women, engaged (although see Morin and Berg, 2001). Influential intermediaries between metropolitan and colonial sites of representation, such as Thomas Carlyle and Matthew Arnold, played particularly significant roles in articulating a certain geographical imagination that was bound up with these trans-imperial debates. In doing so, they helped effect meaningful shifts in the relations of power among metropolitan Britons, British colonizers, and those whom they sought to colonize.

HUMANITARIAN NETWORKS

Bourgeois reformers constructed a British discourse of humanitarianism during the late eighteenth and early nineteenth centuries due, at least in part, to their opposition to aristocratic hegemony at both colonial and metropolitan sites. In contrast to an aristocratic identity founded on natural hierarchy, heredity and stasis, middle-class British identity was being constructed around a qualified universalist conception of human nature; of the capacity of each individual, given freedom from confining regulations, to progress spiritually and materially, thus contributing to the greater good of society. A number of interwoven programmes, including evangelicalism, patriotism and abolitionism, informed this middle-class moral code and underpinned its diverse political agendas.

Evangelicalism was one means by which metropolitan middle-class groups, marginalized from 'the world of rank and land', could establish their own 'associations and networks', challenging 'the existing apparatus of power' (Davidoff and Hall, 1987: 73). The incorporation of evangelicalism into a set of hegemonic representations, however, was inextricably connected to Britain's imperial expansion and, in particular, to debates over the slave trade. As Thomas Laqueur has argued, within a nascent evangelical morality, the eighteenth-century concept of individual 'virtue' was being superseded by a notion of collective responsibility for the plight of distant others. This shift was manifested in a 'new cluster of narratives' including fiction, coroners' reports and post-mortems, all of which 'came to speak in extraordinarily detailed fashion about the pains and deaths of ordinary people in such a way as to make apparent the causal chains that might connect the actions of its readers with the suffering of its subjects' (Laqueur, 1989: 176).

This spatially telescoped ethics was conditional upon an awareness of the relations between distant peoples forged by modern capitalist practices – practices that were themselves being stretched further across space. Such relations, of course, reached their extremes of brutality and exploitation in the trans-Atlantic slave trade and an evangelical sensibility required urgent political action to obtain redress for its victims (Haskell, 1985). The abolition of the trade in 1807 served both to secure national atonement for the wrongs that Britons had inflicted on the world through their participation in the trade, and to reinforce patriotic discourse by distinguishing freedom-loving Britons from tyrannical Continental Catholics (Colley, 1992; Oldfield, 1998).

As well as consolidating a particular kind of evangelical Protestant nationalism, abolitionism gave rise to new, spatially extensive techniques of political mobilization. While planters in the West Indies, traders operating out of Bristol and Liverpool, London merchants and parliamentary representatives liaised to defend the trade, the anti-slavery campaign was supported by Baptist missionaries in the West Indies, Quakers in Britain and America, evangelical businessmen and middle-class women in the British provinces, reformist Members of Parliament in London and, for a brief period, large numbers of working-class radicals in Britain's industrial and agricultural towns. The London-based Committee for the Abolition of the Slave Trade mobilized this trans-Atlantic network through books, pamphlets, prints and artefacts, using all the resources that modern print capitalism, the 'birth of consumer society' and the growth of the 'public sphere' put at its disposal (Habermas, 1989; Turley, 1991: 5). This anti-slavery network would be inherited and deployed through the remainder of the nineteenth century by humanitarians interested in the welfare not only of slaves, but of all colonized peoples.

Perhaps one of the most profound instances of bourgeois-led reform 'at home' was the Poor Law Reform Act of 1834. It can usefully be seen, however, in conjunction with colonial developments, and, in particular, with the abolition of slavery itself. The Act was passed during the same year as the emancipation of Britain's colonial slaves and was a manifestation of the same discourse of proper relations between employers and employees. Poor Law reform and the abolition of slavery were each measures designed to head off labourers' revolts by encouraging 'self-exertion'. In each case, this would be achieved 'by forcing "free" labour onto a competitive market', constructing on the one hand, 'a world of autonomous individuals contracting freely', and on the other, 'a landscape of moral discipline and government' (Driver, 1993: 18–19). In Britain that landscape would be filled with workhouses constructed as much like prisons as possible. In colonies like Jamaica and the Cape, it would be peopled by freed slaves who would remain on their masters' farms and plantations, serving a further four years' 'apprenticeship', in order that they might learn the responsibilities of freedom (Holt, 1992).

As far as middle-class British reformers were concerned, then, the enslaved abroad and the poor at home 'occupied similar moral space' and had to be treated in similar, if never identical ways (Daunton and Halpern, 1999: 4). At both metropolitan and colonial sites, bourgeois humanitarians claimed sovereignty over those whom they sought to protect. As Laqueur points out, humanitarians spoke 'more authoritatively for the sufferings of the wronged than those who suffer[ed] [could] speak for themselves' (1989: 179). In speaking for the British labouring classes and the freed slaves of empire, it was by no means a humanitarian intention to elevate them to an equal status in society.

> They would be free to pursue their own self-interest but not free to reject the cultural conditioning that defined what that self-interest should be. They would have opportunities for social mobility, but only after they learned their proper place. (Holt, 1992: 53)

In pursuing a reformist, humanitarian agenda that challenged both aristocratic arrogance and working-class presumption, the trans-imperial British bourgeoisie were simultaneously clarifying 'who was most fit to rule, at home and abroad' (Stoler and Cooper, 1997: 3).

HUMANITARIANS IN THE CAPE

Dr John Philip, superintendent of the London Missionary Society, articulated humanitarian discourse most consistently and eloquently in the early nineteenth-century Cape Colony. John Fairbairn, Philip's son-in-law and the editor of a liberal Cape Town newspaper, was his most influential ally. Both these men were opposed to the military, aristocratic culture through which the Cape was governed. Fairbairn wrote: 'If England is determined to use us only as a depot for the dregs of her Aristocracy – if her surplus Idlers are to be quartered upon us at this rate – we would ... advise our countrymen to avoid these shores' (*South African Commercial Advertiser*, 19 April 1826). But both men were, if anything, even more vehemently opposed to the practices of some 4,000 settlers, who had emigrated from Britain to the Cape frontier as part of a government-sponsored scheme in 1820.

By the mid-1830s, a number of these settlers were investing their capital in the booming enterprise of wool production and export to British mills. They were encroaching eastwards from the colony onto the lands of the independent

Xhosa in search of more grazing land. Philip wrote of his concerns to an American friend:

> the colonists will think of nothing but an extension of territory and more land, so long as they can hope that they will be indulged in their wishes ... the extension of the colonial frontier is attended with ... the destruction of the natives who have been killed in defending their territories, or have perished by the evils which have followed their expulsion. (in Porter, 1999: 353)

In 1835–7, the eastern Cape frontier became a battleground, both in a literal sense as a coalition of Xhosa chiefdoms launched an attack on the settlers in an endeavour to reclaim lost land, and in a metaphorical sense, as contests erupted between and among settlers, officials and humanitarians over the morality of British colonialism in the region.

THE HUMANITARIAN APOTHEOSIS

Once news of the Xhosa attack on the colony reached Britain in 1835, Philip's most useful metropolitan contact, and leader of the parliamentary abolitionists, Thomas Fowell Buxton, realized that it provided an opportunity to bring the attention of metropolitan groups to bear directly on the provocations that had caused it. He moved successfully in Parliament for an enquiry into the practices of British colonialism on the Cape frontier and elsewhere. As the humanitarian former Attorney General of New South Wales, Saxe Bannister, acknowledged when drawing on comparative material from New South Wales and Canada:

> the evils combated [in the Cape] are not confined to one spot, and therefore are unlikely to originate in mere local circumstances ... on the contrary, they are so widely spread as to indicate a deeply rooted origin in our general government of distant dependencies. (Bannister, 1830: 7)

Buxton's Select Committee on Aborigines accordingly brought the relations between officials, settlers and indigenous peoples not just in the Cape, but across southern Africa, the Canadas, Newfoundland, New South Wales, Van Diemen's Land (Tasmania), New Zealand and the South Sea Islands, to the attention of politicians and the public at the 'centre' of empire.

Whether in 'the south and west of Africa, Australia, the islands in the Pacific Ocean, a very extensive district of South America', or in the 'immense tract which constitutes the most northerly part of the American continent', the Committee concluded that:

> the intercourse of Europeans in general, without any exception in favour of the subjects of Great Britain, has been, unless when attended by missionary exertions, a source of many calamities to uncivilized nations. Too often

> their territory has been usurped; their property seized; their numbers diminished; their character debased; the spread of civilization impeded. (*British Parliamentary Papers*, 1837: 5)

The hearings of the Select Committee influenced the Colonial Secretary, Lord Glenelg, himself a member of the reforming Clapham Sect of evangelicals, to appoint Protectors of Aborigines in all the settler colonies, and to renounce the annexation of an extra 7,000 square miles of Xhosa territory that had been seized by the Cape's Governor, Sir Benjamin D'Urban, as punishment for the Xhosa attack. The Secretary of State informed D'Urban that:

> The cost of the war is the least of the causes of regret the continuation of the war would cause the people of Great Britain. Indeed, it is a melancholy and humiliating but an indisputable truth that the contiguity of the subjects of the nations of Christendom with uncivilized tribes has invariably produced wretchedness and decay and not seldom the utter extermination of the weaker party. (in Vigne, 1998: 38)

SETTLER NETWORKS

British settlers in the eastern Cape, many of whom had claimed new farms in the annexed Xhosa territory, felt that their best chance of countering humanitarian representations lay in forging connections with an oppositional Tory counter-discourse in Britain and in making common cause with settlers in other expanding colonies. *The Times* was the leading anti-humanitarian organ within metropolitan politics and also represented the interests of the commercial enterprises trading with Cape Town and Port Elizabeth. In it, the settlers found their most influential metropolitan voice. The paper warned that if reports of an intended withdrawal from the territory seized in the war 'be true, and the savage be permitted to triumph in his deeds of atrocity by any concessions, this signal of our weakness will not be lost upon him'. While withdrawal would certainly be 'destructive to a trade of considerable magnitude', the paper's stated main concern, like that of the Aborigines Committee, was of a more universal nature: 'when civilization and barbarism meet, a shock will be felt, and is the liberal cabinet of Downing – street to decree, in their excessive devotion to a mistaken philanthropy, that the former is to give way?' (*The Times*, 5 January 1836). With Cape settler newspapers such as the *Graham's Town Journal* being extensively extracted and commented upon not just in metropolitan papers, but in the Australian and New Zealand settler presses, colonists in all of these sites, who were waging their own struggles against the Protectors of Aborigines and other forms of humanitarian 'interference', were able to co-ordinate counter-representations of their own. These were founded on a partially 'scientific' rationale for racially exploitative material practice (Lester, 2002a).

Nevertheless, the withdrawal of British troops from Xhosa territory took place and the settlers' mouthpiece, the *Graham's Town Journal* raged that the imperial government seemed to have

> deliberately considered how public opinion in this part of the colony might be most outraged, defied and insulted ... we can scarcely persuade ourselves that ... the subjects of a free, powerful, and enlightened country could thus be treated with such monstrous cruelty and injustice. (26 January 1837, 2 February 1837)

The unsettling prevalence of bourgeois humanitarian discourse in Britain not only derailed immediate settler capitalist projects of expansion onto Xhosa land in the Cape; it also destabilized settlers' notion of 'home'. While most settlers continued to refer to Britain, and specifically to their various places of origin or residence prior to their emigration as 'home', the threat posed by hegemonic metropolitan currents of thought prompted a greater sense of displacement. As one of the most vocal of the settlers complained, Philip and his local and metropolitan humanitarian allies:

> with the assiduity of purpose that Satan himself might envy, have gained their object in persuading our countrymen, to whom we looked for sympathy and succour, that we are monsters. England, instead of protecting us, accuses us, who were born and bred in her bosom, and have the like feelings as the rest of her sons, of cruelty and oppression. (Bowker, 1864: 2)

Such feelings of wounded loyalty, betrayed memory and severed connection, created an instability in British settlers' notions of belonging and a rupture in their narratives of origin that could be countered only by the project of refashioning metropolitan 'public opinion' (see Gooder and Jacobs, this volume).

HUMANITARIAN DISILLUSIONMENT

Much to the subsequent relief of the British settlers in the eastern Cape and elsewhere, the late 1830s marked the beginnings of a truly trans-imperial sense of disillusionment with the humanitarian notion that 'unreclaimed' human subjectivities could be rapidly transformed. This disillusionment with colonized people's capacity to learn the lessons of freedom and civilization began with the experience of the abolition of slavery, and its roots can be located within the ethnocentric and class-bound ontology of humanitarian discourse itself. Abolitionists and their supporters had assumed that, while some freed labourers in the West Indies would make a success of independent peasant agriculture, most would progress towards civilization and 'culture' through continued, disciplined and productive labour on the plantations, and through the adoption of 'respectable', British forms of Christianity (Holt, 1992: 280). Within a few years of emancipation, however, roughly half the black labour force moved off the plantations to cultivate individually owned plots of land. The spread of myalistic forms of Christianity proved a further grave disappointment to the self-proclaimed liberators of the slaves.

As Thomas Holt points out, 'the answer to the question what went wrong in Jamaica ... had consequences beyond its particular boundaries and in domains other than the economic'. It seemed apparent to many humanitarians that, 'released from the restraints of the plantation before new values and social aspirations took hold, the freed people had ... moved ... beyond the reach of civilizing forces, and reverted to African barbarism' (Holt, 1992: 116–17, 146). If humanitarians themselves expressed disillusionment at the results of emancipation in the West Indies, planters and their metropolitan supporters capitalized on the 'lesson'. 'Throughout the 1840s – in parliamentary hearings and debates, in memorials to the Queen, in the popular press – planters succeeded in drumming their particular construction of West Indian reality into British consciousness with little effective rebuttal' (Holt, 1992: 280). Since Jamaican blacks were apparently 'incapable of self-direction and inner restraint', the planters seemed to have proved their point that 'they must be subjected to external controllers. Having failed to master themselves, they must have masters' (ibid.).

Despite a smoother economic transition, the dominant post-emancipation discourse in the Cape was fashioned in conjunction with that in the West Indies. Even William Elliot, Chair of the London Missionary Society and one of the leading metropolitan humanitarian campaigners, wrote that 'the authority of the missionary had been diminished' in the Cape since emancipation, because the freed slaves and indigenous Khoesan escaping their masters on the mission stations 'prefer abundant leisure and unrestrained freedom to those habits of industry and those salutary restraints, which must be sustained and submitted to in ordinary social life' (in Bank, 1999: 374).

If emancipation of the Cape's 'coloured' population had 'failed', subsequent endeavours to pursue the recommendations of the Aborigines Committee concerning other parts of Africa were also to prove disastrous within the very terms of humanitarian discourse. In 1841, Buxton helped organize the Niger expedition 'to attack slavery at its source' by introducing Christianity and 'legitimate commerce' to those parts of Africa most blighted by the practice. The expedition failed miserably as most of the Europeans died of malaria (Brantlinger, 1986). Charles Dickens constructed the exercise as 'the prime example of philanthropic folly' (Lorimer, 1978: 116). In a piece entitled *The Niger Expedition*, Dickens wrote:

> The history of this Expedition is the history of the Past in reference to the heated visions of philanthropists ... to change the customs even of civilised men ... is ... a most difficult and slow proceeding; but to do this by ignorant and savage races, is a work which, like the progressive changes of the globe itself, requires a stretch of years that dazzles in the looking at. (in Brantlinger, 1986: 193)

'News' from the settlers of the eastern Cape frontier during the 1840s reinforced this conviction of the intractability of the African. It contributed to a shift in the terms of imperial debate that facilitated not only the passage of Masters and Servants laws to re-establish controls over freed slaves in a number of colonies, but also the renewed colonization of the Xhosa. With humanitarian-inspired treaties regulating the relationships between Xhosa chiefs and colonial officials, the eastern Cape settlers, and the *Graham's Town Journal* in particular, took the lead in marshalling new representations of humanitarian failures among the

Xhosa and conveying them to Britain and other colonies, where they inflected other local accounts of intractable racial difference (Lester, 2002a). It was through this means that settlers pursued the project of refashioning dominant metropolitan understandings of 'their' colonial space, re-stitching their frayed bonds with 'home'.

Well after the withdrawal of troops from the newly annexed Xhosa territory, settlers continued to organize a series of petitions to the King and subsequently the Queen, to the House of Commons and to the Colonial Secretary, bemoaning missionary and humanitarian 'misrepresentations' (including Grisbrook, 1846). Through the 1840s, the *Graham's Town Journal* published a litany of accounts of stock losses, robberies and murders apparently committed by the Xhosa against unoffending colonists. These accounts were excerpted in metropolitan newspapers such as *The Times*, and circulated among government officials by the settlers' metropolitan allies, most notably by the merchants with whom they traded. The continuing 'plunder' of the colonial margins was represented as proof positive that humanitarian 'experiments' in dealing with the Xhosa were not only misguided, but also fundamentally dangerous. Rather than the frontier being the space of British provocations as the Select Committee had imagined, settlers established through the *Graham's Town Journal* that *their* frontier was a 'space of terror' inflicted by the Xhosa (Taussig, 1992).

When, in 1846, a new governor breached the treaties with the Xhosa chiefs, they were provoked once again to attack the colony. This time, the 'hostile' Xhosa had no British advocates, colonial or metropolitan. The war was almost universally seen as a manifestation of the humanitarians' naivety in assuming that the Xhosa could be civilized, at least in the short term, and of the Xhosa's unwillingness, if not incapacity to 'learn'. The recently occupied territory was conquered once more and re-annexed as British Kaffraria (Lester, 2001).

It was in their transformed representations of the Xhosa and of a 'just' frontier policy during and after this latest war that the Cape humanitarians' loss of faith in an earlier model of colonialism was most dramatically demonstrated. Fairbairn's personal political transition, thought to be 'so very strange!' by Philip's daughter back in England, was indicative (in Mostert, 1992: 872). After the 1846–7 war, Fairbairn, as other humanitarians were beginning to do, rejected his earlier 'idealism'. He now formulated a less sympathetic and more utilitarian political economy. Describing the Xhosa's act of defiance as a 'betrayal', Fairbairn insisted that 'The Caffres have forfeited all claim to forbearance'. It was now necessary to:

> add Cafferland to the dependencies of the Cape . . . both chiefs and people have to learn that the effects of an unjust war are not to end with the termination of actual resistance in the field. They have forced the British government most reluctantly to declare, that not victory but conquest is to be the end of this outbreak. (in Kirk, 1972: 151)

In reassessing the Xhosa's aptitude for civilization within a liberal frame of reference, Fairbairn was carrying out a manoeuvre that was to become characteristic of a 'turn' in liberal thinking within the empire as a whole. He connected the threat posed to colonial Britons by 'uncivilized barbarians' like the Xhosa with that posed to the metropolitan middle classes by the unassimilated elements in British society. Arguing effectively that the middle-classes' accumulation of capital was 'the root of all that strengthens the state and adorns society', he vehemently condemned 'the Chartist rabble' in England at the same time as he dismissed the Xhosa's claim to self-determination. (Kirk, 1972: 57)

INTERSECTIONS: RACE AND CLASS, COLONY AND METROPOLE

Colonial representations like those of the reconstituted Fairbairn became more potent in mid-nineteenth-century Britain precisely because they intersected with, and helped to reformulate, British domestic discourses of class, ethnic and gender difference. In turn, these refashioned discourses underpinned practices of racial domination in the colonies. Respected spokesmen for the British bourgeoisie were becoming frustrated by the 1840s with humanitarian liberalism, insofar as it pertained to Britain itself. Through the reforms that had already taken place, the wealthiest and most 'respectable' of Britain's middle classes had been effectively incorporated within the governing elite. As Evans (1996: 223) argues, 'government based on property [had] not only survived but was strengthened thereby'. The propertied classes feared that further reform might give 'proletarian hordes' the opportunity of exploiting 'bourgeois democracy to make socialism', a spectre that loomed especially large during the unsettling years of Chartist activity in the late 1830s and 1840s (Holt, 1992: 180).

There were a number of indications of a shift in dominant ideas of proper moral and governmental authority associated with this new middle-class orientation. By the late 1830s, for instance, Whig journals such as the *Edinburgh Review* 'were already showing a marked decline in their reforming attitudes, above all through an unquestioned acceptance of the dogmas of political economy'. When presented with the massive Chartist petition of 1842, the reformer Macaulay responded: 'Civilization rests upon the security of property, and to give the vote to those without property would be destructive of the whole of society' (in Saville, 1994: 37–9). The economic crisis and the events of the famine in Ireland in the 1840s, the revolutionary turmoil on the European continent in 1848, and the later association between Fenianism and English radicalism, served only to harden alliances within the propertied classes, and to reinforce demands for the more effective policing of politically radical labouring class elements (Saville, 1994; Thompson, 1988).

Bourgeois reaction in Britain, however, was intimately connected with the struggles that settlers were waging against humanitarian liberalism in the colonies. Colonial emigrants had long sought to emphasize the dangers that they faced when confronting 'unregenerate' groups in the imperial periphery, and they felt that they had lessons to teach the respectable middle classes of Britain about the inherently 'irreclaimable' nature of certain social groups. It was no coincidence that, by the mid-1860s, the *Saturday Review* was pointing out: 'There is too much disposition in English society so far to share . . . Colonial prejudice' (in Lorimer, 1978: 199).

While 'mid-Victorian householders [in Britain] did not require the visible distinctions of race to assign a marked place to their servants' (Lorimer, 1978: 105), 'a repertoire of racial and imperial metaphors' was nevertheless 'deployed to clarify class distinctions' (Stoler, 1995: 104). In the face of continued working-class mobilization, the Liberal Party first attempted to draw a line between those workers who had realistic ambitions to 'respectability', and who were thus deserving of the vote, and the remainder, who were not. In the event, the Tories extended the franchise to 'registered and respectable' working men through the 1867 Reform Act. The concession had the effect of separating those men among the 'lower orders' who could most safely be absorbed into the politics of the ruling classes from the 'residuum', the roughly one-third of the male population, and women, who were still considered to be unfit to exercise citizenship. However, the metropolitan contest over the franchise in the late 1860s was bound up with discussion of irredeemable racial difference in the colonies. In particular, the political debate 'at home' coincided with that over the Morant Bay revolt in Jamaica (Holt, 1992; C. Hall, 1994; Hall *et al.*, 2000).

On the one hand, the radical demonstrators meeting the recalled Governor Eyre, who had been condemned by humanitarians for his violent excesses in repressing the revolt, 'linked [his] brutal repression of Jamaican blacks with the newly inaugurated Tory government's repression of the Hyde Park demonstration [in favour of franchise reform]' (Holt, 1992: 306). On the other hand, though, arrayed against the humanitarians and radicals who condemned Eyre, were men who sought to consolidate and protect white male bourgeois power at each site. For these men, the links between colonial and metropolitan relations of dominance were just as important, but they drew very different conclusions from them. The Morant Bay revolt had taught them, as the *Pall Mall Gazette* put it, that:

> securing civil rights to a people is one thing, and conferring on them political privileges is another; that all races and all classes are entitled to justice, but that all are not fit or ready for self-government; that to many ... giving them to themselves, as we have done, is simply the cruellest and laziest neglect. (in Bolt, 1971: 87)

Through the new property qualifications, not only poorer casual labourers in Britain, but groups such as women, gypsies, criminals and the transient Irish, continued to be defined as unfit for citizenship, just as were the blacks of the empire. Indeed, these metropolitan groups were often represented in popular periodicals, in the speeches and writings of bourgeois spokesmen, and in the accounts of scientific racists in overtly racialized terms (Stepan, 1982; Stoler, 1995; Thorne, 1999). In the way that colonized groups like the Xhosa and others stood in relation to colonial settlers, many of these domestic categories could be referred to as a 'gigantic evil' that 'threatens the civilization to which it is a reproach, is a standing danger to the middle and upper classes, and tends to the deterioration of the race' (*Wesleyan Methodist Magazine*, in Lorimer, 1978: 80).

By the late 1860s, then, the racial differences represented by settlers were intersecting powerfully in Britain not only with dominant representations of class, but with revised notions of gender, ethnicity and criminality. Settlers in the Cape and elsewhere were no longer marginalized by hegemonic metropolitan discourses as they had been in the 1830s. They were not only deriving legitimation from more reactive metropolitan discourses of class, ethnic and gender distinction; they were actively contributing to the debates surrounding them, and thus to their refinement.

THOMAS CARLYLE AND MATTHEW ARNOLD

Thomas Carlyle and Matthew Arnold each played crucial roles in bringing about the trans-imperial discursive shift away from humanitarian liberalism and towards a more reactionary discourse of race and class difference. They did so largely by fashioning conduits through which settler representations could further inform popular metropolitan notions and vice versa. Carlyle's main endeavour, and an extremely influential one, was to reformulate liberal ideology in such a way that it could accommodate ideas of 'natural' difference between properly governing classes and their 'others'. As Catherine Hall (1992, 1994) has shown, his diatribe on the inherent limitations of freed Jamaican slaves, prompted by his personal connections with Jamaican planters, was critical to this reformulation. In his *Discourses on the Negro* (subsequently *Nigger*) *Question* (1849), Carlyle channelled the Jamaican planters' imagery of former slaves 'sitting . . . with their beautiful muzzles up to their ears in pumpkins . . . grinders and incisor teeth ready for ever new work . . . while the sugar crops rot around them uncut', to metropolitan audiences. He addressed the freed labour force directly on behalf of their former masters:

> You are not 'slaves' now; nor do I wish, if it can be avoided, to see you slaves again; but decidedly you have to be servants to those that are born *wiser* that you, that are born the lords of you; servants to the whites, if they *are* (as what mortal can doubt they are?) born wiser than you. (in Holt, 1992: 280–1)

As Holt (ibid.: 282) puts it, 'here was the slaveholder's propaganda in the mouth of one of Britain's most prominent men of letters'.

The lesson of emancipation in Jamaica was one that Carlyle felt had a direct relevance 'at home'. As the 'noisy, turbulent, irreclaimable savagery' of the Irish proved, it was 'not the colour of the skin that determines the savagery of the man'. Rather, it was willful rebellion against 'the laws of Nature'. The only 'true liberty' for those afflicted by such the condition of savagery, be they black Jamaican, Irish or even English, was 'the indisputable and perpetual *right* to be compelled, by the real proprietors of . . . the land, to do competent work for his living. This is the everlasting duty of all men, black or white, who are born into this world' (in Holt, 1992: 281–2).

In Carlyle's *Shooting Niagara*, the dangers posed by colonial humanitarians, and by extending the vote to the metropolitan labouring classes, were represented as being one and the same (C. Hall, 1994). But Carlyle served further to undermine the evangelical humanitarianism that had attained such power in the 1830s through his assault on the sentimentalism, naivety and other-worldliness of missionaries and liberal reformers. Indeed, the risible picture that he painted of missionaries concerned with the sufferings of distant savages, while those English men and women who *were* reclaimable starved through misgovernment, was perhaps his most powerful appeal.

It was largely through the ridicule of humanitarians by eminent figures such as Carlyle and Dickens, with his *Bleak House* character Mrs Jellyby, and her overwhelming concern for the savages of a fictitious African kingdom, that the meaning of words such as 'sentiment' and 'sentimentalist' shifted during the mid-nineteenth century. Having been 'a positive sense of a strong emotion which prompted the individual into action' in the 1830s, the concept of sentiment by the 1860s became

> tinged with hypocrisy, a mere self-indulgence of the emotions; and a sentimentalist became a week-kneed, impractical individual who, in the words of Carlyle, was particularly associated with the 'spoutings, anti-spoutings, and interminable jangle and babble of Exeter Hall [the annual meeting place of the main missionary societies]'. (Lorimer, 1978: 113; Comaroff and Comaroff, 1991: 50–1)

The utility of Carlyle's arguments, not just for West Indies planters, but also for settlers in the Cape, and the fact of their trans-imperial deployment, is testified by John Mitford Bowker. Among all the Cape's colonists, he drew most explicitly upon Carlyle's work to articulate notions that had long been held less systematically within the settler community. Bowker was particularly fond of quoting from Carlyle's *Past and Present* (1843). In this book, Carlyle emphasized the humanitarians' failure to change the stereotyped freed slave figure of 'Quashee', who, 'educated now *for half a century*, seems to have no sense in him' (in Bowker, 1864: 123). It was his knowledge of Carlyle's influence in Britain that enabled Bowker to state with confidence that:

> Aborigines' protection societies, Anti-slavery societies, mission institutions, as at present conducted, are things of naught. Savage nations must be taught to fear and respect, to *stand in awe* of a nation whose manners and customs, whose religion, it is beneficial and desirable for them to adopt . . . we must prove to these people that we are their superiors before we can ever hope for much good to be done among them, by conquering them if no milder means are effectual. (ibid.: 131)

This was a message that the Cape Colonial government had already accepted, and that the metropolitan government would also confirm during the 1850s, when they wholeheartedly approved of the repressive measures adopted by the military government in British Kaffraria (Lester, 2001).

While Carlyle was presenting not only the Jamaican planters, but also communities such as the Cape settlers, with a new and especially influential mouthpiece in Britain, and a conduit by which their racial discourse could inflect dominant metropolitan notions and policies, Matthew Arnold was heaping further scorn on the settlers' enemies. Like Carlyle, Arnold was opposed to labouring class enfranchisement in Britain. He too attacked 'naïve' and dangerous humanitarian notions of individual rights. Believing that 'great and pregnant elements of difference . . . lie in race', Arnold insisted on the 'English race's' need for discipline and on the rejection of 'sentiment' (Hall, 1994: 13). He was particularly well placed to become a protagonist in the very public controversy over the Bishop of Natal, John Colenso's, published analysis of parts of the Old Testament in 1862.

By the late 1850s, Colenso had already raised the hackles of many other missionaries and most settlers in Natal and the Cape, first, because of his opposition to the tactic of threatening everlasting punishment in order to terrorize potential converts, and, second, because of his tolerance of polygamy. In the early 1860s though, Colenso's Zulu translator, William Ngidi, was encouraging him to ask more fundamental questions about spiritual belief and conversion (Guy, 1997). Not content with advising on Zulu linguistics, Ngidi insisted on interrogating certain biblical passages, pointing out their contradictions and absurdities, and presenting Colenso with insoluble difficulties in their interpretation. In Colenso's published analysis, Ngidi's influence was acknowledged alongside that of European intellectuals who had similarly destabilized the notion of the Bible as objective historical truth. Following his experience with Ngidi's questioning, Colenso looked forward to the day when:

> we shall be able . . . to meet the Mahomedan and Brahmin and Buddhist, as well as the untutored savage of South Africa and the South Pacific, on other and better terms than we now do, being no longer obliged to maintain every part of the Bible as an infallible record of past history, and every word as the sacred utterance of the Spirit of God. (Colenso, 1862: 150)

Colenso's 'heresy' of relativism, ultimately confirmed when he was excommunicated by the Bishop of Cape Town, prompted a settler newspaper, the *Natal Witness*, to pen the ditty:

> A Bishop there was of Natal,
> Who had a Zulu for a pal,
> Said the native 'Look here,
> 'Ain't the Pentateuch queer?'
> Which converted my Lord of Natal.

More damaging to Colenso's reputation than local settler satire was the profound metropolitan debate over religious belief and culture that his writings prompted. Arnold took it upon himself to demolish Colenso's pretensions to be a biblical scholar or, indeed, a respected intellectual in any sense. 'Literary criticism has to try the book of the Bishop of Natal, which all England is now reading. It has to try it in respect of the influence which it is naturally calculated to exercise on the culture of England or Europe' (Arnold, 1863: 243). What worried Arnold was the effect that Colenso's attempt to render the Bible intelligible to Africans and other subordinates might have on domestic class relations. His fears were expressed in the same terms as Carlyle's: 'The highly instructed few, and not the scantily instructed many', he asserted, 'will ever be the organ to the human race of knowledge and truth. Knowledge and truth, in the full sense of the words, are not attainable by the great mass of the human race at all' (in Guy, 1997: 239). Thus, Arnold's well-publicized attack on Colenso was not only 'a smirk at a Christian bishop who takes seriously the beliefs of the other', but also a reaction to the democratic demands of Britain's own poor, but increasingly assertive, labouring classes (Guy, 1997: 239). It was ultimately Arnold's dogged pursuit of the logical flaws and pedantic preoccupations in Colenso's account that did most to reduce the former Bishop to a laughing stock. Much to the satisfaction of the majority of Natal's and the Cape's settlers, Colenso was soon ostracized from polite social circles, both in South Africa and Britain.

Long-held settler representations, such as those that were reformulated and re-presented for metropolitan consumption by Carlyle and Arnold, became more powerful in mid-nineteenth-century Britain because they articulated a language of inherent difference in which domestic class and gender relations could now be more conveniently framed. They helped establish, as Stoler puts it, 'a "mobile" discourse of empire that designated eligibility for citizenship, class membership, and gendered assignments to race'. Together, settlers' constructions of the colonized, and domestic bourgeois constructions of the uneducated and unreconstructed labouring classes, 'captured in one sustained image internal threats to the health and well-being of [the] social body' (Stoler, 1995: 127–8). In turn, the affirmation of such colonial notions in Britain allowed D'Urban's successors as Cape governors to attempt the imposition of pervasive systems of territorial segregation, taxation and cultural repression on the Xhosa during the late nineteenth century, with barely a murmer of protest being heard in the corridors of imperial power (Lester, 2001).

CONCLUSION

The utterances of some of the key personalities who figure in this account were situated within circuits of thought that traversed a diverse and dynamic, but interconnected imperial terrain. In the 1830s, John Philip reproduced a discourse of humanitarian concern that had been constructed through connections with the middle-class reform movement in Britain, but also with abolitionists in the West Indies and North America. At the same time, vocal eastern Cape settlers like Bowker communicated with, and devised strategy alongside, their counterparts engaged in the material production of commodities and the control of black bodies in the West Indies, Australia, New Zealand and elsewhere. Both men were influenced by, and sought to influence, powerful metropolitan contacts.

In the nineteenth century, then, the Cape Colony was one among other imperial sites in which contests were being waged over relationships between the propertied and propertyless, whites and blacks, men and women. It was connected to each of these sites, both materially and discursively. During moments of imperial crisis in particular, colonial representations of the Xhosa were considered in the light of West Indian planters' portrayals of former slaves and British bourgeois ideas of the labouring classes, among other 'subaltern' groups. As far as most 'respectable' colonial Britons were concerned, this mutual consideration of the empire's subordinated peoples in itself helped generate a collective consciousness of being part of a British bourgeois diaspora defined by its distinction from various sets of 'aborigines' and from the disreputable, poor 'at home'.

In the 1830s, a consideration of metropolitan and colonial conditions within a single, middle-class frame of reference had held out positive agendas for reform at both sites. The newly ascendant and reforming propertied classes in Britain could conceive of rosy prospects for the inner salvation of slaves and indigenes in the colonies, on the one hand, and the lower classes in Britain, on the other. The newly colonizing settlers who sought to resist humanitarian interference in 'their' affairs were marginalized, as were their metropolitan advocates. From the mid-nineteenth century, however, the same intersection of colonial and metropolitan concerns created a more reactionary hegemonic discourse. The entrenched propertied classes 'at home' now agreed with planters in the West Indies and settler capitalists in places like the Cape that there were certain natural and irredeemable distinctions between social groups, defined by race, class and gender. Such conclusions were not derived through the projection of metropolitan concerns and anxieties into colonial space, but through continual transactions between bourgeois subjects in metropolitan and colonial sites.

While this chapter has centred on a specific set of relations between propertied, male, 'British' subjects in the Cape, Jamaica and Britain, it has some broader ramifications for postcolonial work in geography. First, its emphasis on the spatiality of colonial discourse construction (and not in the abstract terms in which spatial metaphors are often deployed by postcolonial theorists) helps us to move beyond the primarily temporal frame in which colonialism and postcolonialism are often discussed. Rather, we can conceive of colonial and postcolonial places and practices being simultaneously and mutually constructed through extensive, if uneven, transnational circuits of exchange. The broad geographies of connection that characterized the empire thus helped condition the seemingly more parochial and insular relations forged in any one imperial site. Both imperial and local historiographies will have to be re-written with histories of connection in mind if this insight is to be fully developed.

Second, an appreciation of the multiple and conflicting colonial projects that were pursued through transnational circuits in the past will enable us to challenge the complacent assumption 'that we already know very well what the oppressive coordinates of [the colonial] legacy are, and that this legacy constituted a recognizable, if not unchanging, bundle throughout the decades of postcolonial history' (Stoler and Cooper, 1997: 34). An understanding of the political contests that fashioned and destabilized hegemonic colonial discourses in the nineteenth-century should equip us better to comprehend the equally contested engagements shaping postcolonial interventions. In particular, perhaps, a reconsideration of early nineteenth century humanitarianism's reflexive formation against more virulently racist counter-discourses, and its more inclusive political agenda, when weighed against its ethnocentric, bourgeois ontology, could provide a useful point of departure for discussions about the ethics of contemporary humanitarian intervention in an even more globalized world (Lester, forthcoming b).

Third, the conception of discursive networks simultaneously and persistently configuring both metropolitan and colonial societies helps us disrupt the metropole/colony, back then out there/here and now, centre/periphery binaries, which still characterize popular understanding of the imperial and postimperial world. That disruption in turn, of course, has implications for postcolonial senses of identity. As Massey argues, 'The identity of places' and the people who live in them 'is very much bound up with the *histories* that are told of them, *how* those histories are told, and which history turns out to be dominant'. One of the things that is at issue in the writing of new histories is 'recharacterizing' metropolitan places such as Britain by 'redrawing [their] connections', acknowledging 'that what has come together, in this place, now, is a conjunction of many histories and many spaces', including those of formerly colonized as well as colonizing peoples (Massey, 1995: 186). Recognizing in this way that 'the imperium at the heart of the nation-state' was 'not an entity *sui generis*', but one created in association with the diverse fates of Xhosa, Aborigines, Maori, black Jamaicans and so on, may, ultimately, be a step towards the displacement of ethnically and racially exclusive narratives of contemporary British identity (Burton, 2000: 147–8).

3

IMPERIALISM, SEXUALITY AND SPACE

PURITY MOVEMENTS IN THE BRITISH EMPIRE

Richard Phillips

> Those who have studied a map of the British Empire, in connection with the question of the State Regulation of Vice, must have noted the apparent solidarity of the Empire on the side of evil. (Dyer, the *Sentinel*, January 1886: 7)

Campaigning for the repeal of certain laws that regulated prostitution in the British Empire, Alfred Dyer brought a geographical dimension to imperial sexuality politics. He elucidated geographies of regulation both in sweeping claims such as those quoted above, and in detailed maps and descriptions (Figure 3.1). These polemical geographies caricatured the spatial relationships between imperialism and the regulation of sexuality. However, they also suggested the critical potential of spatializing the analysis of relationships between imperialism and regulation, and more generally between imperialism and sexuality. Since Dyer's maps were deployed in specific campaigns against regulation, they also demonstrated the potential of critical geographies of imperialism and sexuality for interventions in sexuality and postcolonial politics. In both senses, they present important points of departure, for postcolonial geographies of regulation and more generally of sexualities. This chapter builds upon the (limited) geographical literature on imperialism and sexuality and draws upon historical and other postcolonial studies of the same, as well as some original empirical material. It charts and systematizes a postcolonial geography of regulation and resistance, and more generally of imperialism and sexuality.

Sexualities and sexual life have become prominent in postcolonial histories and geographies because they illuminate an important and, until recently, neglected dimension of colonialism and because of their recursive relationship with imperialism and imperial power.[1] Geographers have begun to acknowledge and examine the significance of space for the construction, performance and broader regulation of sexualities (Bell and Valentine, 1995). They have generally concentrated on urban and Western sexual geographies, but have recently

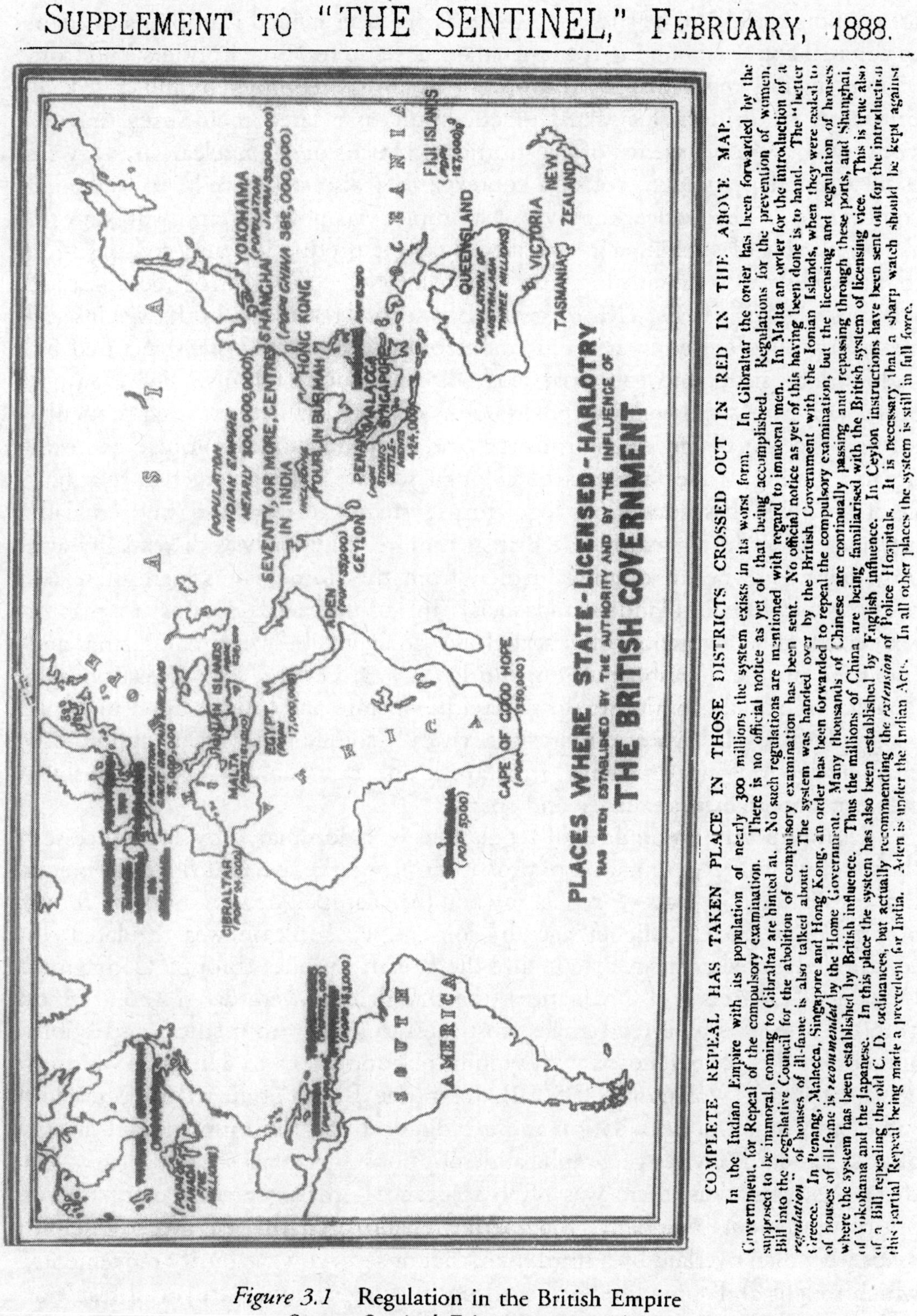

Figure 3.1 Regulation in the British Empire
Source: *Sentinel*, February 1888: 14

devoted some critical attention to non-metropolitan – rural and/or colonial – sexualities (Howell, 2000; Phillips and Watt, 2000). In history and postcolonial studies, the analysis of sexuality and imperialism is more advanced. Hyam argues that: 'The expansion of Europe was not only a matter of Christianity and commerce, it was also a matter of copulation and concubinage' (1990: 2).

Developing the claim, he shows how sexual practices helped Europeans to adapt to colonial contexts, ranging from penal outposts to resource frontiers, and from regions mainly resettled by Europeans to others conquered and ruled by European minorities. But sexual practices and associated socio-sexual institutions, ranging from systems of prostitution to forms of the nuclear family, were more than adaptations to colonial contexts; they also structured and facilitated colonizations. The nuclear family, for example, was not only an institution for the regulation of sexuality; it was also a unit of production and consumption that served small-scale farming, and was therefore a pillar of many colonization schemes (Harris, 1977). More generally, sexual relations, both within and between groups of colonizing and colonized peoples, were both structured by, and in turn structured, imperial and colonial social relations. For example, Stoler (1995) has shown how constructions of race, which structured particular forms of colonialism, were produced and reproduced in colonial contexts, notably through the regulation of colonial sexual and reproductive relations. Levine (1994) has identified regulatory systems at disparate but crucially interlocking locations within the British Empire. The analysis of sexuality and imperialism has been extended further, from the immediate sphere of sexual relations between individuals and social (including racial) groups, to that of sexualized and metaphorically sexual relationships between colonizing and colonized peoples (Kabbani, 1986; Aldrich, 1993; Lewis, 1996). Relationships between imperialism and sexuality therefore operate and impact upon multiple geographical levels. By examining systematically some of these geographies, this chapter develops a conceptual framework for the analysis of relationships between imperialism, sexuality and space.

British imperial geographies of regulation were dominated by two processes: the state and military regulation of prostitution, and the social purity movements that resisted such 'repressive' regulation and then campaigned for 'positive' forms of regulation, such as higher ages of consent. Prostitution was regulated, in certain designated areas in Britain and the British Empire, through Contagious Diseases (CD) Acts and Ordinances (the British Acts were dated 1864, 1866, 1869). These laws required female prostitutes to submit to medical inspections and confined those diagnosed with syphilis or gonorrhoea to detention wards of 'lock hospitals' (Walkowitz, 1980: 2). Josephine Butler argued that regulation subjected women to degradation and exploitation and institutionalized a moral double standard. Dyer's geographical descriptions and maps showed that where there was regulation, there was often resistance – the geography of first-wave purity movements broadly, if imperfectly, mirrored that of regulation. Both maps were then overlaid by a third map, that of second-wave purity movements, which sought and sometimes achieved positive legislation. Partly as a result of such campaigns, CD laws were repealed and positive legislation passed throughout much of the Empire. For example, regulation Bills were defeated in South Australia in 1869 and 1875 and regulation laws were suspended in Britain in 1883 and in India after 1886. The (female, heterosexual) age of consent was raised in such disparate locations as Australia (most colonies), Britain and India at around the same time (in South Australia and Britain from thirteen to sixteen in 1885, and in India from ten to twelve in 1891) (Engels, 1983; Mason, 1995).

The patterns of regulation and purity raise complex questions about geography, imperialism and sexuality. Mapping and interpreting imperial and colonial geographies of regulation, Levine has addressed the question of why CD laws appeared – in interestingly different forms – in different parts of the Empire at around the same time. Although much has been written about purity movements in Britain, Europe and the USA, colonial geographies of resistance to regulation and of second-wave purity movements have attracted less critical and empirical attention. The questions they pose are similar to those addressed by Levine: why did purity movements emerge and make an impact in some places and not others? More generally, what light does the geography of those movements throw upon relationships between imperialism and sexuality? To examine how legal frameworks, moral discourses and campaign strategies were extended across time and space, it is necessary to identify a geography of networks and international (or intercolonial) relations. The imperial geography of purity campaigns is paralleled by that of other social and political networks (see Lester and Bell, this volume). To examine why purity movements emerged and were successful in certain places more than others, it is necessary to identify and compare those geographical contexts, for example, to compare and contrast the political agency of the people who lived there and to distinguish their potential influence over the political process. Comparative research, which draws together and juxtaposes what Edward Said (1993: 1) terms the 'overlapping territories' and 'intertwined histories' of imperialism, reveals the interconnectedness of disparate imperial locations and critically excavates those 'geographies that appear in the margins and between the lines of the cultural archive' (Gregory, 2000: 614). Finally, to examine why purity movements targeted and were more successful in certain places and types of places, it is also necessary to understand something of the geographical imaginary that constructed certain places as pure or impure and, therefore, as unsuitable or suitable for 'purification'. These three geographies, relating to networks, and to material and metaphorical spaces, are examined in the following sections.

INTERNATIONAL AND INTERCOLONIAL NETWORKS

The coincidence around the British Empire of projects and developments suggests that purity activists did not always act independently (Engels, 1983). On the contrary, they communicated and cooperated with each other, through international and intercolonial networks of activism. Purity campaign journals published in London or Toronto, and purity meetings held in Adelaide or Bombay, for example, generally targeted local and national systems of regulation, but did so within international and intercolonial frameworks. For example, the *Sentinel* reported and encouraged purity-related interventions in Britain and around the Empire. It ran regular features on developments in London and other parts of England, but also Wales and Ireland, Canada and India. Its coverage corresponded to the geographical distribution and networks of activists and correspondents. These individual and organizational campaign networks, which facilitated the exchange of information and ideas, structured the temporal and spatial extension of purity movements.

One function of campaign networks was to facilitate the diffusion of purity movements from metropolitan to non-metropolitan locations. Although I argue that purity campaigns did not simply diffuse outwards from the mother country, through campaign networks, that is sometimes what happened. Butler (1887: 5) advised British purity campaigners to consider whether they had 'any connection, direct or indirect, with missions, any correspondences or friends in the Colonies'. Many followed her advice and concentrated their overseas interests on the British Empire, where they felt a sense of responsibility and/or political opportunity, and where they understood the official language and felt they understood the political and legislative terrain. These purity activists criticized the British government for directly or indirectly imposing CD Acts and Ordinances in British colonies (Van Heyningen, 1984; White, 1990; Warren, 1993). To some, such as Butler (1879: 29; 1887), regulation revealed the more general immorality of colonialism and the more general tendency of 'Englishman to destroy, to enslave, to domineer'. To others, it represented a corrupted form of colonialism (Taylor, 1883: 19). It would be simplistic to label some purity campaigners anti-imperial and others imperial reformers (Burton, 1994), but whether they sought ultimately to dismantle or to reform imperialism, many such campaigners asserted and reproduced the general power of British people over their colonized counterparts. They regarded themselves as the leaders of – not just participants in – a movement that spanned the English-speaking world and the British Empire. Ellice Hopkins, who wrote booklets for the White Cross League (a purity society), boasted of her overseas sales figures (Barrett, 1907), and took credit for a 'movement that has roused the whole nation, and has spread to the antipodes' (Hopkins, 1904: 6). Imperial in scope and attitude, these movements reflected – for they were produced by and in turn produced – the geographies and power relations of imperialism.

The export of British purity movements sometimes involved travel and was therefore closely and recursively related to geographies of imperial travel and migration. For example, when Dyer left England for India in 1888, exchanging his editorship of the *Sentinel* for that of the *Bombay Guardian*, he took many of his political ideas and strategies with him and deployed them in the service of a similar political agenda. This revolved around fighting local CD laws and seeking to raise the age of consent. In India, Dyer participated in an established campaign network, which broadly reproduced British sexuality politics. In the *Bombay Guardian* – 'a radical nonconformist journal' (Ballhatchet, 1980: 115) – Dyer 'wrote strongly, against every kind of social unrighteousness. The liquor traffic, the opium traffic and the vice traffic all came under the editorial lash' (Kiek, 1927: 243). As an editor and journalist, he borrowed many of the tactics that had been used by campaign journalists in England (Ballhatchet, 1980). He also co-founded a vigilance committee in Bombay, which was modelled on similar committees formed previously in Britain and around the Empire. Finally, Dyer and particularly his wife Helen did what they could to help Indian activists who were fighting what they perceived to be similar battles. For example, they endorsed Pandita Ramabai's struggle for the rights of Indian women, and Helen produced a sympathetic biography of the Indian campaigner, with a preface that asked British readers to support her work (Dyer, 1900).

Imperial campaign networks did not always involve the transfer of political agendas and strategies from Britain to her spheres of imperial influence. For example, Ramabai saw herself not as an agent of essentially British purity politics, but rather as an independent and critical Indian activist, whose relationship with British people and ideas was never subordinate. By refocusing attention from the perspectives of the Dyers to those of certain Indian activists, it is possible to explore ways in which British ideas were not simply imported to imperial contexts, but variously resisted, appropriated and supplemented. Ramabai's support in Britain (as in other Western countries, particularly the USA) derived in part from her ability to translate her projects for the benefit of British (and those other national) audiences, to present her ideas self-effacingly as their ideas (for example, by criticizing Hindu customs in a letter to the London *Times*) and doing so from the perspective of an Indian Christian (Kosambi, 1993). Supporting a rise in the age of consent, Ramabai was allied with British missionaries and the British Indian government, but she was never their pawn. Although converted to Christianity and educated partly in Britain, she came frequently into conflict with the Church of England and she opposed what she regarded as exploitative British colonialism in India (Burton, 1998). Ramabai's intervention, comprised of local agency situated within and supported by an international network of contacts, suggests that purity campaign networks were dispersed rather than simply Anglocentric and hierarchical. Thus, although they often mirrored the spatial order of imperialism, campaign networks did not necessarily concentrate power in the centre. Hunt shows that important Victorian moral regulation projects in Britain and the USA were directed as much from below as above, socially and politically. He argues that agency was 'dispersed' socially and geographically, and 'that moral regulation movements form an interconnected web of discourses, symbols and practices exhibiting persistent continuities that stretch across time and place' (Hunt, 1985: 9).

The dispersal of campaign networks is illustrated, in the first instance, by the dependence of British purity activists upon ideas and strategies that were imported from overseas. Many of them co-operated with colleagues overseas, particularly those in continental countries such as France and Belgium that had longer histories than Britain's of state regulation of prostitution and of resistance to such regulation (Fawcett and Turner, 1927: 41). The (British) National Vigilance Association (NVA) 'found that to keep the work on watertight national lines would at the best achieve only partial success' (NVA, 1935: 5–6). British activists participated in, but did not lead, European purity movements. Butler, who worked with colleagues in Belgium, Switzerland, France and elsewhere, advised prospective British activists to learn languages such as French, and to acquaint themselves with 'the efforts and conflicts of reformers of other lands' (Butler, 1879: 34).

The dispersal of agency within campaign networks in the British Empire is illustrated further through the biography and influence of another promoter of the Indian Age of Consent Act. Like Dyer, Behramji M. Malabari appropriated some of the techniques of British campaign journalism, but he did so to promote what might be termed an Indian rather than a British agenda in India. Partly through his editorship of the *Indian Spectator*, and most prominently in the seven-year period before the Indian Age of Consent Act was passed, Malabari mounted a 'raging campaign through the press for removing the abuses and evils in Hindu society' (Parthasarathy, 1989: 54). Burton (1998: 160) suggests that 'Historians of late-Victorian Britain will recognize Malabari's use of the urban press corps to reflect and produce anxiety about the sexual activities of women and girls as strikingly parallel to W.T. Stead's agitation in the *Pall Mall Gazette*.' The articles that appeared in London's *Pall Mall Gazette*, which played an important part in promoting the Criminal Law Amendment Act (1885), had been reported around the world. They were then appropriated and adapted to local settings and concerns, as far afield as Europe, North America, Australasia and India (see, for example, the *Sentinel*, March 1889) by journalists such as Malabari. Beyond his newspaper work, Malabari also campaigned through his network of contacts. For example, he secured introductions to, and lobbied, 'some of the leading citizens of Bombay' (Singh, 1914: 42), notably officials in the British Indian government. Malabari's contacts were also useful to him in 1890 when he visited London and lobbied parliamentarians and other influential figures in his age of consent campaign.

The dispersal of agency within campaign networks was also apparent in colonial resettlement societies such as Canada and Australia, where British and American individuals and organizations were particularly influential. Valverde (1991: 16) asserts, in her book on Canadian social purity movements, that 'It would be impossible here to detail all the forms and channels of English and American influence on Canadian ideas about social and moral reform.' In Australia, similarly, much of the content of social purity movements could be traced to English and American sources. Regulation bills, put before and sometimes passed by responsible colonial governments, were generally modelled directly or indirectly on their British counterparts. Colonial purity activists, such as the Reverend Joseph Coles Kirby in South Australia, depended heavily upon arguments imported from Britain, accurately prefaced with 'no pretence to originality' (Kirby, 1882: 3). That said, general arguments were actively appropriated and deployed in the creation of local, colonial and national social purity movements, which were conceived as more than variants on a British model. Kirby concluded three lectures on social purity with a call to action: 'Let South Australia show a lead resolute and effective', which might be an example 'to Australasia and to the whole British Empire' (Kirby, 1882: 45). To this end, and not simply to execute essentially British politics, he worked within campaign networks to promote the South Australian and wider purity cause. His regular correspondents included Benjamin Scott (a leading purity activist in London) and Dyer, whom he visited in India. Kirby was also a prolific correspondent of the *Sentinel*, which published his regular letters and articles and chronicled the progress of the South Australian Purity Society. In this manner, Kirby was able to inform British campaigners of his projects and to win their support, and also to influence public opinion in South Australia itself where the *Sentinel* was also read. The mutual rather than subservient nature of Kirby's relationship with British campaigners was demonstrated when, in Britain in 1891, he shared a platform with Josephine Butler and W.T. Stead, and 'was asked to say a few words as representing the social reformers of

Australia' (Kiek, 1927: 232). As the *Sentinel* put it, 'If action in Great Britain has been an encouragement to our friends in Australasia, they may be assured that their action is in return an encouragement to us here.' Kirby acknowledged the assistance of his British and international colleagues for the information and advice they had sent (*Sentinel*, February 1886: 24), but he ultimately attributed success in South Australia to the efforts of South Australians.

Although the empire-wide geography of purity draws some attention to the intercolonial dimensions of purity campaign networks, campaigners generally concentrated most of their attention on national and colonial networks and projects. For example, although Kirby visited Dyer in India and Butler and Stead in London, and although he maintained regular contact with British and international campaigners through the *Sentinel*, he devoted most of his time and energy to Australia and participated mainly in Australian colonial and national campaigns and networks. In India, too, campaigners maintained inter-colonial contacts but increasingly forged internal, national networks. Indeed, Heimsath (1962) argues that Malabari turned the age of consent campaign into India's first *national* cultural political campaign. In Britain, also, purity movements were organized on mostly national lines, in the form of the Ladies' National Association and the NVA, for example. The national, colonial and local contexts that purity movements addressed, in which they were situated and between which they spread, are thus of some significance.

CONTEXTS: NATIONAL AND LOCAL PURITY MOVEMENTS

Although a number of regulatory systems and purity politics spread widely throughout the British Empire, there were also many differences between the laws and ordinances that were enacted, the ways in which they were enforced, the ways in which they were received locally, and the ways in which reactive and/or pro-active purity campaigning emerged and brought about change. The latter was influenced by a number of contextual factors, including: political structures that influenced individuals' and groups' potential to influence locally applicable legislation; the presence or absence in a region of military personnel and influence; and broader cultural factors including attitudes towards sexuality and morality.

First, since purity movements revolved around relatively formal regulatory systems and political interventions (in each case involving the state), the geography of purity movements reflected variations in the imperial state and in the relationship between that state and the people who lived under it. The complex historical geography and eclecticism of imperial state formation meant that British imperial states did different things – with respect to the regulation of sexualities, for example – in different times and places (Overton, 1987; Ogborn, 1993). Different types of colonial states had different approaches to the regulation of prostitution. Stoler (1991: 63) generalizes that, in terms of their sexualized race relations and their racialized systems for regulating sexualities:

> Colonies based on small administrative centres of Europeans (as on Africa's Gold Coast) differed from plantation colonies with sizeable enclave

European communities (as in Malaya and Sumatra), and still more from settler colonies (as in Algeria) with large and very heterogeneous, permanent European populations.

She argues that the formal and informal systems of regulation were correspondingly variable. Regulation was an important pillar of imperial and colonial states that were governed by male-dominated white minorities, particularly where those men (low-ranking British soldiers or Dutch plantation workers, for example) were expected to remain single, neither bringing European wives nor marrying local women. Regulation was less important, but by no means absent in resettlement colonies where European men had more opportunity to marry and, therefore, less interest in local prostitutes and other women (McGrath, 1984; Lewis, 1997). The agenda for intervention by purity activists and others to change such systems was correspondingly variable. Where there was regulation, as in India for example, there also tended to be reactive purity campaigns. Where regulation was less established (for example, in many Australian colonies), there were sometimes preventative (opposing CD Bills) or proactive (seeking positive legislation) purity campaigns, and in most of prewar Sub-Saharan Africa there were no purity campaigns at all.

These different types of colonies also had different political structures and consequently different channels for political intervention. In the late-Victorian period, British resettlement colonies generally elected their own governments, whereas white-minority colonies and other imperial possessions were generally ruled directly by the central and/or local British government. The majority of people in Canada and Australia had some form of access to political channels (Ward, 1976), whereas few in India or British Africa had such direct or indirect influence. Thus, for example, Butler argued that British women must defend the interests of Indian prostitutes because those women could not represent themselves. The question of subaltern resistance, of whether women such as these were able to 'speak', for example to resist regulation through more informal channels than those followed by purity campaigners, has been the subject of much debate among postcolonial critics (Spivak, 1988). These debates address interrelated questions of gender and class, which are relevant to understandings of social purity movements. Western women played important, often leading parts in the purity movements, campaigning for change both locally and overseas (Phillips, 1999b). Their efforts were not evenly distributed. In the late-Victorian period, British women who took an interest in overseas affairs paid disproportionate attention to India (Burton, 1998). Those who lived overseas focused their attention on the areas where they lived; areas of established white settlement (Australia, for example) and white minority rule (such as India), rather than settlement frontiers and more recent territorial acquisitions (much of Africa, in particular). Indeed, many women's participation in purity campaigns was broadly consistent with their prescribed role as moralizers who would raise the tone of colonial life. Although British colonial women cannot be so neatly characterized because their relationships to imperialism were ambivalent (Callaway, 1987; Blunt, 1994), the conformity between the general and specifically colonial gender identities that were mapped out for them, and the role of a purity campaigner, provided these women with a niche in which to participate in purity campaigns. In contrast, colonized women were not accorded the same ability to raise the moral tone of colonies because they were not generally regarded as potential wives for British men (Hyam, 1990), because they were identified with sexuality rather than morality (Kabbani, 1986), and because they generally had no formal role in the political process. However, some colonized women did find ways to influence and lobby voters, legislators and law enforcement agencies and thereby intervene in relatively formal political arenas. Some Indian women and men (such as Ramabai and Malabari) exercised formal political influence, largely by virtue of their privileged social positions. The influence of elite Indians notwithstanding, a general contrast can be made between white-dominated resettlement colonies, where popular purity movements composed of both men and women were able to develop and make an impact, and colonies ruled by white minorities, where such organizations and individuals were more constrained and where colonized women were often most constrained of all.

Geographies of regulation and purity were also structured by the presence and particular geographies of other imperial institutions, particularly the military. The variable geography of CD legislation mirrored that of militarization: generally, the stronger the military presence, the stronger the lobby for, and enforcement of, this form of regulation, and the stronger the resistance from purity activists. In Britain, CD Acts applied only to certain designated military zones such as garrison and naval towns. In the Empire, CD laws applied most firmly to militarized zones. The correlation between geographies of British imperial militarization and regulation, and correspondingly of resistance to such regulation, is illustrated at different geographical scales, ranging from that of the world to that of a particular imperial region (such as India), to that of a militarized imperial location (such as a cantonment in India). Dyer's map of regulation and repeal (Figure 3.1) reveals a correlation between the imperial geography of regulation and that of purity-related resistance; both tended to concentrate in the most heavily militarized parts of the British Empire. The national and local correlation between militarization, regulation and purity-related resistance was demonstrated in a national map of the Indian Empire, entitled 'India's curse and Britain's shame', which depicted 'seventy-two centres where the British government has established the abomination of legalized impurity' (Figure 3.2) (*Sentinel*, July 1887: 1). Understandings of localized relationships between militarism and purity were represented, for example, on a site map that depicted 'The government versus the gospel at Bareilly' (Figure 3.3). This map, sketched in 1887 by Alfred Dyer, was intended to show 'how lust is forced upon the British soldier, and how the native population is corrupted, by the British government in India'. The caption explained:

> While the Temperance tent is in a comparatively obscure corner, the tents of the Government harlots confront the troops from morning to night, separated from their own tents only by a public thoroughfare, without any buildings or trees intervening. It will be observed that the encampment of the Government harlots as shown in this plan, is in full view of the

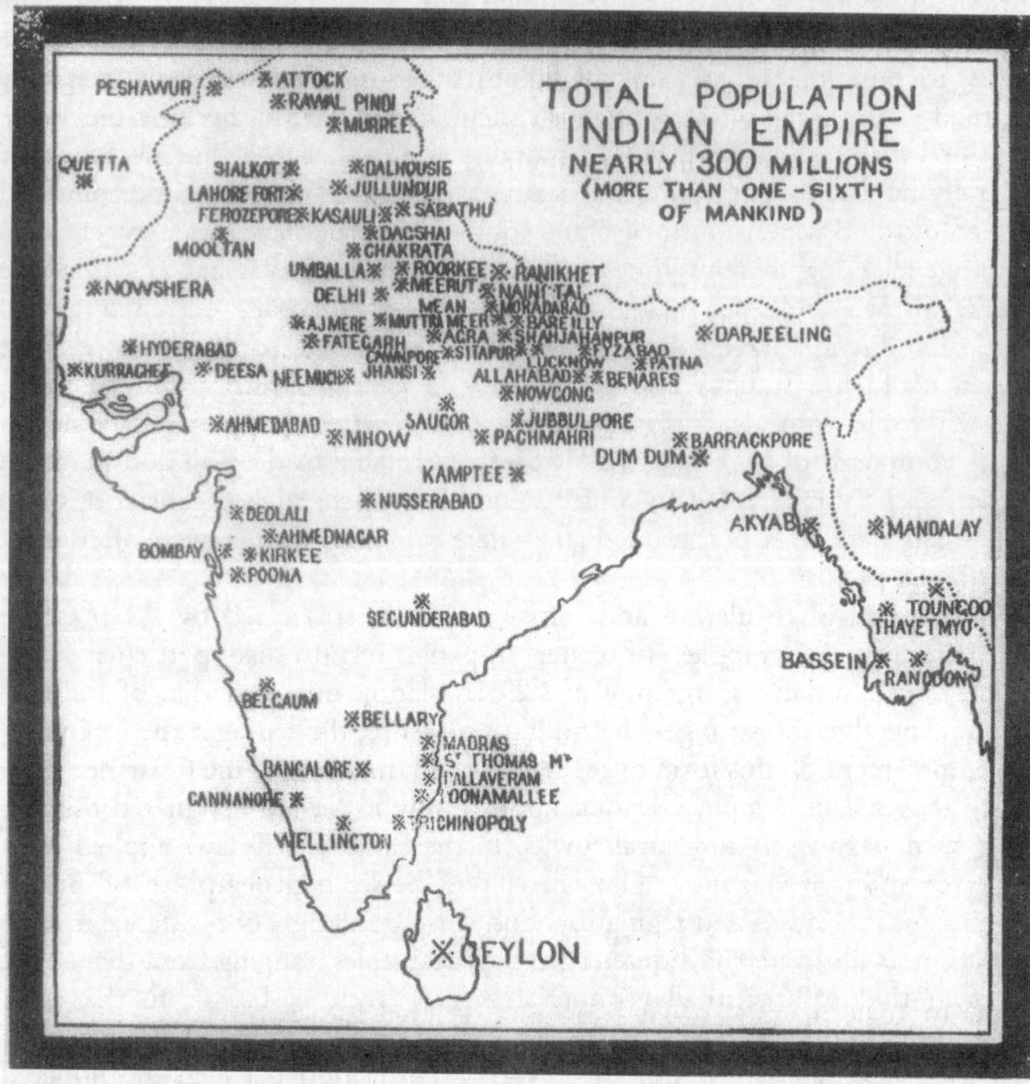

SEVENTY-FIVE OF THE CENTRES IN WHICH STATE-LICENSED-HARLOTRY HAS BEEN ESTABLISHED BY THE BRITISH GOVERNMENT IN THE INDIAN EMPIRE.*

Figure 3.2 Regulation in India
Source: *Sentinel*, March 1888: 27

> entrance to the native Christian Church. A school is also held in that building. (*Sentinel*, March 1888: 27)

Conversely, outside military zones, CD laws had less impact and purity activists had a different agenda. In South Australia, the failure of CD Bills (*South Australian Register*, 10 November 1869) might be explained, in part, by the low levels of militarization in the colony. Nineteenth-century South Australia had neither garrison towns nor naval ports and remained almost completely untouched by formal military presence throughout the century. An opponent of CD legislation in South Australia told the Assembly:

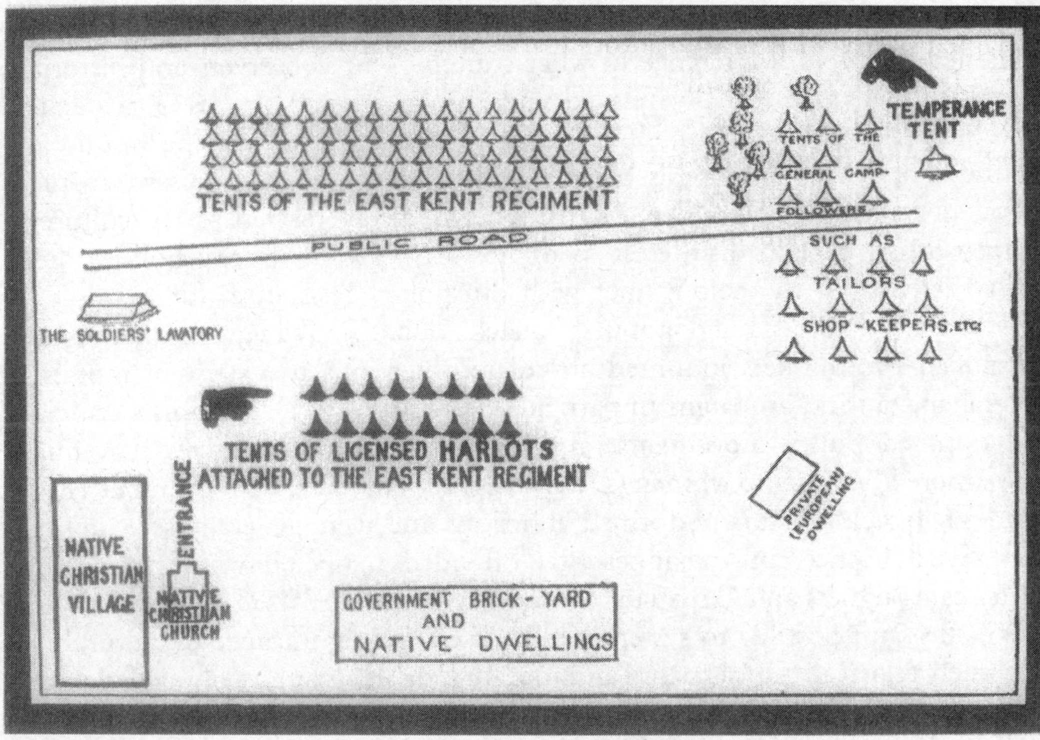

THE GOVERNMENT *VERSUS* THE GOSPEL AT BAREILLY.
(Sketch taken on the spot by Mr. Alfred S. Dyer, Dec. 30th, 1887.)

Figure 3.3 Regulation at Bareilly
Source: *Sentinel*, March 1888: 26

> There might be some excuse or argument in favour of the [CD] Bill if we had soldiers stationed here, who were debarred from marriage except with the consent of their officers ... but here we had no such cause for legislation. (South Australian Parliamentary Debates [SAPD], 8 September 1875: 982)

Without a strong military presence, South Australia lacked both military prostitution and it lacked a military lobby, which in other places promoted such legislation.

A third contextual factor influencing the imperial geography of regulation and purity movements was associated more with cultural geographies, which encompassed situated and variable attitudes to moral and sexual questions. The age of consent, for example, meant very different things in the different cultural contexts of India, England and Australia, and in each of these places it meant different things to different people. Within Australia, for example, different colonies assumed different positions on possible changes to the age of consent. Purity campaigners in South Australia were more successful than their counterparts in New South Wales in persuading fellow colonists and Members of the Legislative Assembly and Council that the age of consent should be raised (in the former colony the age was raised to sixteen in 1885, while in the latter it remained as low as fourteen until 1910). The weakness of proactive purity movements in New South Wales, and particularly its major city, might be explained partly with reference to what contemporary observers and historians have identified as a sexually relaxed and secular culture. In 1873, a detailed survey entitled *Vice and its Victims in Sydney* argued that 'the youth and manhood of Sydney are rapidly being corrupted' by sexually permissive attitudes prevalent in the city (Woolley, 1873). This allegedly relaxed sexual culture in Sydney might explain disinterest in or hostility towards purity politics there. Purity activists in the colony met with outspoken resistance, for example by Freethinkers, feminists and popular 'quack' doctors. Sydney's numerous and outspoken Freethinkers mounted articulate objections to Christian morals in general and purity campaigns in particular (Phillips, 1981). Feminists criticized and opposed purity movements, arguing for secular alternatives that might prove more liberating to women (*Daily Telegraph*, Sydney, 22 November 1893). Sydney's 'quack' doctors performed abortions and were generally seen to sanction sexual licence, in a manner that offended many conventional doctors, purity campaigners and Christians (*Australian Christian World*, Sydney, 19 June 1896). It is not possible to systematically assess the significance of cultural factors, such as attitudes to sexuality and morality, on geographies of regulation and purity in New South Wales, and certainly not the British Empire, in the space available here. This discussion does, however, shift the terms of this debate from aspects of material context (of the state, the military, and so on) to more evidently subjective and imaginative geographies. The latter are not always measurable or tangible, but are nevertheless of real significance in politics of regulation and purity.

IMAGINATIVE SPACES

In this discussion of cultural contexts, a number of factors have been introduced, albeit without explanation of the mechanisms that may have linked them to regulatory systems and purity movements. One such mechanism was the deployment of arguments about sexual and moral geographies by legislators, medical and legal experts, purity campaigners and others. Imaginatively, certain spaces and types of spaces and environmental attributes were associated with sexuality and immorality, or with innocence and morality, and arguments about specific and generic spaces were used to argue for geographically variable and targeted systems of sexual regulation. In this manner, the imaginative spaces of sexuality and morality played a part in structuring systems of regulation and purity movements.

A distinction between urban vice and rural virtue – a principal dimension of imaginative sexual geography – was deployed in generic and specific forms in purity politics within the British Empire to argue for variable and targeted forms of regulation. Commonly, big cities have been associated with sexual impurity or 'worldliness', as well as with other broadly negative characteristics like alienation, rootlessness, poverty, immorality and ill health. Meanwhile, rural and provincial places have been associated with 'innocence, and simple virtue' (Williams, 1985: 1) and with positive qualities like stability, morality, healthfulness, contentment and beauty. Not universally, but conventionally, the city is associated with vice, the country with purity. Williams (1985) shows that this moral geography has changed over time, adapting for example to industrialization and to constantly changing political contexts. When purity activists wanted to establish the need for positive legislation, for example in New South Wales, they invoked sexualized urban imagery, associated generically with cities and seaports. In 1899, the London *Church Times* explained that 'Sydney is a seaport, with all the usual vices and temptations of seaport towns.' The paper went on to suggest that 'A visitor to Sydney cannot fail to be struck by the fact of shameless immorality displayed in the streets of the city at nightfall' (*Church Times*, 5 May 1899: 527). The conviction that Sydney was a sexually promiscuous city inspired a number of projects ranging from inner-city church extensions and missions among prostitutes, to urban regeneration ('purification') schemes (Mayne, 1982). Conversely, some of those who opposed forms of regulation did so by arguing that their cities were smaller, their colonies more rural. One politician moved successfully to suspend a CD Bill in South Australia partly by arguing that 'a measure of this kind might be suitable for *large towns* in England, such as Chatham, Deptford, and Portsmouth ... but it would not be required here' (my emphasis) (SAPD, 19 October1869: 603). These were not only towns, of course, but also ports for commercial and naval fleets and this doubled their imaginative sexualization. This moral geographical discourse illustrates the manner in which English imaginative geographies were applied to, and sometimes distinguished from, colonial cities, which were then regarded as places of absolute or relative immorality and regulated accordingly.

Purity discourse also invoked conventionally sexualized Orientalist imaginative geographies. The erotic Orient, variants of which were depicted by British, French and other Western painters, writers, travellers, anthropologists and geographers, divided the world into West and East and generally identified the latter with (among other things) sexual perversity and excess (Kabbani, 1986). The boundaries of the erotic Orient, as variable as those of the more general Orient, sometimes defined a precise and large area, as for example in Richard Burton's 'Sotadic Zone' (Burton, 1885–86; Phillips, 1999a), and sometimes defined a vague and/or smaller area. In each case this encompassed the Arab world (Kabbani, 1986), possibly with the Mediterranean (Aldrich, 1993) and/or parts of sub-Saharan Africa (McClintock, 1995). The imaginative sexualization of the South and/or East was linked to correlations, some quasi-scientific, others more overtly ideological, between sexuality, race and environmental attributes such as climate. Correlations between climate and sexual passions, sometimes loosely attributed to scientific sources and to environmental determinist philosophy (Livingstone, 1991), were invoked to justify geographical variations in systems of regulation and in purity-related interventions. It was argued that, partly for climatic reasons, puberty came earlier in Australia and, therefore, that a lower age of consent should apply there. Politicians highlighted differences between Britain and New South Wales, arguing that warmth and prosperity brought early maturity in the colony, which necessitated lower ages of consent there (New South Wales Parliamentary Debates [NSWPD], 19 September 1905: 2250). Arguments about climate and sexuality were also used to justify stronger forms of regulation in warmer regions. One commentator, lamenting the repeal of CD Acts in India, argued that sexually transmitted diseases were a particular threat there, since 'Men's blood in the tropics is hotter than in colder climes' (Verax, 1895: 2). The correlation between heat and sexual passion was linked, in part, to racialized conceptions of sexuality. While the warm South and exoticized East were sexualized, so were their non-white inhabitants. Indeed, constructions of race revolved around the construction of sexual and moral differences. For example, it has been argued that the white majority in Melbourne distanced themselves from the city's Chinatown, a space that, with its combination of urbanity and racial otherness, was doubly associated with immorality (McConville, 1985). The racialization of sexuality, and its significance for the construction of regulatory systems, took a different form in British Africa, where neither regulation nor purity politics made much headway. This may be attributed partly to imperial constructions of Africans as the primitive, sexual others of their European counterparts. A footnote to Burton's *Nights* illustrates this tendency to caricature black African men as primitively and even bestially sexual (see also Jackson, 1994):

> Debauched women prefer negroes on account of the size of their parts. I measured one man in Somali-land who, when quiescent, numbered nearly six inches. This is a characteristic of the negro race and of African animals; e.g. the horse. (Burton, 1885: 6)

White (1991: 176) argues that prevailing British 'ideas about African sexuality' made 'officials believe that English legislation was inappropriate for Africa'; they 'consistently saw African sexual behaviour as something beyond legislation'. In other words, she argues that eroticized imaginative geographies structured British attitudes towards potential regulation and purity politics at different locations throughout the Empire.

Finally, while imaginatively sexualized and immoral geographies were deployed in purity politics, their opposites were also imagined and articulated as purified utopian spaces that might be achieved through purity campaigns for sexual and moral reform. Said has observed that, to Orientalists such as Richard Burton, the desert:

> appears historically as barren and retarded as it is geographically; the Arabian desert is thus considered to be a locale about which one can make statements regarding the past in exactly the same form (and with the same content) that one makes them regarding the present. (1979: 283)

Of course, utopian writers are concerned ultimately with the future; Richard Burton's desert writing presents something of a sexual libertarian utopia, a space in which sexual behaviour was subject neither to unjust laws nor to prudish morality (Phillips, 1999a). Richard's wife, Isabel, also deployed utopian desert images but in order to propose, albeit tentatively, ideas about sexual purity (Phillips, 1999b). Isabel described real and imaginary travel to pure spaces, especially the desert – an important site of biblical spiritual journeys. As she explained, 'I yearn for the desert to recover the purity of my mind' (Burton,

1875: 1–2). In other writing, she produced images of purity and challenged images of impurity in the context of a broader cultural politics of purity (Phillips, 1999b). For example, her descriptions of the harem and Turkish bath lifted the 'veil' on the erotic East and threw cold water on a Western sexual fantasy, putting something pure – in this case something wholesome and domestic – in its place (see also Melman, 1992). Her purity rhetoric may be situated within a broader discourse, which invoked often conventional signifiers of purity. If impurity was signified by large cities and seaports, southern and eastern countries, hot climates and dark skins, then purity was signified by the opposite of all this, for example by an English or Welsh country cottage or a Canadian family farm (Davies, 1996). Images such as these were deployed effectively by purity campaigners (Valverde, 1991).

Geographical images of purity and impurity do not always accurately represent sexual geography, although they retain a mythical force, which fends off empirical contradiction (for example, by historians such as Davies, 1996), and ensures an ongoing significance in cultural politics of purity. Thus, while they are distinct, real and imaginary sexual geographies are recursively related (Phillips, 2000). Although immediately focused on sexuality, these real and imaginary geographies must also be situated more broadly with reference to their cultural and material contexts. Williams links the imagined geography of the country and city back into material concerns and relationships between these two regions: 'the relations are not only of ideas, but of rent and interest, of situation and power; a wider system' (1985: 7). Sexualized imaginative geographies should be seen not as matters of sexuality and morality *per se*, but as constituents of a broader economy of power and difference. This point has been developed by critics of sexualized Orientalism, but might be extended to the interpretation of other sexualized geographies. It is important, therefore, to reconnect geographies of sexuality politics with broader questions of imperialism.

CONCLUSION

This chapter has made some preliminary suggestions regarding the imperial and colonial locations in which people in the British Empire were able to intervene with respect to the regulation of sexuality. It has outlined a geography of the contested regulation of sexuality, albeit one which may raise more questions than it answers. It outlines ways in which people's location, in a broadly imperial and colonial sense, structured both the way in which their sexuality (and that of people around them) was regulated, and also the opportunities that they (and those around them) had to intervene with respect to that regulation. Location, in this respect, comprised campaign networks, political and cultural contexts, and imaginative geographies. Research, structured around this three-fold system, may go some way to explaining why purity movements emerged and made an impact in some places more than others. This may then complement emerging descriptions and interpretations of imperial geographies of regulation, which tend to emphasize the workings of the imperial state (and its political, legal and military components) more than the interventions of purity activists and others.

The geography of purity movements in the British Empire was uneven. It was not, however, structured simply by imperial power over colonial people and places. The geographies of campaign networks suggest that interventions were spatially dispersed, extending to a series of non-metropolitan sites. This suggestion ties in with arguments that have been made by others regarding imperial and colonial geographies of sexuality and regulation (Stoler, 1995; Howell, 2000). I have argued elsewhere that colonial spaces could be productive, rather than merely receptive, with respect to constructions of, and systems for, regulating sexuality (Phillips, forthcoming 2002). But, since purity movements were dominated by relatively formal political interventions, the geography of purity movements was uneven and reflected that of conventional social and political power. Imperial purity movements were dominated by people who were formally enfranchised, and by adults, white settlers, community leaders, doctors and other professionals. White women played an important part in these movements, partly because they were directly affected by regulation in ways that they found objectionable and also partly because, at least for middle-class British women, their gender identities provided latitude to participate in this particular political arena. People on the margins had less scope to intervene and were less likely to do so. This raises further questions about how people outside the social and spatial spheres of purity activism may have engaged in sexuality politics, if not always through formal channels. It also raises questions about subaltern resistance, about how Indian women or Chinese Australians, for example, might have resisted their sexualization and regulation by a colonial state and raises questions about the wider significance of marginalized – provincialized, colonized and other non-metropolitan – people and places in politics of the regulation of sexuality (Phillips and Watt, 2000). How, for example, while they were unable to prevent the British Government from raising the age of consent in their country, were Indian people able to render the legislation unworkable (Kosambi, 1991)? The geography of purity must therefore be set alongside other geographies of formal and informal, intentional and unintentional politics of the regulation of sexuality.

Finally, I have suggested ways in which imperial geographies structured interventions in sexuality politics, but the reverse was also true; interventions in sexuality politics (re)produced imperial geographies. By illustrating ways in which they did so, it is possible to suggest the broader significance of interventions in sexuality politics. For example, by promoting changes to the age of consent, purity campaigners in South Australia helped to redefine some of the parameters of the nuclear family, perhaps the most important building block of their agricultural colonial society. By successfully resisting legislation that would have regulated prostitution in certain parts of South Australia, they helped to determine where in Adelaide a prostitute or other woman could go, with or without risk of police harassment. They thereby helped to define the gendered and sexualized geography of that colonial city. In addition to shaping significant details of colonial life, purity movements also played some part in broader imperial processes. Stoler (1991) has shown how the production and regulation of sexuality structured and reproduced particular colonial formations. With reference to racially structured colonialism in the Dutch East Indies and French

Indochina, she has shown how racial boundaries were produced, policed (often nervously) and naturalized (not always convincingly), partly through the tight regulation of sexuality. The relationship between purity movements and imperialism is more ambivalent. However, through their role in producing a differentiated sexual and moral geography, and in contesting the manner in which certain sexualized and marginalized people and places within that geography should be regulated, purity campaigners played an important part in the contestation and reproduction of social and spatial centres and margins, which were themselves fundamental to imperialism.

ACKNOWLEDGEMENTS

This research was funded by the British Academy. I would like to thank Mike Ingham, Alison Blunt and Cheryl McEwan for their comments on a draft of this chapter.

4

INQUIRIES AS POSTCOLONIAL DEVICES

THE CARNEGIE CORPORATION AND POVERTY IN SOUTH AFRICA

Morag Bell

In a recent critique of development studies and the postcolonial, Christine Sylvester (1999: 718) argues that the latter frequently offers more in the way of 'new-fangled language than food'. In its preoccupation with the colonial past, material concerns and pressing contemporary priorities including problems of global poverty, are rarely addressed except in an over-abstracted language (Dirlik, 1994; Simon, 1998). As a result, postcolonialism appears to offer little in the way of 'useful' knowledge beyond the intellectual authority bestowed by the academy. Notwithstanding these criticisms, Sylvester emphasizes that post-colonial agendas can be 'orientated to issues of material well-being that matter on the ground'. She highlights the freedom exercised by postcolonial writers to criticize 'creeds of progress openly', to draw on 'types of data' including imaginative literature little used by development studies, and, in moving 'in between the colonial and postcolonial spaces of many locations', to demonstrate 'the ways in which agents of development have been restructured and penetrated by colonised peoples' (1999:713). Building on these opportunities, this chapter explores some links between postcolonialism and the study of poverty. In doing so, it moves beyond questions of how the postcolonial is variously represented and interpreted (see Sidaway, this volume). Its purpose is to examine how our investigations may be framed and enhanced by drawing on the data sources and critical insights offered by postcolonial perspectives.

The chapter focuses on meanings of 'useful' knowledge about poverty in particular places at a specific time, namely, in South Africa and the USA during the final years of apartheid. It concentrates on the part played by an inquiry into poverty funded by the Carnegie Corporation of New York, which became known as the Second Carnegie Inquiry. In examining the significance or 'usefulness' of the Inquiry, rather than focus on the detail of its content (although this is important), my purpose is to examine the processes by which knowledge of poverty was constructed and communicated to various publics during the 1980s. In analysing these processes, attention is directed to the complex encounters within and between North and South that stimulated and shaped them. I examine the connections forged between the Carnegie Corporation, one of the largest international philanthropic trusts with its headquarters in New York, and a group of public intellectuals in South Africa, together with the network of relations within the respective territories which they drew upon and which influenced their activities.

In adopting this focus, the chapter questions some established assumptions about institutional knowledge and Western cultural power. Numerous critiques of international institutions highlight the exclusive and exclusionary professional circuits with which these institutions are associated, and the persistence in international debate of epistemologies rooted in the North. The chapter suggests that by shifting the focus from institutions to the practices in which they are engaged in particular times and places, including the instigation and implementation of inquiries, it is possible to refine these interpretations. Although inquiries are rooted in Western governmental practices, the chapter questions the extent to which they are necessarily an exclusive instrument of western cultural control. Rather, it is argued that by reference to postcolonial interpretations of representation, power and voice, the complex character and 'usefulness' of this cultural device in specific contexts can be explored. By tracing the origins and spatial genealogy of an inquiry over a period of ten years, and by examining the moods and motivations underpinning it, the chapter suggests that some of the subtle modes of power shaping North–South interactions can be identified. In the case of the Carnegie Inquiry, reference is made to the power of uncertainty within both the North and South in stimulating a form of inquiry that became characterized as a co-operative endeavour. The chapter examines how the meaning of this concept evolved as the Inquiry proceeded, the usefulness of this representation to groups within the South, and the ways in which the activities underpinning it became both creative and enabling.

NORTH–SOUTH ENCOUNTERS AND THE POSTCOLONIAL

Co-operative enterprises

Postcolonial perspectives have introduced some important themes and ethical considerations into studies of North–South interactions. Although this work is varied and there are difficulties in identifying common ground, collectively it provides a more decentred framework for conceptualizing these interactions than orthodox Western-centric approaches. In challenging the concept of the west as an enclosed entity, postcolonial critiques raise key questions about power, representation and voice. They seek to move beyond a notion of power as a one-way relationship between dominant and dominated, and point to the need to rethink the sites and agents of knowledge and representation beyond those customarily associated with the West/North (Crush, 1995; Rattansi, 1997; Slater, 1998). Within this framework, the concept of co-operative endeavour provides a focus for investigation. Co-operation in a range of spheres across established political and institutional boundaries is widely employed to exemplify sets of relations and forms of conduct which enshrine a decentred approach to the exercise of power and the production of knowledge. Implicit in the concept is the assumption that knowledge is partial and contingent and that there is value in engaging with dissenting voices and unorthodox views. Within science, Akira Iriye (1997) argues that since the early twentieth-century co-operation across national boundaries has formed an important part of cultural internationalism. In transcending geopolitical relations, he suggests that scientific exchanges have frequently challenged contemporary inequalities in the distribution of geopolitical power. Within the development field, the widespread use of 'partnerships with developing countries' in recent policy documents on international aid implies a similar decentred approach (DFID, 1997, 2000).

Many commentators are unconvinced. Although co-operation and partnership as ideas and ideals have a postcolonial appeal, as a set of practices, the evidence is weak. Questions arise over 'ownership' of ideas in debate and the spatialities of power over representation. In Edward Said's (1983) exploration of travelling theory, he discusses how the movement of ideas and theories between cultures involves processes of representation and institutionalization that are different from those at the point of origin. For institutions located in the North the interpretation of international interchange as 'co-operation across' may disguise the complex spatial genealogies of ideas and the significance of the countries of the South as a key source of these ideas. It may also overlook the very different ways in which this interchange is represented in other institutional and spatial settings (Slater and Bell, 2002). Notwithstanding the appeal of co-operative endeavour as an idea, evidence suggests that it frequently operates to exclude certain regions and social groups and tends to reproduce modes of 'power over' the South in particular. The extent to which this is necessarily so requires close examination. It is suggested here that a postcolonial framework provides scope to evaluate, in particular times and places, the meaning and significance of 'co-operation across' established boundaries. It prompts new questions about the spatial and temporal contexts within which the concept is created and sustained, including by and for whom and for what purpose it is inspired. It also provides scope to trace the spatial genealogy of specific interactions with which cooperative endeavour is associated.

As a focus for examining ideas and practices in terms of origins and travellings, an inquiry into poverty provides the point of convergence here. In terms of contexts, reference is made to the influence of a prevailing atmosphere of uncertainty in both the North and the South in stimulating and shaping it.

Uncertainty – decentring cultural power

As mood or attitude, doubt and uncertainty have been widely used to characterize contemporary times in the countries of the North in particular. In an era of supposedly unprecedented change, this mood is widely interpreted as a function of broader changes in global conditions. For some writers, these anxieties are the product of a decisive historical shift in prevailing beliefs, material conditions, orientations in space and time and in relational values (Bauman, 1997; Beck, 1999). Contemporary global processes are associated with unprecedented interactions between spaces and cultures. The 'disorientating' effects are linked, in the west at least, with an end to established intellectual and social orders and a challenge to fixed identities of nation, class and 'race' (Williams, 1997). Other commentators are sceptical of the newness implicit in this representation of our times. Although a tendency to discredit the old in order to privilege the new may be an inherently modernist instinct, it is argued that the search for both collective and personal control in an unstable and uncertain world has been a consistent feature of western modernity (Osborne, 1995; Lash *et al.*, 1996). For many critics this characterization of the present also marginalizes the experiences of the countries of the South where conditions of uncertainty, risk and anxiety have been, and remain, for the majority of the world's population an essential part of daily survival (Simon, 1998) and where the continuities between past and present are as significant as any discontinuities (Escobar, 2001).

Representations of the present in terms of 'disjuncture' are directly linked to treatments of time and the past. Disjuncture suggests a rupture or break with the past. As a mode of interpretation, it may be deployed, as above, to define distinctive epochal shifts or separate moments in time. Periodization does, however, tend to be based upon the identification of major public events frequently associated with the West. Moreover, it implies the principle of linear change and serial time, an approach to history that has been challenged both within and beyond the West (Chakrabarty, 1992a; McClintock, 1992). The notion of disjuncture also characterizes particular relations between past and present. In an era of 'time–space compression' for many social theorists the 'disjunctured past' is 'beyond recovery' (Dodgshon, 1999: 611). There is a sense of liberation or freedom from its burden. This characterization does, however, reinforce a recent tendency in Western social thought to prioritize spatial over temporal analysis and with this, the assumption that time can no longer play a significant role in the interpretation of contemporary social processes. Postcolonial critiques challenge Western modes of representing and interpreting the past. They also question the relative neglect of temporal analysis in the wake of the spatialization of social theory. In doing so they provide an alternative framework for conceptualizing uncertainty.

In postcolonial critiques disjuncture or a 'disjunctive present' (Bhabha, 1994: 254) relates to the notion of classificatory disorder, namely, to the undermining or disorganization of established histories or narratives of cultures written in 'homogeneous serial time'. Building on Dipesh Chakrabarty's (1992a) insistence on provincializing Europe in critiques of history, postcolonial perspectives seek to break down familiar chains of signification by focusing on systems of reference other than those produced by and for the West. In the practice of 're-writing' the past, the notion of rupture or break relates to the sites and agents of knowledge and representation. For many societies this practice has formed part of a process of recovery and restorative justice in the aftermath of European imperialism (Werbner, 1998). But it is also profoundly important for histories within the west in highlighting the mutuality in identity formation between colonizer and colonized, globalizer and globalized, and in undermining the binary oppositions implicit in these dualities (Chun, 2000). For Ali Rattansi (1997), a mood of uncertainty in the North can be linked to this classificatory disorder. In the aftermath of the imperial past, he identifies within the former metropoles a pervasive sense of postcolonial doubt over the nature of the encounter between former colonizers and colonized and over how this encounter is conceptualized and represented. Contrary to those poststructural critics for whom history is beyond recovery and the past is redundant in explanations of the present (Dodgshon, 1999), postcolonial interpretations of time affirm the importance of alternative histories *for* the present (Said, 2000). Recovering these alternative histories has assumed a special significance recently in South Africa.

The following analysis draws together and also seeks to move beyond the broad critiques discussed above. It argues that there is a need to ground them in experiences. Specifically there is value in examining how concepts of co-operation, uncertainty and time are interpreted by different groups in certain spatial and temporal contexts and the significance of these interpretations for particular practices. In defining contexts, rather than focus on either the countries of the North or the South as these critiques tend to do, it is argued that they may also cut across North and South.

SOUTH AFRICA'S TRANSFORMATION

In April 1994 for the first time, South Africa held democratic elections on the basis of one-person-one-vote. In and beyond the country, they were interpreted as a decisive historical moment in the creation of the 'New South Africa'. For the Government of National Unity a central feature of the transition from apartheid to post-apartheid political orders was the formulation of strategies through which to confront the legacies of the apartheid past. These included not only new programmes of reconstruction and development but also initiatives through which the traumatic experiences of apartheid could be publicly recorded. The Truth and Reconciliation Commission, established in 1996, provided a particular focus for remembering. Its victim-centred approach enabled thousands of hitherto voiceless and powerless people across the country to recount their experiences of gross human rights violations (Boraine, 2000). In addition, within the academy there is a commitment to exposing and analysing the country's bitterly contested past. This academic research builds on a stream of critical indigenous scholarship, which gained momentum during the final years of apartheid. The Carnegie Inquiry into poverty formed part of this critical scholarship. Analysis of the Inquiry contributes to the contemporary process of recounting and recovering. It focuses on how, during the 1980s, uncertainty as mood and co-operation as practice were experienced by and drew together different groups across North and South and how these concepts held certain meanings and assumed a particular significance for them. In doing so it is possible to demonstrate how an inquiry as a seemingly orthodox cultural device came to enshrine postcolonial qualities as a mode of resistance to apartheid.

Inquiring into poverty

> Poverty is like an illness – it is complex – its different forms need to be described and understood. (Wilson, 1986: 5)

> Visual images have helped shape our view of Africa. The haunting looks of starving children mobilized support for relief to Ethiopia. The brutality of authorities in Soweto and Alexandra has made apartheid an American cause as well as an African one. These images play to the emotions, generating a simple, almost visceral response. They do nothing, however, to explain the causes of famine or the intricacies of a political and economic system. (William B. Hamilton, 8 June 1986: 6)

In his monumental study, *The African Poor*, the historian John Iliffe (1987) argued that close analysis of human impoverishment had profoundly important practical *and* intellectual implications. It provided an important opportunity to move away from elitist colonial histories and the parochial nature of the national histories that replaced them. Although there were difficulties in finding a usable definition of poverty, Iliffe acknowledged the significance of numerous country studies carried out during the 1970s and 1980s by agencies including the International Labour Organization and the World Bank, and what he described as 'the massive Carnegie Inquiry into poverty and development in southern Africa' (ibid.: 1). The words by Francis Wilson recorded above are taken from the findings of this 'massive Inquiry'. William B. Hamilton's comments, quoted in the *Washington Post Magazine,* represent one response to the Inquiry, the findings of which were widely disseminated in the countries of the North, including the USA, in the second half of the 1980s.

Contexts

On 4 April 1984, the recently appointed President of the Carnegie Corporation circulated a memo to a small delegation from the Corporation that was about to embark on a visit to South Africa. They were to attend a conference in Cape Town that formed part of the Second Inquiry. He wrote:

> I find myself intrigued and troubled by our impending visit. Why are we going? What have we been trying to do? How can we assess the prospects for a useful role there in terms of fundamental democratic values? ... Perhaps the visit can help to resolve our ambivalence ... I do not assume that we will carry on a program in South Africa indefinitely ... Much will depend on our assessment of the potential for specific socially useful interventions.[1]

The uncertainty implicit in the President's memo derived in part from the timing of the Inquiry. It was carried out during the 10 years of acute tension and unrest that characterized South Africa between the entry of P.W. Botha to the position of Prime Minister and the release of Nelson Mandela from prison in February 1990. It also echoed a broader unease. In contrast to the confidence and optimism typically associated with Western scientific culture, his words communicated the insecurities of modernity; not least doubts over the meaning of 'progress' and the moral rectitude of Northern interventionist practices in the countries of the South. Within the Corporation it was a period of debate and reflection over its role in Africa and South Africa in particular.

Support by the Corporation during the 1980s for what became the Second Carnegie Inquiry into Poverty and Development in Southern Africa can be interpreted as one in a long history of projects funded by this philanthropic trust in the continent dating back to the late 1920s. Indeed, one of its earliest ventures into Africa took the form of the first Carnegie Inquiry. Conducted in South Africa during the late 1920s, it had been entitled a Commission of Investigation into the Poor White Problem, and was popularly known as the Poor White Study. The Second Inquiry also had a powerful contemporary resonance. Initiated at the conclusion of a decade in which the United Nations had placed priority on meeting basic human needs, it can be interpreted as one of a series of country studies conducted at the time with a view to promoting an internationalist humanitarian ideology (Iliffe, 1987). With its focus on poverty, the Inquiry brought together the latest international development priority with an established concern of Western philanthropy, namely, poverty alleviation. However, for the initiators of the Inquiry, it occupied a more specific place in history and the present in which the Corporation's association with South Africa at this particular time was crucial in shaping both the character of the Inquiry and the identity of the Corporation.

The launching of the Second Inquiry marked the renewal of the Corporation's involvement in South Africa after a period of some 30 years. Following World War II, the Corporation had redirected its resources from South Africa to the countries of the Commonwealth, including those parts of Africa where political independence from Britain was being secured. By the late 1970s the strategy of the Corporation had shifted as South Africa was drawn into the Corporation's orbit once again. Far from an 'unknown' territory in the popular international imagination, following the Soweto riots and the death of Steve Biko, South Africa had become a major focus of global media attention as a morally repugnant state (Tapscott, 1995). Within the country, the rise of P.W. Botha to the premiership in 1978 was followed by the introduction of a new reformist rhetoric by the ruling elite with a view to restructuring the system.

Institutional relations

Support for the Inquiry by the Corporation represented a form of transgressive institutional conduct in which a degree of humility and reflexivity were important characteristics. The Corporation's involvement in the country came under attack from opponents of apartheid in America who argued that such involvement lent legitimacy and respectability to the regime. By contrast, for Alan Pifer, the Corporation's President, it built on the spirit of the Corporation's Charter. As if to counter the muted condemnation of apartheid by the American and British administrations at this time (O'Tuathail, 1992), by the late 1970s the Corporation had reopened a selective programme in the country with the specific objective of supporting 'the first glimmerings of a prospect for peaceful change'. As part of this, support for a 'scientific analysis' of poverty offered scope to produce 'useful' knowledge that would not only further discredit the system but would also contribute to promoting 'new' times within the country (Carnegie Corporation, 1980: 4).

This dual objective appealed to members of the Corporation and many groups working to end apartheid in South Africa. It gave a Second Inquiry strategic significance as a legitimate expression of North–South 'co-operation' and solidarity in the interests of democratic values and racial equality. As part of a discourse of social justice and political transformation, it offered not only the opportunity to underline the failure of successive apartheid regimes to confront the evidence of inequality within South African society as a whole, as opposed to a small section of it, but more optimistically, scope to support 'some new system' (Carnegie Corporation, 1980: 4). In combining condemnation with a commitment to social action, it also chimed with a particular concern of Alan Pifer who, on becoming President in 1967, and in response to urban riots and the civil rights movement in America during the 1960s, had sought to make poverty a major focus of the Corporation's programme.

Crucially, pressure for the Inquiry came not from the Corporation but from prominent anti-apartheid intellectuals within South Africa. The Inquiry's principal architect in South Africa, Professor Francis Wilson, recalls that although the possibility of a second Carnegie Inquiry had been discussed within the country many times since the 1930s, and indeed the Corporation had received numerous requests, by the late 1970s the circumstances were right. The Corporation's new director of the international programme, David Hood, was travelling through southern Africa actively seeking research proposals at a time when the apartheid regime continued to deny the scale and nature of poverty within its territory. Clearly, for both the Corporation as funding agency and those responsible for designing the Inquiry in South Africa, there were compelling internal processes of justification which, while somewhat different, were nevertheless compatible.

Ideas and designs – continuities / discontinuities

The Inquiry quite specifically built on the concept of co-operative endeavour. For the Corporation, the transfer of resources from New York to South Africa was a strategically important gesture. It symbolized a form of inter-continental solidarity and identification with an already well-established intellectual traffic in radical ideas within and beyond that country. But for the Corporation, the form of institutional co-operation across the two continents was also crucial in determining its acceptability within South Africa. It was essential that the Corporation was free from any implications of ethnocentric control. In defining its role beyond providing funds, Alan Pifer made this point clear in his 1980 presidential report:

> Trying to affect change in another country, especially one as complex as South Africa, is ... something that must be approached with considerable sensitivity, a great deal of humility and enough skepticism about the relevance of American experience to know that this country cannot be held up as an unquestioned model for South Africa, however useful certain pieces of our experience may be. (Carnegie Corporation, 1980: 14)

His emphasis was on differences between the two territories rather than on common ground. Moreover, in openly acknowledging the climate of political uncertainty that accompanied P.W. Botha's early years in office, and the Corporation's own lack of detailed knowledge and experience of the country, he and the trustees affirmed that it was within South Africa rather than outside it that the necessary expertise lay. Responsibility for designing, stimulating and co-ordinating the Inquiry was assigned to Professor Francis Wilson and the Southern Africa Labour and Development Research Unit (*Saldru*), University of Cape Town (UCT). One of South Africa's oldest and most prestigious institutions of higher education for the white population, it had become among its most outspoken critics of apartheid (Jansen, 1991).

The credibility of the study to a range of competing interests in South Africa depended on establishing a form of critical inquiry which would genuinely look forward, and over which the apartheid regime would have no control. Political anxieties over the position of the researchers as public intellectuals, and uncertainties over how the Inquiry might be shaped and implemented, proved to be an enabling process for those involved. The institutional arrangements finally reached and the cultural technologies used in the research process evolved over a period of two years and as a result of detailed consultation between members of the Corporation, various black, English- and Afrikaans-speaking groups and Francis Wilson who was appointed consultant to the Corporation in 1980. In effect, it was the outcome of lengthy debate over the form and purpose of the Inquiry rather than fixed at the outset. Wilson recalls that during his initial consultations across the country in 1980 prior to the launching of the Inquiry, clear differences of opinion emerged. The majority of white South Africans to whom he spoke were excited about the idea and requested all the facts and information that could be gathered. By contrast, many black South Africans were deeply sceptical about the need 'to spend real dollars discovering this poverty'; they wanted action (personal communication, 31 March 1998).

Deploying the past

The outcome was an Inquiry of hybrid character. On one level, it was conformist; on another, it was transgressive and transformative. Its conformist character is reflected in the common ground that was deliberately sought with the first Inquiry conducted some 50 years previously. Within the public domain the principle of historical continuity was actively employed as a validation strategy. At a time of acute political tension in South Africa when radical voices, including participants in the Inquiry, sought to break with the past, two features of this earlier Inquiry were profoundly important in ensuring that a second could take place; time was used as a landmark in the numerical recording of social change; a similar institutional language and cultural technologies were employed.

For the purposes of national publicity, a gap of 50 years since the Poor White Study offered a legitimate reason for a follow-up study of broader character but with similar objectives. An emphasis on the funding body as an independent philanthropic foundation that had supported educational activities in South Africa over that same period, was intended to counter criticisms that those involved in South Africa had been co-opted in the interests of capital and that the Corporation was a mere agent of US foreign policy. In terms of institutional language, much was made of its importance as a 'scientific' study. Defined by

Francis Wilson in a national press release on 14 April 1982, as the collection and collation of up-to-date 'facts' on poverty and the process of impoverishment, debate over the major causes, and the production of proposed strategies against it, the language bore strong similarities to that of the Poor White Study. Co-ordinated like its predecessor by an academic institution and retaining the label of a formal Inquiry based on co-operation between a range of agencies, this arrangement also gave it, like its predecessor, the status of an official investigation and public legitimacy through its independence from official manipulation.

However, this deliberate deployment of continuity for the purposes of external consumption facilitated a profoundly different kind of Inquiry from its predecessor and one that apartheid sympathizers could not easily discredit. Thus an orthodox image of the university as the intellectual space for politically neutral, objective science was used to full effect. In an interview for the *Sunday Times* of South Africa (18 April 1982), Wilson emphasized the Inquiry's role in uncovering the facts about poverty and of UCT as 'an independent university' acting as a public forum for debate about these facts which would be of interest to 'people right across the political spectrum'. But in their production, this same setting provided a protected space, a laboratory, within which to experiment. Following a gap of a half-century and within an international intellectual environment openly hostile to the universal applicability of epistemologies rooted in the North, the second study specifically recast concepts of useful knowledge, scientific practice and the nature of expertise. Prior to its formal launch in April 1992, Francis Wilson spent a period of six months travelling the country and consulting a wide range of different people, notably those who were banned, in order to ensure that the subject matter, design and conduct of the Inquiry would be widely accepted.

In defining its scope, although in the 1980s poverty was endured primarily by the black population, in seeking to minimize the notion of a separate and exclusive ethnic category of poverty with or without the right to vote, the study was not confined to a specific demographic group. Moreover, rather than adopt a specific definition of the concept, the complex meanings and manifestations of poverty were elicited in the research process (Wentzel, 1982). Equally, in the details of its internal design the notion of a commission involving a few 'wise persons' charged with responsibility for conducting the research and compiling reports, was replaced by a more inclusive study (Wilson, 1983: 5). In contrast to the prevailing technocratic policy discourse which sought to perpetuate the notion of development as a science guided by the objectivity of the scientific method, in the process of knowledge production, notation and dissemination, the imperatives were social critique, plurality and participation. Equally, the boundaries of useful knowledge were redefined and democratized as the study encouraged participation beyond the spheres of academe and professional practitioners to include also those closest to the experience of poverty such as social workers and community leaders.

Networks of exchange

Thus the form of the Inquiry was neither carefully planned at the outset, nor an initial condition for funding. Unlike the Poor White Study, which depended on established networks for its implementation, contributors to the Second Inquiry produced diverse circuits of knowledge as part of the research process. Over 400 people from across the country and from neighbouring states in Southern Africa were involved. The results of their investigations were recorded in written form and the contents of the papers were communicated to the contributors through an 'interactive network' between them. Francis Wilson records that the possibility of building up this network 'emerged as one of the most exciting aspects of the Inquiry'.[2] Participants were brought together at a public conference hosted by the University of Cape Town from 13–19 April 1984. Deemed to be an appropriate means through which to consolidate the Inquiry as a 'co-operative venture', the conference offered a forum for debating and disseminating the findings from the various investigations and a basis for practical action. In eschewing disciplinary traditions both the research design and conference structure combined a thematic and a spatial approach. Thus the relationship between poverty and, for example, the law, education, food and nutrition policy, the Church and the allocation of public funds was combined with detailed analysis of poverty in particular localities.

The conference provided a forum for a study that was designed to be inclusive and including. It was intended as a form of co-operative science that transcended disciplinary boundaries and a co-operative experience that extended beyond the boundaries of the academy. By 1984, it involved many activists who had recently been unbanned. In effect, it formed an essential part of the research process where the participants, while disagreeing on many issues, were nevertheless afforded the opportunity to present, debate and represent their views. At the conference a variety of settings were made available for this purpose and different media (written, oral, visual) were encouraged including verbal presentations, a film festival and a photographic exhibition. The 1984 conference enshrined what were to become three prominent features of the Inquiry, namely, a dynamic research process in which the participation was broadly based and evolved gradually through consultation. The conference also came to reflect a fourth important feature of the Inquiry, the widespread public reaction to it both within South Africa and beyond.

Dissent and critique

It was the staging of this major and unprecedented event in Cape Town that attracted the initial attention of the international press. In exposing the extent of poverty at such a public forum, the evidence was reported in the *Guardian* (16 April 1984), the *International Herald Tribune* (23 April 1984) and the *Star Overseas Edition* (30 April 1984). It also provoked comment and criticism from different groups in South Africa. Some black organizations argued that it was largely conducted, and the conference hosted, by white liberals. From the initial consultation phase, however, Wilson and his colleagues had deliberately sought to ensure that it had a 'real black centre of gravity' and indeed 25 per cent of the papers were produced by black authors. While Wilson emphasized that this was 'not as it should be', it was nevertheless 'a lot better than it had ever been before' (personal communication, 31 March 1998). Criticism of the Inquiry and the public conference came also from government officials. During a debate in

Parliament (14 April 1984), the Minister of Health suggested that its findings might have some merit if they were evaluated on scientific grounds and not used to make political points. The *Natal Daily News* (15 April 1984) reported that a National Party member had ridiculed the study as 'flagrantly unscientific, naive and one-sided'. Similar criticisms were made by the Prime Minister, P.W. Botha in a statement to the House of Assembly on 14 May 1984, in which he stated, 'I find it remarkable that a Carnegie investigation of poverty should be carried out in South Africa when the great continent of Africa is dying of hunger.' In condemning the study for its supposedly misleading assumptions, he voiced the impressions held by many white South Africans about their country at this time. The extent of alarmist press reporting on the findings of the Inquiry within South Africa both during and after the conference confirms this level of ignorance, or unwillingness to acknowledge the depth of poverty.

For the Corporation itself, as the Inquiry proceeded there were doubts and anxieties. Conducted during what Ellen Lagemann (1989) defines as a strategic phase in the Corporation's grant-making and initiated in 1980 under the presidency of Alan Pifer, it was carried out under the new President, David Hamburg (1982–97), for whom the value of the programme in South Africa was in doubt. I return to the memo circulated by him with which this section of the chapter began. Issued on the eve of a visit by himself and six trustees of the Corporation to the 1984 Conference in Cape Town, a gathering that was central to the process and outcome of the Second Inquiry, it captured his deep unease over the credibility of Carnegie in South Africa. In particular, it reflected the tensions between a desire to support those groups openly hostile to apartheid but with limited material power to destroy it, and the need to fulfil the terms of the Corporation's grant-giving. Writing to members of the Delegation, the President concluded:

> Perhaps most important, will people in and out of government be inspired to use some of the information presented at the meeting to improve the lot of the poor? ... Can we hope for some long-term response from the Government? Would we be able to recognise the role of the Poverty Project if it happened?[3]

In line with the wishes of the Corporation's founder, Andrew Carnegie, for the new President it was the practical impact of the Inquiry that would determine the future of the Carnegie programme in South Africa; it should be 'socially useful' within the country and be absorbed into public consciousness within the countries of the North.

The President's candid remarks highlight what became a crucial feature of the Inquiry, namely, its significance for the identity of the Corporation. For its officials and trustees, the Inquiry was viewed as a learning experience. The President's address on the final day of the 1984 conference ranged widely over twentieth-century North–South relations and the role of the Corporation in these. Focusing on the 'astounding' advances in institutionalized science and technology and the potential benefits to human well-being, he also eschewed scientific determinism by reaffirming the power of science and technology not merely to relieve but also to increase human suffering. The latter, he argued, was a 'root cause of human impoverishment, and a dilemma that has reached crisis proportions in South Africa'.[4] Within this context, he returned to the First Inquiry and the constructive role of time in shaping the Corporation's subsequent activities. Widely credited as having assisted in the process of alleviating poverty among the Poor Whites, Hamburg also openly acknowledged its failure, 'like most of mankind in that era, to recognize fully the humanity of black Africans ... They were ... dimly viewed as peripheral to human society.'

For the Corporation the Second Inquiry had been approached with humility. There was much praise for the skill of those responsible within South Africa and for its innovative nature in view of the 'hostile political atmosphere' within which it was conducted. Hamburg and his colleagues had already publicly distanced the Corporation from US policy towards South Africa at this time. According to Hamburg, the study documented the many faces of poverty to an extent 'rarely achieved in any country' and 'the participants ... deserve our respect and admiration'.[5] In addressing an issue inextricably linked to the humanity of all people, he emphasized that the findings should have significance throughout the world. A psychiatrist by training, Hamburg drew particular attention to the complex position of science in society. The South African study he argued, like similar studies of poverty in other parts of the world, emphasized that notwithstanding the 'prodigious capabilities' of the human species for 'technical skill', the elimination of human impoverishment depended upon confronting the 'ubiquitous tendencies toward prejudice, ethnocentrism and violent conflict'.[6] As President of one of the most powerful American philanthropic institutions, Hamburg also challenged the comfortable assumption that poverty happens 'elsewhere' by referring specifically to the importance of the Inquiry within the USA where the Corporation supported work 'to illuminate and overcome' the multiple dimensions of 'human impoverishment'.[7]

Dissemination

During the 1980s, the Inquiry as a cultural device had multiple influences. For the participants, the research process offered scope for a public indictment of apartheid and a means by which to discuss openly alternative strategies. For the sponsor of the Inquiry, it defined a set of connections across continents in which South Africa was cast as strategically important. It was a suitable location in Africa within which to promote the Corporation's international objectives. For those who learned of the Inquiry outside South Africa, it offered a structured way of rendering meaningful the history and contemporary struggles of a specific country and its people. Following the 1984 conference and with financial support from the Corporation, the Inquiry's findings were widely disseminated through the remainder of the 1980s. Two major publications followed. In 1986, *South Africa: The Cordoned Heart* was published. It documented and illustrated through the photographs displayed at the 1984 conference, the conditions of poverty primarily affecting the black population (Wilson, 1986). In 1989, Francis Wilson and Mamphela Ramphele produced a major report on the main findings of the Inquiry. Entitled *Uprooting Poverty: The South African Challenge*, it was widely reviewed in the South African and the international press.

Of the various media used to communicate the findings of the Inquiry beyond the country, the militant and emphatic qualities of the photographs were among the most powerful. At the request of the Corporation's trustees notably Avery Russell, the photographic exhibition displayed at the 1984 conference in Cape Town toured within South Africa and beyond. It was shown in London's Photographers' Gallery for one month in April 1986 in conjunction with a retrospective collection by the leading South African photographer, David Goldblatt. The former then toured the UK with support from Christian Aid and Oxfam. It subsequently moved to the USA. With the Corporation's assistance, the International Center of Photography, New York University, in conjunction with the Centre for Documentary Photography, Duke University, launched a two-month exhibit of 60 photographs from 9 May to 22 June, 1986. Following this display in New York, with further funding from the Corporation the exhibition travelled to 25 cities around the country over a nine-year period (Carnegie Corporation, 1991). The final presentation was at the Schomberg Center for Research in Black Culture in New York City. It took place in April 1994 to coincide with the founding elections in South Africa and was seen by more than 25,000 people.

CONCLUSION

Postcolonialism has been characterized as a redemptive doctrine in its ability to challenge and question established truths. In unsettling conventional classificatory schemes and identities it is associated with the 'disorientations' of the present. It has also been criticized for its failure to fulfil this exalted position. It is nevertheless acknowledged that postcolonial perspectives can offer critical insights on issues of material well-being and of contemporary global concern. This chapter has sought to explore these links. By reference to a particular cultural device, an inquiry, and a specific context within which it was used to examine poverty, the analysis has demonstrated the complexities and subtleties of institutional knowledge, identity and power. In doing so, it has harnessed and built upon some postcolonial interpretations of space and time.

Tracing the spatial genealogy of ideas is central to the postcolonial as critique. In the opening years of this new century, poverty is once again on the agenda of Northern institutions including philanthropic trusts. Within contemporary South Africa it is a crucial political and moral concern. But as a thematic priority it is not new. The Second Carnegie Inquiry into poverty can be interpreted as a specific case in the complex global histories and geographies of this concept. Conducted at a particular moment in North–South relations, it represents one of many national poverty studies initiated during the 1970s and 1980s. But it also has a more specific significance. As the cruel legacies of apartheid are confronted by the present post-apartheid government, remembering past atrocities and injustices has also been interpreted as crucial to South Africa's future as a new and united nation. The Carnegie Inquiry is integral to the histories and geographies of inequality and resistance. At a time when physical violence and unrest had rendered much of South Africa ungovernable, the Inquiry reflected the strategic use of 'facts' to undermine the apartheid system. Moreover, although funded by a Northern trust and carrying its name, the inspiration and initiative came entirely from within South Africa.

Analysis of the Inquiry has focused on its significance as socially useful knowledge. Thus questions have been raised about how, by whom and for what purpose it was produced and communicated. A supposedly orthodox device, emphasis has been placed on its unorthodoxy, that is, its role in raising public awareness of human impoverishment at a time in South Africa when the nature and extent of poverty were widely ignored or denied by the white population at least. Within this context, the Inquiry has been viewed and examined not as a specific event with a single documentary outcome but as a series of dynamic interactions within and across the North–South divide. By tracing its dynamics over a period of some 10 years it has been demonstrated that much may lie behind a supposedly conventional investigation and the details of its content. The evidence challenges established assumptions about the authority and moral certainty underpinning the actions of Northern institutions. It highlights how in particular circumstances, multiple sites and agents of knowledge may be involved, and that complex and subtle power relations may operate within and across the countries of the North and South.

In examining how the Inquiry came to be represented as a co-operative endeavour, particular attention has been given to the ways in which its formulation and implementation were inspired by the experience of uncertainty. In other words, co-operation has been interpreted not as a point of departure but as the outcome of a convergence of circumstances, which drew together the New York-based Corporation and anti-apartheid groups in South Africa and which enabled the latter to conduct a series of transgressive practices. Thus, in contrast to those critics who pathologize uncertainty as a chronic weakness, the focus has been on its creative and enabling power. In the case of the Carnegie Inquiry, it prompted a hybrid study, in which an appeal to conventional practices within the public domain disguised inner transgressive processes. Thus strategic uses of the past, of scientific 'objectivity', and of 'respected' cultural technologies, to validate the study in public, disguised hidden networks of knowledge and modes of representing poverty that promoted public debate and political action; in effect, networks and modes of representation that were transgressive and transformative.

The significance of the Inquiry within a postcolonial framework can therefore be assessed on a number of levels. While extensive publicity was given to its findings in the national and international press, an important achievement in itself at the time, the power of the Inquiry lies as much in the hidden, unexpected and long-term as in the immediate, public and obvious. None of the participants and least of all its architects would argue that it made a significant contribution to ending apartheid beyond further discrediting the system. But as 'useful' knowledge, more important although less obvious at the time, was the research process itself in giving a voice to those to whom it had been denied, in anticipation of a post-apartheid future. Indeed, several of the participants who, immediately prior to the Inquiry, were banned, came to hold senior positions in the post-apartheid administration.

As an exercise in North–South co-operation, for this influential Northern trust the study was also important in unexpected ways. Granted its credibility was enhanced by a major dissemination exercise that extended well beyond South Africa into Europe and North America during the 1980s. But this public image obscures the internal debates extending over some 10 years, and the genuine anxieties of some of its leading decision-makers, over the position of the New York-based Corporation as funding body and supporter of radical social science activists in South Africa. Here was an institution which, through its venture into 'the unknown', became quite effectively harnessed by public intellectuals in the South; began cautiously resourcing a preliminary investigation in 1980; on the eve of the Inquiry's first major public hearing in 1984 remained unsure how it should proceed; but which, as a result of this public hearing, sustained a South Africa programme linked directly to the Inquiry until 1990. In his valedictory report to the Corporation in 1996 the President, David Hamburg, recalled 'the extraordinary experience of the Second Carnegie Inquiry' as one of the major features of his presidency.[8]

ACKNOWLEDGEMENTS

This chapter is based on research carried out in Cape Town and New York with financial support from Loughborough University and from the Wellcome Trust for the History of Medicine. Columbia University Rare Book and Manuscript Library provided access to the files of the Carnegie Corporation of New York. My thanks to Professor Francis Wilson, University of Cape Town, for making available to me material associated with the Second Carnegie Inquiry and for invaluable discussions.

PART II

URBAN ORDER, CITIZENSHIP AND SPECTACLE

INTRODUCTION TO PART II

The chapters in Part II all raise, either explicitly or implicitly, issues about urban, national and imperial citizenship. The chapters by Satish Kumar, Mark McGuinness and Jenny Robinson ground theoretical issues of racialized subjectivity in the materialities of imperial/postcolonial urban spaces. Kumar explores aspects of racialized and class-based subjectivity in his essay on the ordering, sanitation and segregation of urban colonial space in Madras from the late sixteenth century until 1941. He argues that the invocation of various forms of law and regulation helped to create a special form of colonial urban civil society, which sought its identity by remaining aloof and separate from rural India. In this way urban space was not only made representational, but also nostalgic and hygienic and riven with conflicts of interests. Kumar explores how class became an overriding issue along with 'race' in maintaining difference and how a discursive space co-existed with representational space, which ordered segregation in a hierarchical space along caste, class and 'race' lines.

Mark McGuinness explores renewed concern for and interest in 'race' and ethnicity in contemporary Britain. This chapter interrogates emerging policy responses to the disturbances in de-industrialized northern towns during the summer of 2001 and, in particular, how they relate to debates about post-colonial citizenship and difference. The theme of 'misreading' difference that McGuinness argues is apparent in these debates is further developed by examining attempts by geographers to re-read and re-write the city to account for racial diversity. In this sense, McGuinness further explains some of the issues raised in Sidaway's chapter by using postcolonial theory to expose and critique the unwitting ethnocentrism of contemporary geographical knowledge. He uses critiques of whiteness to expose the taken-for-granted white norms that inform the practices of contemporary academic geography. Geographers still carry out studies of difference and hybridity in the most obvious sites of non-white migration while whiteness itself remains transparent to the critical scholarly gaze. Thus the chapter argues that despite the embracing of postcolonialism by geographers, the discipline stills lacks a fundamentally decolonized geographical language through which to speak about the world, and about difference in particular. Like Sidaway, therefore, McGuinness problematizes the relationship between geography and postcolonialism and poses challenging questions for the discipline.

Jenny Robinson draws on similar themes in her discussion of Johannesburg's 1936 Empire Exhibition, which celebrated the city's half-century and the achievements of South Africa within an imperial frame. In this racialized context, the modern city could be seen as racially exclusive, but Robinson demonstrates that while the historiography of the South African city emphasizes the segregation of African people on the outskirts of the city, the Empire Exhibition brought into view a potential common city space. The enthusiasm of

African people for visiting the Exhibition, and their participation in various exhibits and displays marked both Empire and the city as at least to some extent a 'terrain common to whites and non-whites' (Said, 1993), allowing Robinson to explore the 'overlapping territories' of the postcolonial city. Like McGuinness, Robinson is concerned with whiteness and its encounter with racialized others, in this case how white South Africans interacted with and responded to the diversity of histories and cultures on display at an imperial exhibition. By exploring the intersubjective geographies of white identities in this specific context, therefore, Robinson develops an argument that responds in many ways to the critique outlined by McGuinness, but in rather different ways. More broadly, Robinson reflects upon the spatialities of postcolonialism, their implications for a postcolonial politics, and the possibilities that a more sympathetic reading of whiteness might hold for the post-apartheid city.

Ideas about urban spectacle and postcolonialism are further discussed by Marcus Power in the context of the contemporary politics of decolonization in Portugal. Like Robinson, Power uses a postcolonial framework to examine Portugal's EXPO '98, exploring how memories of imperial spaces and places are woven into nostalgic conceptions of national difference and of national history. He critiques the continuing seductiveness of empire in Portugal's national imaginary, the erasure of more problematic colonial histories and the continuing marginalization of the formerly colonized voice in these histories.

5

THE EVOLUTION OF SPATIAL ORDERING IN COLONIAL MADRAS

M. Satish Kumar

Madras (now known as Chennai) is a postcolonial city illustrating historical continuity in disjuncture across multiple precolonial and colonial spaces. Postcolonial urban space is not simply a physical entity, but is also a relational identity, created by interactions across traditional, premodern and modern spatial boundaries and between the colonized and the colonizer. How were colonial spatial multiplicities layered and transformed into a spatial unity? What were the moral imperatives of this enterprise? Colonization captured space and therefore established boundaries across which there were multiple interactions. Such forms of multilayered spatiality were socially produced. This space was also used to project moral standards and gradations of cultural appropriateness in time. Spatial appropriations were premised, therefore, on specific moral, economic and political strategies of conquest.

This chapter analyses the importance of boundaries and the resultant spaces in colonial Madras. Major differences existed between the indigenous precolonial and colonial urban spaces in the city. The evolution of spatial ordering in Madras illustrates a definitive trajectory between the initial precolonial imprint and colonized urban space, segregated by imperial, colonial and indigenous identities.

Discourses on urban space and its construction and planning were always invested with intense political and cultural significance. In this respect, the political economy of urban growth cannot be addressed outside the scope of the moral and cultural agenda so visible in the rise of imperialism. Colonial urban practices, therefore, reflected these imperatives and invariably ended up as fragmented and disjointed because of constant shifts in imperial policy. Postcolonialism thus confronts the spatiality of imperial and colonial control.

The postcolonial predicament forces an assimilation of interpretations of inscribed urban space with that of politics of imperialism/colonialisms and links with indigenous cultural politics. However, as Driver (2001: 8) notes: 'postcolonial criticism has frequently given way to an essentialised model of colonial discourse which obscures the heterogeneous, contingent and conflictual character of imperial projects and it might be more useful to construe them as articulations of practices.' The question then is how to investigate the historical geographies of the colonized world in a postcolonial context based on such practices and spatial strategies. Colonial urban forms and spaces were constantly resurrected and reworked to express the aspirations of the imperial metropolis.

It is instructive in examining the postcolonial to study how Madras negotiated its precolonial past. Imperial inscriptions were grafted onto the urban space of Madras, which was essentially a product of the struggle between imperial powers, their colonial aspirations and indigenous traditions. It was not a simple transfer of imperial spatial ideas to the colonized world (Yeoh, 1996). The translation of metropolitan notions of imperialism within the colonies was mediated by the effective use of spatial technologies of town planning, taxation, municipalization, or spatial ordering and moral and socio-cultural ordering. In this respect, imperial projects were generally imposed on territories with complete disregard for the existing indigenous spatial configurations of history, land and people. The changes that took place were always drastic and related to the imperatives of colonial projects and practices, leaving the indigenous fractured and contested without being assimilated. The project of 'civilizing' and 'othering' went hand in hand in this colonial enterprise (Loomba, 1998).

The urban 'spatial strategies' (Gregory, 1994: 168–75) invoked became crucial in describing the contestations associated with the evolution of Madras. Spatial continuity is largely a cultural construct of the precolonial imprint, which was forcibly transformed by mercantile and colonial imperatives, with race as a signifier. The city became a space for assimilating differences. Duncan (1990), Jacobs (1996) and Duncan and Gregory (1999) have all emphasized the importance of the politics of cultural representation in space. While this process of assimilation was clearly visible, it is not contradictory to argue that spatial boundaries were created and normalized as essential. By focusing on hybridity, postcolonial studies in geography have constantly undermined the idea that important boundaries existed in colonial space. My contention, using the case of Madras, is that even in assimilative spaces, boundaries were entrenched and important.

COLONIAL URBAN SPACE

The ideology of the Raj posited a duality between rural and urban, in which urban life was seen as orderly, hygienic, scientific, superior, and civilized. Municipal by-laws and rules were used to bring order to indiscipline (Anderson, 1992). Indeed, precolonial local urban taxation (for example, the *hundi* or *octroi* taxes) was adopted and re-adapted to current conditions. Relentless surveillance of everyday behaviour and vigilance over popular conduct became the order of the day. This was a civilizing project, which called for 'moral ordering', 'spatial' or 'municipal ordering', and 'sanitization' or 'social and cultural ordering'. Omnipresent policing and other forms of surveillance constantly reinforced the conceptual boundaries between newly imposed legality and illegality. Rules bordered on absurdity to prevent the precarious order from disintegrating into chaos (Anderson, 1868: 26). More importantly, ideas of public space introduced by the British administration were also conveniently internalized by the Indian elite (Anderson, 1992; Chakrabarty, 1992b; Kaviraj, 1997).

In Madras, separate Black and White Towns emerged as Europeans established fortified settlements exclusively for non-native residence. Natives migrating from the rural areas and pre-colonial temple towns to work in the new settlement resided in the surrounding area, which came to be known as the Black Town. These separate 'Towns' introduced a sense of hierarchized space that had not existed in the indigenous urban centres, although it was common in village communities. The social intermixing of races was extremely limited, occurring only among a small number of the Indian elite and among domestic servants. Parks and open spaces illustrated the deliberate methods to maintain distance and preserve the environment of the White Town from being polluted. This was particularly true in the case of the *maidan* or Company's Garden (grand parks used for ceremonial purposes in the colonial port cities). Use of these places was limited to the British and the indigenous elite, illustrating the regulation of distance. Colonial urban space denoted officialdom where new manners of accountability and representation became standard features of the time.

The development of colonial cities, with the coalescence of indigenous and new colonial spaces, sparked fears of miscegenation (Kaviraj, 1997: 94). For the first time, there were new opportunities for the newly educated indigenous middle class to break the shackles of narrowly defined caste and class barriers. A new colonial civil society was created with a clear spatial impress of public and private space. This meant that despite attempts to segregate colonizers and colonized through actual spatial boundaries, notional spatial boundaries could constantly be transgressed by the indigenous population and, at times, by the colonialists themselves. The division between inside and outside and private and public involved a 'metaphorical' use of space for delineating boundaries. However, cultural practices were responsible for negotiating these notional and actual boundaries, which were not fixed and shifted position under different political circumstances and time.

In Madras, space for different communities became communally constructed. Hindus, Muslims, Armenians, Portuguese, Catholics and Protestants and those from right- and left-handed castes all occupied separate spaces, based on criteria of race, purity and pollution. The Black Town was represented by the colonial administration as a repellent space, a space of dirt and disorder. This colonial perception was based on three kinds of fear, which can be delineated as moral, political, and sanitary uncertainties. Morally and politically, the 'bazaar' and the contiguous Black Town were seen as a den of debauchery, full of greed, lies, flies, mosquitoes and gossip in which the ignorant and superstitious interacted and rebellions were plotted. As Kaviraj (1997) observes, colonial cultural politics transformed open spaces into public spaces and redefined urbanism.

In appropriating urban space, the imposition of a spatial order defined a regulated usage, functions and habitation within an expanding urban space – the city. The preoccupation with public and private can be related to the fact that '[u]nlike pre-colonial efforts to police public space, the colonial doctrine of nuisance was closely wedded to a regime of private property' (Anderson, 1992: 4). The growth of the city reflected intensified suburban property speculation. Inter-mingling in uses of space, especially in relation to commerce, transcended the formal dichotomization of White and Black Towns. With the gradual transformation of the older village order, conflicts around issues of unequal social status (exemplified by differences between elites and the lower orders) intensified. These became acute after the 1850s, when 'wealth and status, rather than caste alone' were increasingly noted as the factors determining social mobility (Ludden, 1978: 517–19). There was a struggle between the upcoming urban artisans and the merchant castes (Hossain, 1979). The *mirasdars* (traditional rural elite) petitioned the colonial government for greater control of their lands and privileges (Appadurai, 1974; Lewandowski, 1975, 1977; Roche, 1975; Neild, 1979). Neild (1979) established that private property in land had emerged in this region long before the advent of the British.

Initially there was a rigid enforcement of legalized segregation in Madras, contrary to Home's belief (1997). The British colonialists did not reside in the original Black Town. The first Black Town was Mylapore, where Portuguese of mixed parentage lived alongside the indigenous population. However, with the expansion of the population, houses were rented to European merchants who were trading with the Company, and they started to encroach into the native part of the city. By 1710, with the expansion of the White Town, Portuguese, Armenians, and native Christians were encouraged to settle in the Black Town (Lewandowski, 1977: 201). The majority of the British business houses and administration buildings were in the colonial core. Wealthier Indians had retail business and merchant houses in the White Town, whereas others such as *dubashes* (those speaking two languages) and *shroffs* (money lenders) worked as clerks. By the end of the nineteenth century, an increasing number of wealthier Indians (and their domestics) resided in the White Town. Thus, while a notional divide between the colonizers and the colonized was established in the White and Black townships, in reality there was far greater fluidity between both populations residing in the city.

The existence of Black and White Towns indicated perceived oppositions and ethnic divisions between Indians and Europeans. In fact, the Black Town was also divided along religious, regional language, race, caste, and class lines. Within an Indian lexicon, the *mohalla, ward, wadi, bazaar, chawl* or neighbourhood and streets (*gallis*, lane, and alley) had strong spatial identities. Neighbourhood identities were very complex. Unlike Bombay, village-like neighbourhoods in Madras *co-existed* with colonial urban forms (Masselos, 1991; Chandavarkar, 1994). Neighbourhoods were segregated by function and caste (Barlow, 1921; Roche, 1975; Chakrabarty, 1992b; Kaviraj, 1997). The power of the state and colonial economy was mediated through templates of urban space in the form of government buildings, places of worship, railway stations and dockyards. Cities, therefore, contained both familiar and unfamiliar spaces for both the colonizer and the colonized – as a locality or *pada* (Chakrabarty, 1992b; Kaviraj, 1997) and as an *adda*, or a private space in a public domain (Chakrabarty, 1999).

Black and White Towns were beachheads between different universes. Forms of labour and spatial organization introduced under the municipal government and by Public Works' projects helped to create new social identities (Lanchester, 1916; Bhatia, 1965; Roche, 1975; Lewandowski, 1975 and 1977). The new colonial cultural and symbolic spaces, and public and private spaces of work and residence, were not imbued with ritual religious significance. The introduction of factory production systems introduced new divisions of labour and created new scope for social discourse and new constructs of performativity between the colonizers and the colonized as well as among the colonized themselves. The regulation of housing, recreational and commercial space was clearly spatially segregated. This was instrumental in contributing to the institutionalization of social and racial categories. Colonialism re-appropriated the classic caste segmentation of Indian spatial constructs onto colonial urban space. As Kaviraj maintains, the colonial urban built environment was not only a complex space but was continually reinterpreted in everyday usages (1997: 84–5).

Modernity became a cultural project for the control of spaces and for the renegotiation of anxieties between and among ethnically diverse races and communities in Madras. The urban form that emerged was a product of intense conflict and complicity of interests, which were played out in imperial spaces well beyond the frontiers of the limited Raj.

MADRAS TOWN PLANNING

The ethics of colonial town planning suggested that one could not have access to a properly planned town unless one was 'morally' qualified to utilize its public spaces. Rules and regulations were therefore necessary since human beings were imperfect. As Figure 5.1 shows, there were zones of difference between various ethnic communities. No fewer than 33 caste-based occupations practised in the city, many of which were highly specialized, were recognized as occurring in particular urban spaces (Figure 5.2). Most maps from the early seventeenth century represented caste and ethnic divisions in urban space.

In the seventeenth century, the Fort area was the commercial centre of the city, while various residential quarters of the city developed later (Lanchester, 1916). Before the advent of railways, business, employment, worship and education were located in distinct areas in Madras. Railway construction furthered the disruption of neighbourhood boundaries, but afterwards railway lines acted as new boundaries between which communities re-organized themselves. Overcrowding in the Black Town was not for economic reasons but social ones. Communities of one specific caste, religion, and trade occupied a given urban space. Any modification of this space was resisted, as it was contingent upon caste affiliations and related trades. This socially constructed space became a constraint for planning purposes. Rural occupations in the Black Towns continued to co-exist with urban ones, while rural activities such as keeping cattle were marginalized. Schemes to improve traffic conditions and remove slums involved the inevitable destruction of property. Thus, the greater social and functional differentiation of the colonial urban centre contrasted with the multifunctional and socially heterogeneous character of the temple towns incorporated into Madras.

The formal distinction between city and countryside gradually acquired substance through the operation of separate administration, institutions and local regulations. The road and railway network helped to further coalesce the city and to strengthen the orientation of the suburbs towards the urban centre

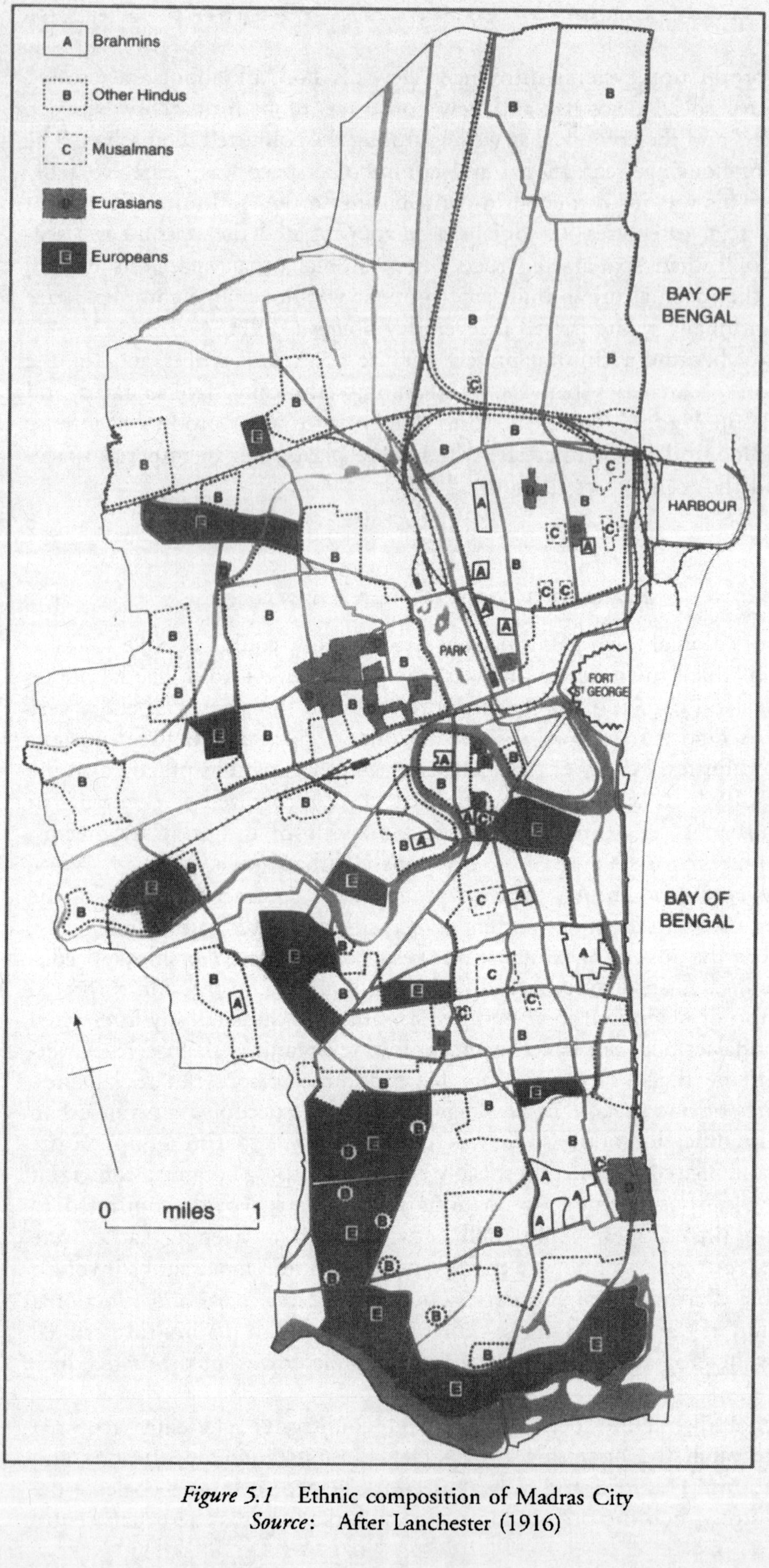

Figure 5.1 Ethnic composition of Madras City
Source: After Lanchester (1916)

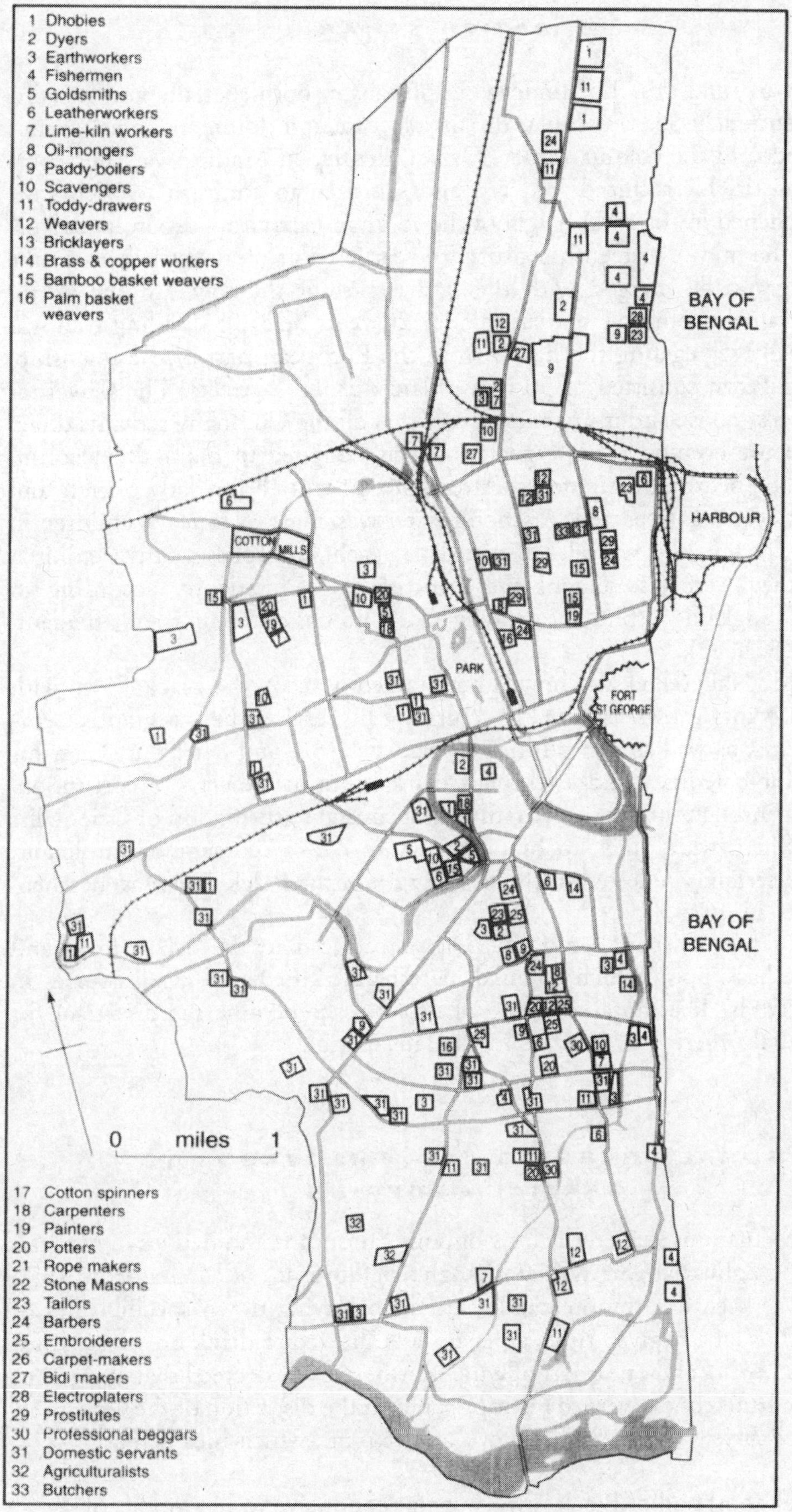

Figure 5.2 Occupational distribution of Madras City
Source: After Lanchester (1916)

rather than to rural ties. The underlying pluralism, both spatially and socially, remained entrenched in a colonial urban structure and dominant social groups were sucked into the colonial order. Urban identity in Madras was thus complex, pluralistic, hierarchized, ordered and sanitized to conform to a colonial order entrenched in the rural neighbourhood of an expanding urban landscape.

During the mid-seventeenth century, the earliest European settlement in the Fort area gradually merged with the native part of the town in the north. Madras became a common spatial unit for 20 years before a dividing wall was built, spatially segregating the native from the European part of the township. The White Town consisted of 50 houses laid out in 12 streets. The Governor had the largest house and it was mandatory that all the Company servants dined together in the evening. This expectation was designed to maintain decorum and discipline befitting their status. Attendance at church for daily prayers and Sunday sermons was expected. A schoolmaster was engaged to teach children in the White Town: 'He was also directed to teach Portuguese native children provided they were also taught the principles of Christianity according to Church of England despite the heavily Catholic character of the settlement' (Talboys, 1878: 53).

The Pedda Naik (chief watchman) maintained peace in the Black Town with 20 native servants known as *peons*. In return for his services, he was granted rent-free rice fields, as well as petty duties on rice, fish, oil, and betel nut. Later his office became hereditary and 'eventually drifted into native ways of corruption' (ibid.: 53). Throughout the records, there is a constant affirmation of Orientalist attitudes, which were quick to brand an entire race as corrupt or intolerant. These were certainly reflected in the description of the Black Town as 'heathen' by Dr Fryer in 1674.

Thus, a sense of 'spatial morality' was introduced in the urban form and became the basis upon which colonial 'paternalism' mediated all discourses in colonial Madras. The moral ordering of urban space became the precursor for intense spatial ordering of Madras in the later period.

MORAL ORDERING AS A PRECURSOR TO SPATIAL ORDERING

Rules and regulations shaped the lives of both Europeans and natives in Madras. As a strict disciplinarian, Sir William Langhorn, Governor of Madras from 1672 to 1678, was keen to promote public morals by laying down specific rules of conduct. Thus, at any given time, a person was allowed to drink only half a pint of brandy or *arrack* and one quart of wine. Further, it was decreed that all persons addicted to drunkenness were to be imprisoned at the discretion of the Governor. There was a curfew in the White Town after 8 p.m., which meant that:

> The neighbourhood of Black town was not conducive to the morals of the Fort. The younger men would climb over the walls at night time, and indulge in a round of dissipation. There were houses of entertainment known as Punch houses – took the name from an Indian drink concocted

> by the convivial factors at Surat ... It was also ordained that all persons swearing, cursing, or blaspheming the sacred name of Almighty God should pay a fine. (Talboys, 1878: 54, 65)

Soldiers were used (before the advent of a police force) to suppress drunken disorders. Debtors were also severely punished. Native debtors were dealt with by having their ears cut off, being whipped and banished from the settlement and, in extreme cases, transported as slaves. Most of the European offenders were imprisoned before being deported since the Governor did not have the power of life and death over these subjects (Love, 1913: II).

There was general concern for the state of sexual morality in the settlement. A letter written to the Court of Directors in 1676 highlights the duality of biased sexual politics in the city of Madras:

> Most of the women are popish Christian and if those that marry them do not fall onto the former inconveniences, they hardly escape being seduced by their wives or wives' families into popery. I wish your worship may consider it be not responsible to inhibit such marriages for the children turn either into infidels or popish. I do also wish there was more inspection taken what persons you send over into these places for these come hither some 1000 murderers, men stealers, some popish. Some come over under notions of a single persons and unmarried, who yet have wives in England and here married to others and lived in adultery and some on the other hand have come over as married persons of whom there was strange suspicion they were never married. (Talboys, 1878: 69)

On the question of marriage between different races there were severe reservations but also ambivalences reflected in the discourse, which exposed the anxieties of race, religion and gender in the colonial politics of Madras City. The presence of Portuguese Catholic women posed a dilemma; they would 'prevent wickedness' by encouraging soldiers and other colonialists to marry, but their religious affiliation posed difficulties in the upbringing of children. It is clear that mixed religion marriages were preferred to Indian alliances. Race was therefore a more crucial factor than religion and this tendency was accentuated as the eighteenth century progressed.

THE MUNICIPALITY: SPATIAL ORDERING OF THE 'OTHER'

Moral ordering gradually led to spatial ordering via the instruments of municipal administration. Municipal governance, which discriminated between the native and the European settlements, was essentially a colonial invention. According to Hill, before the advent of the European colonialists there was no municipal administration. The autocratic village policeman, the *Kotwal*, administered the precolonial towns. Popham's Police Plan to regulate the city of Madras in 1786 envisaged improving the health and cleanliness of the town, fraud prevention, and the naming of every street:

> Its name marked in English and in the Country Languages; its Inhabitants, Europeans, Armenians, Portuguese, &c., as well as Natives, registered with their Trades &c., a List of the Shops in each Trade, where situated and by whom kept and each Shopkeeper's name marked over the door; such Lists to be kept by the Bailiffs of each ward ... Every Birth and Burial to be noticed in a Book kept by those who are under the Police Master, and a General report made to him thereof, with an Account of the arrival and departure of all Strangers ... The Licensing and restraining the number of all Houses and places for the sale of Arrack or other Spirituous Liquors ... and of carriages and Animals used for drawing them. (Love, 1913, III: 310–11)

A Mayor and corporation had been established in Madras in 1687 under James II. This corporation had the function of levying taxes, building a school, a guildhall, a gaol, and other necessary buildings. The Mayor's authority included power to try civil and criminal cases. Later, the Charter Act of 1793 created municipal administration under the control of the Governor General. Unlike Calcutta, the Madras Act IX of 1865 was a political landmark, providing for nominally democratic representation of the city inhabitants.

Taxation without representation had been a feature of previous municipal administration in Madras. In 1678, Masters, the then Governor of Madras, had succeeded in raising taxes not for repairs or fortifications, but for promoting the sanitation of the Black Town. However, demands for raising taxes were met with petitions from the unconvinced natives. They appealed to the Governor and Council:

> The inhabitants of this town declare that it is now 40 years and upwards from the foundation of the fort and that they were invited to people and increase the town upon the word and favour of the English under whom they have lived received many honours and favours without paying any tribute or rent. Only in the time of the past Governor, Mr. Masters, who imposed a tax upon arrack, and upon paddy and causing us to pay for cleaning the streets. We are poor people and lived upon our labour and trouble. This town having the fame and this called the place of charity. Signed by the heads of several castes: Chuliars, painters, tailors, husbandsmen, coolies, washers, barbers, pariahs, comities, oil makers, fruiters, shepherds, potmakers, muckwars, tiaga, cavaree, nugabunds, pally, goldsmiths, chitties, and weavers. (Talboys, 1878: 83)

The inhabitants of the Black Town refused to pay the tax and were threatened with personal ruin and banishment by the colonial authorities. Eventually, the petitioners paid up and, ultimately, a new Governor abolished the tax in 1781.

There was further turmoil when the construction of the Black Town rampart was in progress. The government wanted to defray the cost by taxing the native inhabitants again, claiming Quit Rent and Scavenger's Duty. These taxes had not been sanctioned in Britain and there were protests against such an unjust imposition.

The post of Superintendent of Lands was created to assess all Company lands, identify the rightful owners, the number of buildings, bills of sale, and deeds as proof of authentication of the right of possession. There were regulations regarding the hiring of servants and their wages. The Board of Police was set up to inspect the *bazaars* (markets), to regulate the prices of goods sold there, and to prevent fraud in weights and measures. Taxes were levied on the exercise of professions, arts, trades, on buildings and lands, water and drainage, lighting, vehicles (with and without springs) and on animals entering municipal limits. Town duties were also raised on consumer goods and there were restrictions on the sale of such goods outside designated markets.

Thus, there was a considerable differentiation in the degree of intervention by the colonial municipal government and in the methods by which spatial control was maintained. Spatial ordering of the 'Other' reinforced the boundaries between native and European communities and attempted to regulate myriad elements of urban life and tax inhabitants for the privilege.

SANITARY OR 'SOCIAL-CULTURAL' ORDERING OF THE 'OTHER'

In colonial terms the 'filth and nastiness' of the Black Town had to be eradicated. The Superintendent of Lands checked encroachments not only in the Black Town but also on every road and village around Madras. From time to time, during the additional fortification of the Fort, native and even European buildings were demolished. In line with sanitation principles there was a perceived need for cultural ordering of native life in the Black Town. The Sanitary Commission of 1864 simply reinforced Popham's Police Plan of May 1786. The Inspector of Nuisance (an Indian) was appointed to determine levels of hygiene on a daily basis, as well as to educate the natives in cleaning, personal hygiene and in the prevention of nuisance. It was believed that: 'lessons they would teach of the advantages of obedience to a few simple sanitary laws would in course of time lead the people to adapt of themselves measures calculated to place their village communities under improved sanitary condition' (Ranking, 1869: 2). The Collector noted that: 'The Inspectors I would appoint to certain groups or circles of villages ... This class of men need not be highly educated. They would merely be required to know what are 'nuisances' to spy them out and report upon them' (ibid.: 4). In keeping with this, the sale of unwholesome food was banned. Hogs and swine were banned from the streets. Dogs too, were a threat to health. Inspectors were instructed to kill unlicensed dogs and a reward was instituted for every carcass.

Sanitary ordering involved the construction and execution of permanent drainage works, water supply, paving, maintenance of roads and general town improvements. Nuisance Inspectors were under the paternalistic purview of the Superintendent of Lands (a European) who was explicitly referred to as a 'Moral Agent' to check evil misuse of power by native subordinates, illustrating the conflation of the moral and the sanitary types of order by the colonial authorities. In promoting sanitation efforts, the Presidency government was not interested in providing funds to maintain the salubrity of the native colony. It was keen that funds for expenditure should come from municipal and local budgets. This resulted in the absolute neglect of the native towns since there were no surplus funds remaining after the completion of conservancy projects in the White Town.

Fairs, festivals, and even the movements of religious pilgrims were controlled due to fears of disease spreading to the military cantonments. The Madras Sanitary Regulations made elaborate provisions for the prevention of cholera during native festivals. Native migrants to Madras from infected areas were excessively policed, put under close surveillance, and issued with 'passports'; and emergency powers were introduced to summarily punish both male and female 'offenders'. By 1869, every conceivable agglomeration was brought under systematic sanitary control.

Sanitation rules frequently resulted in surveillance of the population, leading to oppression and extortion by the police and sanitary inspectors. Moreover, natives were made to pay for being under surveillance. Paternalistic and moralistic overtones in colonial policy were clearly self-evident, despite government assertions that they did not intend to interfere with the religious observances of its people. Yet, the other equally compelling reason was to exert control over them and gain the practical advantages of enforced conservancy from which the entire population was said to benefit.

During a plague outbreak in 1898, restrictions were imposed on the movement of people from infected areas. Every household and medical practitioner was required to report evidence of plague symptoms to the Health Officer or Sanitary Inspector. These officers possessed unlimited power to enter any building for the purposes of inspection. The holding of fairs and festivals was restricted and officers could prohibit the movement of people during the outbreak, for example, by refusing to issue railway tickets. There were three types of plague 'camps' established to contain the disease. The first were encampments for the isolation and treatment of persons suffering or suspected to be suffering from plague. The second were 'Suspect' camps for those who came into contact with plague sufferers who were detained under surveillance; and the third were 'Health' camps for persons who were required to vacate buildings and ground under plague regulations and those who were unable to procure alternative accommodation. The methods of land (or building) acquisition 'required' for plague camps illustrate the limits on property rights in the Black Town and the high-handed methods of control considered necessary by the colonial authorities. Owners were not entitled to compensation, only a rent fixed by the government. Any building or place considered 'overcrowded' in the opinion of the Health Officer (and thus liable to plague infection) could be cleared overnight, or the number of occupants arbitrarily reduced. Premises used for the supply and preparation of food or drinks were closed down, and laundry restrictions were enforced. Those who refused to comply with regulations faced interrogation and detention. Violation entailed punishment.

Strict burial regulations were also enforced on the native population. Routes for funeral processions were prescribed which avoided the White Town and those areas that might be a threat to the health of soldiers in the cantonment.

There was a prohibition on, and an enforcement of, burials in specific sites away from traditional sites. Regulations included instructions on the depth of burial sites and even the ritual bathing of dead bodies was regulated. While the autopsy of any corpse was optional, in case of non-production of a medical certificate the death would automatically be classified as a plague case, leading to strict segregation of family members and the disinfection of dwellings. These regulations assisted in the planning of Madras City only after the colonial moral ordering had been established.

Social and cultural ordering was accompanied by constant rhetoric concerning the need to take the 'people' into the confidence of government and over the nature of the plague measures, yet the methods were authoritarian. The only concession was the recognition of communal identities, since Hindu and Muslim staff were used to deal with their respective communities. However, lurking suspicion about native compliance and understanding was always used as an excuse for heavy-handed enforcement.

CONCLUSION

The evolution of spatial ordering in colonial Madras was premised on interconnected processes. Moral ordering was established at the earliest stages of colonial intervention determining spatial ordering. The project of 'civilizing' and 'othering' was much in evidence in Madras, achieved by a variety of colonial spatial strategies including taxation, town planning and municipalization. Spatial boundaries existed between discontinuous rural and urban spaces and between the contiguous White and Black Towns of Madras. The spatial boundaries between the precolonial and colonial were constantly normalized, particularly in relation to racial identity. These boundaries were perceived as fixed, but were in reality constantly transgressed and fluid. However, the transgression and negotiation of boundaries did not imply that spatial identities were hybridized, although they were multi-layered. The spatial layout of Madras illustrated the manner in which the pre-colonial was constantly negotiating its relation to colonial urban space.

The colonial city attempted to superimpose order on an ever-widening suburbia, including a number of villages and temple towns that co-existed (with their own parallel lifestyles) within Madras. The decline of traditional trades and the advent of railways in the city increasingly geared its functions towards the colonial powers rather than for the natives of 'Madrasapattam'. Both the native and European elites connived to acquire property from the traditional landowners, allowing prime land and a highly salubrious climate to prevail for the colonizer. At the same time, spatial expansion was always at the cost of native sites.

The evolution of urban settlement actually began in the precolonial period (Raman, 1957; Neild, 1979) and not in the nineteenth century as commonly believed. Occasionally, native voices struggled to make themselves heard in the midst of the officiality and morality of imperial and colonial discourses. The colonial construction of Madras was part of the civilizing project that called for a 'moral ordering' to be followed by 'spatial' or municipal ordering, sanitization or 'social and cultural ordering'. Colonial imperatives meant that moral ordering always preceded 'spatial' ordering. These imperatives included the forging of new racial identities among the colonizers as well as among the natives and the implied (Protestant) Christianization of the population, both Portuguese and native. Urban space was racialized as well as segmented into class, caste, and communal divisions and used to project new moral standards.

Municipalization was a colonial invention and there were protests from the indigenous population. Laws of sanitation were invoked to order the social and cultural attributes of a non-modern society, utilizing surveillance to enforce conservancy as essential in the Black Town, bringing order to otherwise 'docile' natives. Additional taxation was imposed to continue the beautification of the White Town, and superficially to improve the Black Town. Colonial administrators tended to display obsessive tendencies in measures to control the movement of pilgrims, vagrants and suspected plague victims, ably aided by the collaborationist native bourgeoisie. Colonial regulations were unsympathetic to indigenous sensibilities, and class, gender, and caste were subsumed into racial identities and conveniently ignored. Thus, urban space was made nostalgic, hierarchized, and hygienic, characteristics that drew upon the conflicts and complicity of interests among natives and Europeans, while spatial boundaries apparently imposed by the colonial order were in fact reinforced by indigenous responses to colonial intervention. The assumed assimilative spaces of the colonial city often remained entrenched in pre-colonial tradition due to, and in spite of, colonial impositions.

ACKNOWLEDGEMENTS

I would like to thank Emma Alexander for help with various drafts. Comments from Alison Blunt, Cheryl McEwan, Nuala Johnson, James Ryan and David Livingstone were extremely useful. I also benefited from discussions with Dipesh Chakrabarty, James Duncan and Sudipta Kaviraj. Maura Pringle and Gill Alexander kindly produced the maps.

6

GEOGRAPHIES WITH A DIFFERENCE?

CITIZENSHIP AND DIFFERENCE IN POSTCOLONIAL URBAN SPACES

Mark McGuinness

When Labour Party leader Tony Blair entered Downing Street as Prime Minister on that memorable, sun-drenched, morning in May 1997, expectations across Britain were high. Continued strong economic performance, declining unemployment, and renewed investment in public services throughout the first term seemed to affirm the promise that 'things can only get better'. A Labour government that had vowed to tackle social exclusion, poverty and racism was the most popular government in living memory. But within weeks of the Labour Party's unprecedented second successive landslide victory in June 2001 the rosy glow of New Britain was suddenly dimmed. On a scale not seen since the early 1980s, years of high unemployment, social division and a deeply unpopular Conservative administration, disturbances erupted in a series of towns and cities across the north of England. Focused on Burnley, Bradford and most bitterly in Oldham, all towns with large concentrations of ethnic minority populations, there was a serious collapse of law and order for a number of nights. Following the high-profile and deeply controversial conclusions of the long-awaited Stephen Lawrence Inquiry (Macpherson, 1999), suggesting that London's Metropolitan Police Force suffered from an 'institutional racism' leading to the failure to properly investigate the brutal and racist murder of a young black man in April 1993, the issue of 'race' was once more placed very firmly in the centre of British political debate.

This chapter is written in the context of this renewed concern for and interest in race and ethnicity. In the first half of what follows, the emerging policy responses to the events in northern England in 2001 are outlined and examined. Policy-makers and their advisers have begun to talk in serious terms once more of the nature and extent of *citizenship* in Britain. Mirroring similar concerns about inclusion and participation during the postwar period of the construction of the welfare state, which are also examined here, the reports into the causes of these events and the conceptualization of the problem by politicians, attaches blame to a series of missing identifications and commonalities amongst those who became unruly. This description of a lack of a full sense of citizenship amongst particular social groups is pursued for there is, I suggest, too tight, too automatic, a fit between this lack of citizenship and the ethnic and racial geography of postcolonial urban Britain. Noting the differences (of skin colour, of language, of religion) of this urban population from 'mainstream' (read: white, English-speaking, Christian) culture, I argue, is not quite the same thing as noting a lack of citizenship.

The second half of the chapter follows this theme of misreading *difference.* Here, I look at another constituency's interest in race and ethnicity, that of professional, academic geographers. There has been a recent and welcome interest in the nature and experience of difference in urban lives. Making many intellectual strides forward, particularly regarding the non-essential nature of place and of personal identities, there has been a growing band of geographers re-reading and re-writing the city to account and more accurately reflect the increasingly racially and ethnically diverse nature of the urban population and, thus, the urban experience. Following on from a discussion of emerging work suggesting the increasingly fragmented nature of white ethnicities and its impact in contemporary geographical literatures, I examine one such powerful re-reading of the city. Such work strikes many successes, yet retains at least one serious limitation that echoes those explored in the first part of the chapter. I conclude that this difference is conceptualized as a series of easily recognizable differences such as skin colour, language, religion, dress and foods. Such 'differences' only actually register as differences if they are studied from the seemingly homogeneous and stable platform of 'mainstream' white urban (and suburban) culture.

UNRULY CITIZENS

In the story of postcolonial Britain, the 'mill towns' of northern England that hit the headlines in 2001 are of more than a passing interest. These medium-sized, quite old urban settlements were the home of the UK's textile industry, which had been based on the processing of cottons grown across the British Empire, in particular in British India. They had largely been dependent upon cheap imports of cotton from the Empire overseas. In the years of post-war labour shortage, migrant workers from the Indian subcontinent began to arrive in these urban areas in large numbers. But the dismantling of the Empire, which permitted this influx of new migrants, also undermined the staple activities of the textile industries upon which these local economies were dependent. With the Imperial Preference withdrawn, the price of imported cotton lost competitiveness and a gradual process of stagnation and decline took hold of the mill towns.

The disturbances of the summer of 2001 were, in large part, the continuation of a discontent felt right through the post-war period and that so spectacularly burst into popular consciousness during the years of mass unemployment and disenfranchisement in the early 1980s. Urban uprising from Berlin to Belgrade,

Soweto to south Lancashire, has always been political (Gooding-Williams, 1993), and the history of postwar, postcolonial Britain is regularly punctuated by such urban uprisings. Within critical cultural and urban theory, 'The Empire Strikes Back' became firmly established as a regulating metaphor for this phenomenon (CCCS, 1982) firmly placing the blame, if this could be so easily and fully apportioned, upon the end of Empire and the economic and social marginalization of newly migrant workers and their families in the declining urban cores of deindustrializing Britain.

However, among those with a stake in such matters, the novelty of the uprisings of 2001 is that the main participants were previously ascribed – in the dominant white imagination anyway – to the category of 'model minority'. The migrants from India, Pakistan and, later, Bangladesh had, during the turbulent 1980s, been held up by all right- (and Right-) thinking policy-makers and politicians as the grist to the assimilationist mill. Pointing to the many handy examples of the full embracing of Western capitalist values in the economic sphere and the strong 'family' orientation of 'Asian culture', such core values were lauded by prominent politicians and policy-makers. It was this 'industriousness' that marked out the Asian experience as somehow different and more 'integrated' than that of the dangerous black body that arrived on the *Windrush* from the 1950s onwards. African and African-Caribbean black bodies were read through rather different metaphors of a rampant and dangerous physicality and sexuality and the thinness of their moral and social fibre (Haymes, 1995; Hall *et al.*, 1978).

The Asian urban working-class male, though always present in these uprisings was never held in quite such suspicion. (White) politicians from all sides roundly praised the strong family values, ethos of hard-work and self-motivation, coupled with educational success for a large number of young Asians which contributed widely to the belief (or at least the hope) that, unlike the African-Caribbean community, Asians were content to do their best to fit in with 'mainstream British culture and society'. Such values were of course heavily promoted during the decade of the 1980s, which was characterized by an emphasis on family and self-sufficiency, anti-state and pro-market rhetoric.

The events of the summer of 2001 demonstrated the illogical, deceptive and politically unacceptable nature of these arguments. The eruption of violence in apparently 'quiet' (to whom?) medium-sized urban areas of predominantly Asian settlement in response to symbolic and actual violence and hate-attacks from members of far-right organizations, and the alleged non-reaction (even complicity) of local police forces, brought the limitations of such simplistic and cosy conceptualizations of British racial and ethnic dynamics, and their interrelation with geographies of class, gender and deindustrialization, into acute focus. With such diverse and conflicting experiences, the geography of postcolonial urban Britain could no longer be written in such convenient and superficial terms.

Citizenship and Social Welfare

The recognition of continued racism and the renewed visibility of urban struggle have all formed the backdrop to recent innovations in policy orientations towards urban life and culture. Viewed *in toto*, this shift represents a renewed concern with the nature and status of citizenship. In the context of new dynamics of race and ethnicity in turn-of-the-century postcolonial Britain that I have outlined above, there has been a significant increase in concerns for greater integration and participation in 'mainstream culture' by the migrant communities in ordinary places like the mill towns. Although it is unclear where this debate is heading, at the time of writing a heated debate rages over the plans of the current UK Home Secretary, David Blunkett, to refashion citizenship for those already here, and to subject new applicants to 'citizenship classes'. Due to the geography of Britain's postcolonial in-migration, these plans will clearly influence and frame the trajectory of urban racial and ethnic politics. The cities and peoples of postcolonial Britain are of course the arenas in which these very debates will eventually be played out.

Citizenship and the rights and responsibilities of the citizen are not, however, new arrivals on the horizon of debates about social inclusion. Indeed, the post-war period of simultaneous decolonization and welfare statism has, for some, been interpreted as a programme of securing a series of rights equally due to each and every member of society. Based on the influential writings of T.H. Marshall, the construction and evolution of the British welfare state have been seen as the embodiment of just this principle. As Hughes has it:

> Marshall's interpretation of the rise and subsequent consolidation of a social democratic welfare state in the post-war UK was optimistic about the possibilities of social inclusion and the avoidance of class conflict through the rise of a third form of citizenship, namely social citizenship, following the earlier evolution of two other crucial forms of citizenship (legal and political). (1998: 10)

Understanding the reconstruction period as one framed by the emergence of this 'third form' of citizenship has interesting parallels with current debates about the 'dislocation' of migrant communities in contemporary Britain. It is clear that by responding to the fears and extremes of the periods both during and before the Second World War, times characterized by mass unemployment, social and economic disenfranchisement and disillusionment with the status quo, the elusive sense of social inclusion was to be sought through the citizen's active participation in the social realm and through equality of access to social goods such as better housing, healthcare, and education. Equal access to a range of important social goods would, it was argued, reduce social divisions. Social stability through common practices and identification was thus the objective. Marshall himself is very clear about this, arguing that social citizenship would require:

> a direct sense of community membership based on loyalty to a civilisation which is a common possession. It is a loyalty of free men endowed with rights and protected by a common law. Its growth is stimulated both by the struggle to win those rights and by their enjoyment when won. (Marshall, 1950: 40–1, quoted in Hughes, 1998: 13)

The newly founded welfare state was thus seen as a means of disseminating this sense of inclusion and belonging right through society through the provision of common social goods and common social practices. This sense of commonality resonates through these debates, and should be seen as an attempt to secure a measure of social stability through the provision of social goods and the promotion of common identifications and of shared ownership and values.

This principle of an inclusive social citizenship through the universalist provision of social goods, however, disguised a rather different reality for some of these theoretically equal citizens. The implied citizenry to be served and included in the new welfare state constructed in the years after Beveridge's influential report (Beveridge, 1942), was, of course, never homogeneous. Universalism implied a 'one-size-fits-all' mentality; inclusion was one side of these new social practices, exclusion was the other. Hughes suggests that:

> the quintessential new 'Beveridgean citizen' was the fully employed (and insured) married, white, able-bodied, male worker. Other categories of people included women, ethnic minorities, disabled people, children and the elderly, who, though not excluded from the welfare state, were subject to hierarchically organised forms of state welfare. (1998: 31)

In other words, securing universalist social citizenship actually implied a uniformity that not all social groups could so easily adopt or adapt to. In fact, at least half of the population could be said to have a problematic relationship to these categories: women were among the principal social groups holding a subordinate and potentially disenfranchisable position in relation to this 'universal' citizenship. The influx of migrant black labour into Britain's urban areas was another such 'subordinate' social group, and their experiences of this period still resonate in the contemporary period. Williams argues that:

> The welfare state became central to the reconstruction of post-war Britain . . ., built with the the bricks of the family, and the mortar of national unity, by the labour of low-paid women and newly arrived black workers. Ironically it was often these groups of workers to whom the benefits of the new welfare state were restricted: black male workers may have built council houses, but discriminating allocation criteria meant that they weren't eligible to live in them. (1993: 85)

Thus the urban renewal of the old industrial cities is one that is intimately intertwined with and implicated in the problematic nature of this social citizenship. Black in-migrants were thus relegated to the private rented sector and Britain's depopulating urban cores were gradually repopulated and reconfigured as newly migrant populations negotiated urban rented accommodation markets and white British culture. This was the other side of the universalist social citizenship that characterizes *white* writings of the period. Early postcolonial black literature articulates this quite different experience of a postwar urban Britain beginning to spatially and socially fragment. Sam Selvon's ([1956]

1995) book *The Lonely Londoners* is a careful and reflective fictional tale based on the experience of the new Caribbean male migrants as they arrive in urban Britain and perhaps defines the experience of the period: difficulties over access to accommodation, work and welfare are themes that run through the book. For these black *and* British citizens, everyday life was a constant oscillation between inclusion in some social processes and exclusion from others, such as work and welfare. Nowhere was this more so than in the arena of housing, a theme captured beautifully in Wole Soyinka's 1962 poem *Telephone Conversation*:

> The price seemed reasonable, location
> Indifferent. The landlady swore she lived
> Off premises. Nothing remained
> But self-confession. 'Madam,' I warned,
> 'I hate a wasted journey – I am African.'
> Silence. Silenced transmission of
> Pressurized good-breeding. Voice, when it came,
> Lipstick coated, long gold-rolled
> Cigarette-holder pipped. Caught I was foully.
> 'HOW DARK?' ... I had not misheard ... 'ARE YOU LIGHT
> OR VERY DARK?' Button B, Button A. Stench
> Of rancid breath of public hide-and-speak.
> Red booth. Red pillar box. Red double-tiered
> Omnibus squelching tar. It *was* real! Shamed
> By ill-mannered silence, surrender
> Pushed dumbfounded to beg simplification.
> Considerate she was, varying the emphasis –
> 'ARE YOU DARK? OR VERY LIGHT?' Revelation came.
> 'You mean – like plain or milk chocolate?'
> (Soyinka, 1962 in Moore and Beier, 1968: 144)

This striking passage illustrates the reality (for some) of the universalist, inclusive citizenship upon which urban and national social renewal were based. The unevenness of the application of this model of Marshallian social citizenship, where the rights of the citizen to communicate (symbolized by the red telephone and post boxes) and of spatial mobility (in the form of the public transportation of the quintessential red London double decker bus), are not matched by equal and open access to the primary social good of accommodation. The myth is exposed: indeed the heightening of the redness of the highly visible features of the urban infrastructure suggests the embarrassment felt at the yawning gap between a noble ideal, and the suspicion of the exclusion of the black-skinned citizen. Soyinka's poem perhaps represents the experience of the many thousands of black migrant workers on the doorsteps of respectable urban middle-class and white landlords and landladies. Social citizenship through equal and full access to the range of social goods that defined this process thus remained elusive and, for many, rather more mythical than actual. Such experiences of urban culture and racism most, necessarily, form the basis of contemporary debates on citizenship and the public realm.

Citizenship and Culture

Concerns about social inclusion and senses of belonging thus structured many of the debates surrounding the construction of the welfare state in postwar Britain. As I have explored above, the virtues of social citizenship were extolled as a means of providing those with a sense of social isolation and exclusion with a sense of shared ownership and a 'common bond'. In the late twentieth and early twenty-first centuries (a period, interestingly, marked by the careful renegotiation of that same welfare settlement) the nature of citizenship has once more been high on the political agenda and the subject of much public discourse. This is a debate very much about our cities and the people who live in them. In the context of an increasingly multi-racial and postcolonial urban society, this has also become a debate very much marked by a series of assumptions regarding 'race', ethnicity and social exclusion. As already noted, the changing racial and ethnic composition of urban Britain was brought into ever sharper focus by the series of urban disturbances in the summer of 2001. As we shall now see, the nature and qualities of citizenship also lie at the heart of these discussions of postcolonial urban Britain.

Following the tensions of the summer period, the Home Office commissioned the Community Cohesion Review Team (CCRT) to review and develop the series of inquiries that took place following the disturbances. Chaired by Ted Cantle, the team published its findings in December 2001 (CCRT, 2001). Their report made shocking reading for liberals and conservatives alike. Concentrating on the 'physical segregation' that they found in urban Britain, the team argued that 'separate educational arrangements, community and voluntary bodies, employment, places of worship, language, social and cultural networks, means that many communities operate on the basis of a series of parallel lives' (ibid.: 9). This is clearly of concern since such arrangements do little to 'promote meaningful interchanges' between the diverse constituencies that compose postcolonial Britain. Building on critiques of Marshallian models explored above, the team suggested that the sense of social citizenship, so dear to the universalist welfare state had failed to cohere in the towns and cities of contemporary multi-racial Britain.

The ultimate destiny of this report is unclear at this early stage and I do not here have the space to look in detail at its recommendations. However, I want to focus on what the deployment of the notion of citizenship, introduced in this report and more fully developed by the Home Secretary David Blunkett in his response to the CCRT's report, can tell us about developing understandings of postcolonial urban Britain. After considering the evidence put before them, the CCRT concluded that:

> There has been little attempt to develop clear values which focus on what it means to be a citizen of modern multi-racial Britain and many still look backwards to some supposedly halcyon days of a mono-cultural society, or alternatively look to their country of origin for some form of identity. (CCRT, 2001: 9)

As Home Secretary, David Blunkett commissioned the report and gave his response to its findings in a keynote speech to a group of Asian community leaders in Balsall Heath in central Birmingham. Balsall Heath is an ethnically diverse area of predominantly Pakistani Muslim population and also one marked by high levels of urban deprivation. It is a prime example of the new postcolonial urban Britain, recent regeneration and anti-prostitution efforts displaying high levels of community solidarity and identity, a point which no doubt did not escape the media planners at work in the Home Office. Echoing mid-twentieth-century articulations of the problems of social exclusion and dislocation, Blunkett's response centres on the core concept of citizenship and 'core values'. 'Whilst the violence and social disorder we saw in our towns and cities was inexcusable,' he began, 'the reports show that behind the disturbances lie serious social problems':

> There is a large measure of agreement that in the areas affected, communities are fractured and polarised. Significant Government investment is going into the regeneration of these communities, to underpin equality of opportunity and hope for the future. But communities need social cohesion as well as social justice. Today's reports show that too many of our towns and cities lack any sense of civic identity or shared values. Young people, in particular, are alienated and disengaged from much of the society around them, including the leadership of their communities. (Blunkett, 2001).

The theme of social fragmentation, 'fractured' and 'polarized' communities, runs right through both the CCRT report and Blunkett's response to it. Towns and cities are places lacking any sense of 'civic identity' or 'shared values'. Urban Britain is once again seen as a place in crisis, 'lacking' a sense of ownership and inclusion. Blunkett calls for 'a wide public debate on what citizenship and community belonging should mean in this country'. The key difference between what I would term the 'crisis of citizenship' in our times as opposed to during the construction of the welfare state explored above, is the foregrounding of cultural and ethnic difference. The following remarkable passage from his response to the CCRT reports highlights the emergence of new, more 'cultural', forms of citizenship:

> people should have the wherewithal, such as the ability to speak English, to participate fully in society. This is not 'linguistic colonialism' as my critics allege – it is about opportunity and inclusion. And just as we seek to defeat racism, so we must protect the rights and duties of all citizens, and confront practices and beliefs that hold them back, particularly women. This is not cultural conformity. There is no contradiction between retaining a distinct cultural identity and identifying with Britain. (ibid.)

So that while the CCRT report 'show[s] that we have failed to promote cohesive communities and common citizenship in the UK' there is potentially an emerging concern in policy circles with attending to a *universal* respect for *difference*: 'citizenship means finding a common place for diverse cultures and beliefs, consistent with the core values we uphold'. This is an interesting shift of emphasis away from forms of social citizenship to be underwritten by the state, through the provision of a universal (in principle anyway) social welfare package, towards a rather different form of citizenship rooted in everyday practices and respect for cultural diversity and values. This diversity, however, seems only to be registered and recognized in the framework of 'core values' that 'we' uphold. Here, the problem rests on a feeling that respect for difference is one held together by a core structure of citizenship that is pre-defined and requires the erosion of some differences, in particular those of language. In other words, this call pulls both ways, both towards difference (of culture, of ethnicity) and towards homogeneity (core values and common language).

Obviously, this is some distance from the universalist dreams of the social citizenship agenda and mirrors recent intellectual attempts to capture the nature of the crisis of citizenship. In his examination of 'the cultural rights of citizenship', McGuigan, for example, suggests that:

> With the premature announcement of the eclipse of the nation-state, the retreat from a welfare-state model of social entitlements and the accelerated migration, frequently illegal, from poor to rich nations, the status of citizenship has been dislocated. Universalism and particularism vie with one another to define the role of the citizen. Again, modernist pieties are called into question. Simultaneously, demands are made to extend the scope of citizenship beyond the economic, social and political rights that have been 'won' over the past 200 years to the cultural, the assumption being that in one way another we may speak of the cultural rights of citizenship. (1996: 136)

For McGuigan, the nature of citizenship in public discourse is one that engages with the societal and cultural changes that characterize everyday experience of contemporary towns and cities. Citizenship, with its Western and European heritage, thus struggles continually to adapt to new circumstances, attempting to reconcile its universalist ideals with its uneven realities. The emerging forms of cultural citizenship encounter exactly this tension between the universal and the particular, between commonality and difference that structures the evolution of British urban and cultural policy. The intertwining of race, migration and national identity is characteristic of contemporary citizenship debates: '[The cultural rights of citizenship] clearly meet up with "race" insofar as it raises questions concerning "naturalisation" and "integration", whether in terms of assimilating "the Other" to a host community or respecting difference in more or less official manner.' Such important issues clearly resonate strongly in the current debates in the UK surrounding urban politics and social inclusion. The CCRT report and David Blunkett's kick-starting of the debate on citizenship obviously have underpinning them the increasing racial and ethnic diversity of postcolonial Britain. This in no way suggests that Blunkett's call for a citizenship debate in the context of the changing cultural geography of urban Britain is limited only to urban policy applications. In October 2001, newspapers reported that Blunkett was considering the introduction of 'citizenship classes' for new migrants, where would-be citizens would be obliged to learn English and demonstrate a basic grasp of British history and culture. As Blunkett explained: 'I believe we need to educate new migrants in citizenship and help them to develop an understanding of our language, democracy and culture' (*Guardian*, 26 October 2001). This new and uncertain agenda follows on from Blunkett's earlier work as Education Secretary following the Labour Party's historic 1997 election victory. Here, he established the Advisory Group on Citizenship (AGC) and following the recommendations of the final report (AGC, 1998), 'citizenship education' is currently being introduced in all state schools in England and Wales. Citizenship, then, is firmly back on the political agenda, in education, in cultural politics, and in urban policy.

Citizenship is a concept that at two key points in the recent evolution of postcolonial Britain has been a central organizing discourse and suggests an interpretation that sees 'lack' of citizenship and common culture as the root of the urban disenfranchisement and disorder that reared its head once more in the summer of 2001. The city, the 'natural' home of the citizen, is more than a neutral stage on which citizenship debates are played out. The changing nature of urban life and urban culture, is, by the turn of the century, seen to be part of the problem itself – the sense of isolation, alienation and disengagement felt by many minority communities and the sense of frustration felt by policy-makers concerning themselves with the 'urban problem'. The call for a renewed sense of citizenship, as I have shown above, is contradictory and deeply problematic, yet offers clear and convincing evidence of the continued link – at least in the minds of policy-makers and their advisers – made between *race* and *urban space* in postcolonial Britain.

WHERE'S THE DIFFERENCE? RACE, THE CITY AND ACADEMIC URBAN GEOGRAPHY

What I want to do now is to shift my focus away from finely tuned policy debates towards the practices of 'professional' academic geographers. While the close discursive connection remains, in what follows I outline a different story yet one which still implies this connection between the city, race and ethnicity in the postcolonial imagination. This discussion of contemporary academic British geography is one that follows closely recent debates on the nature of white identities and the construction of difference. In order to study ethnic difference, it is argued, the geographical imagination is drawn to places of highly marked ethnic difference, most notably the presence of black faces and black culture. In so doing, of course, the visibility and ethnicities of what remains a predominantly white discipline escape unmarked. What is offered here therefore is a critique informed by emerging research on white ethnicities and what such work can say about the contemporary practice of academic geography.

There has been a recent upsurge of interest in 'whiteness' both within and beyond geography (including Bonnett, 1996b, 1997, 1998a, 1998b; Sidaway, 1997; Jackson, 1998). Like other studies of ethnicity and identity, work on whiteness seeks to problematize it as a *specific* social construction and provides us with a furthering of important critiques of static notions of ethnicity and identity that clearly follows and informs other important work across the social sciences (see, for example, Mercer, 1990; Rutherford, 1990; Hall, 1992b).

The growing body of work in British academic geography that informs questions of hybridity, identity and difference is drawn toward a particular range of sites through which this new critical geography is then dutifully demonstrated. Visibly marked places of difference have become the conventional sites of empirical observation and investigation for this new geography. In particular, London's visible ethnic diversity has been investigated in a wide range of current writing on the subject from a variety of approaches (e.g. King 1990; Sassen 1991; Massey 1994; Jacobs 1996; May 1996a, 1996b), and other similar sites of visible difference in Britain and around the world have also been the focus of much academic attention.

These geographies are offered as colourful empirical demonstrations of the cultural cosmopolitanism that is the contemporary Western moment of post-colonialism. This has largely been important work that is part of an attempt to bring those at the margins back into cultural and political discussion, to put an end to the denial of the other's difference. However, we should not forget that this commitment to a liberal 'politics of difference' is not always a straightforwardly progressive and desirable trend but often represents the continuation of older forms of exclusion, appropriation, and social differentiation (hooks, 1992; May, 1996a). As this 'new cultural class' of gentrifiers and middle-class professionals (including a fair number of geography academics) invent, appropriate and rework imaginary geographies, visible differences (in food, language, dress, etc.) in the city become commodified and reduced to little more than the 'spice' that can 'liven up the dull dish that is mainstream white culture' (hooks, 1992: 21). It is, in fact, only recently that geographers have begun to engage and discuss whiteness, drawing on lessons from 'White Studies'.

What is 'White Studies'?

Richard Dyer's now seminal (1988) piece on representations of whiteness in British and American cinema has had a considerable impact on the emergence of the field of White Studies. Encapsulating many of the concerns of this agenda, Dyer succinctly described whiteness as 'a subject that, much of the time as I've been writing it, seems not to be there as a subject at all'. He suggests a kind of omnipresent quality, simultaneously an 'emptiness, absence, [and] denial [yet] seeming to be nothing in particular' (Dyer, 1988: 44). Dyer's essay is an important marker in the development of this research agenda, increasingly referred to – somewhat problematically – as White Studies. Established 'race geographers' are now, at last, beginning to think more closely about whiteness in much the same way as the more conventionally considered 'marginal' identities. Jackson has recently argued that: 'whilst there have been numerous studies of the social construction of racialised minorities, [there has been only a] much more gradual recognition that these arguments apply with equal force to the construction of dominant categories and majority groups' (1998: 99). This recent work has provided a useful platform, but these are only beginnings and much remains to be resolved. There is, for example, the important concern that White Studies is too specifically North American, too tightly bound into a specific and highly particular race–gender–class dynamic. What this amounts to is that, even when at their most incisive, White Studies approaches may assume a 'cultural' norm while seeking to displace an 'ethnic' norm. Gabriel (1996), for example, found very different meanings and responses generated by UK and American audiences to the film *Falling Down*, a crucial text in the White Studies canon, rather than any straightforward cultural similarity where one can be 'read off' the other (see also Gabriel, 1994: 3–4). Bonnett has developed work that 'draws from, but is not dominated by, American perspectives' (1996b: 152); also see 1998a). Others have signalled caution regarding the way that much of this literature seems driven by a 'me-too-ism' (Dyer, 1988; Jackson, 1998). 'The margins' are sought after either/both as a means of denying the privilege of the white self in a racist society, or as a means of making 'normal' white existence more interesting, more 'alive' (see Dyer, 1988). Somewhat related to this is the suggestion that the White Studies agenda too easily slips into negative forms of guilt rather than a positive reconfiguration of whiteness showing awareness of its own difference and that of others.

Writing about the turn to histories of colonialism in contemporary geography, Clive Barnett makes a useful point about 'theoretically inclined' critical geographers who, he thinks, have been 'busy grabbing their share of colonial guilt' (1995: 418). He suggests that the renewed interest in geography's past, while demonstrating a heightened critical awareness of the inherent violence of the Western geographical imagination, also acts as 'a way of avoiding looking in the most obvious places' (ibid.: 419) and genuinely interrogating the discipline as it stands today.

It is this thought that I feel best articulates my uneasiness with these 'new' geographies of postcolonial Britain. Demonstrating diversity in multi-ethnic places like Kilburn High Road without paying adequate attention to the historical and contemporary whiteness of the discipline might just lead down two conceptual 'blind alleys'. First, the geographer's finger may too eagerly and unproblematically be pointed at the geo-emporic inner cities of late twentieth-century Britain, suggesting a kind of 'new exoticism'. Second, if hybridity is always demonstrated in these multi-ethnic areas, whiteness is allowed to remain untouched, unmarked, not an ethnicity at all – just 'normal'.

Kilburn High Road revisited

Bonnett (1997: 199) issues an important challenge to 'those geographers concerned with issues of "racial and ethnic difference"'. In attending to the situatedness of all forms of knowledge, it has become something of a commonplace to argue that our cultures and ethnicities mark each and every one of us in different ways and, visibly or not, form the basis of our interactions and interpretations of the world. With this in mind, I offer an alternative reading of a widely acclaimed example of geographical scholarship to illustrate my point.

In Massey's (1994) remarkable essay 'A Global Sense of Place', we read about the unevenness of the whole process of increased mobility of capital, goods, and labour. She argues, quite rightly, that we need 'more socially formed, socially evaluative and differentiated' (ibid.: 150) understandings of these processes, since 'different social groups and different individuals are placed in very distinct ways in relation to these flows and interconnections' (ibid.: 149). All of this is carefully argued through a vivid and affectionate sketch of daily life in her locality, Kilburn in North London, 'a pretty ordinary place' (ibid.: 152).

She tells us how, in Kilburn, she can buy an Irish newspaper or an Indian sari, see posters for both Eamon Morrisey and Rekha. In Kilburn, you can chat with people of many faiths or of none at all. She describes how the area's links to the wider world bring about a fascinating postcolonial possibility, where a Teresa Gleeson and a Chouman Hassan can both be winners in local lotteries in the same week. 'It is (or it ought to be)', she concludes, 'impossible even to begin thinking about Kilburn High Road without bringing into play half the world and a considerable amount of British imperialist history' (ibid.: 154). Black faces, brown faces, white faces all living, working, shopping side by side. The 'chaotic mix' (ibid.: 153) of Kilburn, with its immense diversity and richness of different cultures, she ably deconstructs with characteristic skill, care and responsibility.

My problem with this, however, is that 'difference' is very easy to spot in this multi-ethnic area, and Massey herself counterposes the cosmopolitan diversity of Kilburn with the 'relatively stable and homogeneous community (at least in popular imagery) of a small mining village' (ibid.: 153–4). She goes on to raise questions of differentiated experiences of such 'homogeneous' places, particularly gendered experiences. Quite; but perhaps we are also to assume that she also means white community, acting as the stable background against which she contrasts the 'chaotic mix' of the place of the other? The invisibility of this signifier represents the commonsensical, normalized and unremarkable (or at least unremarked) constructions of whiteness.

Why not also look at the supposedly homogeneous white spaces of postcolonial Britain with equal vigour? If there is to be more meaningful talk about ethnicity in the contemporary British context, analyses are required that offer the potential for us to do just that. The deconstruction of places like Massey's mining villages cannot be simply abstracted from such (admittedly skilful) analyses of obvious sites of difference like Kilburn because difference is, of course, about more than that which is marked (and this is usually marked by the white eye anyway). Might there be just the possibility that a continued (if unintentional) Eurocentrism persists, where the normalizing white eye associates hybridity with blackness, assuming whiteness to be so much less hybrid, less interesting, that it does not even remark upon it?

We might also consider Massey's own markings, as she walks along Kilburn High Road. Of course, each step is marked by her profession, gender, class, ethnicity, education (and much else). Would this street look the same to everyone regardless of who they were, the languages that they spoke and the colour of their skin? Is it, reading her text, reasonable to assume that if you were marked differently to our geographer that you might well 'see' things quite differently? Might it be that the same sources of Massey's pleasure could also be the source of another's fear or distrust? In her attempt to 'genderize' the notion of diaspora, Anthias asks,

> to what extent do women of all social classes and groupings have access to 'global' thinking, on the one hand, and to what extent do specific gendered

social relations lead to a greater incentive for grasping the global mettle, on the other? (1998: 571)

Such questions are fundamental to any 'proper analysis' of places like Kilburn High Road. Massey's narrative is of course a particular, located, privileged description of contemporary urban Britain and, as I have noted, this is implicit in the text anyway. My argument is, therefore, not that Massey is unaware of these issues – indeed, in the piece referred to here she is more aware than most of differential locations (her 'power-geometry') – but that the Kilburn High Road Experience that she describes could easily be seen as a very particular white Western construction of a world of difference. Kilburn is not a 'pretty ordinary place' (whatever one would look like). In its range of visible and marked cultures and ethnicities, it is actually quite specific. She takes on some clearly very sophisticated ideas of postcolonial existence and then describes a geo-emporium of difference, perhaps reproducing some older white mythologies about the West and its centrality (Young, 1990).

This echoes some of May's concerns about the new urban *flâneur*. He describes how a new cultural class consumes the differences the city contains, 'prid[ing] themselves on their liberal attitudes. Special pride is taken in their interest in and understanding of other cultures' (May, 1996a: 61). The exotic is appropriated through a 'politics of difference' that is not automatically about a progressive sense of other cultures or places but may, in effect, represent a contemporary reworking of the Cook's Tour of old, where difference is 'reduced to the sights of an afternoon stroll' (May, 1996b: 208). While Massey could hardly be accused of any simple exoticism or Orientalism in her afternoon stroll down Kilburn High Road, the concern is that such descriptions belie an unproblematic sense of white self and, to borrow from Laura Donaldson, a 'passive collusion' with a racist culture that allows those with a certain skin colour to pass unhindered and without remark (1993: 1).

In setting course for 'the inner cities' to talk about race and hybridity, an unproblematized whiteness is at best left untouched, at worst re-centred. Destabilizing whiteness means doing this type of geography in a whole range of different places. Might such predominantly white places as the British New Towns and the seemingly endless suburbs of Middle Britain also be sites of an equally dynamic and (perhaps) exciting reinvention of postcolonial ethnicities? In the manner that these places represent specific visions/versions of white identities as a response to a rapidly changing post-war British economy and society, they most certainly could be interpreted in these same ways. But if the only literature available to geographers is that on areas of 'chaotic mixing', it might not seem so obvious. Not to me anyway. This is more than a methodological posturing or an intellectual exercise, but represents a systematic challenge to the misidentification of postcolonial identity with the spaces of non-white migration and visibility.

If the study of postcolonial Britain remains tied to these exceptionally marked places, there is the suggestion of a failure to appreciate the depth to which white identities and spatial norms continue to define everyday lives and professional practices, such as those of contemporary British geography. It, rather unfortunately, evades some of the most crucial and critical interrogations that the recent intellectual trends discussed above have raised. The study of difference in geography – even of the most decent and critical brand – needs to break the seemingly exclusive focus on these areas. The residents of postcolonial Britain do not only live in places like Kilburn High Road, but also in the 'White Highlands' (Bonnett, 1996b) of Middle Britain that post-war planning and post-imperial restructuring have created.

CONCLUSION

Dyer suggests that 'White domination is reproduced by the way that white people colonise the definition of normal' (1988: 45). Geographers and policy-makers, whatever their characteristics and identifications, need to confront the simple conflation of difference with blackness/non-whiteness and its location and association with urban spaces. This difference, it would seem, can only be seen on the street where it jumps out, reads 'different' newspapers, wears 'different' clothes and eats 'different foods', while remaining blind to the difference of the Invisible White Man and Woman who live in high-rise blocks and behind the uPVC windows, net curtains and neatly trimmed hedges of white suburbia.

Throughout this chapter, I have explored such imaginative connections made between race and ethnicity and urban spaces in two quite different geographical discourses. The policy and political musings, focusing on the nature and delivery of citizenship, actively map the same territory as the academic writings, inexorably drawn toward the easily differenced (and distanced?) territory of postcolonial urban spaces. Put at its plainest, they both construct a geography of difference (of welfare status, language, skin colour, clothing, food and religion) which is urbanized, written into particular spaces of the city. The problem is, in both cases, the eye falls on the black city. In both of these postcolonial urban geographies, residues and echoes of older, less progressive uses of and exercises of the geographical imagination remain.

This is a very difficult line for me to tread. Those whose words and actions I have covered in this chapter are clearly not racist scum. I am in no doubt that they clearly believe that they work for the common good rather than for the forces of evil, and there is much of value here. My main concern here has been to show that whether we look at renewed citizenship debates or the writings of urban geographers we come across contradiction, tension and change. These *geographies of the postcolonial* are drawn, as if by tractor-beam, towards a few urban spaces where the novelty of chaotic difference excites the eye, ear, tongue, and nose and I am uncomfortable with that. I think *postcolonial geographies* should cast everything 'known' about cities, citizenship, difference and the practice of geography itself to the four winds. To me, doing postcolonial geography means doing geography *differently*.

Writing in the immediate aftermath of Blunkett's call for common citizenship through common language, Vikram Dodd of the *Guardian* observed that:

> Those least likely to have a grasp of English are the elderly and women who come here for arranged marriages. Look at the TV footage of the rioters. There is a striking absence of Zimmer frames, of hijabs and salwar kameez. Those rioting were young men, with a pretty good grasp of English, integrated enough to have the odd drink, spliff and be clad in Nike's finest. (Dodd, 2001: 13)

Racism, poverty, and hopelessness, it is suggested, lie at the root of this particular urban problem rather than 'linguistic ability'. While I feel elated that someone has the sense to point out that 'Mr Blunkett has not just failed to grasp the right end of the stick, he has failed to grab the right stick' (Dodd, 2001), I am uncomfortable because I know there is some sense in what Blunkett is proposing. Yet Dodd is surely correct to conclude that 'the grafitti in these areas of segregation do not attack ethnic minorities for their inability to decline verbs properly. They attack on the basis of skin colour' (ibid.). Similarly, that the study of hybridity and difference in academic urban geography has been primarily carried out in some of the most empirically obvious sites of non-white migration is not only unfortunate, but would seem to lend support to Bonnett's contention that whiteness still continues 'to have an extraordinary power to appear transparent before the scholarly gaze' (1997: 194). Maybe, as they are very fond of saying on the streets of a rapidly transforming postcolonial Birmingham these days, 'it's time for a change'.

ACKNOWLEDGEMENT

The final section of this chapter is a revised version of my paper 'Geography matters? Whiteness and contemporary geography', *Area*, 32, 2, 225–30, 2000. It is reproduced here with the kind permission of Blackwell Publishing.

7

(POST)COLONIAL GEOGRAPHIES AT JOHANNESBURG'S EMPIRE EXHIBITION, 1936

Jenny Robinson

In July 1936, two months before the Empire Exhibition was due to open, several newspapers ran a double-page article entitled, 'Family Robinson, Can they do the Empire Exhibition for £3- a day?' The article captured what it might be like for a family on a modest income to spend the day at the Exhibition, adding up what it would cost to enter the grounds and to see some of the attractions that charged a separate entrance fee, to go on rides, or play at side-shows in the amusements park, to get into the ice-skating rink, to eat at one of the restaurants, and to purchase some of the goods on display. Mom and Dad Robinson might even consider going back one evening to one of the many plays or performances held in the concert hall or arena. Over the course of the Exhibition (from 15 September 1936 to 8 January 1937), many journalists and other visitors reported on their experiences at the Exhibition. They noted down their favourite exhibits, recounted tales of meetings and occurrences, explained how it made them think and feel about things like Empire and nation, and also described their reactions to other people and cultures they encountered there.

The Exhibition brought together displays from all parts of South Africa and the British Empire, assembling people, objects, images, models and technology from all over the world. For 'average' white South African families like the Robinsons, and for many white and black visitors, the Exhibition offered an opportunity to see and reflect on their country, on their fellow country-people's achievements and histories, and on the more distant landscapes and products of other colonial contexts. The Exhibition grounds enabled many South Africans and some foreigners to wander among bits and pieces of their country and commonwealth, and to observe and meet some of their fellow countrymen and women in a wide range of re-created settings.

In this chapter I reflect on the nature of these meetings and what they might have meant for visitors and exhibitors. I also consider what the range of interactions enabled and provoked by the Exhibition might imply for broader understandings of the formation of white identities in relation to others, in this case, colonized African people. In bringing together people and objects from such a range of contexts, the Exhibition, as a space of assembly, allowed people to experience together diverse interactions that might otherwise have been kept apart in space and time. Or perhaps the Exhibition simply heightened the experience of those interactions which anyway characterized the co-existence and co-presence of different settings and experiences within the colonial context and, more especially, within the South African city.

This chapter places most of its emphasis on white experiences of the exhibition, rather than on black visitors' responses. I have written elsewhere on African participation at the Exhibition where I note that African people participated in the exhibition, not only as performers or exhibitors and, in some cases, as exhibits themselves, but also as enthusiastic visitors (Robinson, 1999). But in many ways, the assumed audience of the exhibit was white South Africa, and there was much written about how the Exhibition would influence and benefit white visitors. Most of the accessible written accounts of visits are by white reporters or visitors. I use this imbalance in the sources as an opportunity to excavate aspects of how white South Africans interacted with, and responded to, the diversity of histories and cultures on display at the Exhibition.

(POST)COLONIAL RELATIONS

An important starting point in reflecting on the meaning of the Exhibition for white visitors must be the ways in which (post-)colonial interactions have been theorized more broadly. The geography of these interactions in South Africa as well as the distinctive setting of the Exhibition draws attention to questions surrounding the spatiality of (post)colonial interactions and subjectivities. Colonizing and colonized subjects are widely understood to be mutually involved in making histories and geographies in colonial and postcolonial contexts (Gilroy, 1993a; Jacobs, 1996; Lester, 1998). With intertwined pasts and presents (Said, 1983), white and black cultures and identities are seen to be shaping one another in significant ways.

My discussion of South African white identities in the encounters of the Empire Exhibition draws inspiration from a wider postcolonial literature in two ways. First, it recognizes that colonialism was always a partial and fragile project, framed as much through the agency and contributions of colonized people as through the dominating ambitions of various colonizing actors; and thus in some ways always prefiguring the postcolonial moment (Thomas, 1994). Second, in exploring relations between colonizer and colonized, postcolonial scholarship has drawn psychoanalytic literary scholarship (Bhabha, 1993; Low, 1996) and historical research (Schwartz, 1994) into an uneasy relationship. I explore the intense emotional registers of (post)colonial relationships within a specific historical context, suggesting ways beyond the rather universalizing efforts of psychoanalytic theory (McClintock, 1995; Lane, 1998).

Not only have white colonizers played a part in the emergence of culturally hybrid colonized subjects (Bhabha's 'mimic men', perhaps), but the long history of colonial encounters means that what is felt to be white, western or perhaps British has already been shaped by many different engagements with indigenous people in different contexts (Schwartz, 1994; Stoler, 1995; Hamilton, 1998). In South Africa by the time of the Exhibition, there had been many shifts in relations among colonized and colonizers over a long history of interaction, and across diverse regions of the country (Marks and Trapido, 1987; Elphick and Giliomee, 1989). Some aspects of interactions were governed by law and government policy, others shaped more by cultural conventions and practices. Most historians see the emergence of firmer racialized distinctions in South Africa occurring around the turn of the twentieth century, associated with the rise of a segregationist ideology (Cell, 1982). By the time of the Exhibition, these divisive relations between white and black South Africans had yet to be subject to the exhaustive legal regulation of apartheid. But many of the cornerstones of apartheid legislation (controls on the movements of African people, their rights to residence in different parts of the country, or different areas of the city, restrictions on the right to representation or property ownership) already existed in some form. In some cases, these were simply not effectively or nationally implemented. Against the backdrop of increasing legal restrictions on African rights, the Exhibition provides an opportunity to consider the nature of more informal interactions between white and black people at this time.

In the face of these significant historical changes in relations between colonizer and colonized, postcolonial theory has been prone to make quite universalizing statements about the nature and dynamics of these interactions. Psychoanalytically informed accounts are perhaps most formulaic, although also perhaps most suggestive, in their assessment of the dynamic tension underpinning the complexities and ambivalences which have shaped (post-)colonial relations. For Homi Bhabha (1993), for example, responses of desire and disgust, or fear and fascination, arise together in colonial contexts where cultural interpretations of differences of skin and culture are mediated by apparently more universal dynamics of self and other (mis)recognition (Lane, 1998).

Many postcolonial accounts grapple with the perplexing co-existence of aggression and affection that characterizes many colonial encounters. Psychoanalytical analyses suggest that, far from being contradictory, these ambivalences arise together. For example, for white colonizers, the racist politics of misrecognition means that recognition of fellow humanity and abjected aspects of oneself are simultaneously located in colonial 'others' (Bhabha, 1993; Low, 1996). Historians have usefully cautioned against universalizing accounts of quite different colonial contexts, though. In earlier periods, power imbalances were perhaps far less than in late nineteenth- and twentieth-century encounters, and attitudes to people in other cultures changed substantially across the long historical sweep of Western colonial encounters. Early European travellers were more likely to be overawed by the cultures they encountered, than supremely confident of their superiority (Schwartz, 1994).

More importantly for the purposes of this chapter, in later periods of colonization, there were also considerable variations among different people involved in colonial enterprises in their attitudes towards different colonized peoples. Settlers, missionaries, administrators, soldiers, and religious groups all had different experiences to draw on, and different values and learning shaped their encounters (Thomas, 1994). In the South African context it has recently been acknowledged that certain individuals may have had more sympathy and interest in African people and culture than historians have tended to allow. Carolyn

Hamilton's (1998) study of Shaka Zulu argues that some key white administrators and historians of Zulu culture developed a substantial knowledge of and respect for Zulu traditions, language and people. She suggests that through these men, many contemporary understandings of Zulu history and culture have been shaped not by Western impositions, but by the significant input of indigenous knowledge. More broadly, the sympathetic approaches of ordinary white people and even some native administrators and apartheid legislators at the often coercive front line of white relations with Africans (Robinson, 1996; Atkins, 1993) point to the co-existence within South African society of a range of responses to African people and cultures (Lester, 1998, and this volume).

My account of responses to the 1936 Empire Exhibition involves thinking more about how to interpret this diversity of responses. Such responses are differentiated not only by social class, language or ethnicity but, as Bhabha (1993) and McClintock (1995) suggest, marked also by unresolved interior divisions in individual subjects' attitudes and emotions. I argue that responses of white people to the Exhibition were shaped by the specific historical circumstances of their interactions with African people in South Africa at the time. These would have been various, although mostly laden with relations of white domination, but included relatively intimate relations in households, on farms, mission stations, on streets and in workplaces. White domination, while usually present, was negotiated in complex and often subtle ways, with plenty of agency on the part of African people, and depended on the context of the interaction (Comaroff and Comaroff, 1995). The city in South Africa, as in other colonial contexts (see Kumar and Phillips, this volume), may have been racially differentiated (and in 1936, the city was not yet divided in the harsh fashion of apartheid years); but it was also the site of numerous interactions and encounters. Imaginative geographies of the city also tied its inhabitants together in a mutual world, albeit one often physically separated (Low, 1996; Robinson, 1998).

Many commentators on postcolonial relations take the same view of these relations as Saul Dubow, writing of scientific and popular assessments of Khoisan people's place in human history. He notes of the display of 'Bushmen' at the Exhibition that: 'Such entertainment played an important role in the construction of racial stereotypes: it provided the observer with the means to distance or pathologise the unfamiliar "other", while at the same time affirming or normalising the familiar self' (Dubow, 1995: 24). The element of Bhabha's psychoanalytic dynamic that Dubow misses here is the placing of self-recognition on the side of the 'other' as well: both the splitting off of the hated parts of the self onto the degraded other, and the recognition of common humanity, and valued parts of the self in the other too. My assessment of the responses to the Exhibition is that even this more complicated psychodynamic account misses the diversity of responses that these encounters provoked. I specifically explore the kinds of responses which white people made to the 'Bushmen' exhibit. Not only were these responses at least as complex as the schema outline by Bhabha, but they were also shaped by more than the interiority of personal psychical motivations. In their historical location in a society already shaped by many different kinds of encounters and co-existences, the encounters staged at the Exhibition also require a more contextual understanding.

A DAY AT THE EXHIBITION

In this section I explore, in a simple narrative fashion, what it might have been like for the family Robinson, if they, like so many of Johannesburg's population, had in fact made their way to the Empire Exhibition at the Showgrounds in late 1936. I keep the narrative at a quite personal level, and in fact draw on a few of my own imaginings as to what it might have been like if my own 'family Robinson' had been there. It was of course amusing to me to find the average family with my own name. I decided to use it here as a way to keep the characters close to me, although this has obvious dangers. I imagine that it might lead people to think I had over-identified with the characters, been overly sympathetic, and read back into their worlds my own concerns and anxieties. But on balance I find it a useful strategy to hold on to the possibility that white visitors to the Exhibition had a range of emotional responses to places and people they encountered, and it especially helped to keep at bay my very modern sensibility which tends to limit whiteness to a strategy of domination. I have composed the narrative from newspaper reports, photographs, letters to newspapers and some published personal accounts of visits to the Exhibition. The sources are footnoted here to keep the narrative intact, but can be read as an alternative 'voice-over' of events.

There would have been a few days at the beginning of the Exhibition when the Robinsons would have stayed at home – unseasonably cold weather kept most people away long enough to make the organizers really worried.[1] But then summer finally hit and public holidays drew much bigger crowds than expected – the family could well have gone home hungry and thirsty as long queues meant that almost everything had run out by the late afternoon.[2] Whenever they chose to go, the family would have probably taken a tram downtown, and embarked on the special tram service to the entrance on Empire Road. The tramdriver may well have been looking at the excited children with some envy. He would have to wait for a day off to be able to go in to the grounds, even though he drove up to the entrance dozens of times a day.[3]

Mom would have to fork out 6/- for entrance tickets[4] but even as they were standing in the queue to get in they would have been marvelling at the grand entrance, flags flying and the most contemporary stylish architecture towering over them. Perhaps they felt proud of such a modern development in their city.[5] As they passed through the turnstiles, they would have been counted as one of the 1.75 million visitors over three months. Perhaps one of Mrs Robinson's friends sold them the ticket – and exchanged some words about the long hours she was working. Looking down the tree-lined avenue ('Prosperity Avenue') the Tower of Light would have caught their eye. Knowing from the newspapers that lots of people met there, perhaps Mom interrupted Johnny and Carol to instruct them to wait at the base of the Tower if they were to get separated in the crowds. And the sweet shops nearby the Tower probably interested the kids more – an incentive to get lost and spend their pocket money unsupervised![6]

Johnny immediately nagged his father to take him to the map of the world and to see the model cars that his friends had told him were in the British government pavilion. They made their way there, a bit confused by the map in the brochure, but they'd seen plenty of photographs of the rather sombre building in the papers. The children spent ages leaning over the edge of the world map set in the ground, following the lights as ships and planes made their way around the British Empire, trying to find Johannesburg and wondering how these models moved around.[7] As Johnny and his father pored over the models of cars and planes, Mom thought perhaps she could persuade Carol to go to the Women's Exhibit. Annoyed at having to do girl things,[8] Carol went along and was quickly absorbed in the Afrikaans women's displays of crafts – sweet koeksisters and women in strange old Voortrekker bonnets she recognized from her history books. She saw one of the girls from her neighbourhood and went over to chat while Mom found her Women's Institute friends who had arranged a display of old quilts and the work of some winners of a regional needlework competition.

They met up with the others at the kiosk for a cool drink and made their way around the South African government building. The children were soon bored, but Mom steered them to the Durban model, where they found the hotel they had stayed in for a couple of days the previous Christmas, when they had visited her sister in Pietermaritzburg.[9] Johnny and Carol pored over all the different buildings in Durban, trying to recognize where they'd been. The sea even had waves in it and they both agreed this was the best exhibit so far.[10] Dragging Dad away from chatting to his buddies from the City Health Department, part of the Johannesburg Municipality's display, they decided there was just time before lunch to go and see the Victoria Falls model, one of two exhibits they had decided they could afford to pay to see. After lunch (sandwiches and tea at the Grill Room, they passed by the Bien Donne restaurant – where they spotted Dad's boss – and howled at the cost of a cup of tea (2s 6d),[11] more than the whole family's lunch), they headed for the Bushman Camp, which they'd read all about in newspapers and magazines. They stopped briefly at the Swazi Kraal, passing a group of young boys being chased by one of the Swazi men. It turned out they had taken a photograph without permission and without paying the small fee which the Swazi group were charging.[12] Johnny flinched as they ran by, wondering why this large man in head-dress and skins was looking so angry. Carol walked around a bit bored, eager to get to the Bushman camp, and afraid they might miss something. Dad tried to draw the kids' attention to some of the objects which were lying around the kraal, struggling to remember their Zulu names which he had learnt from an uncle in Natal. The children got tired of his halting efforts and dragged him off to the Bushman Camp. The story of their visit continues below.

PUTTING EMOTION INTO BUSINESS AND NATION

At the gathering to bid farewell to Mr Bellasis, who had been on secondment from the British Federation of Industries for two years in Johannesburg to organize the Empire Exhibition, the Mayor commented that he 'had created a city of dreams and a fairyland in Johannesburg' (*The Cape Argus*, 18 November 1936). The Empire Exhibition captured the imagination and stirred the emotions of many people who visited it – like John and Carol in my story. But it was also a work of the imagination of its makers. Before I move on to draw out the diverse emotional reactions which the staging of empire provoked in visitors, let me draw a picture of the imaginative work which went in to making this 'city of dreams'.

Writing in a local journal, *The Outspan* (12 April 1935), Bellasis outlined 'Points That Must Be Considered In Planning An Exhibition'. Quoting Said Kiralfy, the 'king of showmen', who had organized the original White City Franco-British Exhibition of 1908, he noted that 'Your exhibition is a failure if people do not pause and exclaim with wonder the moment they step inside the entrance gates.' Bellasis commented that:

> If the public are genuinely staggered during the first few seconds then half the battle is won. The public, stunned and dazzled by the glory that overwhelmed them on arrival, are blind to numbers of little faults and defects. The first impression remains with them for quite a while.

Behind this wondrous visage, long and hard work had to be put in by the organizers not only to prepare the grounds but also to get exhibitors, checking that the exhibits and the goods promoted were appropriate for the country and for the aims of the exhibition. As Bellasis continued:

> The Buenos Aires exhibition [which he had recently staged] was a trade fair, pure and simple, but the aim of South Africa's exhibition is educative as much as anything else. About half of the exhibition will be commercial, about half non-commercial. Its aims may be summarised briefly thus: (a) To educate South Africans about South Africa; (b) to educate the world about South Africa; (c) to let Great Britain and the other Dominions come in and educate us about what they can do ... Nothing of this nature has been attempted since Wembley in 1924–1925.

Certainly, some aspects of the Exhibition were directed at promoting business and trade for South Africa and other British dominions and colonies. Putting the 'emotion into business' (*The Star*, 27 November 1936) was how Bellasis saw the work of the exhibition – but it was also expected to play a part in the emotional life of (mostly white) South African citizens. Part of the success of the exhibition was judged in its providing a source of pleasure and fascination for visitors, but it was also meant to achieve more serious emotional work around building a sense of nation, instilling a pride in South Africa's achievements and for, some of its promoters at least, to instil a sense of belonging to the British Empire.

As H. J. Crocker, Director of Publicity in Johannesburg, outlined in a promotional speech, the exhibition aimed at

> not only stimulating present inter-Commonwealth trade relations, but serving to create new desired and extended markets upon a foundation of knowledge transmitted by visual display ... [It would be] ... an ensemble of irresistible appeal to business people throughout the Commonwealth ... We plan too to invest it with the life and colour peculiar to the African

> scene . . . The popular appeal of the 1936 Exhibition will be heightened by modern amusement devices on a big scale; bands, concerts, dances and pageantry; gardens on Empire and of the Union; an art gallery and courts devoted to popular science, education, sociology, handicraft and home-craft, and it is conservatively estimated that the public attendance will exceed a million and a half. (*The Municipal Magazine,* March 1935)

Beginning as an attempt to promote South African industry and commerce as early as 1928, and subsequently linked to the celebration of Johannesburg's Jubilee Year, the Exhibition also became the object of nation-building hopes when government support was successfully achieved. But it was not an easy time to be linking South African nation-building to the Empire. The Fusion government had been formed in late 1934, which was an alliance between the Empire-oriented South Africa Party and the more republican United South African Nationalist Party, or the United Party. Davenport (1978: 218) notes that this alliance was 'born of a common desire to settle the constitutional relationships within the Empire and to pull South Africa out of economic crisis'. The Empire Exhibition certainly embodied such ambitions, although the presence of republican nationalists in the Fusion government made it difficult for the organizers to arrange diplomatic and financial support without substantial lobbying.

Nonetheless, opposition to the Empire links promoted by the Exhibition was relatively marginal. Throughout this period, Afrikaner cultural and economic associations were slowly building up support for the Nationalists, but, as Dan O'Meara (1996: 41–2) observes:

> The elaboration of this new Christian-national ideology of the 1930s and 1940s was an almost purely intellectual affair, conducted in the inner circles of party, press, Broederbond and church. The broad mass of Afrikaans-speakers displayed scant interest in these abstruse philosophical/theological debates. Neither did they manifest great support for the NP. The majority of Afrikaners voted for General Hertzog's UP in 1938 [and] 1943.

The low level of Afrikaner nationalist opposition to the Empire Exhibition reflected this, as did the enthusiastic participation of various Afrikaner cultural organizations in the Exhibition. What were to be key Afrikaner nationalist symbols – an oxwagon destined to head the re-enactment of the Great Trek in 1838, and a model of the planned Boer Memorial outside Pretoria – both received prominent coverage at the Exhibition. Some Afrikaner observers even glossed the Exhibition as evidence of the 'vitality which might be expected of a young nation' (*Die Volkstem,* 16 September 1936).

The Pretoria News (16 September 1936) made the link between the Exhibition and national politics explicit in an editorial entitled 'A dream comes true':

> The country is enjoying prosperity, after union without unity, now people are optimistic. In the political sphere a great dream has come true. The Union of provinces has become a union of hearts, insecurity has given place to faith in the future, and destructive waste is transformed into

> constructive opposition. We hail the Empire Exhibition as the first fruits of the new spirit in industry and commerce; the equivalent upon the material place of the spiritual change wrought by fusion in the political sphere. There were always dreamers in trade and industry, too, and their dream has now come true. Through the Exhibition, they have put the Union 'on the map'.

The organizers were not to be disappointed, then. Commentators from all backgrounds were suitably impressed with the standard of exhibits and the general beauty of the grounds. The Exhibition made many writers contemplate the state of the nation – its development, and its achievements in many fields of industry and culture. The Exhibition itself was seen as a reflection of progress in South Africa – and the achievement of doing this in Africa was frequently remarked on. In this respect, as the organizers had hoped, the Exhibition also made white people think in quite personal ways about their location in Africa and the pasts on which they drew in understanding their place here.

If the Exhibition was designed to inspire South Africans to a stronger sense of national identity, one of the most popular and more unusual exhibits in the grounds played an important if unexpected role in this. A group of people were brought to the exhibition from the Kalahari by a well-known Game Hunter, Donald Bain, and exhibited as some of the last remaining 'pure' type of bushmen in the country. Many accounts noted that people were fascinated by the idea of the Bushmen, and intrigued by the detailed information which the organizers broadcast at the 'kraal' where some of the group of Bushmen spent each day, dancing, posing for photographs, and occasionally meeting visitors and well-wishers. As with many of the Exhibition entrepreneurs around the world who arranged for people of various backgrounds to be displayed at world fairs and exhibitions, the success of the spectacle depended on substantial authorization from 'science' (Lindfors, 1999).

The following section of the chapter draws together some responses to the Bushmen 'exhibit', from those involved in organizing it, validating its authenticity, safeguarding the well-being of the people involved and, finally, those visiting the staged events at the Exhibition. There were of course many other displays of artefacts, art and performances at the exhibition, but the Bushmen example illustrates my main point: that the responses and attitudes of visitors to the Exhibition were far from uniform or unambiguous, even in the case of perhaps the most disturbing and objectifying kind of encounter made possible by the Exhibition, the display of people.

THE EXHIBITION AS MEETING PLACE/S: 'BANTOE, BOESMAN ... EN WITMAN'[13]

One commentator, writing in an Afrikaans newspaper, *Die Burger*, imagined a number of different African groups meeting at the Exhibition. The maVenda ironworkers stirred him to suggest that, as when visiting game reserves or the Bushmen camp, to see traditional ironworkers practising their ancient crafts would make observers feel as if they had had a glimpse of pure nature. More than this, he suggested that the experience 'is just as if you are looking at the entrance to a road which would lead you to the understanding of the puzzle of your own origins', providing a look at 'the nature and soul of this Africa of which we are adopted children, we who are white people'. 'Truly,' he wrote of the encounter between a 'Zulu' (more likely Swazi) Induna and the 'bushmen',

> here Africa has brought before you her different efforts to form Homo sapiens ... They are her true children – and what are we then? If that old spookliedjie (lit. ghost-tune) that the Bushmen are now singing with their welcome dance for the Induna; if the Kaffir dance group with their war cries; if that is all the voice of South Africa,[14] what then is our part in this? Bushmen, Hottentot, Kaffir, Whiteman, look at each other – what will the future hold for them?

Another commentator noted that the replica of the Great Zimbabwe in its mystery contrasted with the modern buildings elsewhere in the Exhibition, and with the 'traditional' Cape Dutch building: 'Zimbabwe reminds its onlooker of our purely African past; these old homesteads of the Europe that was once our home' (*Cape Argus*, 15 September 1936).

In a way, this set of reflections seems to support postcolonial assessments of relations between colonizer and colonized as tied to the colonizer's own sense of self – placing the 'other' on the side of nature and history. Scientific thought about 'Bushmen' at the time emphasized their distinctive place in human history, as supposed 'living fossils'. In the topical search for the 'missing link' in human evolution from ape to humankind, the 'Bushmen' or 'Boskop' race, played a significant role. Skeletons and skulls of recently deceased people were analysed in the Cape and in Britain, and one of the leading lights in this sphere of research, Raymond Dart of the University of Witwatersrand, had determined that a recent finding of an ancient skull could be placed as one of the missing links in the evolutionary chain (Dubow, 1995). Dart also accompanied Donald Bain on his expedition to the Kalahari Desert to gather and study the group of 'Bushmen' for the Empire Exhibition. As Dart wrote in a paper drafted after his visit to Bain's camp in the Kalahari, 'They are, as it were, living fossils, representatives of the primitive state of all mankind, mementoes of our own primaeval past' (Dart, n.d.: 2).

This interest in 'origins' then, as evidenced by the article in *Die Burger*, was shaped by popularized scientific debates of the time. But it also spoke to some other questions about the place of white South Africans in a continent that had seemingly been inhabited since the beginnings of time by people who were still there. How they were to get along over the years following the Exhibition was indeed a profound question. The intertwining of the scientific placing of the 'Bushmen' as living evidence of ancient evolution with questioning how white people were to live among, and face the future with, African people speaks to the framing concern of this chapter. The interest in, perhaps even 'fascination' with, the 'Bushmen' on the part of white people took place at a number of different registers (in this case, science, politics and personal wonder), and was shaped by a range of pre-existing contextual inter-relationships.

Stories about the 'Bushmen' coming to Johannesburg became popular fare in newspapers before the Exhibition. Two contrasting narratives from former police officers illuminate this point. Both had worked in South West Africa for some time and had plenty of contact with 'Bushmen' and took the opportunity of the planned exhibit to tell some stories about their experiences. One former police officer (N. Ousley-Stanley writing in *The Star*, 26 October 1935, 'If the Bushmen Come to Town') warned that the Bushmen were dangerous people, whose poisoned arrows and criminal activities gave him plenty of trouble in his time in the territories, and led to his shooting and being attacked by a group of renegade cattle raiders. He thought it would be hard to convince the Bushmen to come to Johannesburg. He imagined them considering whether to come Johannesburg or not, whether they would consider the hunting and meat to be good there, or whether money or tobacco would offer more of an incentive for the trip. He thought it beyond basic humanitarian values to force the Bushmen to come, and suggested that there had been reports of individuals dying in prison. He thought they would need grooming, for display, or their habit of not bathing, and smearing themselves in fat, would make them upsetting for visitors. Despite his role in chasing down and imprisoning Bushmen cattle raiders, and his assessment that 'Civilisation is not for them', he articulated an understanding of Bushmen as human and self-determining, noting, for example, that the raiding party he was involved in apprehending was motivated by opposition to the restrictive legislation affecting Bushmen. He recorded some intricate cultural practices, which he seemed personally eager to know more about.

The other officer (James Hope writing in the *Sunday Times*, 24 November 1935, 'Bits about the Bushmen') told rather more warm-hearted tales, but equally demonstrated his knowledge and understanding of distinctive Bushmen customs. He related two incidents, both of which rest on a patient interaction with local people. In one, he recounts drawing on an African interpreter to assist a Bushman whose store of drinking water had been stolen – a death sentence in the desert. The complexities of transcultural communication speak of an administrator eager to understand a world quite different from his own, and a plaintiff and translator who consider it worth the effort to communicate with this helpful officer. This recognition of common humanity and respectful engagement across different languages and cultures is nonetheless lined with a set of paternalistic assumptions, which are what make the article's 'humour' work for the reader, even if the author demonstrates his more detailed knowledge of the situation – the simple Bushman complaining, for example, that he is 'dead', as a result of his water being stolen; or, in the other incident, his comment on a craftsman he met:

> If this had not been in Africa I should have mistaken for a gnome the small figure that squatted there. His eyes glistened, and tiny cracks ran like spider webs over his face ... good fellowship glowed like a welcome warmth from his whole being. 'Good morning, White man', he smiled from his work.

These may be read as strong fantasies of belonging to 'Africa' (the same fantasies which motivated the writer in *Die Burger*), but they also reflect the practicalities of many decades of close interaction between settlers and indigenous people.

Visitors to the Exhibition would not be arriving with a blank slate to view human spectacles, but were quite likely to view the performance of difference, which they were (more or less) familiar with on a routine basis in their everyday lives. The resources for interpreting these exhibited differences were already available to visitors (such as the Robinsons), and could have varied from indulgent paternalism to fearful admiration or dismissal. To appreciate the social meaning and impact of the display at the Empire Exhibition it is necessary to recognize this variety of responses.

The distinctive physical body of the 'Bushmen' attracted much of the attention of the crowd at the Exhibition, and of the scientists, who described the group as 'pedomorphic', a supposedly formal, technical term to capture a range of physical and social characteristics of the group (Dart, n.d.: 5: 'we draw in the Bushmen, as it were, from the eternal fountain of youth'). For visitors to the Exhibition, these 'child-like' features evoked interest and sympathy. But, like the police officers, there was a great deal of interest in understanding distinctive aspects of Bushman culture and language, something which white people in many walks of life would have had to consider in relation to people of different cultural backgrounds with whom they had regular interactions. The arrangements made for the visit of the Bushmen group also show the significance of pre-existing modes of interaction between white and African people, especially in the world of administration and popular cultural or scientific knowledge.

Bain's efforts to bring the group to the Exhibition were hampered by the concerns of the Native Affairs Department officials, some of whom felt that Bain was seeking personal gain from exploiting the Bushmen.[15] They were anxious that the group should be well treated during their stay in Johannesburg, and sought assurances from Bain and the Exhibition organizers concerning their welfare. In return, Bain suggested that:

> One must, however, make allowances for him [Smit, the Native administration official] in that I feel sure that he is quite ignorant of the fact that the Bushmen are being exploited, persecuted and brutally treated by every native, Bastard and degenerate European whom these people have the misfortune to encounter. (Gordon, 1992)[16]

Bain's motivations for promoting the Bushman exhibit were closely tied to his ambition to have a reserve declared where they could be 'protected' and their distinctive and apparently deeply significant physical form and way of life 'preserved'. His enthusiasms were not self-interested. As Gordon (2000) recounts, he bankrupted himself in his quest for the declaration of a Bushman reserve. But they were certainly paternalistic, as Bain (together with a committee of scientists and political figures) determined, within the framework of territorial segregation and subdivision common in South Africa at the time, that this was the best solution for these people.[17] Whether the group he assembled saw this as the best solution for themselves is hard to ascertain (although Bain does claim their support). It is perhaps also worth noting that under the new post-apartheid government, arrangements were made for the transfer of land to the descendants of this group, including at least one person who had been at the Empire

Exhibition. In the context of diminishing opportunities for survival, ongoing killings and imprisonments, and increasingly exploitative interactions with white settlers, the relatively benign plans of Bain might have seemed a reasonable path for people in the group to tread for a while (Gordon, 1992).

Although the Exhibition was portrayed as including the last remaining 'pure' type of Bushmen, there was fairly open discussion about the many different interactions which people in this group had had with other cultures in the region, including intermarriage with Africans and Europeans. Bain was reported to observe that only about 30 of the group brought to the exhibition were 'pure-bred specimens of the old Cape Bushmen type, who were stated to be extinct several years ago'. The other 40 were described as 'cross breeds' but were members of the families who refused to be left behind (*Sunday Express*, 18 October 1936). Much of the media coverage focused on the idea, suggested by Ousley-Stanley in his story of a year before, that 'The Bushmen and their primitive customs will astonish the city, but not nearly as much as the city will astonish the Bushmen.' Both directions of this statement, often underpinning headline media coverage of the group's visit to Johannesburg, were inaccurate – and this was quite public knowledge. Bain's commentary at the exhibit made clear mention of the contacts which the group had had with many different elements of 'modern' life over the years – enough that among them were people who spoke both Afrikaans and African languages. As he managed to persuade a number of Bushmen in the region of his camp to join him, he wrote back to Dart, preparing to make the trip to the Kalahari:

> By that time I shall have all the Bushmen collected which are available in this area, and I shall sit down and 'work' them until it is time for me to depart for Johannesburg. [I have about 70 in the camp,] among whom some are very fine specimens but the majority are useless . . . The sorting out process is one of my chief problems . . . The Bushmen of this neighbourhood are a far more desirable type, for Exhibition purposes, than . . . any of the other tribes. *They are what the public will expect to see*, and may be disappointed at the rather insignificant type of the North . . . [On the other hand they have lost their individuality,] and for some time have been forced into frequent contact with the Europeans, Hottentots and Baastards . . . younger ones have grown up in a semi-civilised environment and in several instances have even lost the use of the language. Some speak Bushman, some a mixture of Bushman and Hottentots and others speak Bushman, Hottentot and Afrikaans as well. Those that are farthest away wear the typical Bushman costume and those that are living in the neighbourhood of the outlying farms wear any old thing they can pick up. Practically no ornaments are worn by any of them . . . *Now at the moment my main object is to get them dressed correctly* and that is my reason for making a trip to Ghanzi where I hope to obtain the necessary skin mantles, ornaments etc.[18]

Lengthy accounts of the Camp in the Kalahari were published in newspapers (including *Rand Daily Mail*, July 1936) and, although they made it seem exciting on the basis of the exotic differences of the Bushmen group, it was also clear from these reports, as well as from Bain's letters, that the Bushmen shaped the encounters in significant ways; or, as one of the scientists put it, 'I found them all as avidly interested in us as we were in them' (*The Star*, 7 July 1936).

The scientists involved in the project had come in for some criticism, with the Native Affairs officials describing them as 'cold-blooded'. Dart had written directly to the officials suggesting that the group's welfare was the province of the administration, and that the scientists would seek to have the group brought to Johannesburg in order to be able to examine them more closely in the interests of science. Science in practice, though, was far from cold-blooded. The trip to the Kalahari threw the team of eminent scientists into a world of complex social relations, which were seldom beyond the control of the 'bushmen' people themselves. The scientists were to certify this collection of living human specimens as of the 'purest type' of Bushman through physical examination and linguistic and other social studies. But their interactions were made possible as much by the learnings of the assembled group, such as their facility in different languages, as through their own professional expertise. The interactions in the desert were driven as much by the Bushmen's agenda (in terms of who wished to travel to Johannesburg, or whether people would sing into the recorder or not) as that of Bain and the scientists. The suggestion that the process whereby the group was gathered and brought to the exhibition involved their being 'denigrated, humiliated, dehumanized and exploited' (Lindfors, 1999: x), while clearly accurate at one level, needs further detailed historical investigation. Part of the answer depends on what happened at the Exhibition – how were the group understood and engaged with by the visitors?

'THE ROBINSONS' MEET THE BUSHMEN

Now is a good time to return to the family Robinson as they make their way into the Bushmen 'camp'. What would they have seen? Some comments on the camp suggested that the place looked a bit pathetic, but Bain had ensured that the initially drab environment was spruced up with some reeds against the corrugated iron backdrop. There were a number of grass huts and a stone shelter for the people should it rain or hail and Bain had also asked for a loudspeaker and microphone so that he could explain everything to the crowds of visitors (*Natal Advertiser* 18 September 1936). Photographs show the group milling around, occasionally dancing, interacting with spectators (asking for cigarettes, looking in mirrors, watching things that were going on, such as a sculptor at work, and meetings between the leader and various dignitaries or visitors). By all accounts the camp was well attended, so Carol and Johnny would have had to be quite determined to make their way to the front. They probably arrived in the middle of the commentary, which a tall man (Bain) was shouting out through a megaphone:

> The purpose I had in mind, when I brought these people out of the Kalahari, was to make propaganda, to build up public knowledge so they have a good understanding of the unremitting war that these children of

> Nature fight and lose against nature, man and animal. Regardless of whether they are primitive or wicked, these individuals are also living human beings, and if reserves for animals can be created, why can we not stand together and make a reserve for these poor people and save them from certain extinction? I want to turn the attention of everyone here to the individuals who stand before you ... The old figure right in the front is Abram, head of these Bushmen ... he has been thoroughly investigated by scientists and everyone thinks that he is anything from 99 to 109 years old ... He can speak good Afrikaans, a language he learnt when he was in the jail as a result of trespassing the Shooting Laws.[19]

Carol walked around the camp to look more closely at the little children playing nearby. She came running back, saying, 'It's lovely how they all sing and talk, the children are so cute – and cheeky, when I got close to them they jumped up and caught my face and said, "I kiss you"!! This is the best thing I've seen!'[20] Dad was wondering aloud about looking at human beings in a camp like this – was it right to stare at people, the way you would at monkeys?[21] Bain went on, explaining the ways in which Bushmen hunted, prepared poisoned arrows and lived in small family groups, without tribe or nation. He described some of the clothing and decorations they were wearing and explained how their simple shelters were suited to moving around the desert. Abram and his daughter both spoke into the microphone, so that everyone could hear their language, with its many different click sounds – more than the few Zulu clicks which Dad and their maid Minah had taught them. The group had now formed a circle and started to dance – Bain said, 'The feet are not picked up as high as in the Bantu dances (which they had all seen around the town) but are more shuffled over the sand.'

After the talk and dancing were over, Abram spotted someone in the crowd smoking and went over to ask for a cigarette. As they were leaving, a woman was setting up a stand to make sculptures of the young women in the group. Johnny and Carol wanted to stay, but it had been a long day, and the Bushmen were starting to put on their blankets and sit closer to the shelter. The sun was about to go down and the night air was getting colder. It was time to go home.

CONCLUSION: POSTCOLONIAL RELATIONS AND GEOGRAPHIES

It is unusual to write a relatively sympathetic account of white people's engagements with African people in South Africa. My intention here has not been to suggest that all interactions surrounding the Exhibition, and specifically the Bushmen exhibit, were sympathetic and generous. It is certainly the case that the dominant relations shaping the encounters in and around the 'Bushmen' camp were racializing, objectifying and infantalizing. Science, racial domination and white cultural superiority framed the meaning of the event. As Gordon puts it:

> The narratives used by both Bain and the pageant familiarised, exoticised, and ambiguously defined Bushman as victims in need of protection, but at

> the same time debased them. They also played a pivotal role by telling of a heroic ascent toward the natural goal: white middle class society. (2000: 285)

But slipping the tale a little closer to the experience of being at the Exhibition, there is more to take account of in the interactions staged at the Exhibition. White identities, like all others, are formed relationally, and are dynamic and contradictory (see McGuinness, this volume; Bonnett, 2000). The evidence in this chapter suggests that it would be a mistake, though, to read white identities as solely about recognizing the self through the abjection of the other. While that was certainly going on, a dynamic and multi-faceted set of responses have been reported here, which reinforces pleas for a more historical and nuanced account of colonizer-colonized relations.

There was a measure of self-reflection going on around the Bushmen camp. The concern with origins and belonging, as well as the self-interest of scientists, who sought to 'preserve' culture and physiology to study the origins of humanity, were all about white people seeing themselves in the mirror of the other (Bhabha, 1993; Low, 1996). This particular mirror was one constructed around physical forms, an unusual language – and an engaging and interested group of people. Some discomfort with the idea that people were being presented for viewing was assuaged by the context – the idea that the group was seeking support for a reserve. The animal/human dichotomy was firmly decided on the side of humanity – although the associations with animals were present, shaping people's responses, and their concerns. Alongside this, though, was a set of concerns for the people on view – about their well-being during their stay, concerns that their culture was headed for extinction and support for the idea that the group should have a secure place to live. Of course this slotted well into the contemporary plans of the government to allocate reserves to all African groups and deprive them of rights to land ownership elsewhere. But it also spoke of the recognition of common humanity, and a compassionate concern, although, as Gordon (2000) points out, this never translated into funding for the venture when it ran into trouble later on.

Some of the fascinations with differences cut across divisions between adults and children, English and Afrikaans speakers. Many people spoke of the games Bushmen children played with the mirror and were impressed with the dancing, language and their different stature. White adults were also impressed by a validation of their superiority: the imagined astonishment of the group at the big modern city of Johannesburg (and this was something many of the white schoolchildren from rural areas were themselves impressed by). The other side of this, though, was a general interest in the details of the Bushmen's lives, languages and history. As in Bhabha's account of the psychodynamics of colonial relations, the 'other' was a site not only for recognizing the abject aspects of oneself; but also for identifying a common humanity calling for compassion and mutual recognition of some kind.

My aim in this chapter has been to destabilize too simple a story of white experiences and identities as only about one side of this equation: abjection, hatred and fear. Certainly these were present and profoundly shaped South

African politics and cities for decades after the exhibition. But there was also present, in reports of this and other aspects of the Exhibition, moments of more compassionate and interested engagement by white people with the performances, productions and stories of African people. More than this, (post)colonial relations were diverse and bore the traces of the variety of historical situations in which white and black people met across the South African landscape. The invitation, then, is to move beyond the dynamic, if limiting binary of the psychoanalytic desire/disgust dualism as a basis for understanding (post)colonial relations, to a more historical and contextual account, albeit one still alert to emotional dynamics and processes of identification.

Finally, if domination was not the whole tale of these encounters, then perhaps there are more resources on hand to build postapartheid society and to refashion South African cities, than is sometimes imagined. These diverse resources of personal and cultural identification, available to South Africans in 1936 as a product of contextual encounters, are I suspect, even more widely available in postapartheid South Africa. Scholars and commentators could do more to look for them (even in unlikely places), rather than reproduce too easily a narrative about separation and disdain in colonial contexts.

8

EXPLODING THE MYTH OF PORTUGAL'S 'MARITIME DESTINY'

A POSTCOLONIAL VOYAGE THROUGH EXPO '98

Marcus Power

> This is the year of Portugal. A year in which the Portuguese have a greater pride in being Portuguese. 500 years ago we brought new worlds to the world, sharing discoveries, knowledge and cultures . . . Indelibly connected with the seas and the world . . . actively participating in the scientific study of the Oceans . . . EXPO '98 is a magnificent vessel anchored in the Tagus which generously invites you to discover the wonders of the Oceans With EXPO '98 an entire country joins an ancestral spirit of discovery and sharing, opening to the world, the worlds here present. This country is Portugal. (António Gutteres, Prime Minister of Portugal, 1998)

For the organization responsible for staging the last world's fair of the twentieth century in Lisbon in 1998, the primary objective of the Exposition was to offer visitors the chance to return to the cultural heritage of Portugal's imperial discoveries in the fifteenth and sixteenth centuries. The Portuguese contribution to the Exposition was dependent on stories of a number of Portuguese maritime adventurers who had supposedly been involved in events 'decisive to the construction of the modern world'. The Prime Minister's notion of a geographical gift of 'new worlds', and of a Portuguese 'ancestral spirit of discovery and sharing', was strongly characteristic of the way in which EXPO '98 (itself a 'magnificent vessel') disseminated the idea of an indelible national connection to the seas. The historical and geographical narratives constructed at EXPO '98 advanced a particular representation of Europe's imperial adventure (and of Portugal's imperial discoveries) that arguably necessitates some form of postcolonial critique.

Contemporary notions of *Portugalidade* (Portugueseness) register the legacies of Portuguese imperial discovery in profound ways. The discoveries (e.g. India) and discoverers (e.g. Vasco da Gama) have become crucial geographical components of a contemporary national imagination of Portugal's imperial past. National coins and banknotes still feature portraits of explorers, whilst the national flag displays a navigational sphere at its centre and the national anthem begins with the words '*heróis do mar, nobre povo*' ('heroes of the sea, noble people') (Sidaway, 1999b). This chapter explores how memories of imperial spaces and places are woven into nostalgic conceptions of national difference, themselves grounded upon the spatial displacement that was the 'voyage of discovery'.

In the official visitors guide to EXPO '98, António Mega Ferreira, President of *Parque EXPO*, recalled that:

> As often happens in Portugal, it was over a lunch of codfish and red wine that the writer and commission chairman, Vasco Graça Moura, and I ... decided that the fifth centenary of Vasco da Gama's voyage to India by sea could warrant a great festival of a universal nature ... A purely historical viewpoint was put aside and the theme [of the Oceans] was addressed in the light of its prospects for the future. (António Mega Ferreira, 1998)

But the *Parque EXPO* Commission largely failed to set aside a 'purely historical perspective'. A concern for the Commemoration of the Discoveries had in effect been institutionalized, over a decade prior to the Exposition, by the establishment of the *Commissão Nacional para a Comemoração dos Descobrimentos Portugueses* (CNCDP, 2000), a national commemorative commission sponsored by the government. The spatiality of imperial discourses was powerfully represented at EXPO '98 with its concern to recreate the material effects of imperial discovery, to restage the imperial 'discovering' of overseas territory by an exclusive band of male Portuguese 'adventurers'. The material geographies of the exposition deserve further attention in that they (quite literally) explore the condition(s) of postcoloniality in contemporary Portugal and emphasize how nostalgia for a lost age of discovery was expressed, alongside a desire to illustrate the dynamic and innovative nature of Portuguese capitalism, before a trans-national corporate audience. This chapter seeks to destabilize the imaginative geographies of Portuguese empire that were recreated at EXPO '98. Although a predominantly Lisbon-centred view of these imaginative geographies is discussed here, a key objective is to pose questions about how historical hierarchies of colonial centres and margins structured the Exposition of Empire in 1998.

In staging EXPO '98, Portugal was constructed as a 'prosperous and go-ahead country' focused on the future and not held back by its history as a colonial power or dependent on that past for contemporary inspiration and the affirmation of its national identity. Nonetheless, *Parque EXPO* offered visitors to Lisbon between 22 May and 30 September 1998 the chance to learn about the country's imperial discoveries, to join in the 'spirit' of imperial exploration, and to follow in the footsteps of Pedro Cabral, Bartolomeu Dias or Vasco da Gama while simultaneously embracing future responsibility for the world's oceans. How, in 1998, was this 'ancestral spirit of discovery' important to national belonging and identity or to having a 'greater pride in being Portuguese'? As flamboyant and flexible institutions of display (Harvey, 1995), World Fairs have been constructed as sites of opportunity and innovation but require continuities, identities and traditions in order to represent the world, the nation and citizenship, as in EXPO '92 in Seville:

> Change and progress, however, are only visible in a context which also marks continuities and traditions. Thus, although the idioms of power in EXPO '92 were quite openly directed to a corporate model of the nation-state, to the global competition for markets and control of the most advanced information technologies; the values of culture, tradition and identity were also central to national exhibits. (Harvey, 1995: 87)

EXPO '98 represented an incredibly expensive and intensive 'national' effort for the Portuguese into which the equivalent of some £1.5 billion was invested over nearly a decade (Wheeler, 1998). The Exposition attracted some 10.5 million visitors which, although some way short of the predicted 15 million visitors, was still viewed largely as a success in allowing the country to transform the image of Portugal overseas. Special collections of national coins and stamps were offered throughout 1998 in association with the Exposition organizers, including one series launched by the national postal service (CTT) on Vasco da Gama showing his departure from Lisbon, his Armada at sea and the rounding of the Cape of Good Hope (*EXPO '98 Informação*, 1998). The site chosen for the Exposition was also adjacent to the Vasco da Gama bridge which stretches 10 kms across the River Tagus, the largest civil engineering project of its kind in Europe and more expensive than the Channel Tunnel. Even 'Gil', EXPO '98's official logo and mascot, was based on a symbol of the era of Portuguese navigation and discovery. The idea for 'Gil', a cartoon character rendering a drop of ocean water, was based on Portuguese navigator Gil Eanes, who rounded the Cape of Good Hope in 1434.

The construction of the Exposition was also seen as intimately linked to wider urban and regional regeneration plans for transport and communications infrastructures and local urban and regional economies. Portuguese planners claimed to have learned from the Spanish experience at Seville in 1992 where planning and construction were seen as inefficient and ineffective in the longer term and where the 'commemorative dimension' had been viewed as 'highly ambivalent' (Gristwood, 1999: 21). To this end, the Portuguese Pavilion itself, the centrepiece of Portugal's contribution to the Exposition, has since become the site of a permanent industrial exposition and cultural centre, and numerous Portuguese state officials have spoken of regeneration in the Portuguese national economy as a consequence of EXPO's wider national 'impetus'.

In addition to stressing the wider economic and ecological benefits of the Exposition, the organizing committee was also keen to stress the differences between EXPO '98 and its predecessors (particularly EXPO '92 in Seville) many of which were criticized as restricted 'nationalist or imperial ventures'. EXPO '92 represented 'a crucial statement of identity' for Spain (Harvey, 1995: 88), where the central theme had also been the 'Age of Discovery'. In contrast, the contribution of EXPO '98 was intended to be global, benefiting not just local urban and regional spaces through longer term sustainable development plans, but by raising international consciousness of the need to conserve oceanic resources. The official guidebook at EXPO '98 outlines the idea that the organizers were 'unconcerned' with constructing proud narratives of Portuguese imperial history:

> The first Universal expositions were mainly industrial and trade fairs. They underlined technical progress, national pride and imperial values. In our days a national component has become predominant. The great powers now compete at a symbolic level, *affirming their power through the magnificence of their representations* ... Anxieties and hopes, monsters and myths, technological developments and questions in search for answers, evoking the past and anticipating the future, these are the issues on which EXPO '98 is based. After all the very same stuff that our dreams are made of. (*EXPO '98, The Official Visitors Guide*: 27; emphasis added)

EXPO '98, as the 'stuff of dreams', would not be confined by the desire to project imperial values or by simplistic 'nationalist' considerations but would rather be driven by higher causes and wider issues that face 'all mankind'. Through the magnificence of its representations, supported by the very latest in technology, EXPO '98 projected a national and international vision of the Portuguese as European pioneers, as a nation that responded to its destiny (and a 'longing for the sea'). In so doing Portugal is shown to have bestowed upon all humanity, through a process of sharing and mutual discovery, the gift of geographical and scientific knowledges of the Oceans. In the words of Portuguese President Jorge Sampaio, EXPO '98 began by welcoming all cultures to one of Europe's oldest nations:

> Welcome to Portugal, a country with a history of many centuries, a language spoken by many people, a culture of many horizons. A European, Atlantic and Mediterranean country. The country which greets you, is a country of freedom, open to modernisation, a nation which left its imprint and many memories in all continents and made the sea its own destiny because, as Fernando Pessoa once put it, 'It heard the present sound of that future/sea the voice of the earth longing for the sea.' (Jorge Sampaio, President of the Portuguese Republic, 1998)

The reference to the imprints of Portuguese culture and memories, stretching across all continents, is highly reminiscent of the language of António Salazar, President of the fascist dictatorship the *Estado Novo* (New State) that dominated Portuguese affairs between 1926 and 1974. It could be argued that the Portuguese, far from trying to embrace the future and set aside a 'purely historical perspective' (Ferreira, 1998), actively turned to the history of its empire, particularly the late fifteenth and early sixteenth centuries, in search of the reaffirmation of what it meant to be Portuguese at the end of the twentieth century. For the Portuguese, the evocation of this past was a necessary precondition for anticipating a national and global future. This 'voice of the earth longing for the sea' was an important part of the assumptions EXPO '98 made about Portugal's imperial adventures. Continuities from previous World Fairs can be traced to EXPO '98, where National Pavilions remained the central focus (alongside transnational corporations) and nationalist discourses were crucial given that the World Expositions can still be considered a 'technology of contemporary nationhood' (Harvey, 1995: 89).

Earlier colonial expositions held in Portugal were also in a sense dominated by the theme of the 'age of discovery' and are discussed here in the first part of the chapter, which attempts to develop an understanding of the historical role of Portuguese expositions (particularly those concerned with geographical discovery) in the making of national cultural identities. The importance of the Lisbon Geographical Society to what Salazar called the 'internal colonization' of Portugal and to the building of national moral cohesion, is also an important part of this history. EXPO '98 was by no means the first exposition in Portugal to incorporate a discursive structure centred upon the idea and the memory of 'pioneers' like Vasco da Gama. Values of culture, tradition and identity were central to a variety of colonial expositions in Portugal; in Lisbon in 1998 they were again foregrounded, forming a backdrop of tradition and continuity used to illustrate Portugal's contemporary control of advanced technologies and its corporate 'successes'.

MYTHIFIED NARRATIVES OF PORTUGUESE IMPERIALISM: EXPOSING 'COLONIAL CULTURE' (1865–1940)

The first World Fair was held in London in 1851 where mass production was on show in the very fabric of the event (Harvey, 1995) and where high capital and empire were proudly celebrated (MacKenzie, 1988). As 'spectacular articulations of modernity' (Pred, 1995: 31), these new forms of mass spectacle constituted 'popular phantasmagorias of patriotism and consumerism that glorified capitalism's technological progress' (Buck-Morss, 1989: 323). Culture and technology were the objects on display and participation came at a high cost to exhibiting nations, motivated by their desire to expand economic and political power. Allied to these motivations, Gristwood argues that each exposition offered:

> the visual expression of a mythified narrative of history, of progress toward a legitimated present and utopian future. Indeed the cities and states involved become both entrepreneur and customer in a commodity fairyland, *customer* in the sense that they 'buy into' the discourses promulgated by these events – high technology as a panacea for underdevelopment. (1996: 6)

By the late nineteenth century these expositions had reached their apogee (Greenhalgh, 1989). Portugal was represented at most of the major international expositions throughout this period where colonial cultures and modern technologies were displayed. The staging of large-scale international Expositions within Portugal began with the *Exposição Universal* of 1865 held in Porto. A society for the promotion of the Exposition (the *Sociedade do Palácio de Crystal Portugense*) was established and resolved in November 1864 to celebrate 'an ostentatious party' in a permanent building made of stone, iron and crystal. The Universal Exposition of 1865 was primarily an expression of Portuguese modernity and civilization, celebrating national industries alongside the 'pacifying' work of Portuguese missionaries.

The more explicitly 'nationalist' kind of Exposition commenced with the beginnings of the *Estado Novo* regime in Portugal that established a *Secretariado de Propaganda Nacional* (National Propaganda Secretariat – SPN) to market the policy and ideology of the fascist dictatorship. From the beginning of the 1930s, the New State set about an emergency plan of building national moral cohesion, attempting to institutionalize *Portugalidade* in the process (Ferreira, 1996). One seemingly logical extension of this propaganda work was the idea for an *Exposição Colonial* (Colonial Exposition) in Porto in 1934 that came from the international exhibitions in Paris in preceding years. Henrique Galvão, who led the organizational commissions for the Colonial Exposition of 1934 and the later Imperial Expositions of 1940, had argued that there was a growing need in Portugal to increase national 'sentiments' for the overseas empire, the *Ultramar*, thereby increasing popular understanding of imperial endeavours.

The *Agência Geral das Colónias* (General Agency of the Colonies), with which Galvão was involved, organized small demonstrations across Portugal from 1933 seeking to influence public opinion about the colonies whilst the Ministry of Colonies organized fairs and exhibitions within the colonies themselves to demonstrate Portuguese imperial unity. The colonies were seen by Salazar's regime as a central way of bringing political stability and order to Portugal, hence the need to increase popular knowledge, support and understanding of the colonial mission. The Exhibition followed the *Acto Colonial*, appended to the 1933 Constitution, which aimed to restructure a range of political, economic and social relations between the metropole and the colonies (Wheeler, 1993). The Act and the Exposition were also accompanied by a large number of novels and short stories set in Africa and depicting colonial themes, published throughout the 1930s and 1940s, which also contributed to Salazar's project of 'internal colonization' (Ferreira, 1996: 140).

Galvão described the Colonial Exposition of 1934 as 'the first lesson in colonialism given to the Portuguese people' (Galvão, 1934: 16). The 1934 Exposition was constructed instead in such a way as to stress the unity of the Empire. Colonies were represented within themed technical areas rather than through individual pavilions. Differences between the colonies were explained in terms of differences in resources, climate or in terms of the nature of Portuguese colonization in each 'Imperial theatre'. The organizing commission included officials from the Ministry of the Colonies, the *Agência Geral* and the Navy and Army, industrial representatives and City councillors, and also officials from the colonial states. According to Article two of the legal decree brought by the Ministry of the Colonies, which established the objectives of the Exposition:

> The Exposition will be organized with essentially practical criteria, demonstrating the extension, intensity and effects of the Portuguese colonizing action, the resources, economic activities of the Empire and possibilities of strengthening the commercial relations between the various parts of the nation. (*Diário do Governo*, 1933)

Each colony was allowed to open a credit account during the economic year 1933–34 in order to allow them to prepare. Every colony was represented individually in a single themed day and a number of excursions were organized. There were also numerous ceremonial occasions during the exposition such as the *Cortejo Colonial*, commemorations of the Portuguese Imperial effort and of the taking of particular colonial possessions. The *Cortejo Colonial* was the final stage of the Exposition, a grand Colonial parade, led by a number of key officials of the New State, which wound its way through the streets of Porto to an emotional climax at a monument to the five continents in which Portuguese colonization had become a reality (*Exposição Colonial Portuguesa*, 1934). Over one million Portuguese visitors attended. '*Vamos ver os Pretos*' ('let's go see the Blacks') was the desire articulated by many of them, according to Galvão's commemorative album, although colonial subjects had been exhibited in parks in downtown Lisbon before 1934 (Saraiva, 1990; see also Robinson, this volume). There was also a session on 'The Portuguese discoverers' and one relating to 'The Tragic-Maritime story' of Portugal. Upon its conclusion, the Exposition was declared a 'grand national triumph', an important moral victory for Portuguese imperial unity.

In 1940, the *Exposição do Mundo Português* (Exposition of the Portuguese World) represented a further intensification of imperial propaganda and sought to illustrate the 'modernization' and progressiveness of Portugal since the 'national revolution' in 1926. Offered in 'testimony and support of the national consciousness' (de Castro, 1956), the exhibition housed a number of decorative sculptures of navigators like Vasco da Gama and Fernando Magalhães. The aim was to symbolize the spirit of discovery and to construct this as something that was irrevocably woven into the ancestral fabric of the nation, part of Portugal's 'indelible connection' to the seas. It also aimed to celebrate the 'soul of the nation' and the consequence of 'colonizing action' that it had inspired.

For the New State and its 'provincial' representatives, these Expositions represented a colonial lesson of the highest moral value, illustrating the 'values and heroisms of the *Patria*', demonstrating the effort in terms of 'lives, dedications and sacrifices made in the name of maintaining Portugal's historic heritage'. Several maps were produced for this exposition, including an illuminated map showing the geographical routes of the Portuguese voyages of discovery and others depicting successful military campaigns or trade routes. The exposition terminated in a *Sala do Acto Colonial*, which aimed to represent unity and continuity and contained a picture of Salazar by the exit with a legend above it reading 'Solidarity, Unity and Nationalism, here is the trinity of principles in which the Imperial idea is enshrined' (Galvão, 1934).

Trophies and arms used in Empire were on display as well. Other rooms showed *Escudos* (currency) from the eight colonies or detailed the history of the military occupation of Guinea, India and Timor. One gallery dealt specifically with the administrative organization of the colonies and included a section on the Lisbon Geographical Society and 'Colonial Culture'. This raises some important questions about the interconnections between geographical knowledges and changing colonial discourses of nationalism and imperialism in Portugal. In most of the national and international Expositions with which Portugal was involved, the Lisbon Geographical Society contributed substantially to the preparation of material to be exhibited. The Society's role in the formation of 'colonial culture' was represented in the 1934 Exposition as indispensable to the nation. In the strategic reformulation and revaluation of prior discourses of colonial culture, the *Sociedade de Geografia de Lisboa* (SGL) was an important part of the historical, political and cultural contexts (Barata, 1985). The SGL provided many of the maps of discoverers' routes, or luminous maps of navigation, conquest and exploration used by the Portuguese in the eighteenth and nineteenth centuries. The SGL was also involved with EXPO '98, but the National Commission for the Discoveries (CNCDP) had a more direct and central influence on the shape and content of the exposition and on the Portuguese pavilion in particular. Here, Portuguese geographers, navigators and cartographers were celebrated and commemorated for their gift to humanity and European modernity with technology that António Ferro (President of the Propaganda Secretariat) could never have imagined and in a way that would have made him very proud. In presenting Vasco da Gama as the epitome and personification of the Portuguese spirit of maritime discovery, the organizers of EXPO '98 were (albeit in very different historical, political and cultural contexts) buying into very similar nationalist discourses to those that had animated the *Exposição Colonial* of 1934 or the *Exposição da Ocupação Portuguesa* in 1940.

DECONSTRUCTING THE MYTH OF THE PORTUGUESE AS 'CONSTRUCTORS OF THE OCEANS'

Visitors to EXPO '98 were almost immediately (and thereafter quite frequently) reminded of the contribution of Portuguese navigators and explorers, botanists and cartographers during the beginnings of Europe's imperial adventure. Vasco da Gama's image adorned the tickets used to enter the Exposition itself. Visitors not arriving at the specially constructed connection to the Lisbon metro system, the *Estação do Oriente* (Station of the Orient), might have crossed the River Tejo on their way to EXPO '98, and thus travelled across the Vasco da Gama bridge to reach an area of the Lisbon docks once utilized by Portuguese naval vessels destined for the Empire. On the *Day of Portugal* in June, a naval parade was organized opposite the exhibition and the Vasco da Gama memorial regatta also culminated here.

The Exposition was illustrated throughout by numerous images of 'Gil' (Eanes) and also included the *Garcia de Orta* gardens, which were named after the Portuguese botanical doctor (1501–68) and contained 400 species of plants from all around each of the former colonies. From the range of tropical vegetation assembled in these gardens the Vasco da Gama tower could be seen, towering high above the exhibition and facing toward the Tagus, adjoining the *Pavilhão da Europa* (European pavilion) housing European Union representatives. Within this Pavilion was a section entitled 'Vasco da Gama revisits the EU after 501 years' where Vasco da Gama ('in spirit') returns to Lisbon, slightly 'confused by the size of the buildings' and 'deeply curious as to what happened to his Europe' (Pavilhão da Europa, 1998). The 'spirit' of da Gama was regularly used to represent a wide variety of (often contradictory) values and ideals throughout EXPO '98 and was eventually almost as omnipotent as the Exposition's logo and mascot. Vasco da

Gama even came to the aid of Slovakia, a nation conscious that its participation in a world exposition about the Oceans was potentially problematic:

> Today is Slovakia's National Day at EXPO '98. For a country without a sea, Slovakia's participation in the exposition of the oceans could have troubled its representatives from the beginning . . . The problem was solved in the following way: 'Discover Slovakia with the help of Vasco da Gama,' says the Pavilion in the North International Area. This proposal is carried out in the centre of the pavilion, where the floor and the walls are covered in black stone, giving the idea of an enigmatic and secret space. Vasco da Gama stands there at the brow of a fifteenth-century ship. Suddenly the lights go out and the Portuguese navigator starts to move and speak: 'we are going to learn about this country,' says the man who reached India 500 years ago by sailing around Africa. (*Diário de Noticias,* 1998: 6)

When a fifteenth-century ship carrying da Gama offers to help you 'Discover Slovakia' and navigate a passage through a Slovakian national history, it is difficult not to be struck by the bizarre nature of the involvement of Portugal's most famous imperial voyager. Throughout EXPO '98, an enigmatic da Gama is constructed as a central figure in European discovery and modernity and in Portugal's contribution to the emergence of Europe and European knowledges, yet a contribution that the world has yet to fully recognize: the role and importance of one of Portugal's most ambitious and enlightened ambassadors for European trade. As Haraway (1991) shows in her work on museums, celebratory public exhibits do more then simply represent people and places, they recreate the object of attention in a perfect and desirable form.

This interpretation of the history of Portuguese imperial discovery and discoverers as if they were somehow part of a neglected chapter of European history was best illustrated in the *Pavilhão do Conhecimentos dos Mares* (Knowledge of the Seas Pavilion). This attraction, divided into five sections, was designed to illustrate the process of discovering the seas, where the overwhelming centre of attention (particularly in the discussion of the fifteenth and sixteenth centuries) is Europe, European knowledge, histories and scientific discoverers. The transition between the various sections of the exhibit was to be made by means of an intermediate sector honouring Magellan's circumnavigation of the world. His route was drawn on a large globe, suggesting a parallel between the corridor just crossed by the visitors and the Straits in the extreme meridian of South America. At the centre was a film called *Oceans and Utopias*, which explored the 'fears, myths, monsters and hopes' associated with the sea.

The *Pavilhão de Portugal* (Portuguese pavilion) also screened a film that explores the myths and monsters of Portugal's imperial past, entitled *A Viagem* (The Voyage) and based on the characters depicted in the famous Namban screens (seventeeth-century illustrations painted by the Japanese). The Portuguese pavilion was located on the site of the Olivais dock, a central location within the EXPO '98 site (see Figure 8.1) where the general theme was the contribution of the Portuguese to the discovery and conquest of the oceans. Having passed below a sign above the entrance to the first section recognizing that 'Portugal

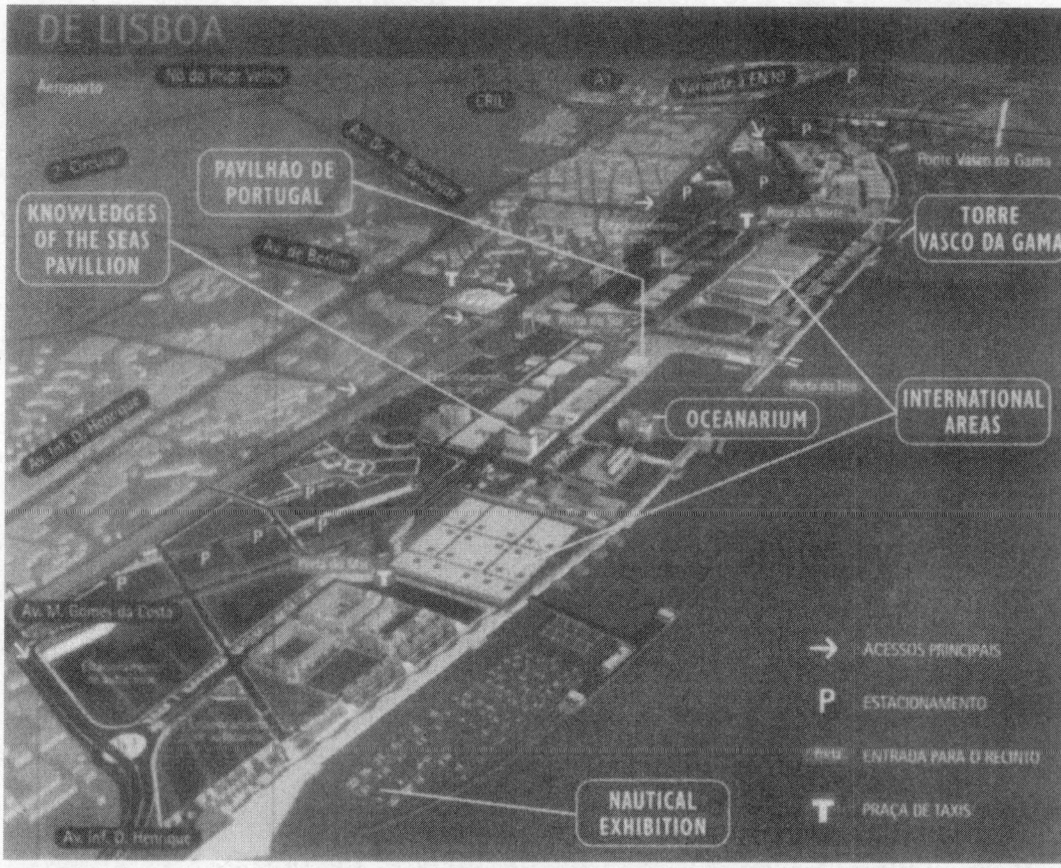

Figure 8.1 The EXPO '98 site, Lisbon
Source: Adapted from *Visão*, 1998

gave knowledge of the seas to all humanity', the first nucleus of the exhibition was entitled 'Myths, dreams and realities'. It featured *A Viagem*, which depicted the arrival of the Portuguese in Asia and their introduction of items such as chairs, rifles and eye glasses to their 'hosts'. A central objective of the Pavilion, according to Head of the organizing Commissariat, Simonetta Luz Afonso, was to convey the idea of the Portuguese as 'constructors' or 'builders' of the oceans:

> I would like to leave the Portuguese the pride of having been the constructors of the oceans, in the sense of communication between peoples and in search of knowledge. It is also important though that this 'pride' collaborates in the creation of new perspectives. (Simonetta Luz Afonso, 1996: 22–7)

In this 1996 interview with the publication *História*, Simonetta Afonso refers on several occasions to the need to avoid what she calls a 'luso-centric' vision of the discoveries and to create 'new perspectives'. A national pavilion that seeks primarily to position Portugal as having a fundamental role as 'builder of the Oceans' or as a 'pioneer' of oceanic routes was also seen as something that could 'free' Portuguese historiographies of the Discoveries from the overwhelming centricity of Portugal:

> Portugal ... was a pioneer of Oceanic routes ... It seems to me extremely important to benefit from this grand thematic, to give knowledge to the world and free this from a certain luso-centrism that characterizes some contemporary historiography, [identifying] a sense of the purpose of Portugal, precisely in the discovery of these Oceanic routes, in knowledges of the land and as the designer of the first correct maps of the world that we know today ... [Portugal] had a fundamental role in a determined period of world History that nobody can deny. (ibid.)

What the *Pavilhão de Portugal* illustrated perhaps most effectively was the deep significance of the Discoveries to the national historical imagination(s) of Portugal and to contemporary senses of *Portugalidade*. The pavilion also illustrated the contention that Empire has a rather 'shallow grave' in Portugal (de Figueiredo, 1999). Just as the Discoveries themselves had strengthened national consciousness in Portugal during this romanticized age of discovery, so their celebration and commemoration in 1998 would seek to reaffirm the national sense of belonging:

> [W]e cannot attribute to Portugal a luso-centric vision, but we can place/position ourselves as pioneers of the discovery of the oceans, with all the implications that this has ... Portugal affirmed its own sense of identity and it was developed through the conquest of the Oceans and the opening of worlds. I believe the visitor to our pavilion wants to know the Portuguese culture at the time of the Discoveries. (ibid.)

But this was precisely where EXPO '98 fell silent, in that it was only a very selective range of the 'implications' of Portugal's 'pioneering' role that were being remembered and celebrated. In this sense, the Exposition is best viewed as forming part of a long and proud national tradition of exhibitions, which prioritized the era of the *Descobrimentos Portugueses*. Thus the Portuguese pavilion was part of a tradition of attempts to imply that this spirit of discovery and curiosity about the oceans was particular to the Portuguese or irrevocably woven into the national cultural fabric. It is also worth remembering that the Exposition, particularly the *Pavilhão de Portugal,* offered a sanitized and unbloodied history of imperial adventure, saying little about the thousands of slaves and convicts, for example, who were used to sail ships in much of the sixteenth and seventeenth centuries.

The organizers of EXPO '98 promised an 'expanded vision' of the imperial discoveries but what was actually available was a particular version of events, which arguably says more about the Portuguese and the constituents of their national identity than it does about the Portuguese contribution to European enlightenment. As Macedo (1996: 131) suggests, each time there is historical reflection upon the Discoveries, they are in a sense moving a little further away, as they become re-imagined and re-invented:

> The Portuguese pioneers of Europe's imperial adventure (though the Portuguese were not alone in this) projected their own desires, fears, ideas, phantoms, superstitions – in short, their 'imaginary' – onto the things and people they encountered. It should be noted that the Latin word *invenire*, to come upon, and hence to find or to discover, is also the root of 'to invent,' or 'to imagine'. (ibid.)

As the Discoveries were remembered and commemorated at EXPO '98, so this imperial past of adventure and discovery was 'nationalized', re-imagined for the nation. EXPO '98 constructed a particular 'discursive purchase' on the culture of the Discoveries which was in turn heavily marked by the idea of the Exposition as the last of its kind in the twentieth century, as situated 'on the threshold of the Millennium' (Gutteres, 1998).

Even though all of the former colonies had national representations at EXPO '98, many had quite restricted remits, which prevented alternative histories of the Discoveries (and their longer term consequences) from being fully explored. The *Pavilhão de Moçambique* (Mozambique Pavilion), costing $1.25 million, was a good example of this, seeking largely to identify the country as an emerging market with rich natural resources. The delegation was initially widely criticized in Mozambique, particularly for the high costs associated with insuring the exhibits (such as the 'Maconde Christ'). Thematic videos, books, cassettes and music were available and a selection of arts and crafts were drawn from each area of the country. Artist Malangatana Valente Nguenha decorated the outer pavilion with a mural and his work also formed part of a wider cultural programme that had included the national song and dance company (Cuambe, 1998).

On the Mozambique national day, the Minister of Culture, Mateus Katupha, claimed to have 'paralysed Lisbon' and gone some way toward dismantling the negative international image of the country. EXPO '98 would help 'to situate Mozambique in the international concert of nations', and to show how the country had prospered in peace, stability, development and progress (Katupha cited in Cuambe, 1998). For the President, Joaquim Chissano, EXPO '98 would showcase the economic, cultural and political potential of Mozambique. It would show how the country had emerged from the 'ashes of war' and destabilization to a future of reconciliation and multi-party democracy while improving relations with Portugal (Chissano, 1998). In this sense Mozambique was representative of a number of African pavilions in that a wide range of priorities and objectives, often very different from those of their European counterparts, were behind their decision to participate in the Exposition. In the Universal Exposition in Seville in 1992, Harvey alludes to the stark contrast between some of the major European pavilions and the representations of African nations:

> There was no hyper-reality in the Africa plaza, the representational techniques were stunningly literal. Many national pavilions operated basically as souvenir stalls. Within the African Plaza the objects on sale were barely distinguishable from one nation to the next – wooden animals, printed cloth ... Many of the African nations had wanted to show themselves to the world by bringing fresh samples of their produce ... 'EXPO is not only about culture' they explained. (Harvey, 1995: 102)

Although it would be unfair to suggest that African representations were 'barely distinguishable from one nation to the next', or that each simply offered souvenirs, there is a similarity between EXPO '92 and EXPO '98 since many African delegations sought to separate culture from business, constructing their economies as dynamic emerging markets with unrealized resource material and under-utilized labour sources. The pavilions of Mozambique, Angola, Guinea-Bissau, Cabo Verde and São Tomé were not directly concerned with visions of the Portuguese as 'heroes of the seas, noble people', but with illustrating the emergence of market opportunities alongside the diversity and dynamism of their citizens.

CONCLUSION: 'UNJUST TRIUMPHALISM' IN REMEMBERING THE DISCOVERIES

> History gave prominence to the achievements of the Portuguese in the expansion of the known Universe and their role in promoting one of the most significant processes of the sharing of cultures. Welcome to this adventure of rediscovering the Oceans. (António Costa, Minister of Parliamentary Affairs, 1998)

EXPO '98 offered numerous reminders of the contribution of Portugal and its maritime achievements, which were constructed as events 'decisive to the creation of the modern world'. Re-imagined as the 'sharing of cultures and knowledges', the multiplicity of stories and subjects in Portugal's imperial voyages was overlooked and neglected. History did not magically accord prominence to the achievements of Portugal, as the Minister of Parliamentary Affairs suggests, but this was rather an inevitable outcome of this '(mis)adventure of rediscovering the Oceans' for Portugal. According to Portuguese writer and poet Vasco Graça Moura (1992) it is necessary to avoid 'unjust triumphalism' in the process of remembering the discoveries, to have an 'objective analysis' and a 'critical capacity for understanding the cultural and civilisational significance of the discoveries' (Moura, 1992). These ideas have also been conveyed in some of his poetry, such as in the following extracts from *Crónica* (1997):

> We were always or almost or close to
> Running after uncertain shadows,
> Always dreaming of Indias and Brazils
> And discovering our very own misadventures ...
>
> Memory of coral reddened, by blood and suffering mixed ...
> brings us also entangled in seaweed ...
> won some lost some sailing.
>
> (Vasco Graça Moura, 1997)

Moura refers in his work to Portugal's 'maritime vocation' but he writes of this national 'vocation' as if it were incomplete, as if the spirit of adventure and discovery in Portugal would permanently remain unsatisfied. His work is richly suggestive of a postcolonial critique of EXPO '98 as it opens up an array of uneasy tensions and complex questions about what is commonly taken for granted in nationalist historiographies of this European adventure. António Mega Ferreira, head of the organizing Commission at EXPO '92 in Seville, defined Portugal then as once 'the most secret place in Europe', which, coupled with its extreme geographical location, led to the Portuguese into a constant 'dialogue with the sea':

> In the extreme west of Europe, an extremely ancient country reinvents its destiny. This country is Portugal ... in constant dialogue with the sea ... a country whose historic monuments, reflect the intensity of the Atlantic ... Portugal enlarged itself in the opening of the oceans ... Lisbon is today as it always was, a frontier: between Europe and the Atlantic, between the nostalgia of those that stayed and the anxiety of those that left. (António Mega Ferreira, *Portugal Contemporâneo*, 1992: 1)

Expo '98 offered Portugal a chance to 'reinvent its destiny', to re-stage its historical interactions with the oceans and the peoples and lands they 'discovered' before a global audience, while at the same time reaffirming a national sense of pride in belonging. The discursive construction of the Exposition in the public speeches of state officials was, however, wrought with ambiguities and contradictions. Former President Mario Soares, for example, spoke in 1997 of the need 'to return to the sea' in order to fulfil a twenty-first-century role in the management of the oceans (having just reminded his audience of the significance of Vasco da Gama's voyages). Similarly, Antonio Vitorino, Minister of Culture, spoke in 1997 of how EXPO '98 would contribute to 'the affirmation of Portugal' (Vitorino, 1997: 5).

Vasco da Gama continues, however, to have an 'uncertain historical profile' (Carvalho, 1998) and there have been multiple interpretations of the 'facts' of his life. At a recent exhibition entitled 'Vasco da Gama and India', staged at the Sorbonne by the Calouste Gulbenkian Foundation, seven different images of the navigator/explorer were presented to illustrate the contested nature of his history. Head of the National Commission for the Commemoration of the Discoveries, António Hespanha, once pointed out that more critical interpretations of Portugal's 'voyages of discovery' were necessary: 'History is by nature open to conflictual interpretation and Portugal has to be adult in evaluating such conflictuality without preconceptions' (Hespanha, quoted in Barriga, 1997). Technology, art and science are not the universal goals and values of human endeavour, and not all nations share 'the peculiar preoccupation of modern Western societies with mastering "objects of knowledge" and then publicly commemorating the victory by putting on a show' (Jordanova, 1989: 40). More generally, postcolonial critiques of these histories of the Discoveries should seek to interrogate the historical and geographical re-imaginations of their role in making 'the West' (Sidaway, this volume).

The Indian historian Sanjay Subrahmanyam has attempted to demystify some 'certainties' that have crystallized in what he calls 'western thinking' around Portugal's Discoveries (Subrahmanyam, 1993, 1997). He argues that '[t]he

Europeans didn't discover anything at all. The Indians always knew where India was' (Subrahmanyam, cited in Barriga, 1997: 11). A Mozambican journalist also highlighted the concern of Exposition organizers with the idea of Europe, referring to EXPO '98 as 'Portugal's passport to Europe's senior division' (Lima, 1998: 2) or a 'technique of nationhood' designed to provide a testament to the health of the Portuguese economy before its EU partners. Europe was clearly presented as occupying a space at the centre of the world in the Exposition, although this is not a simple metropole/colony opposition as was the case with earlier World Fairs. One section of the Exposition that seemed almost appropriately named was the section of the Portuguese pavilion 'Myths, dreams and realities'. EXPO '98 illustrated the extent to which contemporary expressions of *Portugalidade* are intimately connected with the myths and dreams of the imperial discoveries if not always with some of the (contested) 'realities'. Ironically, being from and belonging to Portugal, these were based on a sense of 'temporally confined spatial displacement', on a longing for the sea and the era of 'the voyages' overseas in the fifteenth and sixteenth centuries (Madueira, 1995: 18). This can partly be considered a legacy of the New State:

> In the Salazarist period, the constructions of Portuguese 'identity' which accrued to themselves an unquestioned hegemonic status were those which emphasized a national 'specificity', a specific national *difference*. This distinguishing feature of Lusitanian identity finds its most cogent expression in the myth that the Portuguese sense of nationhood is (paradoxically) grounded on a temporally confined spatial displacement: the voyages of discovery. (Madueira, 1995: 18)

Madueira (1995) writes of the 'discreet yet persistent seductiveness' of the residues of empire in Portugal and usefully suggests that further research is needed to explore what influence this continuing seduction has on '(post)-colonial metropolitan narratives'. Postcoloniality in Portugal is profoundly tied up with the 'age of discovery' and with the seductive appeal of these early imperial adventures, today constructed as Portugal's gift to European modernity. Mozambican playwright Mia Couto has argued that the African subjects of Portugal's maritime empire have been marginalized in many recent celebrations and commemorations of Portugal's discoveries. He writes of a 'celebration in waiting' and argues that 'much remains for us to do' (Couto, 1999). EXPO '98 illustrated just how much remains to be done, demonstrating the continued importance of these seductive and nostalgic scriptings of imperial adventure to the very (geographical) imagination of *Portugalidade*.

PART III

HOME, NATION AND IDENTITY

INTRODUCTION TO PART III

Ideas about the spatiality of colonial power and knowledge are interrelated with themes of travel, dwelling and subjectivity, which form the focus of the chapters in Part III. Karen M. Morin and John Wylie explore some of the pertinent debates in these areas by focusing on imperial travel and gendered subjectivity. There is a tendency in much of the current literature on British women's nineteenth-century travel writing to focus on elite women's uneasy or ambivalent relationships with British colonialism and imperialism. Thus, the complex intersections between imperialism and gendered subjectivity in places geographically outside of the formal European colonies are often neglected. In contrast, Morin's analysis in Chapter 9 is centred on North America, which has tended to remain closed to postcolonial critiques. She examines the published volumes of two American magazine correspondents and travel writers who travelled throughout the USA in the later decades of the nineteenth century. The chapter highlights the ways in which these writers articulated both with and against discourses of American expansionism and nationalism, and addresses specifically the intersections of these with notions of women's liberation. It problematizes these more transgressive discourses of Victorian womanhood against more conventional discourses of femininity, drawing out relationships among nineteenth-century liberal, 'first wave' feminism, discourses of femininity, American imperialism and nationhood in the texts of women as they toured the mining areas of the American West. Morin thus engages current debates about the meaning and applicability of a postcolonial critique for the USA.

Gendered subjectivity is also at the core of John Wylie's chapter, which explores the almost canonical forms of nineteenth-century geographical knowledges organized around exploration, 'discovery' and adventure. He critically re-examines the different Antarctic experiences of the Scott and Amundsen expeditions which, despite being historically contiguous occasions of 'imperial' voyaging, were nonetheless radically dissimilar in their enactment of an exploratory ideal. Wylie explores the different negotiations by the two expeditions of the interwoven discourses of polar exploration: their complicity with nationalist (and imperial) sentiment; their appeal to a technocratic vision of 'modernity'; their production of a sublime aesthetics of the polar landscape; their reliance upon an Inuit 'other'; and their performance of an 'heroic' masculinity. Underlying these interwoven discourses was the scaffolding of 'imperial', ethnographic and scientific practices that produced, legitimated (and funded) the very idea of voyaging to the South Pole.

Interrogating colonial and imperial pasts is of critical importance to postcolonial geographies. However, a major criticism of postcolonial theory has been that it tends to be too preoccupied with the past and has failed to say much about postcolonial presents and futures. Meanwhile, new forms of orientalism and neocolonial economic, political and cultural relationships continue to disadvantage formerly colonized countries. This book begins to address some of these issues directly. As the chapters by McGuinness and Power demonstrate, the former metropoles still struggle to deal with the acknowledgement and retention of the uncomfortable memories of colonialism in understanding their own presents and futures. In-migration brought imperial frontiers into the heart of Europe's cities, activating memories of empire, memories of *being white* and the racialized language of the colonial frontier (Schwartz, 1999). The experience of immigration was powerful and shocking for those involved, yet the phenomenon of immigration has worked itself into the urban economies and cultures of the postcolonial metropolis in significant ways. As Schwartz (1999: 271) argues, 'The cultural formations emanating from the margins – from the colonies – create new possibilities for the metropolis as a whole, allowing new pasts to be remembered and new futures imagined.'

Issues such as these demand that we turn our attention to the contemporary effects of decolonization and postcoloniality in both the former colonies and imperial metropoles. Several chapters in this volume attempt to link the past with the present, and those by Dwyer and Gooder and Jacobs focus specifically on the contemporary period to explore the cultural politics of decolonization, identity and contemporary politics of 'race' and reconciliation. Chapter 11 by Dwyer on British-Asian identities is informed by recent work by cultural theorists celebrating difference through the construction of 'new ethnicities', which draw upon experiences of 'hybrid identities' and 'diasporic cultures'. The chapter examines relationships between place and identity by considering how these diasporic identities, which are a product of migration and globalization and which cut across and displace national boundaries, are negotiated in the everyday lives of young British Muslim women. Dwyer focuses upon the question of 'home' through an exploration of how young women negotiate what it means to be British/Asian/Pakistani/Muslim. These meanings are characterized by ambivalence and Dwyer explores the extent to which 'new British Muslim identities' may actively challenge and re-work identifications with Pakistan, emphasizing the contextual global–local nexus within which diasporic identities are negotiated.

In the final chapter, Jane M. Jacobs and Haydie Gooder analyse the officially sanctioned process of reconciliation by which Australians are attempting to find some resolution to the long-standing friction between indigenous and non-indigenous communities resulting from colonialism. They explore this process through an examination of non-indigenous participation in reconciliation initiatives as well as their self-understandings of this 'politics of sympathy'. The chapter pays particular attention to the performative role of apology – in the language of reconciliation, saying 'sorry' – in reconciliation practices. Symbolic calls for official apologies to communities who have suffered historical wrongs are increasingly commonplace around the world, and various governments have engaged in formal apologies that draw upon the apparently humanizing and civilizing potential of an apology. In Australia, the giving of an apology has been strongly resisted by the conservative government, allowing the 'simple' intentions of this word to become yet another site in the on-going contestations between indigenous and non-indigenous Australians. Jacobs and Gooder explore the symbolism of apologizing (and not apologizing), the moral expectations implicit within the gesture of an apology, and what this says about the role of the performative in constituting or calling into being 'the reconciled nation'. By examining the complex circumstances by which an apology to indigenous Australians has been simultaneously sought and resisted, the chapter teases out the complexities of a nation struggling to find a postcolonial subjectivity, and raises issues that are of wider significance for postimperial and postcolonial nations.

9

MINING EMPIRE

JOURNALISTS IN THE AMERICAN WEST, *ca.* 1870

Karen M. Morin

Recent studies of nineteenth-century European women's travel writing have found clear and still growing niches in geography, history, literary criticism, and cultural and postcolonial studies. Across disciplines, much of this literature has focused on elite women's complicity with, but also resistances to, European colonialism and imperialism; on intersections between nineteenth-century Western feminism and colonialism; and on representations or experiences of colonized women. As Jeanne Kay Guelke and I point out in relation to the naturalist writing of nineteenth-century British women travellers (2001), much of the feminist and postcolonial work in geography has deployed women's travel narratives to critique 'empire' and patriarchy, for instance, in connecting imperial travel with gendered subjectivity or in questioning how inclusion of women travellers might reconfigure a historiography of the discipline.

However, feminist and postcolonial critiques of Anglophone travel writing (Morin, 1999) have thus far paid little attention to nineteenth-century American women who travelled in, and wrote about, the USA and its empire-building practices. Such closure would seem to be an outgrowth of more general trends in American studies which posit an 'American exceptionalism' to histories of colonialism and imperialism (after Kaplan, 1993). In this chapter I address some of that closure, examining the published volumes of two widely read, influential American magazine and newspaper correspondents of the late nineteenth century, Miriam Leslie and Sara Lippincott (a.k.a. 'Grace Greenwood'). Both of these women took trans-continental tours of the USA in the 1870s and both wrote travel books about their experiences (Greenwood, 1872; Leslie, 1877).

My analysis concentrates primarily on what these travellers wrote about American national consolidation via the development of large-scale industrial mining in the American West. The women discussed the principal site of mining at that time, the Comstock Lode in Nevada, as well as other mines in Colorado and California. Western mining was then entering a new phase of industrial-scale, technologically advanced operations that relied on both large capital investments and waged labourers. I examine these women's writings about the wealthy mine owners and emerging industrialists of the region who served as their hosts and patrons during their travels, as well as the workers they observed. I analyse the writings of Lippincott and Leslie in terms of their feminist 'reform politics' as well as their 'imperial' politics. Among other issues, I am concerned with how the women deployed reform rhetoric in the cause of exploited mine workers, but also how such rhetoric complicates a straightforward reading of their imperial politics. Imperial development of industrial mining depended on the hierarchies produced out of ethnic, class, and gender differences. The 'internal colonization' processes and practices that these texts supported were integral to American continental expansion.

My ulterior motive here is to situate Lippincott's and Leslie's writings within current debates about the meaning and applicability of a postcolonial critique for the USA. In so doing I make the obvious though still contested assumption that 'colonialism happened' in the USA in the nineteenth century. The travel writings of these women demonstrate potential sites of engagement for feminism, US historical geography, and colonial and postcolonial studies. The texts provide useful sites for exploring the intersections between the women's gendered subjectivity and imperial development in the American West, while also demonstrating potential 'postcolonial' sites of opposition to, or support of, that development.

As I examine the gendered and racialized foundations of the American nation through these texts, I further consider how miners seemed to negotiate their place in the emergent American nation. In that sense I am mindfully working against the potential of re-constituting women travellers as autonomous subjects unilaterally projecting metropolitan understandings of themselves and others onto their reading public. Part of my project thus entails being attuned to the constitutive and dialogical role of Western people and places in the production of these colonial discourses. I agree with Mary Louise Pratt who argues that sensitivity to such interactive processes is essential to avoid falling into the trap of the 'self-privileging imaginary that framed the travel and travel books in the first place' (2001: 280).

AN AMERICAN POSTCOLONIALISM?

In attempting to raise the possibility of a postcolonial critique of the writings of Leslie and Lippincott, one confronts a closure around the concept of postcolonialism in the wider American context that has only recently begun to be addressed (Kaplan, 1993; Hulme, 1995; King, 2000; Rowe, 2000; Singh and Schmidt, 2000). What can now be considered 'orthodox' postcolonial studies focus on the processes and products of European colonialism and imperialism, while American colonial and imperial relations, and the 'American Empire' itself, has remained nearly invisible within this theoretical orientation. As Kaplan (1993: 11–18) points out, there remains 'a resilient paradigm of American exceptionalism' – an ongoing denial of American colonialism and imperialism within postcolonial studies. Castle's recent (2001) anthology of postcolonial discourses, for instance, promises to 'regionalize' works coming out of that field, yet no sustained reflections about US colonialism or imperialism within the USA appear in his book. Instead it focuses on places that are by now familiar case settings for postcolonial critiques – India, Africa, the Caribbean, British settler colonies, and Ireland.

Postcolonialism in an American context is complicated by a number of factors. One is the narrative of heroic Americans who fought a war of independence from Britain and who have thus been seen by many as producing an inherently anticolonial state. When an American 'empire' (of the European sort) is recognized, it is typically only insofar as events that took place from 1898 to 1912, when colonial acquisition and permanent informal control was official US policy; that is, only when US imperialism extended to 'distant' colonizations of foreign peoples such as in the Philippines and Puerto Rico (Kaplan, 1993). To Rowe (2000), however, the USA's experience might best be considered one in which the rhetoric of an 'anticolonial' revolution against the 'old world' was used to justify its own imperial expansion, both against the European powers on the North American continent and in the practice of its own violent internal colonization. In fact, studies of the 'internal colonization' of ethnic minorities and Native peoples have a long genealogy in American Studies, since the 1950s if not before (including Drinnon, 1980, and Tompkins, 1992). The study of American expansionism, empire building, and colonial dispossession is well established in numerous human and environmental fields, including geography (Mitchell and Groves, 1990; Meinig, 1998). Yet these works take little advantage of the insights, theories, concepts, and languages that have come to be associated with postcolonial thought.

The closure around postcolonialism in the US context is further complicated by the contradictions inherent in the 'post' of postcolonialism. If continuing colonial or neocolonial relations in the former European colonies strain the concept of postcolonial, this is perhaps even more the case in an American context. In the US, formal decolonization and nationalist independence movements of the twentieth century – which arguably initiated the identifiable field of postcolonial studies – have little relevance, at least on the surface. But I would emphasize that the problems and limitations of the linear or chronological approach to 'post'-colonial relations is not restricted to the USA. Furthermore, there are critics who align the mid-twentieth-century resistance movements in the USA with other decolonization movements. Gayatri Spivak, for instance, submits that the civil rights struggles of African Americans, Chicano/as, and Native Americans can be considered 'postcolonial', as these movements were modelled on Third World liberation struggles. The 'after' of the colonial in the US context for Jenny Sharpe (2000), on the other hand, represents the neocolonial relations that currently intersect with global capitalism and international divisions of labour, especially with decolonized nations. These theorists, then, collectively focus on the post-war international context in their critique of US postcolonialism, as opposed to the earlier 'internal colonization' models of racial or ethnic exclusions.

It seems essential to keep in mind, nonetheless, that with its historically explicit economic, strategic, and political expansionist policies throughout its history, empire-building in America, if nothing else, has always been 'close to home' (Kaplan, 1993). The consolidation and incorporation of different territories, peoples, languages, and currencies into a 'nation' – making the foreign into the domestic – in the eighteenth and nineteenth centuries forms a key aspect to an American postcolonialism that does not rely on a linear or chronological (twentieth-century) frame. A number of American studies and/or ethnic studies scholars consider the USA ripe for such postcolonial analyses, and they approach it primarily but not exclusively through study of literary texts.

Singh and Schmidt (2000: 4) argue that Native American and other ethnic fiction in the USA reads much like other 'postcolonial literatures', in their 'textual moods, styles, and tendencies'. The racialized and gendered foundations of the 'American nation', as well as postnationalism, are taken up by several postcolonial critics (Pease, 1994; Moon and Davidson, 1995; Feary, 1999), while King (2000) argues that the postcolonial paradigm clearly applies to the USA simply because colonialism occurred in USA and its aftermath has everything to do with American identities, institutions, and idioms.

Although this chapter does not address the removal of Native and Mexican Americans in the areas of Western mines, nor their re-integration as waged labourers, it must be understood that the mineral resource extraction industry fundamentally depended on their tragic land dispossession, co-ordinated primarily through the efforts of the US government, land speculators, and settlers. That arm of 'internal colonization', however, should not be viewed as separate from other, interrelated forms of American and European imperial expansion of the nineteenth century that involved the integration of mining capital, workers, and technology on global, national, and local scales.

Postcolonial critics' consistent and self-conscious sensitivity to colonial discourses draws attention to the representational and cultural politics involved in the production of knowledges about colonial or imperial underclasses produced by them. Among the goals of such work is to decentre metropolitan thought and discourses, and to highlight resistance as read from colonial texts. The 'colonial underclasses' in the case of Western mining includes European (Cornish and Irish) and Chinese immigrants whose experiences and actions were both constrained and broadened by the colonial spaces of the Western mines. How they strategized their own survival amidst the processes of immigration and diaspora effects, changing mining technologies, and labour relations and practices, can be fruitfully read through the texts of these women. My specific intervention suggests that postcolonial approaches to studying 'relations of difference' in colonial and imperial contexts challenges self-evident claims to American national identity and notions of progress and stability embedded within them. The writings of Lippincott and Leslie, then, can serve as a window into some of the larger processes of American internal consolidation of nation – a window, in other words, into the struggles for power to define whom rightfully belongs to 'nation'.

AMERICAN WOMEN WRITING AMERICA

Depending on how one defines 'travel literature', one might usefully expand traditional notions of nineteenth-century American women's travel writing to include narratives that describe minority and ethnic women's experiences of forced removal, immigration, and diaspora. Hundreds of recently reprinted primary works, as well as critical secondary works on nineteenth-century women travelling in America, currently abound. For my purposes here, Georgi-Findlay (1996) provides a useful overview of 100 years of Anglo-American women's narratives of American westward expansion. Women's writing about the American West ranges from immigrant and settler accounts of westward migrations; to the accounts of army wives travelling in an administrative or military capacity with their husbands during the 'Indian wars'; to accounts by tourists on holiday at the newly established national parks; to accounts of missionaries, teachers, and other 'frontier' reformers; to accounts more properly identified as *belles lettres* or fiction. Other writers fit more squarely within what might be termed 'booster' literature – women who travelled with husbands who were hired by the railroads to publicize, promote, and write guidebooks for the western regions, both for future settlers and tourists as well as for future railroad reconnaissance purposes.

In some ways Lippincott and Leslie might be loosely characterized as western boosters, as they both travelled as guests of the railroad companies and their hosts and patrons were among the wealthy mine owners and emerging industrialists of the region. Both were also, though, well-established journalists reporting on the West to their East Coast audiences, and in this sense they were quite exceptional women. In 1880, only 288 of the 12,308 people in the USA identifying themselves as journalists were women (Beasley and Gibbons, 1993: 10). The genres of journalism and travel writing complemented one another during this period, for instance in the ways that women could 'legitimately' contribute to both via the epistolary (letter-writing) form.

One might easily frame Sara Lippincott (1823–1904) (see Figure 9.1), as an 'early Washington correspondent' sympathetic to reform causes. Writing and lecturing under the pseudonym Grace Greenwood, she was a well-known US East Coast journalist, travel correspondent, lecturer, and feminist of her time. While not an active member of the reform or progressive movement proper, Lippincott spoke and wrote on reform issues of the day, including in support of abolition, women's rights, prison reform, and against capital punishment (see Garrett, 1997). Lippincott was one of the earliest newspaperwomen in the USA, for, among others, the *Ladies' Home Journal*, the abolitionist *National Era*, the *Saturday Evening Post*, and the *New York Tribune*. She was the first woman employed by the *New York Times* and was also a writer and editor of children's stories and books of poetry. She supported herself, her daughter, and her husband at times, in a profession that offered few opportunities for women.

Lippincott often wrote in the epistolary form in her newspaper correspondence and travel narratives. A popular speaker, she took several lecture tours through the American West and owned a home in Colorado. *New Life in New Lands: Notes of Travel* (1872) is a compilation of an 18-month series of articles she wrote about her transcontinental railroad trip from Chicago through Colorado, Utah, Nevada, and California between July 1871 and November 1872, originally published in the *New York Times*. In addition to reporting on Western mining, she described railroad travel, landscape scenery, the situation of Native Americans, local political and economic growth issues, and

Figure 9.1 Sara Lippincott (Grace Greenwood), 1879
Source: *Dictionary of Literary Biography*, vol. 43: 303

explorations of Yosemite with John Muir. She also devoted two chapters to Colorado and its future.

Miriam Leslie's personal flair and marriage to Frank Leslie, founder of a chain of popular magazines and newspapers, catapulted her to national consciousness as both a newspaperwoman and eventually print-culture 'empress' (Everett, 1985). Entrepreneur Frank Leslie is known for revolutionizing the illustrated news weekly. His *Leslie's Illustrated Weekly* and *Frank Leslie's Illustrated Newspaper* were among a chain of his magazines and newspapers popular for the technical and artistic quality of the engraved illustrations.

Leslie's wife Miriam (1836–1914) (see Figure 9.2), was a controversial figure by all accounts, a flamboyant socialite who spoke five languages and who most critics seem to agree was a woman most interested in 'conspicuous consumption and personal publicity' (Reinhardt, 1967: 5; also see Stern, 1953, 1972). Her involvement in the Leslie publishing empire included editing *Frank Leslie's Chimney Corner* and *Frank Leslie's Lady's Magazine.* After Frank's death in 1881 Miriam 'saved' the failing business, meanwhile legally changing her name to 'Frank Leslie' to protect the publications from claims by Leslie's sons. In later life she turned to lecturing, apparently beginning her lectures with the acclamation:

Figure 9.2 Miriam Leslie (n.d.)
Reproduced courtesy of the New York Public Library

'Ladies and Gentlemen, I am Frank Leslie.' Whatever or whomever else she might have been, Miriam was a committed feminist and supporter of women's suffrage. She left her fortune of $2 million at her death in 1914 to the suffrage cause (Everett, 1985).

Miriam and Frank, along with an entourage of 12 editors, journalists, and artists, choreographed a widely publicized five-month grand tour of the American West in 1877. Largely financed by the railroad companies in exchange for Leslie's publicity, the trip promoted both the capitalist development of the railroad and Leslie's own publications. The group published the *Illustrated Newspaper* en route, with the aid of a small printing press on board (Stern, 1972). Miriam co-wrote a series of articles about this trip with her husband and his assistant, subsequently compiling some of them into her own *California: A Pleasure Trip from Gotham to the Golden Gate* (1877). Her text covers Chicago, Cheyenne, Denver, Salt Lake City, San Francisco, other parts of California including Yosemite Valley, and Nevada. Leslie interviewed Mormon leader Brigham Young, described visits with railroad magnates and mining speculators in San Francisco, and devoted several chapters to San Francisco's Chinatown. On her return trip she visited the sweltering mines of Nevada's Comstock Lode, and stirred up a 'national scandal' with her negative descriptions of the mining town of Virginia City, Nevada.

Both Lippincott and Leslie were self-proclaimed feminists. At the forefront of their texts were a number of white middle-class women's rights issues such as suffrage, equal pay, and clothing reform. Lippincott asserted that, 'I preach everywhere the gospel of equal wages for equal labour', demonstrating as much when she criticized the unequal gendered wage structure of a watch factory in Chicago (1872: 23–4). Both women praised Wyoming as the first territory to grant women's suffrage (in 1869). In one of the few recent critical analyses of Lippincott's writing, Georgi-Findlay (1996) interprets her persona as that of an Eastern cultured woman travelling alone. According to Georgi-Findlay, Lippincott sought to establish herself within eastern or European literary or journalistic culture, and draws her authority from that speaking position. However, both she and Leslie also deploy the rhetoric of Victorian women's 'moral authority' to speak as feminist advocates of a number of social reform causes.

The social reform causes with which Leslie and Lippincott aligned themselves during their western travels extended to prison reform, temperance, immigrants' and workers' rights, and the rights and conditions of Native women, Chinese prostitutes, and Mormon polygamous wives. Leslie wrote several chapters on San Francisco's Chinatown and condemned Chinese prostitution as the 'enslavement' of 1500 women (1877: 165–6). Leslie concluded that the reform of prostitution-slavery ought to rest on converting the slavemasters; as white men 'owned' the most beautiful women, 'Let us devote what is left of our money and energy and Christian zeal to the conversion of these "gentlemen"' (1877: 167).

While scholars have paid a great deal of attention to nineteenth-century feminist reformers' desire to improve the lives of women they perceived as disenfranchised or exploited (including Pascoe, 1990; Morin, 1998; and Morin and Kay Guelke, 1998), one might consider how the logic and rhetoric of feminist reform aligns with reportage of the Western mining industry. How, if at all, did Leslie and Lippincott extend their reform rhetoric to the miners and their working conditions in the mines?

THE WESTERN MINING EMPIRE

American imperialism supported by mineral resource extraction grew at an unprecedented pace in the American West during the period of these women's travels, and their travels were directly supported by it as well. During the California gold rush of the 1840s many miners worked independently and with little capital investment. By the 1860s, a second phase of industrial mining took hold – large-scale, technologically advanced mining operations that depended upon both large capital investments and waged labourers. This second phase of Western mining was key to American empire building and America's entry into the world economy (Limerick, 1987; Robbins, 1994).

Richard White (1991) outlines two types of American and European investment in the West generally during this period, that of buying stocks in companies and in loaning money, mainly for livestock, farming, lumber, and mining enterprises. While more European money was invested in livestock than mining overall, the move toward large-scale underground and hydraulic mining was accompanied by increased capital input. Numerous scholars have documented the extent to which Western American mining and railroad development depended on capital investments from Europe, mostly Britain, and the cities of the American Northeast. Considerable American, British, and French investments were made in Colorado mining from the 1870s (White, 1991), for instance, and hydraulic mining of gold and quartz in California was heavily capitalized by European and American investors. In Nevada's gold and silver mines, investments came from Britain and East Coast cities, but returns from the Comstock Lode especially helped concentrate wealth in San Francisco for the first time. San Francisco's capitalists had provided the bulk of the initial financing for Western mining ventures, but when these proved inadequate the industry turned to other sources, in the USA and in Europe (Robbins, 1994). Thus the development of industrial capitalism in the American West via mining was tied directly to American foreign relations through the mining industry's dependence on capital from Europe and the American cities of the North East. It was also dependent upon the labour provided by Cornish, Irish, Chinese, and other recent immigrants who worked the mines.

Both Leslie and Lippincott reported enthusiastically on the growth and prosperity of the West. The rhetoric of the 'wild West' typified by men of all classes who displayed unrestrained ambition and greed was reserved for just a few mining towns. Most of the region, though, was portrayed as a 'new West' characterized by order, economic enterprise, urbanity, and extraordinary engineering feats (Georgi-Findlay, 1996). Both Lippincott and Leslie attributed much of this success to the railroad; it brought tourists and immigrants, increased agricultural output, and was 'an immense help toward the development of the mines and mineral resources' (Greenwood, 1872: 115, 388). White (1991) explains that the railroad provided the infrastructure for the economic development of the West generally, both as it demanded timber and coal for its construction, and as it greatly enlarged the West's access to eastern and European markets. The development of the railroad was inseparable from that of industrial-scale mining, as the latter required the transport of large amounts of lower-grade ores, supplies, and technologies. Positive, enthusiastic depictions of railroad travel, food, and society pervade the women's texts. Leslie gushed over the 'national triumph' of the railroad (1877: 109), and Lippincott's final chapter was a tribute to the railroad's role in expanding Colorado's mining industry.

Both Lippincott and Leslie were tied into a 'network of patronage' during their travels (Georgi-Findlay, 1996). Both described numerous encounters with bankers, politicians, executives, industrialists, and especially railroad or mining officials who welcomed them into their homes and invited them on excursions, including into the mines. These men are portrayed as bold, manly, beneficent, paternalistic, and refined. Leslie, for example, visited the San Francisco estate of William Ralston, founder of the Bank of California, who reaped a fortune from Nevada's Comstock Lode in the early 1870s by integrating mines, mills, smelters, railroads, and timber production into a single company. Although she frames her discussion around Ralston's tragic death (a probable suicide following an economic crash), she nonetheless characterizes him sympathetically as a 'self-made man, [who] rose from the smallest beginning', a man who was 'princely' and 'audacious' (1877: 123–5). Men of the Bank of California also feature in Lippincott's text. She described the bank as one of the 'marvellous growths of this marvellous New World', and its bankers as 'distinguished for their uniform courtesy and munificent hospitality' (1872: 194–5).

While both Lippincott and Leslie effused over the development of the railroad, tourism, agri-business, and industry, and the men made rich through them, they also reported sympathetically on the various 'colonial underclasses' produced or displaced by them, such as immigrant ethnic groups from Asia and Europe (although they were much less sympathetic to Native and Mexican Americans already inhabiting the region). In this way their writings about American imperialism and the Western mining frontier intersected with tropes of nineteenth-century American feminism. One significant way in which Victorian gender relations and American imperialism intersected in the women's narratives was in expressions of liberation and/or assimilation of subjugated or oppressed people (Ware, 1992; Burton, 1994). Much of what the travellers wrote about miners drew on this feminist discourse of reform.

The counterpart to the discourse of paternalistic and refined railroad and mining magnates were those of the happy, law-abiding, 'heroic' mine workers who were prospering under such industrialists' care. Lippincott especially invoked the discourse of the romanticized, ideal worker who, like his boss, was first and foremost a gentleman. In Cheyenne, Wyoming, Lippincott claimed that her own escorts, who 'got their weapons ready' in her defence, were a bigger threat to her safety than the miners she encountered. Rather than fulfilling the stereotyped role of 'desperados, violent and foul-mouthed', the miners 'stepped courteously aside', and were 'respectful toward women' (1872: 45–6, 48). Near the mining town of Central, Colorado, Lippincott dined with a group of 'honest miners':

> men in rough clothes and heavy boots, with hard hands and with faces well bronzed, but strong, earnest, intelligent. It was to me a communion with the bravest humanity of the age – the vanguard of civilization and honorable enterprise mining life here is sober and laborious and law-abiding; we, at least, saw no gambling, no drunkenness, no rudeness, no idleness. (1872: 81)

Not all the news from the Western American mining front was positive, however. In a number of ways both Leslie and Lippincott emphasized the damage enacted by industrialized western mining, on the people and on the land. While on the one hand the travellers praised the beneficence of the mine owners who served as their Western guides, on the other they harshly admonished Western mining speculators who were dishonest and greedy and who conducted business in unscrupulous ways. They were 'bloated aristocrats' and 'elegant idlers' (Greenwood, 1872: 231).

Lippincott and Leslie also complicated their images of the gallant and heroic mine workers with those of the severe hardships the labouring men endured in the wretched conditions of the mines. By all accounts the working conditions in some mines of the Comstock Lode were abysmal, with men unable to withstand the heat, ambient air, and labour for more than an hour at a time (Limerick, 1987). Leslie visited the Bonanza gold and silver mine in Virginia City, for instance, witnessing the men enter and return from the shafts. Almost suffocated by the hot, oily smell and steam, and the deafening machines, Leslie herself did not descend the mine, although others of her party did. They later produced a wood engraving depicting the thirsty miners for the newspaper (see Figures 9.3 and 9.4). She described the returning miners as ghastly and fatigued: 'Such a set of ghosts one never saw: pale, exhausted, dripping with water and perspiration, some with their shirts torn off and naked to the waist, all of them haggard and dazed with the long darkness and toil' (1877: 282).

Lippincott, too, described the difficult (though aboveground) working conditions at Clear Creek, Colorado: 'Men are kept at work carting gravel, or wheeling it in barrows, for these sluices. In some places they stood knee-deep in water, dipping up the precious mud. A more slavish business could not well be imagined' (1872: 73). Lippincott was little distressed that large-scale, consolidated mining operations were replacing small-scale, independent ones, though, and declared that 'only large means can insure large results':

Figure 9.3 'Miners refreshing themselves with ice-water in the 1,600-foot level'
Source: From *Frank Leslie's Illustrated Newspaper*, XLVI (30 March 1878): 61.
Underground scene in a Comstock mine.
Reproduced courtesy of the Huntington Library

Figure 9.4 'Nevada miners': scene at Gold Hill, Nevada, *c.* 1865
Reproduced courtesy of the Huntington Library

> 'Boarded-up tunnels and idle windlasses are far oftener indications of the failure of means in the miner than of ore in the mine. The running of railroads into this region, and the consequent reduction in the cost of transportation, labour, and living, will work a great revolution'. (ibid.: 108–9)

One might characterize this mode of writing as one of 'reconciliation' (Georgi-Findlay, 1996). Lippincott attempts to reconcile both the destruction of nature and oppressive labour conditions with an ultimately positive image of large-scale industrial mining – and its accompanying society – as 'honest', orderly, efficient, and, above all, economically prosperous. The costs of empire-building in industrial mining were worthwhile so long as mining involved lawful, brave miners and paternalistic bosses; the landscape was only ugly when greedy speculators made a profit from it.

For her part, Leslie's mode of writing was ultimately less one of reconciliation than one of friction and hostility towards the people and places associated with Western mining. This is not least demonstrated in her admonitions against injustices to Chinese workers, and her concluding chapter that extensively draws out the stereotype of the rough, lawless western mining town of Virginia City, Nevada. The 'national scandal' that it incited has informed numerous of her biographies (Reinhardt, 1967; Stern, 1972; Everett, 1985).

Leslie wrote disparagingly of the 'immoral' atmosphere of Virginia City, emphasizing the existence of only one church but 49 gambling saloons; and a mostly male population with 'very few women, except of the worst class, and as few children' (1877: 278). (In fact, in the boom years of the Comstock Lode, the population of Virginia City grew from 2,306 men and 30 women in 1860, to a 2 : 1 ratio by 1870 [Paul, 1963: 72].) Leslie claimed the need for a police escort to walk around the town at night, even though in other towns and cities in the West she scoffed at such advice. In sum, Virginia City had little to recommend itself:

> To call a place dreary, desolate, homeless, uncomfortable, and wicked is a good deal, but to call it God-forsaken is a good deal more, and in a tolerably large experience of this world's wonders, we never found a place better deserving the title than Virginia City. (1877: 277–80)

Leslie's attack on Virginia City rested on deploying her own 'moral authority' to speak on issues of temperance, gambling, and prostitution. As such, she aligned herself with reform women who presented themselves as moral guardians of others. While Lippincott closed her book with a 'hopeful' depiction of Western imperial development based on an advancing railroad, prospering resource extraction industry, and heroic workers, Leslie's text ended with an image of an ultimately irredeemable West. Unlike the exploited, 'enslaved' Chinese prostitutes in San Francisco, on whose behalf Leslie readily spoke, the prostitutes in Virginia City are simply 'bad' women. In addition, it is in this context of Virginia City that Leslie described the miserable working conditions of the miners. Leslie's alignment with feminist reform doctrines of the day is, thus, considerably more uneven than Lippincott's. Her depiction of an irredeemable West ultimately raises the question, I think, of whether she might be read as somehow resistant to American imperial development in the West; and alternatively, Lippincott, as more complicit with it.

MINING A POSTCOLONIAL WEST

Western American 'resource bonanzas' have been well documented. William Ralston and a small group of men known as the 'bonanza kings' monopolized Western mining capital in San Francisco during this period. Brechin argues that Ralston and his cohorts accomplished this through cheating and deception: 'If it took insider trading, backstabbing, wholesale political corruption, and looting of the public trough to make San Francisco great, [Ralston] was only following accepted custom' (1999: 41). Perhaps as many as 30 per cent of the bonanza kings were foreign born; Paul (1963) characterizes them as superwealthy Irish immigrants who emerged from penniless backgrounds, first coming to California during the gold rush. These are the sort of men whom Lippincott and Leslie endlessly flattered and praised in their travelogues for their honesty, manliness, and paternalism towards workers. The women's texts are thus implicated in struggles for power to define who rightfully belonged to the American 'nation'. Such praise must be viewed as complicit with American imperial development via a particular type of gendered and classed identification with these men.

Lippincott's textual reconciliation of the mining West should also be considered with respect to the class background and ethnic make-up of the labouring miners whom she and Leslie described. At the time of their travels, Cornish, Irish, and Chinese immigrants made up a significant proportion, if not the majority in some locations, of these workers. Bitter resistance to, and exclusions against, Chinese workers infiltrated the most profitable mining areas throughout the mid and later decades of the nineteenth century, in Idaho,

Nevada, and California. Robbins asserts that the Western labour movement itself began on the Comstock (1994). Fears of Chinese replacements caused Cornish workers to strike in Sutter Creek, California, and Virginia City, Nevada. The Chinese, who immigrated to the USA in large numbers beginning in the 1850s, by the 1870s provided the main labour force in the building of the Central Pacific Railroad and also comprised up to half of the miners in Idaho and a quarter in California (Paul, 1963; White, 1991). This amounted to 20,000 workers in California alone, men who primarily worked the abandoned 'placers' of the first phase of mining (essentially above-ground ores, as opposed to the underground or harder-to-reach deposits mined later).

Leslie described Chinese labourers she encountered in Mariposa, California, later in her text admonishing the western mining establishment for its unfair labour practices involving the Chinese more generally: 'The cry of cheap labour so furiously raised against the Chinese, principally by the classes to whom any labour is abhorrent, is as unfounded as it is malicious' (1877: 173). She concluded that the Constitution ensured the right of emigrants to 'a share of that freedom and self-government we are so justly proud of', and that if the Chinese were treated justly, 'Time, the great assimilator' would 'soften the differences' among men (ibid.: 174). Due to exclusions and ethnic prejudices against Chinese workers, however, most of the men that Lippincott and Leslie encountered in the mining camps they visited were recent arrivals from Ireland and Britain.

By 1870, foreign-born workers outnumbered American-born ones in numerous mining centres, including the Comstock Lode and Gilpin County, Colorado. These were principally Cornish and Irish immigrants (Paul, 1963). By 1880 in the Comstock Lode, only 770 of 2,770 mine workers were American-born – the rest were Irish, English, and Canadian. The workers shown in Figure 9.4 (except the Chinese cook) were likely Cornish immigrants, as they dominated in both Virginia City and Gold Hill. Paul (1963) explains that mining was a traditional occupation for Cornish men, and by 1881, one-third to one-half of them had left their depressed circumstances in England, readily finding work in places like Virginia City. White (1991) characterizes the men's labour organizing as based on ethnic rivalries rather than class consciousness, as evidenced by Cornish men breaking the strike against the Irish and American born at the Comstock Lode; the anti-Chinese sentiments in the Comstock Lode; and ethnic tensions between the Cornish and Irish in Butte, Montana.

When one considers the ethnic immigrant composition of much of the West's mining population, which both women's texts explicitly did, Lippincott's rhetorical 'reconciliation' of gallant miners, paternalistic bosses, and difficult working conditions becomes clearer. Industrial mining required formerly self-employed miners and recent immigrants to shift and adapt to a system of waged labour. Lippincott's text can be interpreted as one aiding the imperial development of Western mining in the ways in which she constructs a gendered immigrant workforce: her miners are complacent, hard-working, sober, and lawful. Images of these refined gentlemen, courteous and chivalrous to women, replaced those of the rowdy, roughneck independent miners who would prove too subversive within the new system. Miners' working conditions in Lippincott's text are considerably better than in Leslie's; her own visit to the Comstock Lode entailed an excursion deep underground, an experience which she described as 'very interesting, easy, and instructive ... [a] pleasan[t] walk' (1872: 178). Thus in many ways Lippincott's text fulfilled several tendencies of the feminist reform rhetoric of the day, promising livelihood and prosperity to working-class immigrant men who laboured diligently and adopted temperance and other moral ideals of the middle class. Moreover, continental expansion of the railroad and mining industries was thought to help cultivate these gentlemanly traits.

During their travels, Lippincott and Leslie encountered numerous national, local, and global cultural identities within the borders of the USA, wealthy industrialists as well as working-class men. Rowe (2000) asserts that little has been written connecting American internal colonization with more recognizably colonial ventures in foreign countries. He points out, for instance, that one of the ways that internal colonization moved forward was by aligning certain groups of people with the savagery ascribed to 'foreigners'.

Leslie's workers in Virginia City, and their working conditions, do in fact appear quite 'savage'. While her hopes for the assimilation or domestication of Chinese immigrants demonstrate a link between feminist reform politics and American empire building, the Anglo men and women of Virginia City remain largely un-integrated into that progressive model of empire. One might read Leslie's unredeemable West in a number of ways. Perhaps she was deploying an oppositional strategy against American imperialism, condemning or resisting the unrestrained greed of the men (and some women) who advanced the Comstock boom in particular. Alternatively, one might read her as invoking popular racialized discourses about European and Chinese workers. Might the agitating English workers ultimately prove too incorrigible, especially compared to Chinese workers who were stereotyped as docile and apolitical (owing largely to the indentured servitude under which many came to the USA)? Or, finally, one might read Leslie as rather insecure in her own class identity as a properly genteel, upwardly aspiring member of the *literati*, who required unrefined others against whom to define herself. Bourgeois descriptions of working-class people as unrefined and savage can be understood within a broader class politics. Leslie's attempts to shore up her insecure class identity were even more acute later when she travelled to France and returned, declaring herself a baroness (Everett, 1985).

By contrast, rather than reproduce negative stereotypes of lawless, rowdy western men, Lippincott sought to integrate the mineworkers she met into the American nation. Her feminist reform politics work alongside those of empire-building in that Lippincott explicitly domesticated or assimilated the 'foreign' immigrant (Cornish, Irish) into a courageous and contented worker, located within hospitable working conditions. Promised national inclusion, these foreign men thereby serve as witness to the type of progress possible and indeed inevitable within the industrial-imperial complex of the West and the internal colonizations at work there. Their labour was essential to it.

Finally, though, one must consider how the miners these women observed, talked with, and dined with might themselves have envisioned their inclusion in an expanding American Empire as they negotiated their split European and American identities. How these travel texts might provide a window into the ways they negotiated colonial space for themselves – a space that both limited and broadened their opportunities to embody an emerging labour force. These recent arrivals to the USA were negotiating both their material and cultural survival in the midst of the changing economic and technological landscape of western mining. Within a limited range of possible ways that they might have occupied such colonial spaces – dealing as they were with forced migrations (both trans-Atlantic and within the USA), insecure labour relations, and wretched working conditions – still it seems that numerous sites of their accommodation, appropriation, and resistance to American expansionism can be read from the travel texts.

A heterogeneous range of miners' voices appears in these texts, from the courteous, hard-working gentleman miners in Wyoming and Colorado; to the exhausted, fatigued workers at the Comstock Lode; to the rude, drunken gamblers in the other social spaces of Virginia City. As they encountered and addressed Lippincott and Leslie, the men seem to have deployed their own range of classed and gendered constructs. The women appeared on the scene in the first instance as guests of the emerging Western elite, brought into the spaces of the mines by the owners whose wealth depended on these men's labours. Their attempts to ensure integration into or survival within this uncertain transitional period in Western mining might be achieved through various tactics. For example, to engage a bourgeois gentlemanly demeanour – whether as a straightforward strategy or not – is at once to identify with those owners and travel writers while thereby securing inclusion in the space of the American nation they represented.

On the other hand, to expose the corrupt 'values' of elite culture might be another strategy to ensure one's inclusion in 'nation' – by challenging and revising the principles upon which it has been established. Virginia City, as it turns out, rejected Leslie's depictions of it as a hopeless God-forsaken place and 'spoke back' to her. The editor of the local Virginia City newspaper took his revenge in print. In July 1878 he devoted an entire front page article to criticizing Leslie's character, arguing that she was in no position to judge other women as she herself was (allegedly) illegitimate, engaged in numerous extramarital affairs, and exploited those around her for her own personal gain (Reinhardt, 1967; Stern, 1972). His article was titled, 'Our Female Slanderer, Mrs. Frank Leslie's Book Scandalizing the Families of Virginia City – The History of the Authoress – A Life Drama of Crime and Licentiousness – Startling Developments.'

While it was the editor of the local newspaper who spoke through this account (not miners), his actions in support of the miners and their families articulates with the history of political activism at the Comstock Lode, based as it was, albeit, on ethnic rivalries as well as on class conflict. In addition, the basis of his rhetoric is the double standard historically deployed against successful women who do not adhere to the Victorian domestic ideal. Nonetheless, one might also consider the editor's attempt at exposing and destabilizing Leslie's own claim to 'nation' as opening up a space within which other, alternative paths to it might be imagined. If nothing else, his voice mapped Virginia City as a vortex of competing moralities – and it is clear that the moral high ground that Leslie earlier claimed was not one that she would sustain for long. The editor contributed a measure of instability to Leslie's already punctured public persona. That said, and despite the scandal that his writing provoked and her legal and financial problems after her husband's death in 1880, Leslie's print culture prowess remained ultimately undaunted.

I am in agreement with King (2000: 8) in recognizing, accepting, and interrogating 'the conflicted aspects of postcolonial America [that] should energize rather paralyze critical scholarship.' I have taken a provisional step here in linking these women's travel writing about 'home' to some of the insights of what might now be considered an emergent 'American postcolonialism'. My focus has been on how gender, class, and ethnic politics articulated with discourses of American expansionism and nation building via these travel texts. The integration of mining capital, workers, and technology on a range of scales must be understood as deeply linked with other colonial processes taking place in the nineteenth-century American West. This chapter demonstrates connections among aspects of American literary culture, early feminism, and American empire building. My comments on these American women's writings undoubtedly raise more questions than they answer, and numerous other sites for a postcolonial interpretation of these colonial texts exist. At minimum my point has been to strategically deflect some of postcolonialism's attention onto American soil, where it most certainly belongs.

ACKNOWLEDGEMENTS

Thanks to Brian Page and the editors for their useful comments on an earlier draft of the chapter. My thanks also to Don Mitchell and Arnold Publishers for permission to reprint extracts from my article entitled 'Postcolonialism and Native American Geographies: the letters of Rosalie La Flesche Farley, 1896–1899' from *Cultural Geographies* (formerly *Ecumene*) (2002: 9, 2, 158–80).

10

EARTHLY POLES

THE ANTARCTIC VOYAGES OF SCOTT AND AMUNDSEN

John Wylie

PROLOGUE

Setting sail from northern Europe in the summer of 1910, two expeditions, led by Robert Falcon Scott and Roald Amundsen, voyaged south to Antarctica. They shared the goal of the South Pole, and, traced on the surface of the earth, their southward itineraries also had much in common. Without ever meeting in the same place and time, the voyages of Scott and Amundsen describe two intersecting trajectories; at Madeira and New Zealand, on the open spaces of the sea, and finally at the fulcrum of the Pole itself. Yet rather than highlighting lines of commonality, these contiguities in fact serve to throw into relief the sometimes very different nature of these two expeditions. In following Scott and Amundsen to the Pole, I aim to discuss some aspects of these differences – in particular, differences regarding their conception and execution of Polar exploration. I argue that these expeditions may be conceived as sets of *mobilities* and *visibilities* – in other words, as styles of practice and frameworks of understanding, which evolved in conjunction with the Antarctic landscape. I suggest, from within this interpretative context, that in the end *both* expeditions secured a 'victory' of sorts as regards their practical and imaginative encounters with the Antarctic.

'IMAGINING' ANTARCTICA

In the preface to *Arctic Dreams*, the travel writer Barry Lopez identifies two questions as central to his work: 'How do people imagine the landscapes they find themselves in? How does the land shape the imaginations of those who dwell in it?' (1986: xxvii). The first of these questions has been examined in depth in recent years by cultural geographers and literary and cultural historians interested in the cultures of European travel and exploration (Pratt, 1992; Blunt, 1994; Ryan, 1996; Phillips, 1997; Duncan and Gregory, 1999; Elsner and Rubies, 1999). The second has perhaps received less attention. Clearly, a concern to interrogate the imaginative geographies of exploration and empire has been at the heart of the ongoing critical project of rewriting geographical histories (Driver, 1995). Such a focus upon how non-European places and peoples were imagined and represented by explorers and colonists is important because it enables critical purchase regarding the ways in which a raft of representational devices ('ways of seeing', aesthetic norms, literary conventions, and so on), produced and reflected particular European understandings of selfhood, landscape, nature and 'other' cultures. However, it is also important to recognize that such an analysis itself proceeds from a particular set of epistemological assumptions, in that it identifies a certain strata of produced representations, in the form of variegated texts and images, as being constitutive of 'meaning'. In other words, in tandem with the project of critically interrogating discourses of exploration and empire, there has been a concomitant tendency to position the 'imaginative geographies' of explorers and colonists as the primary locus of the production of meaning and signification. That European explorers travelled laden with the baggage of their home cultures is undeniable, but the difficulty is that such an 'internal' discursive focus perhaps leads to a vision of the landscape wherein exploration is enacted 'as a blank page or an empty stage on which the drama of culture is written and acted out' (Demeritt, 1994: 172). In the most general terms, as Ingold (1995: 66) writes, the epistemological problem here centres upon the supposition 'that worlds are made before they are lived in'.

One point I wish to draw from this is that, on the whole, accounts of early twentieth-century Antarctic exploration exhibit a particular tendency to position and interpret exploratory experience in terms of self-contained discursive ensembles. Two of the more unusual (and successful) recent treatments of Antarctic history, Francis Spufford's (1996) *I May Be Some Time*, and Stephen Pyne's (1988) *The Ice* illustrate the varied ways in which such an understanding surfaces and is sedimented.

Spufford's text, focusing upon Scott's second Antarctic voyage, is a labyrinthine cultural history, concerned to excavate 'an intangible history of assumptions, responses to landscape, cultural fascinations, aesthetic attractions to the cold regions' (1996: 6). The aim is to isolate peculiarly Victorian and Edwardian discursive filigrees in which the image of the polar regions became essential. The narrative spirals towards Scott's *textual* death, when, Spufford argues, 'he knew exactly what to do. A century and more of expectations were to hand, anonymous and virtually instinctive to him: he shaped them. Scarcely a word needed crossing out' (1996: 333).

In apparent contrast, Pyne's *The Ice* seeks to convey a sense of the intense materiality of Antarctica. This he seeks to achieve rhetorically in the prologue:

> Higher-order ice forms collectively compose the entire continent: *the icebergs*: tabular bergs, glacier bergs, ice islands, bergy bits, growlers, brash ice, white ice, blue ice, green ice, dirty ice; *the sea ices*: ice stalactites, pancake ice, frazil ice, grease ice, congelation ice, infiltration ice, undersea ice . . . (1988: 3)

The list of 'ices' continues along a lengthy paragraph, and as the eye scans through the text, the constant repetition of the word 'ice' strains attention and its meaning begins to dissolve. This effect illustrates the lynchpin of Pyne's thesis: that the utter materiality of 'the ice', its absolute presence, is synonymous with its complete absence in terms of 'human meaning'. Thus the possibility of meaningful interaction between self and landscape is denied:

> Explorers ... did not discover the ice so much as the ice allowed them to discover themselves. The ineffable whiteness of the polar plateau became a vast imperfect mirror that reflected back the character of the person and civilization that gazed upon it. (1988: 67)

Here, from an emphasis on the materiality of Antarctica, Pyne arrives at a position close to that of Spufford, where the 'meaning' of the landscape can only be constructed *a priori* in the 'imagination', before the explorer reaches the continent's shores.

What I am highlighting here is a shared intellectual sensibility, characterized by a process of discursive purification, in which mobile and visible practices of exploration, involvements with landscape, are rendered legible through reference to pre-established structures of meaning. Thus, although both Spufford and Pyne are critical of a colonial tendency to imagine Antarctica as a *tabula rasa*, in their own work the landscape still blankly awaits its textualization. What this shows, I would argue, is the need to be attentive to Lopez's second question: 'how does the land shape the imaginations of those who dwell in it?' In other words, it is crucial to index and interrogate the 'eventful', material and sensuous nature of practices of travel and exploration, and the complicit and contributory power of the landscapes through which these practices evolve. With this in mind, it is notable that an understanding of European exploration as a set of intangible encoded meanings has increasingly been inflected, by geographical work on travel, colonialism and imperialism. This is indexed, for example, in Barnett's (1998) call to move away from a 'projection model' of colonial discourse, toward an understanding of the hybridities and relationalities inherent within the contextual specificities of colonial encounters. Similarly, Duncan and Gregory (1999: 3) have stressed the need to acknowledge the 'physicality of representation', a manoeuvre which enables critical focus upon the *practical* forging of representational tropes, and the situated, often multiple and fragmentary nature of this production (see also Driver, 2001; Clayton 2000).

In this sense, I aim to present an account of Scott and Amundsen's exploring which addresses both of Lopez's questions. I attempt an account of these expeditions in which 'discourse' and 'practice' are written as inextricably intertwined and, in which, embodied practices and material landscapes are themselves constitutive of the cultural meanings of exploration. While such an account is not intended to activate or advocate a peculiarly 'geographic' perspective on postcolonial studies of travel and exploration, it is perhaps particularly attentive to the spatialities of exploratory being; in other words to the mutual and dynamic fashioning of selves and landscapes which *is* exploratory enactment. Such a perspective, moreover, has implications regarding the conceptualization of colonial discourse. The postcolonial geographical work referenced above is characterized by an emphasis on the significance of the material contexts, the places and times, in which colonial discourses operate, so arguing against an overly idealist and textual understanding of the manifestation and fuction of such discourse. In this chapter, I extend this argument and position 'context' not as a 'location' in which discourse is materialized, but as itself an active, generative force that is the condition of possibility for the intelligibility and visibility, of colonial discourses. This involves examining respectively the *mobilities* and *visibilities* produced by Scott, Amundsen, and their followers. It involves foregrounding the materiality of Antarctica, and the elemental aspects of the worlds in which the expeditions found themselves. Consequently, and with Lopez's question regarding the land's agency in shaping dwelling in mind, my account pays attention to the climates of sensation characteristic of the two expeditions; their techniques of voyaging and dwelling amidst snow and ice, and their development thereof of specific embodied practices. Therefore, this chapter does not in any sense disavow what are commonly described as the 'imaginative geographies' of exploration, the characteristic ways of being and seeing its enactment produces and reflects, but it rather seeks to understand and locate these cultural formations within their *milieux* of emergence.

MOBILITIES

Voyaging south

Both explorers were in receipt of a vessel; Amundsen the *Fram*, a quasi-national emblem of Norway's Polar prowess, and Scott the *Terra Nova*, a Dundee whaler built for harvesting at high latitudes. Both set sail from their homelands in the northern summer of 1910, and both followed roughly the same route southwards. These similarities indicate the equal belongingness of the British and Norwegian expeditions to a shared framework of early twentieth century exploratory conduct. But I want to suggest that similarities were here accompanied and inflected by differences, especially as regards the nature of the mobilities enacted by the two voyages.

To indicate this, Deleuze and Guatarri's (1988) account of smooth and striated spaces is a useful heuristic model. It is vital to note from the start that the two forms of spatiality 'in fact exist only in mixture'; that is, they are necessary to each other. Yet within this mixing, smooth space and striated space develop distinctive characteristics and distinctive styles of mobility. Within the smooth, mobility is primary, 'the dwelling is subordinate to the journey' (Deleuze and Guattari, 1988: 474, 478). And this mobility is of a 'hidden' or 'guerrilla' type able, by traversing without occupying, by scaling directions above goals, to emerge at any given point. In contrast, striation is goal-oriented, subordinating trajectories to destinations. Reliant upon pivots of habitation for progress, its mobility is dimensional, moving from point to point within a systematized grid of the known and charted.

On 7 June 1910, Amundsen and his crew boarded the *Fram* and sailed 'quietly and unobserved' (Amundsen, 1913: 107) out into the open sea. It was already a voyage labouring under a secret. All save Amundsen and the first mate believed they would loop around Cape Horn and up the west coast of America to the Bering Sea, where they would enter the frozen Arctic Ocean. Their goal, clearly, was the North Pole. But this had been claimed by two American explorers, Robert Peary and Frederick Cook, just the previous year and, with the headlines proclaiming these feats and their disputations before him, Amundsen had decided to *switch Poles* and aim south. It was not until 9 September, lying anchored beyond the reach of officialdom at Madeira in the mid-Atlantic, that Amundsen revealed his intentions to the members of the crew. Remarkably, despite the duplicity they had been subject to, they all agreed to continue south with him aboard the *Fram*. They all agreed to become party to the secret.

More than a straightforward change of direction, I would argue that this pact changed the nature of the Norwegian expedition. It altered the nature of its mobility and it changed the sea itself. From this point onward their voyage would be 'hidden', and propelled by an internal dynamic. The decision to journey south instantiated, in a sense, a smooth space of mobility. Beyond the striations of latitude and longitude, the open surfaces of the sea enabled, guarded and channelled this deterritorialization. In tandem with the element within which they moved, the Norwegians forged a nomadic form of mobility, one transcending means and ends, which would carry them to the shores of Antarctica, and which would then inform the style of their motions across the continent's surface.

In partial contrast, the southward progress of the British Polar expedition under Scott proclaimed a different register of mobility. The *Terra Nova* was launched from British shores by cheering crowds and ringing editorials. It sailed south in staggered stages, touching land several times on the way; at Madeira again, and then Cape Town, Melbourne, and finally Lyttleton on New Zealand's south island. The British expedition thus moved easily and always within the circuits of empire; as Spufford notes:

> Nowhere along the route did the expedition touch any port where English was not the master tongue, where the coins were not the same size and shape and denominated in sterling, where the officers were not fed mutton and sherry at dinners given by local notables and the men could not go to the pub. (1996: 250–1)

The *Terra Nova*'s journey so relied upon *and* performed anew the stitched and settled lattices of imperial space. The distinction to be made here, however, is not one between regimentation and relaxation, or between the official and the outlaw. Scott's party were often to be found in dinner jackets, or standing in ordered lines for inspection, while Amundsen's shunned ports of call and public duties, yet it can be argued that the latter was more 'military' and formal in its tone and routine. From within the mobile, smooth spatiality forged by their pact, the Norwegians produced extremes of organizational efficiency. Amundsen's (1913) brief account of this voyage south is a log of focused activities: carpentry, tinsmithery, ironmongery, and above all the training and sharpening of the dog transport ('if I had one watchword at this time, it was "dogs first and dogs second"', 1913: 108). By contrast, the grid of the familiar through which Scott's expedition moved served as a cocoon in which his party could become forgetful of the impending necessities of Antarctic inhabitation. A phalanx of sub-committees circled indecisively around the essential issue of traction (see Cherry-Garrard, 1939). On the Admiralty's grooved southward route, the *Terra Nova* became a space of informality and even exuberance, as the diary of Edward Wilson, Scott's Chief Scientist and closest friend attests:

> We had a general rag, which means turning an individual's clothes inside out for some imaginary offence. This is known as 'furling topgallant sails' ... the struggle lasted an hour or two, and half of us were nearly naked towards the finish. (1972: 35)

Even before reaching Antarctica, therefore, the British and Norwegian expeditions were caught in a web of contrasts, even contradictions, in terms of the practices which sustained and characterized their trajectories: one 'imperial', yet innocent and maybe complacent; the other nomadic, fugitive, perhaps a little ruthless.

Voyaging in Antarctica

Friction. An odd phrase recurs several times in Amundsen's account of his voyage to the Pole: 'the going was as sticky as fish glue'. What Scott and Amundsen encountered in Antarctica was a terrain composed of frictional differentials, icy surfaces whose firmness, texture and grain varied from day to day, from minute to minute. The entirety of their ambitions resolved down into the style and manner of their contact with these ice formations.

At their coastal bases the ice was capricious, liable to melt and occasionally 'calve' into the sea. Amundsen, perhaps, was fortunate in this regard: perched precariously near the edge where the ice-shelf fronted onto the sea, his hut and transport survived both winter gales and spring thaw intact. Scott, in contrast, suffered a series of bruising encounters with the shifting mosaic of ice and water around his base on Ross Island, 250 miles west. A motorized sledge sank heavily into the sea through ice that was thought firm, and was lost. Returning from their autumn depot journey, several members of the British expedition, along with their pony transport, woke one morning to find themselves adrift on the sea: overnight the landscape had fragmented beneath them. The men were saved; the ponies, helpless in the freezing water, had to be hacked to death with ice-picks.

Further inland, the two expeditions discovered only more ice. But rather than being a blank mirror reflecting back to them their own images and desires (Pyne, 1988), I suggest that these ices were the ontological medium in which the explorers lived and travelled. Ice was the *subject-matter* of Scott and Amundsen's expeditions. More than of each other, more than of their companions, it is *ice* with which their diaries speak, interrogate, and quarrel. As the Arctic explorer Robert Peary (1917: 16) wrote, 'Sledge travelling is the twin of ice navigation, the two together forming polar exploration.' To a greater extent than anywhere else, it was with regard to practices of sledge travelling and ice navigation that the voyages of Scott and Amundsen differed.

Afterwards, reflecting on his journey to the Pole, Amundsen (1913: 186) wrote that 'It is no exaggeration to say that everything went like a well-oiled machine.' Perhaps this *machinic* image captures some of the key elements of the Norwegian traversal of the Antarctic. Their sea voyage south was characterized by a military, regimented air, such that 'on the wall of *Fram*'s charthouse a map of the Antarctic [was hung], with the route to the Pole inked in, and a summary of the expedition's plans . . . every man had a precisely defined role to play' (Huntford, 1985: 287). In a cold memoir, Amundsen (1927: 240) states that 'exploration is a highly technical and serious profession', and this emphasis upon technique, already evident at sea, intensified after the Norwegians had established their Antarctic base and begun to prepare for their southward path. A hallmark of this expedition was an almost obsessive perfectionism regarding the equipment to be taken on the southern journey. Amundsen's published voice, often banal, only really seems to come alive when discussing the *minutiae* of exploration, the incremental day-to-day shaving-off of superfluity, the almost-imperceptible gathering of focus. As an illustration of this attentiveness, Amundsen (1927: 258) would later choose 'the making of such a small item as tent pegs. Johannsen produced some that were the opposite of what such pegs usually are, being flat instead of high. This design was both lighter and stronger than the usual kind.' The accumulation of detail has an almost remorseless quality: 'we had two hundred and fifty reindeer skins prepared by the Eskimos . . . I had watched their preparation myself we had forty ski poles, with ebonite points. The ski-bindings were a combination of the Huitfeldt and Hoyer-Ellefsen bindings' (Amundsen, 1913: 79).

In this way, the Norwegian expedition's advance towards the South Pole took on something of the character of an efficient military operation, drilled, planned, precise. Their movements over the surface had a tight and graceful economy, purged of waste and excess. 'From our winter quarters at Framheim', Amundsen wrote, 'we marched *due south* the whole time' (1913: xii). It was as if a bargain had been struck with the earth's abstract geometry. Supply depots for the return journey from the Pole were laid not at points of convenience, but at every degree of latitude south, dovetailing their progress poleward with the stranglehold of the compass. Men, skis, dogs and sledges found their essences through translation into abstractions: kilometres per hour, sleeping hours, calorific units. To ensure maximum efficiency, Amundsen wrote:

> I made the most careful estimate of the average weight of edible flesh of a dog and its food value when eaten by the others. By these calculations I was able to lay out a schedule of dates upon which dog after dog would be converted from motive power into food. (1927: 260)

However, it is perhaps too easy to become seduced by an easy image of Norwegian technical prowess overcoming environmental obstacles (as, for example, Wheeler, 1996 and Spufford, 1996, are). Amundsen's diaries have a calculating, almost at times robotic quality, but to see this tendency as defining the nature of Norwegian mobility is maybe to mistake effect for cause. In other words, undergirding and enabling this severely logical mode of travelling, there lay a sometimes unspoken repertoire of skill and familiarity. The Norwegian traversal of Antarctica exemplified the power of striation – they gridded the earth – but the condition of this ordering power was its entanglement with, and emergence from, a smooth, nomadic occupancy of landscape. In the most straightforward terms, this reflects the fact that Amundsen, and the majority of his companions, were experienced Arctic travellers. In his technique Amundsen was guided above all by the example of the Inuit, with whom he had dwelt for several years (Amundsen, 1908). Now, at the opposite end of the earth, his journeying was enabled by an appropriation of their equipment and style, their reindeer-fur clothing, their dog-driving, their habitual knowledge of icy surfaces. To these the Norwegians added their own element, skis, forging a mobile synthesis capable of traction in all save the most severe conditions. What is crucial here, I would argue, is that the art of Polar *voyaging* was intertwined with the art of Polar *dwelling*. Such dwelling was nomadic: for occupation and 'command' of the landscape it required continual movement, a 'smooth' sensibility anterior to any division of points and lines, settlements and the paths between them. In essence, Amundsen's Antarctic sojourn could be viewed as an illustration of the argument that to travel well in a hostile environment, one has to be *at home* within it, even when the surface is 'as sticky as fish glue'.

Scott's expedition, by contrast, performed a quite different Antarctic mobility. To Huntford's (1985: 289) vitriolic eye, the difference is obvious and telling: 'Scott . . . was marshalling his forces for a ponderous campaign . . . Amundsen was sailing on a raid.' The argument here is that while Amundsen had 'come to terms' with the polar landscape, Scott, even after his previous Antarctic experience on the *Discovery* expedition (Scott, 1905), had failed to grasp the complexity of its challenge, had failed in the final analysis to grasp its *seriousness*. Yet equally, it could be argued that the opposite was true, and that at the root of all the British expedition's difficulties there lay an all-too-clear awareness of the complex and serious nature of Polar travel. Thus, whereas the Norwegian's response to differential surfaces was the streamlined simplicity of a small, coherent team of men and dogs, Scott chose to answer complexity *with* complexity. As Spufford (1996: 327) notes, 'Scott's plan co-ordinate[d] men, dogs, horses and motor-sledges into a pyramid of effort from whose apex will pop a little team of men aimed at 90° south.'

Thus the British expedition carried onto the shores of Antarctica an idea of laying siege to the Pole, and of a style of voyaging that would not adapt to the ice but rather master its caprices through sustained endeavour. If one mode of transport failed, another would take its place, until eventually the Pole would be breached by the trusted steady rhythm of human strides. This was a process that demanded ingenious running, to assemble the quite different speeds and staminas of men, ponies, dogs and motors into a coherent system. In a rare reference, Scott (1913: 337) compares his plan with Amundsen's, noting, revealingly, that 'any attempt to race must have wrecked my plan', almost as if it were the plan rather than its object which mattered. Later, watching his cavalcade trudge through the numbing ice, he wrote that 'it reminded me of a regatta, or a somewhat disorganised fleet' (Scott, 1913: 350). Before long, the motors, an idea too far in advance of the technology, ground to a final halt. The ponies, wallowing to their hocks in the ice, had to be shot. After an immense expenditure of energy had dissipated into the surface, Scott was left with his own legs and lungs.

In this there is a hint of what I would argue was perhaps the most significant difference between the mobilities enacted by the two expeditions. In contrast to Amundsen's emphasis upon *economy*, Scott's was a mobility based upon *effort*. If the Antarctic was, to British eyes, a hostile and sluggish terrain, then to overcome it all the effort one could muster was required. This was a style and manner of voyaging distinctly at odds with that of the Norwegian expedition, a difference in sensibility which both arose from and found expression within bodily activities and attitudes. The British expedition's style of mobility was dogged and obdurate, they *sweated*, as Scott would repeatedly note ('sweating heavily . . . we were forced to pull very hard' (1913: 446)), whereas, *pace* the Inuit, Amundsen's party were constantly conscious of the need to economize the heat and moisture of their bodies. In *The Birthday Boys*, the novelist Beryl Bainbridge (1996) presents a Scott who prizes strenuousness above all other qualities, and the *strain* of their endeavour is a recurrent theme of his party's voyage southward. And yet this effort was entirely within the compass of their expectations. In fact it was preordained, for Scott's mobility was based upon the need to *overcome* the caprices of the surface, while Amundsen's sought to *abide* within it.

Friction. They may seem featureless, smooth white plains, but the ice sheets of the Great Ice Barrier and Polar Plateau through which both Scott and Amundsen voyaged are characterized by difference rather than uniformity, by change rather than persistence. The surface is corrugated by frozen waves, *sastrugi*, indicating the direction of prevailing winds. But in the shifting light these are often invisible, as one of Scott's companions attests: 'when the sun was obscured the whole surface became dead, shadowless white, so that it was difficult to tell whether the next step would be on higher or lower ground' (Ponting, 1921: 95). For the Norwegians gliding on skis this was occasionally inconvenient, but for the British, often on foot, the everyday act of walking took on a spectral, uncanny quality. One day, the surface 'crust' might sustain heavy boots (even pony hooves), the next, Scott's men might flounder thickly as if through a shallow, viscous sea, wading through 'drift snow like finest flour' (Scott, 1913: 120).

Thus, while Scott's story is remembered as the voyage of a spirit exemplifying a national genius, this was not, *pace* Spufford, simply a matter of the 'inherited' meanings brought to the ice. The vagaries of the surface and his chosen manner of confronting them with feet, legs and lungs are the very stuff of Scott's celebrated final marches: 'Surface snow like desert sand' – 'the surface awful beyond words' – 'an impossible friction on the sledge-runners – pulling for our lives we could scarcely advance' – 'God help us, we can't keep up this pulling, that is certain. Amongst ourselves we are unendingly cheerful, but what each man feels in his heart I can only guess'(Scott, 1913: 564–84).

By contrast, the Norwegian expedition had evolved a mobility in tandem with the ice: a mobile synthesis of cross-country skiing techniques and Inuit indigenous knowledges, which carried them over 700 miles of *terra incognita* to the Pole (Riffenbaugh, 1993). In this sense, they won the battle of mobility between the two expeditions: they reached the Pole a month ahead of Scott, and returned safely. But perhaps Amundsen was even then conscious of the absurdity of this specifically European valuation of the earth's extremities. Having seen that the South Pole was a nothingness unadorned by any flags, he remarked:

> I have never known any man to be placed in such a diametrically opposite position to the goal of his desires. The regions around the North Pole – the North Pole itself – had attracted me from childhood, and here I was at the South Pole. Can anything more absurd be imagined? (Amundsen, 1913: 121)

VISIBILITIES

Both Pyne (1988) and Spufford (1996) present a view of Antarctica as a terrain wholly hostile and resistant to the embrace of European visions, a harsh mirror, reflecting such visions remorselessly back to befuddled explorers or a glinting labyrinth in which European notions of landscape, nature and aesthetic beauty were ruptured and dissolved, often along with the bodies of the explorers themselves. But I want to suggest here that Scott and Amundsen's expeditions *produced* distinctive visions of Antarctica – or that they differentially made Antarctica *visible*. Moreover, this was not the imposition of a raft of alien meanings upon the landscape. Instead it was a *necessity*; a necessary accompaniment to and aspect of styles of polar being. As Ingold (1993: 169) argues, 'It is within the context of . . . attentive involvement in the landscape that the human imagination gets to work in fashioning ideas about it.'

The Norwegian

Returning from one of his regular promenades around the capes and bays surrounding his base on Ross Island, Scott drew a contrast between his local landscape and that which he (correctly) imagined daily confronted the Norwegians:

> A dreary white plain of the Barrier behind and an uninviting stretch of sea-ice in front. With no landmarks, nothing to guide if the light fails, it is probable that they venture but a very short distance from their hut . . . The prospects of such a situation do not smile on us. (1913: 385)

Scott's diaries, pruned of controversial passages for publication, nonetheless contain examples of lucid perception, and this, perhaps, is one of them. Perched upon the exposed edge of the ice-shelf, through the long winter darkness, the Norwegians were ensconced in the hut, their energies turned inward to the perfection of their sledging equipment. Throughout his minutely detailed analysis of this episode, Huntford's (1985) constant theme is that the Norwegians engaged Antarctica through a repertoire of rugged skills familiar from immersion in the harsh coastal and upland environments of their homeland. He writes that the atmosphere at the Norwegian base was somewhere 'between that of a mountain hut and a sealing ship' (Huntford, 1985: 397), echoing an indigenous existence tightly squeezed between sea and mountain. And there is a deal of factual truth in such a characterization: the Norwegians triangulated Antarctica through comparison with skiing conditions in both inland Norway and the

Arctic archipelagos. On first arrival, their diaries register surprise at the familiarity of weather and ice conditions. Until, on their Polar journey, they encountered the Transantarctic Mountains, direct comparison with Norway was impossible, but proof that such a comparison could be made came, oddly, from within Scott's party. Tryggve Gran, one of its members, was a Norwegian employed as a ski instructor. On a lengthy depot journey his diary, in comparison with those of his companions, struck a discordant note. 'The landscape looks a bit like Norway', he first wrote, a little hesitantly, then, growing in confidence as the trip progressed; 'the landscape here is just like Norway' (Gran, 1984: 143–4).

Yet that Antarctica *could* be homely to the Norwegians somehow seems to diminish them, even in the eyes of more recent writers like Thomson (1977: 254), who almost bemusedly notes that in Amundsen's hands, 'the Antarctic becomes a sunny prairie where men are always vigorous and assured'. It seems that the prosaic and the everyday strike a jarring note in such a story for both causal readers and academic critics, running against an assumption that the distant ice-fields will be exotically different. For Huntford (1985) this is a measure of Amundsen's individual genius. Equally, I would argue, it is possible to see such everydayness as congruent with a specifically Norwegian way of being amongst wild elements. Witoszek (1997: 210) notes that Norway was 'a symbolic-iconic *fons et origo* of Romantic ideas of nature', but, she argues, this ran distinctly against a native utilitarian and realist perception of the natural world. In this argument, nineteenth-century Norway was a bastion of rationalist values, actively resisting 'the dark energies of German romantics' (Witoszek, 1997: 219). Both the socio-economic elite (to which Amundsen belonged) and the broader peasant society of farmers and fisher-people (from which he chose most of his companions) thus encountered and appropriated nature with a degree of rational pragmatism. In part, of course, this cultural tendency may be attributed to the harshly rural background of the national psyche but, as Witoszek suggests, a distinctly classical, almost mechanistic understanding of nature's workings informed the beliefs and conduct of nineteenth-century Norwegians.

This is an especial feature of Amundsen's Antarctic diary, wherein the landscape's hazards are presented as cogs and springs within a methodical natural order, and where the necessary, indeed imperative response is prosaic, even subdued. At the Pole, after a celebratory toast, he wrote that 'one gets out of the way of protracted ceremonies in those regions . . . everyday life began again at once' (Amundsen, 1913: 122). In this sense, just as much as Scott, Amundsen *nationalized* Antarctica and so brought it within the compass of his fellow Norwegians' understanding. If there was still a need to sometimes adopt a lyrical tone, this was done via the totemic Nordic myth of Askeladden, the humble mountain dweller whom fortune rewards with the hand of the princess: 'It seems as if the princess is still sleeping in her shining castle. Will we be able to awaken her?' If the Polar journey was to be made intelligible, *visible,* to this audience, it could be analogized to a ski-tour in the Norwegian mountains: 'the going was as good as it possibly could be' (ibid.: 57, 31). It might even be argued that such a characterization of Antarctica was the only one open to Amundsen, the only plausible vision he could distil from the rhythmic, habitual, inward-looking routine of Norwegian Polar being.

The British
A central figure in the British expedition was Scott's Chief Scientist, and closest friend, Dr Edward Wilson. His diary for 20 August 1911 reads as follows: 'Tenth Sunday after Trinity. Blowing still. Church. Spent the day reading the *confessio medici* again' (Wilson, 1972: 163). That these lines *could* be written in the middle of the winter Polar darkness highlights, I would argue, some of the key practices and imaginaries through which Scott's expedition made Antarctica visible. More than a scientific organizer, Wilson was the expedition's spiritual leader, and the majority of the party's core of scientists and naval officers (most of whom were fresh from university) took their cue regarding Antarctica from his idiosyncratic blend of religiosity and empiricism.

Spufford (1996) selects the sublime as the lens through which the British viewed Antarctica, and evidence of this is almost all too easily found. On first sighting the landscape, pleasurable dread assails Scott's second-in-command, Teddy Evans: 'how sinister and relentless the western mountains looked, how cold and unforgiving the foothills, and how ashy grey the sullen icefoots that girt this sad, frozen land' (Evans, 1933: 88). But perhaps such an aesthetic was the standardized shell rather than the kernel of this particular brand of Polar being. In actuality, like the Norwegians, the British expedition dwelt in an Antarctic that was *ordered* rather than chaotic. The difference, however, was that while Amundsen lived in a landscape composed of curiously blended rational and animistic forces, Scott's party lived through a distinctly Christian sense of providence and destiny. The landscape was *fateful.* One of the party wrote of 'feeling . . . in the hands of a Providence or Power. An intelligent man cannot really be satisfied by saying it is a matter of chance' (Debenham, 1982: 140). A distinct echo of this occurs in Wilson's (1972: 109) analysis of the disastrous depot-laying journey, which to him revealed 'a beautifully arranged plan in which each one of us took exactly the moves . . . that an Almighty had intended us to take'. The British expedition not only *discovered* order in the landscape, their daily lives and purposes were guided and shaped by it.

Hints of this subsist deep within Cherry-Garrard's (1939: i) celebrated description of himself and his companions as 'artistic Christians'. This, perhaps, is not just a description of what *explorers* should be. Nor does it signal a criminally anachronistic view of Scott's party as bearers of a chivalric, knightly tradition (as Pyne, 1988, argues). In this specific context 'artistic Christians', I would argue, are what *scientists* should be. For Wilson and his followers, science was an 'art' in that it was a marriage of the human and the natural that revealed a divine order – it was thus an art impelled by theological fervour. Engaged in physiography, geology, and glaciology, Scott's scientists observed the landscape as they observed Sunday Service, and they made Antarctica visible as the ideal terrain for a strenuous anglican empiricism.

Above all, then, the British Polar way of being practised and produced Antarctica as a species of the 'great outdoors'. Perhaps the most significant point about Scott's remarks concerning the situation of the Norwegian base is that he made them after returning from a *walk.* In contrast to the 'dreary stretch' of ice facing Amundsen, the British base on Ross Island opened onto a landscape of contrasts and possibilities: capes, bays, islands, distant mountains. It was a space for walking. Again in contrast to the Norwegian instinct to hibernate and conserve strength, Scott's party was in constant motion through the landscape around their base. These perambulations might be viewed simply as the practices of picturesque travel carried onto the ice. In a deeper sense, however, they were, on this British expedition, means of making oneself Antarctic, and of making Antarctica one's own. In his diary, Wilson (1972: 77) rebuked 'one or two who will stick indoors too much – which is a very great mistake', indicating that outdoor walking was not just a pleasure but a *duty*. Walking was not simply the physical expression of a system of beliefs about nature; it was a practice through which Antarctica became visible as a space of activities which were aesthetically and spiritually healthy. Getting out and about was, for Scott's party, the quintessential means of realizing Antarctica as an intelligible landscape – a landscape of vigour and strain that nurtured the development of artistic Christians. Of course, this sometimes led to mishaps, chronicled with mounting exasperation by Scott as his men variously wandered off in blizzards, went on ill-advised bicycling excursions, and fell off icebergs. But at no stage were such activities curtailed. Indeed, Scott (1913: 207) regarded it as most significant that there is 'no-one who has the least prospect of idleness'. This improving walking and strolling claimed the landscape around their base as theirs; even on arrival Scott noted that its 'vast tracts of rocks for walks' might engender 'a homely feeling' (ibid.: 65, 67).

Even in the end, dying in his tent, it is this Antarctica to which Scott appeals and finds comfort. His 'Message to the Public' is an historic (and histrionic) text which, quite self-consciously, seeks to integrate the expedition within the circuits of heroic national endeavour and a calculated discourse of 'gentlemanly conduct'. But in his letter to his wife he offers a more precise verdict on his expedition: 'how much better it has been than lounging . . . at home'. Even now, it is the getting out in the open, into a nature which forces close study, which seems to matter. Of his baby son, he writes, 'make the boy interested in natural history, if you can; it is better than games . . . Make him a strenuous man' (ibid.: 475).

It is in this sense, I would argue that, despite losing the race to the South Pole, the British expedition won a victory, of sorts. Scott's ultimately straightforward appeals to nation, family, fellowship emerge almost miraculously in the final reel of a complex narrative. They were able to do so not only because a series of discursive structures were there for them to slot into, but also because of the intensity, even the idiosyncrasy, with which the British expedition forged and performed a specific Antarctic sensibility – a particular context of practices through which the continent was made visible. While clearly the Norwegian party was superior in their ability to dwell within and voyage through Antarctica, the British more distinctively *made*, rather than adapted to, the landscape. The same emphasis on effort and strain which resulted in the adoption of a series of misconceived traction systems, nevertheless worked to produce a way for men to be in the landscape that possessed style and conviction. When the bodies of Scott and his companions were discovered by surviving members of the expedition, a cairn surmounted by a cross was constructed over their tent. Another cross was erected on a hilltop near their base. They covered the landscape with crosses, and in doing so revealed the ice as a landscape that moulded, and could be moulded by, a specifically 'physical' artistic and religious sensibility.

CONCLUSION

Scott and Amundsen differed in their enactment of exploration, and these differences profoundly affected the nature of the 'discovery' each made. Amundsen, winning a battle of mobilities, discovered that the South Pole, a dimensionless point in a truly untrodden space, was 'a thing of paradox' (Huntford, 1985: 488), existing only as a fulcrum around which the incessant movement he had devised could pivot. The British expedition discovered Scott's body and, more importantly, his ability to translate the complexities of their Antarctic sojourn into a tale of fellowship, patriotism, and a classically 'understated' British gentlemanness. They discovered that they had made Antarctica visible; that is, they had produced an eventful context of practices and beliefs that appealed and persisted.

From Scott's final letters and diary entries it is perhaps too easy to conclude that Antarctica was 'a principal discursive space in which intrepid British Naval officers could parade the flag . . . the literal emptiness of the place served a British imperial fantasy that celebrated empire' (Bloom, 1993: 3). A retrospective interpretation such as this, like its flip side (the 'imperial' and 'national' discourses which turned Scott into an archetypal British hero), is in fact the result of an *uncritical* acceptance of the meanings which Scott, in death, sought to impose upon the narrative of his voyage. And it is equally unsatisfactory to view Amundsen's voyage as an instance of technical virtuosity, stripped bare of what might be termed the 'conventional' assimilatory urges of European exploration.

I have sought to present what is hopefully a more complex account of the practices and imaginaries that characterized the British and Norwegian expedition's modes of voyaging and dwelling in Antarctica. Of course, such an account is neither definitive nor holistic. Its production has necessarily involved neglecting some of the elements fused into the tale of Scott and Amundsen, for example, the role of geographical institutions such as the Royal Geographical Society in early Antarctic exploration, or, more broadly, the issue of the complex masculinities produced within exploratory conduct. I have described Scott and Amundsen more exactly via a series of differences; differentials as regards styles of being mobile and practices of visibility. Norwegian Polar being involved an ability to be mobile and 'hidden' within the drift and flux of sea and ice; in tandem with the repertoire of familiar polar skills this mobility drew upon, Amundsen found Antarctica to be visible as a known, ordered, almost homely landscape. The British expedition, by contrast, viewed Antarctica as a hostile and sluggish terrain, approachable only through obdurate effort and strain. This rendered the landscape visible on the one hand as providential and fateful but for the same reasons it became also a potentially physically and spiritually healthy space.

In this sense, both Scott and Amundsen made the Antarctic landscape intelligible by gathering it within a known frame of reference. But the aim here has been to show that this discursive movement evolved in tandem with, and was thus predicated upon, a raft of complex, contextually specific embodied practices. Both the British and Norwegian expeditions may thus be understood precisely in terms of ways of being in and of Antarctica, because the meanings and actions of each party were forged and enacted through intense bodily encounters with the landscape itself. In focusing upon these practised contexts, this chapter has sought to contest a commonly voiced understanding of Antarctic exploration as a solipsistic activity, by definition detached from the landscape of its occurrence. In the end, of course, it was the polar landscape itself that assimilated Scott and Amundsen; Scott entombed in the ice, and Amundsen, in the bitter twilight of his life seeming to almost actively seek an icy dissolution, disappearing on a flight across the Arctic.

11

'WHERE ARE YOU FROM?' YOUNG BRITISH MUSLIM WOMEN AND THE MAKING OF 'HOME'

Claire Dwyer

> They [migrants] are irrevocably *translated* ... They are the products of the new diasporas created by the post-colonial migrations. They must learn to inhabit at least two identities, to speak two cultural languages, to translate and negotiate between them. (Hall, 1992a: 310)

This chapter explores the ways in which a group of young British South Asian Muslim women – women who occupy the postcolonial spaces evoked in Hall's description – negotiate their own identities in their everyday lives. My focus is particularly on questions of belonging through a discussion of the meaning and evocation of 'home'. Such questions are at the heart of Hall's (1992a) description of 'cultures of translation' and I begin by unravelling some of the postcolonial geographies implicit in his discussion. The young women whose reflections I examine here occupy a particular place within a postcolonial, multicultural Britain as the British-born daughters of parents who migrated from the postimperial spaces of the Indian subcontinent. They are the 'products' of a particular set of postcolonial migrations set in motion by the operation of social, political and economic interlinkages between the metropolitan core and the (post)colonies. These young women might be described as members of 'new diasporas' (Gilroy, 1993a) whose identity formations are not fixed within one national space but are characterized by 'complicated crossovers and cultural mixes' (Hall, 1992a: 310). Such cross-overs are sustained through a wide variety of familial, imaginative, material and mediated transnational linkages and connections, which stretch across 'diaspora space' (Brah, 1996) linking different (and differently) postcolonial places. These webs of connection are sustained by processes of globalization and cultural exchange (Appadurai, 1990; Featherstone, 1990; Hannerz, 1996) through which economic, political and cultural worlds are increasingly compressed in space–time. Through these processes of connection and cross-over across different postcolonial or diaspora spaces, new ways of thinking about identity and belonging are opened up which challenge the conception of home as fixed or singular. Hall suggests that it is through these 'cultures of translation' or 'cultures of hybridity', produced by such transnational and transcultural linkages, that a postcolonial critique can be developed. He argues that the 'postcolonial' can be read as a 'double inscription', which re-reads

> colonialisation as part of an essentially transnational and transcultural 'global' process [that] produces a decentred, diasporic or global re-writing of earlier nation-centred imperial grand narratives. Its theoretical value lies precisely in its refusal of this 'here' and 'there', 'then' and 'now', 'home' and 'abroad' perspective. (Hall, 1996a: 247)

In this chapter I argue that it is possible to see, through the negotiation of 'new ethnicities' or 'hybrid identities' articulated by these young women, how new forms of national belonging within a postcolonial Britain might be imagined. I will stress that the contestation of 'either/or' models of belonging and the different evocations of 'home' through which these young women narrate their identities is not an individual response to some kind of problematic 'culture clash' but a challenge to reconfigure fixed notions of national or cultural identity.

Much of the inspiration for the theorization of 'new' cultural identities of hybridity and translation has come from literary or cultural representations in novels, films or music. An archetypal example is perhaps the novelist Salman Rushdie who describes himself as a 'translated man' and his novel *The Satanic Verses* 'as a love-song to our mongrel selves' (Rushdie, 1991: 394). In contrast, Les Back (1995) celebrates the 'intermezzo' spaces created by the hybrid musical forms produced by Apache Indian, who traces influences via his Birmingham upbringing, Indian Punjabi heritage and black British friends (see also Sharma et al., 1996). While these cultural interventions provide an important impetus for conceptualizing 'new ethnicities', this chapter explores how such negotiations and translations are made by young people growing up within a specific – and rather unremarkable – suburban locality. It looks at some of the *everyday dilemmas* that individuals face within the social spaces of their lives as young British South Asian women. I argue that identification is best understood as a *practice* of making home, emphasizing the political and contingent ways in which identities are made.

QUESTIONS OF IDENTITY

Identity has been a dominant theme in studies of young British Asian women. In her research on the identities of young South-Asians in Southall in the 1970s, Avtar Brah (1979) was unusual in her decision to focus also on the white contemporaries of her informants emphasizing the ways in which the daily experiences and attitudes of both groups intersected. Instead most accounts are dominated by a conflictual model that defines young British Asians as 'caught between two cultures' (Watson, 1977), inevitably experiencing 'identity crisis' as they choose between two sets of cultural values, between 'South Asian' and 'British' ways of life. As Knott and Khokher (1993) argue, dichotomies such as traditional/Western, religious/secular, parents/peers are often mapped onto a simple binary of 'home' and 'school' (Dwyer, 1999b). The discourse of cultural conflict often seems to rely upon an assimilation model that posits ethnic identity as an inherited trait to be shed or diluted over time and relies upon bi-polar models of identification (Anwar, 1998; Jacobson, 1997). The language of 'cultural conflict' can also slide too easily into culturalist interpretations that find explanations in religious fundamentalism or patriarchal cultures rather than more complex theorizations of the ways in which cultural, social and economic formations are interlinked. As Brah (1993) argues, young South Asian Muslim women become defined as victims of oppressive cultures rather than as individuals with multiple subject positions (see also Ali, 1992). By theorizing identity through languages of 'cultural clash', ethnicity and identity are understood in terms that remain essentialist and static.

More nuanced and carefully situated accounts of the lives of young people in multicultural Britain develop a more complex model of identification. Rather than seeing identities as being a case of simply opposing choices, analytical attention is given to when particular identifications are prioritized in different contexts or how identities are forged within particular places and moments. Eade (1997) illustrates how young British Bengalis in London see themselves as Londoners, British, Bengali, Asian and Muslim – but may choose to prioritize a particular identity at a specific juncture. Eade recognizes the ways in which a reassertion or 're-imagining' (Samad, 1993) of 'new' British Muslim identities has re-worked discourses of belonging for his respondents. These new kinds of identifications draw particularly on transnational imaginaries and networks and are reinvigorated within particular spatial and temporal contexts.[1] As the ethnographies of Alexander (2000), Back (1996) and Gillespie (1995) suggest, the identities of young people are not fixed but are negotiated in and through particular places and may draw upon and re-work a range of cultural influences. Such studies suggest a theorization of ethnicity that is both more complex and more fluid or contextual. Rather than understanding ethnicity as a fixed essence or inheritance it is understood as a positioning or a process, an argument developed in particular in the work of Stuart Hall and his characterization of 'new ethnicities'. Hall argues for an understanding of cultural identities as:

> points of identification, the unstable points of identification or suture, which are made within the discourses of history and culture. Not an essence but a *positioning*. Hence there is always a politics of identity, a politics of position. (Hall, 1990: 226)

I draw on Hall's conceptualization of identity as positioning to explore how the young women interviewed negotiate questions of identity. I begin by exploring how the young women define their identities as compound or 'hybrid' identities and emphasizing the contextual processes through which identities are forged. Through this discussion I highlight questions of politics that are foregrounded by Hall and described by the young women as central to their complex negotiations of identity. The second part of the discussion focuses on the meaning of 'home' exploring how concepts of 'home' are evoked by the young women in the negotiation of their identities.

For many cultural theorists writing about identity the question of 'home' is an important theme. One aspect of this writing has been a celebration of movement, migrancy, nomadism and a multiplicity of 'homes' (Clifford, 1992; Chambers, 1993). Writing about challenges to identity presented by processes of diaspora and globalization, Robins (1991: 41), drawing on Bhabha (1990), describes an oscillation between 'the comforts of tradition' and the 'responsibilities of cultural translation'. Tradition is defined as a return to purity, the recovery of certainty and fixity suggesting a sense of home as fixed, pure and bounded connected to an evocation of 'roots' or 'Heimat (home/land)'. In contrast, translation suggests the renunciation of any retrievable 'lost' cultural purity and evokes a notion of home as multiple and interlocking, belonging to many different 'routes' (Gilroy, 1993a). While cosmopolitan writers like Rushdie might celebrate the possibilities of being a 'translated man', I examine some of the tensions that arise when negotiating between the 'irreconcilable forces of Tradition and Translation' (Hall, 1992a: 311).

My analysis of how these tensions might be understood develops Hall's understanding of identity as positioning through an argument about the practice of *making home*. Here I draw in particular on feminist writings about home and identity. In contrast to the celebration of migrancy or nomadism advocated by Chambers (1993), feminist theorists have articulated a more ambivalent and more grounded theory of home. For example, feminist geographers and others have emphasized the significance of studying home-making, domestic spaces and the evocation of home in the analysis of the colonial and postcolonial geographies of empire (Blunt, 1999, Gowans, 2001). Particularly suggestive for geographers has been the exploration of embodied identities through place (Pratt, 1984) and the theorization of a 'politics of location' (Rich, 1986). Such spaces of identity and resistance are explored in bell hooks' (1990) meditation on the concept of home. Describing her search for a place from which to speak that will incorporate 'not just who I am in the present but where I am coming from', hooks (1990: 146) writes about 'home' as a site of resistance. For hooks, home becomes defined as 'no longer just one place ... it is locations' (1990: 148). Her discussion emphasizes both the socially grounded experience of (gendered and racialized) identity through home and the politics of making home as a political speaking position. Drawing on hooks' argument I suggest that the evocations of 'home' expressed by these young women must be interpreted within a framework that recognizes the tensions between 'tradition' and 'translation' and understands the politics of identity-making. I argue that evocations of 'home' can be interpreted as a practice of *home making* in the discursive process of identity as positioning.

THE RESEARCH CONTEXT

The empirical material upon which this chapter is based was conducted in the suburban town of Hertfield, located north of London, between 1993–4, and involved interviews and group discussions with 49 young women aged between 16 and 19 from two different schools (Dwyer, 1997). Of the 35 participants who identified as Muslim, all but four had parents who had been born in

Pakistan (mainly from the region of Mirpur in Azad Kashmir). Most of the respondents had been born in the UK and all except one had spent most of their lives in Hertfield. The respondents were chosen from two contrasting girls' schools (one selective with predominantly 'white' pupils where Muslim girls made up a small minority, the second a neighbourhood comprehensive where more than 50 per cent of pupils were Asian, mainly of Pakistani heritage) in order to gain a broad spectrum of respondents from different class and family backgrounds. The research included interviewees from all ethnic groups in both schools, as a means by which the contextual process of identity construction might be better understood. However, this chapter draws only on the responses from the Muslim respondents. The research sought to examine how identities were negotiated through the everyday lives of the respondents and considered the intersection of factors such as class, nationality, ethnicity, religious identification, gender, sexuality and locality in the narrative construction of identity (see Dwyer, 1999a, b, c, 2000). A particular interest within the research was to explore the significance of a re-asserted or re-imagined Islamic identity for the respondents (Modood, 1988; Samad, 1993), although this is not the specific focus of this chapter. The primary means by which ideas were explored was through a series of in-depth group discussions, but respondents also participated in individual interviews (see Dwyer, 1999c for further methodological discussion).

'BRITISH BUT NOT BRITISH' ARTICULATING HYBRID IDENTITIES

I begin by exploring how the young women talked about their identities in relation to concepts of national belonging and hybridity. Hybridity is a problematic metaphor. Its biological associations might suggest an outgrowth of two 'stocks' which were previously 'pure' or distinct (for critiques of hybridity see Young, 1994; Anthias, 2000). Instead what is suggested by this metaphor is a sense of fusion, of syncreticism (Shaw and Stewart, 1994), the creation of something new produced from the 'cut 'n' mix' (Hebdige, 1991) of differences. For all of the young women I spoke to this sense of a 'hybrid' identity was very real. When they spoke about national belongings, participants refused to position themselves according to dominant discourses of dichotomous alternatives and instead affirmed a simultaneous British Asian or British Pakistani identity:

Eram: I identify not as a British or an Asian but as a British Asian. I'm an Asian, I've got an Asian background but I've been brought up in British society.

Ghazala: I don't feel British, I feel British but Pakistani but not totally British.

What was important in this articulation was the extent to which individuals affirmed a fused or 'hybrid' identity. For Ghazala to be simply British – *totally British* – would not adequately describe her identity while Eram also asserts that she is not one or the other – British or Asian – but both simultaneously. This conjunction is emphasized in particular when individuals seek to compare themselves with their parents:

Eram: That's another thing where there is confusion ... when our parents misunderstand us. They don't understand. They want to see us as Asian boys and girls and they don't understand that we're British Asians, they miss that word British out.

A 'hybrid' British Asian identity is thus affirmed in opposition to the identities of their parents, which participants were more likely to define as 'pure Pakistani' or 'typical Pakistani'. It is also articulated against exclusionary and racialized constructions of British national belonging:

Eram: One thing I don't like, right, if you're British, and you know that you're British but people don't see you as British, they identify you as Asian. And it's like, I'm British, my ancestors are Asian but I'm British. I've been brought up in this country and all this, I was *born* in this country, so how British can you get? And so people go: 'Oh, she's an Asian.'

Anita: It's because of the colour you are.

Eram: Yeah, that's it, they just go by the colour, they don't know anything about you. They go: 'She's just a Paki'. You know, like that, full stop. At times like that I think you get really angry and you go: OK I'm an Asian, but I identify not as a British or an Asian but as a British Asian, I'm an Asian, I've got an Asian background, but I've been brought up in British society.

Through their articulation of 'hybrid' identities these young women challenged the ways in which racialized constructions of Britishness are exclusionary since, as Anita suggests, they conflate Britishness with constructions of 'whiteness'. In contrast to such representations, the participants themselves produced more complex understandings of how different forms of belonging were constructed. Thus Sonia, reflecting on her own identity, evaluates competing claims:

> I think it's quite difficult actually ... Because I'm a British citizen I was born here, so I wouldn't really say that I was Pakistani. If I came from Pakistan to live here then I would be Pakistani, a Pakistani citizen. And I wouldn't call myself an English person because I'm not, I'm a Muslim so I wouldn't really know.

Sonia's response illustrates the ways in which a British Asian (or British Muslim identity) challenges existing constructions of national belonging. First, she defines being British in terms of place of birth and in terms of citizenship. Thus she defines herself as British, challenging the boundaries of Britishness and asserting the legitimacy of her British identity. Second, she considers her allegiances to Pakistan, the place of her parents' birth, acknowledging the ways in which her British identity is a compound identity, inflected with a distinctive cultural heritage. Third, she suggests the importance of being Muslim for her identity and raises the differences between being 'English', with its associations with Christianity (and implicitly 'whiteness', see Dyer, 1997 and McGuinness, this volume) and being British. Sonia's unpacking of the different elements of her composite identity illustrates how dominant constructions of belonging are made. Thus in dominant discourses belonging as British becomes elided with Englishness and 'whiteness', which are themselves imagined as fixed and stable markers rather than recognized as constructed categories (Bonnett, 1996a).

For these young women, articulating a coherent 'hybrid' identity was both an assertion of their own identities as British and also a challenge to existing boundaries of Britishness. While individuals recognized the ways in which the 'imagined community' (Anderson, 1989) of British belonging was implicitly racialized they also resisted prescribed forms of belonging:

Ghazala: There is always a barrier between you being totally British. You can't ever be British if you're not. If you're Pakistani.
Nazreen: You can say you are, but you're not. [laughs]
Ghazala: You can say, but they wouldn't ... When it comes down to it, they won't accept us as British. [laughs].
Husbana: No, I don't think they do accept us, they'll see us as foreigners and that's it. You know what, I don't think they'll accept us. They'll see us as foreigners I think, even if we did adapt to their culture and everything I still think that they'd see us. They wouldn't accept us.

While the dominant narrative construction of Britain creates racialized boundaries of belonging (Gilroy, 1987), Husbana points out it also relies upon a cultural definition of Britishness – a form of 'cultural racism' (Blaut, 1992) – which suggests that to be British involves giving up her distinctive ethnic and cultural heritage. While Husbana rejects this because she argues it would not change her exclusion, it is also rejected by other respondents because it denies the possibility of 'hybrid identities'.

This discussion has explored the articulation of 'hybrid' identities that are expressed as coherent fusions, as British Asian or British Pakistani. For most of the respondents being British Muslim was synonymous with a British Asian or British Pakistani identity although in different contexts the differences between being 'British Muslim' and 'British Asian' were discussed, as one of the respondents, Ruhi, suggests below (also see Dwyer, 1999a, b). Such identities are coherent to the individuals themselves as it is impossible to affirm only one part of this coherent and syncretic identity. However, such 'an impossibly compound identity' (Gilroy, 1993b: 75) may be difficult to express within the discursive possibilities allowed by bounded conceptions of national belonging. Seeking to define their identity the young women often qualified their explanations or struggled for satisfactory terms:

Eram: You could say that we're half-castes. I mean, it may sound a bit stupid, but I think we're half-castes. We're British and Asian at the same time.

Through these struggles to find satisfactory terms and appropriate languages, both myself and the participants found ourselves using terms like 'past', 'background' and 'ancestors'. If a British Asian identity is coherent, its articulation is caught between ideas of Translation, which suggests many routes and multiple belongings, and an evocation of Tradition, of purity and rooted belonging. While young women, as Eram suggests, articulate a simultaneous British Asian identity, they are caught between demands to 'fix' their identities at particular moments – demands which require a 'fixing' of identity in relation to particular places or *homes*.

One example of this demand to 'fix' identity – to demonstrate a prescribed kind of belonging – is illustrated in the following extract in which Riffat reminds others of the Tebbit 'cricket test',[2] which was supposed to ascertain whether people were properly British:

> Riffat: I don't know, alright, let's talk about cricket, like one MP. If it's Australia and England, I'm like, yeah, but as soon as it's Pakistan and India, I cheer for Pakistan.
>
> Shamin: Yeah . . . I feel like I belong here, but I can't get patriotic about, you know, the Olympic Games [agreement], or the football or something. Because I still feel, it's not the same. Coming from, well, having parents coming from, somewhere else.

While these comments reveal the inadequacies of Norman Tebbit's understanding of Britishness, his request forces both Riffat and Shamin to question where they belong. Discourses of national belonging, which appeal to an essence, a fixing of identity in relation to a rooted evocation of Britain as 'home', contradict the syncretic and fused understanding of a British Asian identity. The undermining of this identity, which is reinforced through these discourses, may also increase a desire to fix and root identities through other essences or 'homes'. As Ien Ang has argued:

> It is this very problem which is constitutive of the idea of diaspora, and from which the idea of diaspora attempts to be a solution, where the adversity of 'where you're at' produces the cultivation of a lost 'where you're from'. (1994: 18)

Ang suggests that the experience of not belonging to one 'home' produces the cultivation of other lost 'homes' – a desire to 'fix' or 'root' one's identity in another place.

EVOCATIONS OF 'HOME': IMAGINING PAKISTAN

The lives of all of the young women I interviewed are structured through many different interlocking global–local connections. Their connections with the place of origin of their parents are both discursive and material. Most of the participants had made visits to Pakistan with their parents and their interconnections with Pakistan were sustained through the visits of relatives to Hertfield.

Biradari networks and reciprocal relationships are particularly important for Mirpuri Pakistanis (Shaw, 1988) and this ensured that the participants were involved in many social activities, such as weddings and religious ceremonies, through which extended family relationships are sustained, also reinvigorating links with Pakistan. At the same time the young women reproduced links to Pakistan particularly through cultural practices such as music, television and video (Gillespie, 1995) and fashion (Bhachu, 1993). These links are complex inter-relationships through which cultures are transformed and reworked, as shown by, for example, the emergence of bhangra music (Back, 1995) and the development of British Asian fashion (Bhachu, forthcoming). Thus the participants were involved in cultural practices and other material exchanges through which their links with Pakistan, their parents' birthplace, were sustained. At the same time these linkages were also reproduced discursively through both parental evocations of Pakistan as 'home' and the participants' own evocations of Pakistan.

During group discussions participants often used the language of 'home' or 'homeland' to talk about Pakistan:

Husbana: I feel that it is my homeland and I have to go there eventually.
Eram: I mean, I would like to live in my own home country but I would like to take everything with me.
Arooj: It is quite nice, I mean I do like it, I mean obviously it's my country.

Evident in these evocations of Pakistan as 'home' are the ways in which it is both matter-of-fact, almost unquestioned, but also ambivalent, as suggested by the hesitancy of the words 'I mean' and 'obviously'. Thus the evocation of Pakistan as 'home' is threaded through with contradictions and ambivalences.

One of the most important ways in which Pakistan was evoked as 'home' was as a source of cultural identity and heritage. This was particularly important for parents, many of whom sought to reinforce gendered expectations that their daughters should remain guardians of the family's cultural integrity through maintenance of cultural practices (see Dwyer, 2000). The young women recognized the ways in which, as future mothers, they were expected to reproduce the parental culture:

Sonia: My mum says when you're at home we speak in our own language. Because we're a family and we're Muslims we speak our own language but ... you know, we don't really bother we just speak in English. [laughs]
Thaira: Because if you speak too much English you might lose your mother tongue, you know.
Sonia: I speak English all the time ... She just gets really mad.
Alia: Actually that's what I'm afraid of because I don't really want to lose my ties ... What about our children and the children after? They'll totally forget, they'll totally forget that they're even Muslim. I mean if we're good mothers we'll obviously tell them. But still, if we're not good at it ourselves, how are we going to teach children?

Sonia: My mum always does that: 'You're going to have kids one day and what are they going to know about your religion ... They won't know nothing.' And maybe it's true and maybe they won't. But then it's up to me, then, isn't it?

This dialogue emphasizes the ways in which expected gender roles reinforce the young women's connections to Pakistan. They are encouraged to look to Pakistan as a source of their religious or cultural identity so that they will be able to impart this cultural knowledge to their children. While some participants resisted these expectations, as Sonia does here, most of them identified Pakistan as the source – or 'root' – of their cultural identity. As Alia continues:

> I am actually a British citizen because I was born here. But I'd actually call myself a Pakistani because that's where I actually come from and I think my roots are actually from there. And I think of that more as my country than I do here, and I want to go back there when I'm older ... It's because of our culture, it's from there, you know, your roots. It was so nice because you know when it's our prayer time ... You can hear it everywhere. It's just so nice, you know. Here you don't expect that. Like when I went there I just naturally became more religious than I used to be.

For Alia, being in Pakistan not only gives her a chance to speak her 'own language' – a fluency which Alia particularly values – but also makes her feel 'naturally' more religious. Thus while links to Pakistan emphasize cultural values, for most participants these were inherently bound up with religious identity. In most cases, and reinforced by parents, cultural competency, such as being able to read or write Urdu, was implicitly linked to maintaining a strong religious identity as a 'good Muslim'. This imagining of Pakistan as 'home' requires that it is a fixed and 'authentic' source of religious and cultural identity – suggesting a return to Tradition, or purity (Robins, 1991).

If dominant discourses about belonging to Britain emphasized exclusion, then another important way in which Pakistan was evoked was as an 'imagined community' within which participants were not defined as racialized outsiders but instead were 'the same':

Zakkya: I just like the atmosphere, you know, all understanding each other.

Husbana: I like the atmosphere, it's so nice ... you've got people there the same colour as you and everything the same as you, you feel more at home.

Recalling their visits to Pakistan, many of the young women explained that their parents were much less concerned about their welfare, and much more likely to let them go out by themselves, than was true in Hertfield:

Alia: I was really surprised, I couldn't believe it. Over here they wouldn't let me go out in that way but I suppose it's because we're all Asians over there. Over here we're just one minority.

Thus the imagination of Pakistan as an 'imagined community' of essentialized sameness is produced in opposition to the essentialized and exclusionary discourses of racialized national belonging in Britain.

Pakistan as 'home' was evoked both as a source of religious and cultural identity and as a place where individuals felt 'at home' because everyone was 'the same'. However, these constructions of Pakistan as 'home' were also inherently unstable and subject to contradiction. If Pakistan is imagined through a discourse of *sameness*, participants' own accounts of their experiences of Pakistan emphasized differences. In particular, they described the differences between rural and urban areas as well as regional and class differences. These differences are evident when Humaira compares her own experience of being in Lahore with Alia's time in Mirpur:

> Humaira: That's just it, you see, she was able to go out and that's in a place like Mirpur. In Lahore, if they find out someone is from Mirpur, they think you're really backward.
> Alia: Oh thanks! [laughter]
> Humaira: No, I'm not saying it's true, I'm just saying that's their mentality ... that's what I don't like about it. Here there isn't so much prejudice about what town you're from as there is there.

Thus debates about the meanings of Pakistan produced instabilities and contradictions. While participants evoked Pakistan as an 'imagined community' within which similarities were emphasized, their own accounts of Pakistan often highlighted differences. Paradoxically, class or regional differences were accentuated when participants recounted their experiences of Pakistan while at school such differences were more likely to be minimized in the construction of shared identities as British Asians.

The sense of contradiction was also evident in relation to the other construction of Pakistan as a 'pure' or 'authentic' source of Tradition (Robins, 1991). For many of the young women, the similarities between Britain and Pakistan were surprising and unsettling. One young woman emphasized her amazement that her cousin, living in Mirpur, had the same designer jeans as she had, while another reflected that Pakistan had become 'just like England':

> Sabrea: Islamabad is just like London. It's got Marks and Spencer and British Home Stores.

These tangible illustrations of the globalized economy provoked contradictions for those participants seeking in Pakistan a site to which they could trace the *roots* of their identity. For some individuals these contradictions undermined Pakistan's value as a source of cultural and, particularly, religious identity. As Ruhi, a participant who had recently adopted a more explicitly Islamic identity, explains:

> They're more Westernized than we are over here ... And I mean they've forgotten like the root and everything it's just all forgotten. I mean ... religion, faith ... it's all just gone.

For Ruhi, Pakistan is a contradictory source of her religious identity because it is no longer 'fixed' or 'pure' but has undergone transformation and change. Her response is to seek Tradition within another home, looking instead towards Saudi Arabia as the spiritual homeland of Islam.

If these examples emphasize some of the contradictions between the imagining of Pakistan as 'home' and participants' own experiences of being in Pakistan, this tension was often reinforced in the feelings of dislocation which the young women described when they visited Pakistan. Often, as Kureishi (1989: 284) has poignantly illustrated, it was precisely through their experience of Pakistan that they became British. As two of the participants reflect:

> Husbana: It's like you're acting to a degree. You are then, yeah, but you're still ... because you've lived in England for such a long time you have to ... fit in, you have to adapt to the way they're living.
>
> Eram: You don't feel that you fit there, you know, that you never did belong there and you never will belong there, you just stick out.

These feelings of dislocation, of not belonging, could be explained in terms of the psychological languages of 'culture clash' as participants struggle to find an identity while being 'caught between two cultures' (Watson, 1977). Instead, I want to argue that, while the evocation of Pakistan as 'home' may be scripted as contradictory and ambivalent, this is within a framework that sees identities as bounded and pure and assumes that identities can be unproblematically rooted or grounded in place.

MAKING HOMES: THE POLITICS OF LOCATION

Hall's discussion of identity as 'positioning' suggests that identities are always in process, always being made rather than fixed or essential. Yet, as Hall suggests, such positionings are always political – made within the discourses of history and culture. I want to develop this idea of a 'politics of position' or a 'politics of location' (Rich, 1986) in order to understand better the ways in which identities, and the evocation of home, are articulated by the young women discussed here. As the participants suggest in their discussions about being British Asian, their British belonging is always subject to scrutiny and question, held in abeyance by others. They are always positioned as outsiders. Their articulation of a British identity – of Britain as home – thus becomes part of a process of refutation, of resistance to this ascription. They assert that Britain is their home: they were born in Britain, they have British citizenship, they belong. At the same time they resist a prescribed belonging to Britain – a narrow definition of belonging requiring the giving up of other allegiances, other identities, other homes. To resist this ascription is to force the acknowledgement of differences, to break down old dichotomies and produce new identities. Thus these young women assert compound or hybrid identities as simultaneously British Asian, British Muslim or British Pakistani.

This reworking of identity demands an acknowledgement of the importance of the politics of positioning and representation. Struggles over the complex and multiple meanings of 'home' are struggles over a location from which to speak – and from which to be. The making of identity is also a process of *making home.* This can be exemplified by considering again the articulation of different 'homes' by the participants. The first account I analyse is from Sonia describing her first visit to Pakistan:

> I went about five years ago. I didn't like it. [Laughs] It was just really different. I went with my sister and we went there for about two months and it was just really horrible. I just didn't like it at all. We were really, really homesick. Ill all the time . . . but since then loads of people have been and they all say it's really nice now. So . . . Maybe I was younger that's why I didn't enjoy myself. I'm hoping to go next year [laughs] for the experience. Maybe I might enjoy myself next year.

In Pakistan – her 'homeland' – Sonia is 'homesick' for Hertfield where she lives. Yet her account of this visit is riven through with doubt about the validity of her own experience and the feeling that she *ought* to have enjoyed it more. She seeks explanations for why she did not enjoy her visit this time and suggests that it might be different the next time. This account suggests the ways in which *making* Pakistan 'home' is part of the narration of Sonia's identity. The feelings of disappointment – even guilt – that she did not enjoy Pakistan reflect Sonia's identification with others at school who have emphasized the importance of Pakistan as a source of identity and she also wants to acknowledge this. Sonia's doubts about the validity of her experience reflect her positioning. Pakistan is part of Sonia's identity and she refuses to allow her negative experiences of Pakistan to undermine this connection.

This positioning in relation to Pakistan – *making* Pakistan home – is also evident in an argument within another group discussion. In this discussion Anisa, the only respondent to have spent most of her life in Pakistan, argues that the social position of women in Pakistan remains very low. Other members of the group, some of whom have never been to Pakistan, strongly resist this argument:

Anisa:	In some countries, like the whole object of religion is defeated by culture and tradition. Like in Pakistan, I've lived there for fourteen years and . . . women there are just treated really badly.
Sara:	That is just tradition . . . The women might get up.
Anisa:	They haven't, because they haven't been allowed by their fathers, their parents, they haven't been allowed.
Riffat:	They are doing it now, they have . . . they are changing.

Here Anisa's claim to know – because she has been there – is rejected by Sara and Riffat both of whom vigorously resist her depiction of the lives of women in Pakistan. What is interesting is not which depiction is correct but how a 'politics of positioning' requires Sara and Riffat to challenge such negative representations of Pakistan. Particularly within the boundaries of the classroom or the social spaces of a school with few Asian pupils it is important for these young women to resist negative portrayals of Pakistan and to produce alternative narratives.

In the process of *making home* in Britain, other places are also *made home* as identities are made, re-made and negotiated. This is a process that is neither contradictory, nor necessarily essentialized. Drawing on Hall (1995), the evocation of Pakistan as 'home' suggests not a return to a mythical or lost 'homeland' or roots but instead a symbolic process of making home. This process is a form of politics, a positioning rooted in historical experience. It is a process that makes possible the narration of syncretic identities – British Asians – that challenges racialized constructions of Britishness, celebrates cultural diversity, and negotiates between Tradition and Translation.

CONCLUSION: POSTCOLONIAL GEOGRAPHIES

Ien Ang (1994) has explained the process of making and remaking her identity as drawing upon, in her case, 'Chineseness' as an 'open signifier' – a resource or material for the creation of new syncretic identities. She argues: 'If I am inescapably Chinese by descent, I am only sometimes Chinese by consent. When and how is a matter of politics' (1994: 18). Although none of the young women I interviewed might have expressed themselves in these terms, Ang articulates the complex ways in which individuals draw upon their ethnic heritage in different ways and provides an understanding of how the predicament between 'Tradition' and 'Translation' might be negotiated. As Ang suggests, identifications are always narrated and negotiated within particular contexts. The identities of the young women represented in this chapter – simultaneously hybrid and coherent – are articulated in and through different times and spaces and always in the context of the contested politics of belonging and resistance. For these young women it is the daily interactions at school, at work, at home and in social spaces such as the shopping mall or youth club that provide the context for negotiations of belonging. Within different contexts individuals respond by negotiating different, and sometimes competing, allegiances. Their responses reflect the complex ways in which new forms of hybrid belonging might be negotiated through practices, such as *making home*, which are about 'using the resources of history, language and culture in the process of becoming rather than being' (Hall, 1996b: 4).

This chapter has concentrated on some of the ways in which the young women interviewed responded to questions about their identity in ways that challenge bounded notions of belonging. Yet it is important also to record other forms of resistance to such forms of belonging, which are to challenge or resist categorization itself. This is suggested in the following comments:

Habiba: Have you noticed that on those equal opportunity forms, yeah, they always have Bangladeshi whatever, whatever? And at the bottom it says you'd rather not say, and I always tick that one. [Laughs]

Sarah: If someone asks 'What are you?' I say: 'I'm a living person' and then they just shut up then. I don't like it when they ask me, because they think that because my dad is Pakistani and my mum is English that I'm a bit of both sort of thing ... I just make a sarcastic comment back to them. I get fed up with it.

Humaira: One girl was asking me, 'Are you a Muslim?' and I said, 'No I'm from Venus!'

While Sarah's comment is made in the context of the group discussion, it could equally have been made to me, the non-Muslim, 'white' researcher. Through my part in initiating these discussions I was also complicit in demanding participants to 'fix' their identities. It is therefore important to conclude by reiterating that the politics of positioning I have referred to in this chapter is so often a requirement demanded from those who are ascribed as 'outsiders' within politicized and racialized discourses of national belonging. This positioning is required not because the identities of the young women themselves are 'in crisis' but instead because of the refusal of others, those at the 'centre', to engage in the re-making or re-thinking of identity. As Hanif Kureishi has argued: 'It is the British, the white British, who have to learn that being British isn't what it was. Now it is a more complex thing, involving new elements' (Kureishi, 1989: 286, see also Parekh, 2000).

Hall (1996a) defines the postcolonial as a process of decentring of the nation-centred grand narrative. He describes the spatial unsettlings invoked by a postcolonial critique whereby places can no longer be imagined as 'here' and 'there' or 'home' and 'abroad'. This definition resonates with the ideas expressed by the young women whose views are represented in this chapter, who refuse to embrace 'either/or' identities and articulate instead hybrid identities, which negotiate belongings to several different 'homes' at one and the same time. Through their making of new British Asian or British Muslim identities these young women challenge dominant narratives of Britishness and are part of the shaping of a postcolonial British identity. These new forms of belonging also require new kinds of postcolonial geographies to negotiate and interpret the complex transnational linkages and diaspora spaces through which the old oppositions between 'home' and 'abroad' or 'global' and 'local' are being re-worked. Such postcolonial geographical analysis needs to be attuned both to the possibilities of new, more complex, globalized material and imaginative geographies and to the politics of place through which individuals negotiate their everyday identities.

ACKNOWLEDGEMENTS

This chapter is based on doctoral research funded by the Economic and Social Research Council (R00429 234082). I remain indebted to the young women who shared their views and ideas with me in the interviews and group discussions. A paper entitled 'Negotiating differences: questions of identity for young British Muslim women' which drew on some material in this chapter was given at the International Conference on Women in the Asia-Pacific Region: Persons, Powers and Politics, August 1997, Singapore and is published in the proceedings of that conference. I am grateful to the organizers of the conference and to the editors of this volume for comments on earlier versions of this chapter.

12

BELONGING AND NON-BELONGING

THE APOLOGY IN A RECONCILING NATION

Haydie Gooder and Jane M. Jacobs

In May 1997, some 1,800 indigenous and settler Australians met at the nation's first official Convention on Reconciliation. The audience waited expectantly as conservative Prime Minister, John Howard, made the speech that would formally open the Convention. They waited for much more than an official opening. That same month the findings of an Inquiry by the Human Rights and Equal Opportunity Commission into the Separation of Aboriginal and Torres Strait Islander Children from their Families had been released in a report entitled *Bringing Them Home* (Commonwealth of Australia, 1997). The Inquiry investigated the painful consequences of the forced removal, in the name of assimilation, of 'half-caste' Aboriginal and Torres Strait Islander children from their families and homes. The Inquiry into the 'Stolen Generation' brought into public view a previously hidden part of the nation's history. In one of its many and wide-ranging recommendations, the Inquiry called for those involved in forced removals (governments, churches, police forces and welfare agencies) to apologize to indigenous Australians. It was the delivery of a formal apology from the nation for which delegates of this inaugural Reconciliation Convention waited.

The Prime Minister was far from oblivious to the expectations of his audience. His speech admitted past injustices to indigenous Australians, what he described as 'the most blemished chapter in our history', an acknowledgment that was met with reserved applause. But the qualification that 'Australians of this generation should not be required to accept guilt and blame for past actions and policies over which they had no control' received jeers from an increasingly dissatisfied audience. Among the admissions and the qualifications, the longed for apology was given:

> Personally, I feel deep sorrow for those of my fellow Australians who suffered injustices under the practices of past generations towards indigenous people. Equally, I am sorry for the hurt and trauma many people here today [strong applause] ... Equally, I am sorry for the hort [*sic*] ... hurt

> and trauma many here today may continue to feel as a consequence of these. (The Reconciliation Convention, *Channel Nine News*, 15 May 1997)

This apology was delivered nervously to an impatient and disgruntled audience. Some had already risen and turned their backs in a gesture of not listening. Although delivered by the central figure of national authority, the Australian Prime Minister, this qualified apology seemed unable to do the work required of it. An apology had been given, but it was considered neither appropriate nor adequate.

This chapter concerns itself with what might usefully be thought of as the affective geography of a postcolonizing nation. We take postcolonialism to refer to the processes by which communities benefiting from, formed through, or subjected by, colonialism come to terms with that fact and its aftermath. The modes for such negotiations might be political, material, symbolic, or any combination thereof. The adjustments effected may be either in terms of recognition or redistribution: that is, postcolonization will just as likely entail altering colonized/colonizer subjectivities (how people are seen and how they see themselves) as it will entail altering who has access to what. Indeed, material reparation often as not proceeds only when certain (conventionally racialized and hierarchical) assumptions held about colonizer and colonized are changed. Psychoanalytic perspectives in postcolonial studies have been especially useful in making sense of such identity questions. They also attune analyses to the irrefutably *emotional* dimension of colonialism and its aftermath. The contact zones created in colonial and postcolonizing contexts are examples of what Anderson and Smith (2001) have recently labelled 'emotionally heightened spaces' in which lives are shaped by the intensities of emotions like loss, hurt, anger, shame, guilt, and resentment. That this is the case helps to makes sense of Leela Gandhi's recent suggestion that postcolonial theory necessarily has a 'therapeutic' role committed to 'a complex project of historical and psychological "recovery"' (Gandhi, 1998: 8). Nowhere is this therapeutic project more evident than in the varied efforts worldwide to engage in rituals of apology, reparation and reconciliation intended to ameliorate the negative effects of colonialism (see Trouillot, 2000).

This chapter charts the struggle by indigenous and non-indigenous Australians to restructure the emotional infrastructure bequeathed by colonialism. We do so by analysing the 'psychic life' of the apology and the broader process of Aboriginal and non-Aboriginal reconciliation in which it is embedded (Butler, 1997). Modern Australia came out of a settler colonialism and this delivers to the present a peculiar basis for current indigenous/non-indigenous relations. Supported by Eurocentric notions of superiority and advancement, settler colonialism presumed indigenous Australians were 'primitive', 'uncivilized', without property. These assumptions underscored the construction of the continent as *terra nullius* (land unoccupied) which, in turn, legitimized initial settlement and allowed those to settle to benefit from a secure sense of sovereign right. For this reason, reconciliation and the apology simultaneously implicate affective and material concerns. As such, they bring into question the very bases of settler belonging and their sense of being 'in place' or 'out of place' in the nation.

In Australia the apology functions alongside other gestural and material efforts associated with reconciliation to make up for past wrongs, to offer some kind of reparation to indigenous Australians for the injuries and losses of colonization. In this context, it is an utterance intended to 'restore to a proper state', 'mend', 'repair', and 'renew' (all meanings of the term 'reparation'). In short, it is a mechanism intended to restructure the emotional infrastructure bequeathed by colonialism, and to lead the nation towards a settled state of co-existence in which both Aboriginal and non-Aboriginal people feel they properly (and equally) belong. It is an utterance that is invested with immense potential as a redistributive force, both material and symbolic. But, as we will show, the call for and giving of an apology has instead produced a range of unsettlements, not least for the subset of settler Australians upon which this chapter focuses.

The call for an apology has been variously received by settler Australians. For some, it has intensified their sense of resentment towards indigenous Australians and the special benefits they are seen to receive as a result of the state's (post-colonizing) policies of redistribution and recognition (see Gelder and Jacobs, 1998, and Jacobs, 1997). Yet the call for an apology, and the failure of the federal government to deliver a 'proper' version of this apology, has also brought together large numbers of settler Australians in a collective expression of sympathy towards Aborigines and Torres Strait Islanders. This is a group we dub the 'sorry people'. In the absence of a proper national apology there has been a proliferation of 'minor' apologies, an unprecedented outpouring of popular sympathy toward indigenous Australians from these 'sorry people'. It is with the mass performative of saying sorry in postcolonizing Australia and how it reconstitutes emotional geographies that this chapter is largely concerned.

One might imagine that 'sorry people' – being non-indigenous, mainly white (and mostly from an Anglo-Celtic background) and largely middle class – are empowered enough by their placement in the structure of a settler nation to be outside of any destabilizing ill-effects that might come from a call for an apology. On the contrary, the reconciliation process implicates these Australians quite specifically. The reconciliation process activates a simplified social structure of colonizer and colonized, even though postwar migrant settlement has already worked to create a nation with far more complex, multicultural social relations (Anderson, 2000). Furthermore, it would appear that certain sectors of non-indigenous Australia are drawn into the emotional work of reconciliation more so than others. The philosopher, Raimond Gaita, has observed that: 'national shame requires an historically deeper and more intense attachment, perhaps more defining attachment to country than citizenship' (2000: 279). He implies that reconciliation specifically draws in those non-indigenous Australians for whom Australia has felt (until now) to be irrefutably 'home'. As historian Dipesh Chakrabarty (2001: 14) argues, reconciliation is commonly understood to be 'between blacks and whites ... and the immigrant can simply take a seat on the side and watch the show'.

There are, then, specific sub-groups of Australians who feel themselves called upon to play a special part in the process of reconciliation. In the context of reconciliation, such settlers have assumed not only feelings of guilt but also the mantle of responsibility for assuaging such feelings in the national collective.

These guilt-afflicted settler Australians feel the legitimacy of their national subjectivity to be compromised (Mulgan, 1998). And as a consequence they begin to experience what we diagnose as a form of settler melancholia. The proliferation of apologies from settler 'sorry people' is a symptom of this melancholia and testifies to the strange (and estranging) rewirings of circuits of power in post-colonizing settler contexts like Australia.

RECONCILING THE NATION

The giving of an appropriate apology has become a central symbolic gesture within the broader project of achieving reconciliation between indigenous and non-indigenous Australians. Reconciliation is the latest in a series of official approaches (forerunners included segregation, assimilation and self-determination) adopted by Australian bureaucracies in their struggle to manage the consequences of colonial occupation. Thought of chronologically, these policy frameworks chart a movement towards the proper recognition of indigenous people and a more equitable distribution of power and resources. Reconciliation is radically different from their policy predecessors that confined their attention to indigenous Australians, usually through the frame of 'the Aboriginal problem'. Distinctively, the policy of reconciliation is directed as much towards non-indigenous as indigenous Australians. It holds that to achieve a reconciled nation, changes need to be effected in the way non-indigenous Australians think and act towards indigenous Australians. In this sense, reconciliation is the first 'Aboriginal policy' to be structured around what might be thought of as the 'settler problem', even though the official title of the overseeing body is the Council for *Aboriginal* Reconciliation.

The first official recommendation for a national policy of reconciliation came out of the 1991 Royal Commission into Aboriginal Deaths in Custody, which investigated the inordinately high level of deaths among incarcerated Aborigines and Torres Strait Islanders. That Commission recommended general political support for a 'reconciliation between the Aboriginal and non-Aboriginal communities in Australia' (Commonwealth of Australia, 1991: 65). The Federal Government then passed the Aboriginal Reconciliation Act (1991) establishing the Council for Aboriginal Reconciliation, comprised of both indigenous and non-indigenous community leaders. The stated goal of the Council for Aboriginal Reconciliation is to assist in producing a 'united Australia' built around mutual recognition and respect between indigenous and non-indigenous Australians (Council for Aboriginal Reconciliation, 1993: 1).

Reconciliation is a self-evident nation-building project. The first major report of the Council for Aboriginal Reconciliation was entitled *Walking Together: The First Steps* and enthuses about the 'marvellous opportunity' reconciliation provides for 'all Australians to be participants in a worth-while nation-building exercise' (Council for Aboriginal Reconciliation, 1994: ix). Central to this objective is a pedagogical programme that targets non-indigenous Australians. The programme seeks to reorganize settler relationships with indigenous Australians by restructuring their understanding of the history of the nation and particularly those assumptions that legitimated settlement. The pedagogical arm of reconciliation takes the heroic story of colonial settlement, and reveals the various acts of dispossession and injustice that underscored it. One of the main manifestations of the work of the Council for Aboriginal Reconciliation is the array of educational publications. Supplementing these are study kits that are available to any member of the public to use as the basis for a 'Learning Circle' from which, it is hoped, would develop a 'Local Reconciliation Group', which actively initiates community-based projects involving both indigenous and non-indigenous people. Encouraged by the Council and armed with the study kits, non-indigenous Australians have voluntarily come together to learn about Aboriginal and Torres Strait Islanders' culture and the history and effects of colonization. This pedagogical function is a kind of 'mnemotechnic', a device for revisiting the past in the hope that a new future will be ordained (Nietzsche, 1989: 61).

RECONCILIATION AND BELONGING

The process of reconciliation is intended to produce a state in which all Australians, whether dispossessed indigenes or settlers, should feel they properly belong in the nation. Yet for indigenes and settlers alike the process of reconciliation is as likely to produce feelings of estrangement as of belonging. In the case of indigenous Australians a newly sanctioned sense of belonging was to be built around altering how they (and their needs) were recognized by other Australians and the State. Undeniably, reconciliation has adjusted how non-indigenous Australians understand indigenous Australians and colonization, yet this has rarely been translated into meaningful material recompense for indigenous Australians.

For many Australians the era of reconciliation has not brought the desired state of settled co-existence. In the first instance, there has been a considerable backlash against the material and political gains flowing from what was popularly perceived to be a 'blanket' recognition of native title. This is despite the fact that native title has neither uniformly increased Aboriginal and Torres access to land nor their rights to be consulted over resource use. The recognition of native title contributed to a wider perception, actively promoted by the conservative government, that Aboriginal and Torres Strait Islander Australians are a 'special interest group' and, consequently, the beneficiaries of excessive 'privilege' (a view which is counter to all existing figures on indigenous health, housing and socio-economic status). Indeed, some settler Australians have come to imagine that it is *they* who are disempowered, marginal and without privilege, that *they* are deprived in relation to indigenous Australians! Furthermore, in coming to terms with a new understanding of the nation, one in which settler heroics has been replaced with colonial brutalities and injustices, some settler Australians have complained about the rise of what has been dubbed 'black armband history'. Like the Prime Minister, they refuse to assume responsibility for past wrongs (see Lloyd, 2000). Such sentiments have fuelled the emergence of a 'new racism' grounded in resentment.

Yet what of sympathetic settler Australians, those who have willingly participated in the supposedly therapeutic restructuring prescribed by reconciliation? For these non-indigenous reconcilers a settled state of co-existence also remains elusive. Reconciliation has instead produced intense feelings of subjection structured through the emotions of shame, guilt and loss. These emotions, in turn, impact upon settler senses of belonging such that they come to feel that they are now (after all these years) an illegitimate presence in a nation they previously, and uncomplicatedly, assumed was home. The historian Peter Read is alarmed by such feelings of 'non-belonging' among such settler Australians, referring to their lack of 'spiritual citizenship': 'While Aboriginal people seem likely to remain second class citizens in *daily life*, it seems that non-Aboriginal people aware of these issues are destined to remain second class citizens of *Aboriginal Australia* – we do not belong' (1998: 175). Evoking the *Bringing Them Home* report, Read suggests that there is an emotional equivalence between the dislocation felt by Aborigines who were once removed from their families and country, and that now felt by settlers exposed to the flow-on effects of postcolonial processes of recognition and redistribution. Read uncannily asks, 'who can – or who is willing – to take the rest of us home?' (1998: 175, see also Read, 2000).

It is in the settler who is touched by guilt that we find the kind of melancholia Judith Butler describes in relation to the psychic life of power in processes of subjection. Adapting the Freudian diagnosis of melancholia, Butler describes the way in which it establishes itself in relation to the loss of an external object or ideal (1997: 179). In the melancholic response, there is a refusal to break the original attachment to the lost object or ideal. Rather, the trace of the lost object/ideal becomes internalized. It is drawn into the ego and, within this inner world, the ego absorbs both the love and the rage felt towards the lost object/ideal. This reconfiguration of the 'topography of the ego' results in self-beratement and guilt (a form of narcissism). In this sense melancholia substitutes 'for an attachment that is broken, gone, or impossible' (Butler 1997: 24). Butler's own deliberations on bad conscience and self-beratement have been usefully and appropriately deployed in understanding processes of subjection in the context of certain disempowered or marginalized groups. The history of colonization in Australia means, of course, that many settler Australians are not prone in relation to indigenous Australians. Yet, as we have suggested, in the process of reconstituting the nation's sense of itself, some settlers come to feel they are an illegitimate presence in relation to indigenous Australians.

A once-certain sense of being-in-the-nation, that feeling flowing from the authority of colonial possession, now seems to be irretrievably delegitimized. Some settler Australians might even imagine themselves as alienated from a category of being-in-the-world – indigeneity – which, under postcolonial conditions, seems to have assumed a legitimacy in excess of that which can be claimed by 'the colonial'. They may even perceive of themselves as lacking something in relation to the *positivity* of indigeneity: be it tradition, authenticity, being 'native born' or (most ironically when one considers the dispossessing circumstances of colonization), continuity of occupation. As Anthony Moran argues, the manifest spirit of reconciliation is a sharing between mutually recognized and respected constituencies, but the latent spirit of reconciliation can easily be a form of envy (1998: 110). (Such settler envy can flourish even when settlers know only too well that actual indigeneity, even under postcolonizing conditions, will *not* guarantee access to traditional lands or secure an empowered place in the reconstituting nation.) In the postcolonizing after-effects of reconciliation a new urgency has arisen. How might the 'dispossessed' settler access that primary belonging over which they now imagine indigeneity lays claim?

Guidance in this quest is offered by one of the Key Issue papers produced by the Council for Aboriginal Reconciliation: *Sharing History: A Sense for All Australians of a Shared Ownership of their History*. The publication argues that through a better understanding of indigenous peoples' history and culture, non-indigenous Australians will be able to 'lengthen and strengthen their association with this land' (Clark, 1994: 1). The document elaborates:

> It is only through indigenous Australians that non-indigenous Australians can claim a long-standing relationship with and deeper understanding of Australia's lands and seas, in a way possible to other nations who have occupied their native soil for thousands of years. (Clark, 1994: 28)

There is little doubt that a central position in this pathway to the new legitimate national subjectivity is given to indigeneity. Secure national selfhood can be retrieved by the 'dispossessed' settler assembling a kind of indigenous equivalence. Indigenous ways of being in the world are called upon to offer a model for settlers who wish to divest themselves of any illegitimacy which derives from their having arrived belatedly. As is often the case in settler fantasies, it is only certain forms of indigenous belonging that come to be incorporated into this reconstituted attachment to the nation. Most notably, it is the 'traditional indigene', that figure who has enjoyed continuous occupation of and intimate association with the land, who forms the template for this authentic belonging. It is a figure fantastically untouched by the very history of colonization and dispossession that the mnemotechnics of reconciliation claims to bring into view. It is an idea of indigeneity that wishes away the fact of colonization.

SORRY BUSINESS

Nicholas Tavuchis, in his consideration of *mea culpa*, notes that 'the production of a satisfactory apology is a delicate and precarious transaction' (1991: vii). This is certainly true of the 'postcolonial apology'. Like reconciliation, which turns to the past in order to imagine a new future, the postcolonial apology requires the offender to 'recall' and be 'mindful' of the past so that he or she might move on to a restored state of being (Tavuchis, 1991: 8). The postcolonial apology cannot simply repudiate colonial wrong doings; it must do the work of transmuting the trespasses against indigenous Australians produced by those doings and their long aftermath. For Tavuchis, the proper apology 'acknowledge[s] the fact of wrong doing, accept[s] ultimate responsibility, express[es] sincere sorrow and regret, and promise[s] not to repeat the offence' (1991: vii). Through this template we can see how the apology of the Prime Minister with which we began this chapter, was so insufficient. Certainly, Prime Minister Howard admitted past wrongs and expressed regret for the suffering felt as a consequence of those wrongs. But he would not allow himself, or others of his time, to claim responsibility for those trespasses. Nor would he let the nation state claim responsibility for the wrongs. This was a personal apology by the Prime Minister of a nation, not a national apology delivered by its elected leader. The Prime Minister's unfit apology was symptomatic of the federal government's fear that an apology is an admission of guilt and, once delivered, it would open the way for unwanted claims for compensation and recompense.

The Inquiry into the Stolen Generation added peculiar impetus to the idea of an apology within the broader framework of reconciliation. The Inquiry was an intensely confrontational moment in the sequence of revisionist memory work being undertaken by the nation. The detailed individual accounts of forced removal, which appeared in the report *Bringing Them Home*, shocked the (non-indigenous) nation (Commonwealth of Australia, 1997). The narrative style of this document made a claim on the nation, calling upon it to listen (Frow, 1998). These stories were not located in some distant colonial past. They came instead from a recent history, the painful effects of which were still clearly evident in the shattered lives of those who testified. Furthermore, the recommendations of the Inquiry were not confined to policy or recompense, in short, to the sphere of government – they also called for symbolic responses, both official and personal, which would acknowledge the nation's responsibility for the removal of children. Specifically, the report called for those organizations directly implicated in the forced removals to deliver appropriately worded apologies to indigenous Australians (Commonwealth of Australia, 1997: Appendix 9, Recommendation 5a, 652). It also recommended that there be a 'National Sorry Day' which would offer both the Stolen Generation and other Australians a chance to remember the pain inflicted on Aborigines and Torres Strait Islanders by past policies. The Inquiry's emphasis on an apology was a response to the many submissions calling for both 'official' and 'community-based' apologies. For example, the Aboriginal and Torres Strait Islander Commission (the sanctioned national political voice of indigenous Australians) submitted that an apology was an 'elementary condition' of reconciliation (Commonwealth of Australia, 1997: Submission 684, 285).

The link between an apology and reconciliation was also expressed in the *Document Towards Reconciliation*, a formal document outlining the key principles upon which reconciliation should be based (Council for Aboriginal Reconciliation, 2000). That document included a formal apology so worded: 'As we walk the journey of healing, one part of the nation apologises and expresses its sorrow and sincere regret for the injustices of the past, so the other part accepts the apologies and forgives' (Council for Aboriginal Reconciliation, 2000, no page). The formal reconciliation *Document* assumes apologizing will function palliatively to create a healed nation. Certainly when the *Draft Document for Reconcilation* circulated during 1999 in a nationwide process of community consultation, there was widespread support for one of the clauses being an apology. Yet it was the inclusion of this very clause in the final *Document Towards Reconciliation* that ultimately jeopardized its ratification by the federal government and, consequently, its adoption as the official collective statement of national reconciliation (Council for Aboriginal Reconciliation, 2000).

It is testimony to the widespread investment in the possibility of this healed nation that, despite the reluctance of the federal government to show the way, so many groups and individuals have apologized to indigenous Australians. Within a year of the release of the *Bringing Them Home* report, a number of State leaders had offered apologies on behalf of their governments and their constituents. Similarly, police forces around the nation began to apologize for their role not only in the implementation of the laws and policies of forcible removal of children but also for their role in having enforced other unjust laws. Perhaps the most rapid response to the call for an apology came from those Church groups that had played such a direct role in the removal and custody of children in the Stolen Generation.

This flurry of official apology-giving amplified the absence of an apology from the Prime Minister on behalf of the government of the day, and the subsequent non-ratification of apology carried in the *Document Towards Reconciliation*. The failed apology given to the Reconciliation Convention once again drew attention to the thing that had not been said by the 'sovereign speaker', the Prime Minister of Australia. Eager to do away with what he saw to be a bothersome issue, the Prime Minister, under the advice of a newly arrived indigenous Member of Parliament, arranged for Federal Parliament to 'express regret' for its part in past wrongs to indigenous Australians. But still this was not enough. Despite the proliferation of 'official' apologies from the various institutions implicated in colonial suffering, the future of a reconciled nation became overly dependent upon the uttering of one word by one man. As Dr Lowitja O'Donoghue, former chair of the Aboriginal and Torres Strait Islander Commission, said in her 2000 Australia Day address:

> I now believe, as do many of my people, that reconciliation will not proceed unless our Prime Minister can bring himself to say that simple 'S word' – Sorry. His refusal to do so on behalf of the Government of the day diminishes him as a person and Australia as a nation. (O'Donoghue, 2000)

THE PEOPLE'S APOLOGY

The various formal apologies from governments and organizations have been accompanied by a proliferation of personal apologies from ordinary Australians. Often referred to as the 'people's apology', this mass apology was in fact closely linked to the emerging state-sanctioned revision of the nation's past as evidenced in the recommendations of both the Royal Commission into Aboriginal Deaths in Custody and the *Bringing Them Home* report. That latter Inquiry, itself responding to submissions received, proposed that mechanisms be established to allow ordinary Australians to apologize. There have been two key mechanisms for the delivery of the mass apology: a national 'Sorry Day' and the 'Sorry Books'. Within these structures there were few limits to the ways personal and collective apologies were performed: footballers wore black armbands; people apologized in virtual sorry books; public walks were organized as 'journeys of healing'; and people even sang at a 'reconcilioke' (a karaoke event dedicated to the process of apology and reconciliation). Some apologies were uttered personally and privately through a modest entry in a Sorry Book. Others were harnessed into nationwide events like the one that delivered healing message sticks from the iconic heart of the nation, Uluru (Ayers Rock), to representatives of the Stolen Generation throughout Australia.

The central sites through which these ordinary apologies have been expressed are the 'Sorry Books'. The first Sorry Book (actually consisting of four volumes) was opened for public signing on Australia Day 1998 at a media event at the Museum of Contemporary Art, Sydney. The book was initiated by Australians for Native Title, a voluntary political group concerned with supporting Aboriginal and Torres Strait efforts to have their Native Title recognized. A number of prominent Australians signed this inaugural Sorry Book. The idea of the Sorry Book captured the imagination of settler Australians and the practice of 'opening' Sorry Books spread rapidly. It flowed through the network of largely non-indigenous political groups that had formed to support Native Title claims and the process of reconciliation. It was taken up by church and other community groups and encouraged by the trade union movement. It spread into schools and onto university campuses and was incorporated into the public face of state institutions like museums, libraries, parliaments and municipal offices. It was embraced by private enterprise with Sorry Books appearing in Body Shops, bookstores and shopping malls. A Sorry Book was even opened in London so that diasporic Australians could offer their apologies. The Sorry Books seemed to be a spontaneous expression of national sympathy, although they were endorsed and supported by both The Human Rights Commission and the Council for Aboriginal Reconciliation.

By May 1998, just four months after the original Sorry Book was opened, it was estimated that over 1,000 Sorry Books had been opened nation-wide and over one million signatures and personal apologies collected (Burton-Taylor, 1998: 11). From the outset a set of specifications for 'proper' Sorry Books had circulated and many of the Books conformed to these specifications. For example, most Sorry Books opened with this statement, taken from the original book:

> By signing my name in this book, I record my deep regret for the injustices suffered by Indigenous Australians as a result of European settlement and, in particular, I offer my personal apology for the hurt and harm caused by the forced removal of children from their families and for the effect of government policy on the human dignity and spirit of Indigenous Australians.
>
> I would also like to record my desire for Reconciliation and for a better future for all our peoples. I make a commitment to a united Australia which respects this land of ours, values Aboriginal and Torres Strait Islander heritage and provides justice and equity for all. (Sorry Books, 1998)

In this statement we see many of the features of the proper apology: the admission of trespass, the implied acknowledgment of responsibility, an expression of regret, and a promise of a future in which injury will not recur. A website and brochures offered additional specifications about the paper quality and size (if possible A4 archive paper set in a ring binder) as well as the type of pen to be provided for signing (a water- and fade-proof, black pigment, ink pen). Of course, such was the enthusiasm for Sorry Books that not all conformed to these specifications. Sorry Books are of all different shapes and sizes. Most are ringbound and hard covered, but some are just flimsy notebooks. There are even Internet Sorry Books, like those at 'Apology Australia' which offer people the opportunity to apologize on-line. Some Books bulge with apologies, but many are over half-empty. Each contains lists of personal apologies; some scribed simply as a signature to the pro-forma apology, others as lengthy and pained admissions of guilt.

The Sorry Books came to play an important part in National Sorry Day. National Sorry Day was organized by a special committee but was supported by the Aboriginal and Torres Strait Islander Commission and the Council for Aboriginal Reconciliation. The first was held on 26 May 1998, the anniversary of the release of the findings of the *Bringing Them Home* report. According to organizers, National Sorry Day was established as a day of remembrance, reconciliation and celebration. It was intended to commemorate those affected by removal, acknowledge and express sorrow for past and present injustices, and celebrate the possibility of a new beginning. Hundreds of civic events and other ceremonies were held around the country. In many cases these events became the focal point for the delivery of apologies, both official and personal. State parliaments and municipal authorities flew the Aboriginal and Torres Strait Islander flags and offered local Aboriginal and Torres Strait Islander groups 'keys' to their cities. Churches joined in ecumenical services and bells tolled in unison citywide. And while on this day many new Sorry Books were opened and signed, so others, filled over the past year, were delivered ceremoniously to Aboriginal and Torres Strait Islander elders as a public performative of the giving of an apology.

Although Sorry Day offered non-indigenous Australians an opportunity to say 'sorry' to indigenous Australians, the initial purpose of the Day was not confined to this sense of the term 'sorry'. There is in Australia also an Aboriginal and Torres Strait Islander sense of 'sorry'. 'Sorry business' refers to events that create great sadness (a death, some other form of loss or a transgression). The experiences of colonization and the Stolen Generation fall squarely into the sphere of 'sorry business'. It is a term also used with reference to the activities engaged in when a community deals with such sad events (including, say, the ceremonies and rites performed to enable those implicated by that loss or transgression to move on). While the Sorry Books seem to meet the non-indigenous need to utter an apology, the Sorry Day was also an event that allowed indigenous people to nationally remember, to grieve and express their sorrow. Both these senses of 'sorry' circulated through the inaugural Sorry Day, each activating different moral registers, each drawing different subjectivities into view, each calling forth quite distinct senses of dispossession and loss.

What investments were there in this day for the settlers who so enthusiastically embraced the opportunity to say sorry? There was a curious self-consciousness in the settler performance of saying sorry. The saying alone was not enough. The utterance needed to be 'proper' and it needed to be 'on record'. 'Proper' apologies, unlike the Prime Minister's apology, had the right wording; they conformed to the structure of fit apology. 'Proper' apologies were written in Books that used the right materials, ones that would ensure that these spontaneous apologies were archived. And archived they have been. Many of the

Sorry Books created through the mass apology are now deposited in the library of the Institute of Aboriginal and Torres Strait Islander Studies, Canberra. 'Proper' apologies were delivered in public ceremonies and events so that both indigenous and non-indigenous Australians could bear witness. 'Proper' apologies, in the form of already signed Books, were ceremoniously returned to local indigenous elders, while others were placed in display cases for people to view. It would seem that for many non-indigenous participants in the Sorry Events it was the *performance* of the apology that was centrally important. One had to be seen to be saying sorry. This self-conscious handling of the terms and conditions of the Sorry Events helped to escort these apologies as quickly as possible onto the reconstituting historical record of the nation. Placing an apology 'on record' is of course a mark of respect towards, and recognition of, the injured party implicated in the apology. But it is also a marking of the change of heart of those delivering the apology. The 'on record' apology is proof of a settler subject actively transforming him or herself from 'colonialist' into that fantasized subject of the postcolonial nation. Perhaps it is unsurprising that one newspaper inadvertently referred to Sorry Day as 'a national day of atonement' (*The Age*, 19 May 1998). Such a slip confirms that standing centre-stage of this event was not the sorrow of the Stolen Generation, but the desires of those settler Australians who sought absolution for past sins.

The inaugural Sorry Day was immensely popular and in the subsequent commemoration event a year later, efforts were made to enlarge that appeal. The 1999 event was called a 'Journey of Healing'. It was a change in name that attempted, first, to make the day a less painful experience for the Stolen Generation. But it was also a name intended to make the event 'more palatable' to those settler Australians who, like the Prime Minister, felt some resistance towards the idea of apologizing. Local communities were invited to devise their own 'journeys of healing', which would encourage mutual recognition, joint commitment and unity between indigenous and settler groups. The reinvention of Sorry Day as a Journey of Healing was an attempt to turn to the event away from the backward-looking apology and towards a forward-looking commemoration. It also sought to ensure that the day was a more widely shared event, that it did not attract only those settler Australians who wanted to relieve their sense of 'bad conscience'. It is noteworthy that the Journey of Healing event was both far less visible (most ceremonies and events were on a smaller scale and were less well reported in the media) and less well attended. How should we interpret this drop in interest in such an event? Had the nation already managed to heal itself? Or was it simply that the transition to 'healing' was not what the settler psyche really required from the giving of an apology?

A SORRY BIND

In her discussion of the psychic life of power Judith Butler refers to the 'sorry bind' of desire, will and subjectivity which come together to constitute 'the terms by which we gain social recognition' (1997: 79). We would like to end our reflections upon the apology in postcolonizing Australia by thinking through this bind in relation to settler subjectivity, and specifically the 'sorry people', those thousands upon thousands of ordinary and not-so-ordinary Australians who uttered their own apologies to indigenous Australians.

Tavuchis has noted that individuals and collectives who apologize 'promiscuously and excessively' often lack a sense of 'autonomy' and 'firm social identity' (1991: 40). In this sense apologies are inextricably linked to what he calls 'membership status'. We have diagnosed a similar dilemma of 'membership status' in the settler Australian in the postcolonizing context of reconciliation. In particular, we have pointed to the way in which the reconciliation process involves a reconstitution of the truth of the nation's past through revelations of the injuries experienced by indigenous Australians. These revelations have brought about a form of 'bad conscience' in settler Australians. Rather than delivering to settler Australians a calm sense of inhabiting a reconciled nation, the revelations present them with a vision of a nation improperly formed. They experience the unsettledness of losing their sense of innocent national selfhood. For settlers so afflicted, the postcolonial apology becomes a lifeline to the restitution of a legitimate sense of belonging.

In general terms the apology works to restore order in circumstances where a certain trespass has occurred and where the apologizing party feels a fall from social grace in relation to the injured party. The postcolonial apology has as its social preliminary a condition in which settler Australians experience themselves as a negativity in relation to the moral positivity of the indigene. In this structure it is the indigene alone that has the power to forgive and, through that forgiveness, restore the wholeness of the settler's sense of proper belonging. This is an utter inversion of the circuit of power by which settlers were historically (colonially) accredited legitimate membership status in the nation. It would appear that indigenous Australians are suddenly enfranchised through the logic of the settler's 'bad conscience', assuming a position as arbiter of the moral community of the postcolonial nation-in-formation. Nietzsche noted that there is a 'voluptuous pleasure' associated with the receipt of compensation for injury and that this pleasure is intensified when the injured party stands, as he put it, 'low' in the social order (Nietzsche, 1989: 65). It is very likely that many indigenous Australians felt pleasure in the delivery of settler apologies following the recommendations of the *Bringing Them Home* report. And it is likely that they have felt their usually precarious status in the nation has been animated in new ways by settler guilt. But it is also true that there was immense sorrow felt by indigenous Australians as their previously unspoken stories of pain and loss began to circulate through the nation. That these stories become a focal point for settler fantasies of atonement, rather than the rationale for material recompense or compensation, is sure to have sorely diminished any pleasures or powers felt by Aborigines and Torres Strait Islanders. And because the move from a 'sorry day' to a 'day of healing' happened without waiting for forgiveness to be uttered, it seems the atoned nation is one where (old) order has indeed been restored.

Lest we imagine the settler apology brings us into a fully postcolonial moment, let us revisit the terms within which this apology is constituted. First, let us recall that the settler apology comes out of a sense of melancholia. Melancholia is in itself a form resistance to change in that it emerges when there is a refusal to accept the lost object/ideal. In short, the settler apology carries with it a resistance to the new state of the social world created by postcolonizing events. In this regard it is important to recall the political effect of the many apologies that were uttered by concerned settlers, not only on their own behalf but also on behalf of others (those who refused to apologize, or did not care about apologizing, or even, like the Prime Minister, apologized often but improperly). Relatedly, let us remember that the apology is as much an act of narcissistic will and desire, as it is an act of humility and humanity. The apology is an utterance that awaits a response of forgiveness. Forgiveness works to eradicate the consequences of the offence and restore some form of social harmony. We might note how inappropriate the term 'restoration' is in colonial contexts. There is not a pre-existing shared moral order to which both parties can return. The mutual participation of indigenes and settlers in an apology marks not a return to a once-held moral order, but the forging of a new one. That this moral order follows the logic of a Judaeo-Christian structure of reconciliation demonstrates just how entangled the colonial and its posts remain. Finally, let us consider what this moral restoration entails in terms of the participating parties. On the one hand, it should diminish the injuries felt by the recipient of the apology by way of the symbolic or material recompense it delivers. On the other hand, the apologizing party has asked the injured party to stop seeing them in the way they are presently seen (Haber, 1991: 24). In other words, and drawing only partially on Povinelli's interpretation of Australia's 'psychic reformation' (1998: 580), the indigenous subject is here asked (despite the past that reconciliation brings into view) to affirm the sorry people's sense of themselves as being 'worthy of love'. In the case of the postcolonial apology settler Australians ask that they no longer be seen as belated arrivals, as illegitimately present, as colonial. In apologizing, settler Australians ask indigenous Australians to see them more as they would like to see themselves: as settlers who properly belong, who have a kind of indigeneity. We might ask whether a situation such as this, where settler subjects are no longer seen as 'settler', is actually a little *too* postcolonial? For at the heart of every apology is a set of truths which should not and cannot be forgotten. And at the heart of indigenous peoples' political power in Australia, as elsewhere, is the claim that they were here first, that they belong. What might be the implications of 'dispossessed' settlers acquiring their own indigenized sense of belonging? Does this mark the beginning of reconciled co-existence, or inaugurate a more penetrating stage of occupation? Indeed, when the settler nation fantasizes about co-existence, is it engaged in remembering or in forgetting?

ACKNOWLEDGEMENTS

An earlier version of this chapter appeared in a special issue of the journal *Interventions: International Journal of Postcolonial Studies* (2002) 2, 2, 229–47. We thank Taylor and Francis Journals for permission to reproduce it. We would also like to thank the following for their very helpful input to this chapter: John Cash; Stephen Cairns; Ken Gelder; Marcia Langton; Fiona Nicoll; Ross Poole; John Rundell. We would also like to thank the Institute of Postcolonial Studies, Melbourne, for providing a stimulating context for presenting and discussing these ideas.

NOTES

CHAPTER 3

1 Since this chapter refers to both formal colonies and colonization, and to the wider range of imperial territories and processes that constituted the British Empire, it will generally be appropriate to use the broader terms – imperial and imperialism – in this chapter (see Johnston *et al.* 2000).

CHAPTER 4

1 Carnegie Corporation of New York archives, Columbia University Rare Book Manuscript Library (subsequently abbreviated to Carnegie Corporation archives). Internal memo from David Hamburg, 4 April 1984.
2 Carnegie Corporation archives. Francis Wilson unpublished memo: 3.
3 Carnegie Corporation archives. Internal memo from David Hamburg, 4 April 1984.
4 Carnegie Corporation archives. Address by David Hamburg, 19 April 1984: 11.
5 Ibid.: 3.
6 Ibid.: 14.
7 Ibid.: 17.
8 Carnegie Corporation *Annual Report* 1996.

CHAPTER 7

1 Report to General Committee by Chairman, Major C. C. Frye, 7 January 1937: 'An unusual prolongation of cold nights in the first two months after opening, followed by a period of exceptional rains, affected our revenue from all sources very materially indeed.'
2 *Rand Daily Mail*, 6 October 1936. The first full public holiday after the opening of the Exhibition (5 October) saw over 100,000 people visit the Exhibition.
3 'The Johannesburg municipal tramwaymen have set vigorous demands to the City Council asking for a day off to visit the EE ... A tramwayman [says] that although he has driven up to the gates of the Exhibition 20 times a day, for a period of two months, he knows nothing of what goes on behind the walls.' *Sunday Express*, 8 November 1936.
4 Of course many children both from Johannesburg and other parts of the country never made it. In many parts of the country, funds were raised to send unaccompanied children to the Exhibition.
5 Major Frye observed that 'The general reaction is, without doubt, one of very pleasant surprise that such a good and attractive Exhibition could have been staged in the Union.' He also noted 'the remarkable and appreciative keenness of the average visitor, whether child or adult.' *The Star*, 14 November 1936.
6 *The Daily Dispatch East London* (6 October 1936) reported that schoolchildren from the town were back from the Exhibition where they had slept on straw mattresses, had ample

food and been very comfortable, although 'some boys had too much pocket money and stuffed themselves with ice-creams, sweets and mineral water, and consequently their normal appetites were affected.'

7 *The Star*, 17 September 1936.

8 A photograph in *Sunday Tribune* (15 November 1936) showed about 10 girls staring at a huge train, some of them crawling around underneath it.

9 'Maritzburg is very poorly represented by a small relief painting. It is a pity that the capital of Natal could not do as well as many of far smaller centres.' *Natal Mercury*, 16 September 1936.

10 25 out of 30 Durban children visiting the Exhibition thought the Durban model one of the best 5 exhibits, followed by 24 who liked the British pavilion, and 13 who enjoyed the Bushmen camp. *Sunday Tribune*, 15 November 1936.

11 Although this did include scones and cake ... Letter to the *Cape Argus*, 23 October 1936.

12 As a schoolchild wrote, 'the Kaffir and Bushmen camps, were extremely popular with our group, especially the last named where we had a lot of fun with the uncultured nature's children from the Kalahari'. *Die Burger* (n.d., 1936).

13 'Bantu, Bushman ... and Whiteman', *Die Burger*, 7 November 1936.

14 In Afrikaans this is 'Die Stem van Suid-Afrika', the title of the Afrikaans national anthem.

15 NTS 338/400 (2) EE Bushmen Camp External Arrangements D. L. Smit to The Minister.

16 Wits University Archives, Raymond Dart papers (WURD) Bains to Maingard, 16 April 1937.

17 WURD Univ. of Wits, Notes on a Proposed Bushman Reserve.

18 WURD Bain to Dart 26 May 1936. Italics added.

19 H. G. Meyer, 'Die Boesmans op die Rykstentoonstelling' in WURD n.d. (1937).

20 As observed in schoolgirls writing in *The Courier*, 11 November 1936, and in the *Rand Daily Mail*, 18 September 1936.

21 'You see them lying around, or sitting, or walking; you see their children constantly and happily playing; you hear the constant chattering of the girls; and they are never still or dozy; they are as lively and busy as a group of bush monkeys with almost as little self-consciousness. Is it terrible, as someone pointed out, to look at such a human zoo? Yes and no, mostly no, is my finding ... With these Bushmen it is different; they may look like animals, but you feel very definitely that they are people. It has been very deeply impressed upon them that the money which everyone is paying to see them there will enable a piece of land, a reserve, to be bought for them. The many spectators are in their view the guests of the boss of their camp ... It looks as if they are having, as the children say, the time of their lives.' (M.E.R. *Die Burger*, 31 October 1936)

CHAPTER 11

1 See Lewis (1994) with reference to the Gulf War and Manzoor (2001) in relation to the events of 11 September 2001. My research was carried out during the conflict in the former Yugoslavia, thus providing another context for the exploration and possible re-invigoration of British Muslim identities.

2 Norman Tebbit, a Conservative government minister, argued that many migrants were disloyal to Britain because they failed to support the English cricket team in matches involving their countries of origin (*Daily Express*, 21 April 1990). It is interesting that this example, which might seem dated to the reader, was raised as relevant by the respondents suggesting the recurrent circulation of such discourses.

BIBLIOGRAPHY

Advisory Group on Citizenship (AGC) (1998) *Education for Citizenship and the Teaching of Democracy in Schools* ('The Crick Report'), London: Qualifications and Curriculum Authority.

Afonso, S. L. (1996) 'Entrevista com Simonetta Luz Afonso', *Visão Magazine*, August: 22–7.

Age, The 'A national day of atonement' (1998) 19 May.

Aglietta, M. (1979) *A Theory of Capitalist Regulation: The US Experience*, London: New Left Books.

Agnew, J. and Corbridge, S. (1995) *Mastering Space. Hegemony, Territory and International Political Economy*, London: Routledge.

Ahmad, A. (1992) *In Theory: Classes, Nations, Literatures*, London: Verso.

Ahmad, A. (1995) 'The politics of literary postcoloniality', *Race and Class*, 36, 1–20.

Alavi, H. (1972) 'The state in postcolonial societies: Pakistan and Bangladesh', *New Left Review*, 74, 59–82.

Aldrich, R. (1993) *The Seduction of the Mediterranean: Writing, Art and Homosexual Fantasy*, London: Routledge.

Alexander, C. (2000) *The Asian Gang: Ethnicity, Identity, Masculinity*, Oxford: Berg.

Ali, Y. (1992) 'Muslim women and the politics of ethnicity and culture in Northern England', in G. Sahgal and N. Yuval-Davis (eds) *Refusing Holy Orders*, London: Virago, 101–23.

Amundsen, R. (1908) *The North-West Passage*, London: John Murray.

Amundsen, R. (1913) *The South Pole*, London: John Murray.

Amundsen, R. (1927) *My Life as an Explorer*, London: Heinemann.

Anderson, B. (1989) *Imagined Communities*, London: Verso.

Anderson, H. L. (1868) Memorandum on Measures Adopted for Sanitary Improvements in India up to the end of 1867, India Office Records, Oriental and India Office Collections, British Library.

Anderson, K. (2000) 'Thinking postnationally: dialogue across multicultural, indigenous and settler spaces', *Annals of the Association of American Geographers*, 90, 2, 381–91.

Anderson, K. and Smith, S. (2001) 'Emotional geographies', *Transactions of the Institute of British Geographers*, 26, 1, 7–9.

Anderson, L. (1986) *The State and Social Transformation in Tunisia and Libya, 1830–1980*, Princeton, NJ: Princeton University Press.

Anderson, M. R. (1992) 'Public nuisance and private purpose: policed environments in British India, 1860–1947', *SOAS Working Paper*, No. 1. School of Oriental and African Studies, University of London.

Ang, I. (1994) 'On not speaking Chinese: postmodern ethnicity and the politics of diaspora', *New Formations*, 24, 1–18.

Anthias, F. (1998) 'Evaluating "Diaspora": beyond ethnicity?', *Sociology*, 32, 3, 557–80.

Anthias, F. (2000) 'New hybridities, old concepts: the limits of "culture" ', *Ethnic and Racial Studies*, 24, 4, 619–41.

Anwar, M. (1998) *Between Cultures: Continuity and Change in the Lives of Young Asians*, London: Routledge.

Appadurai, A. (1974) 'Right and left hand castes in South India', *Indian Economic and Social History Review*, XI, Nos. 2–3, 216–59.

Appadurai, A. (1990) 'Disjuncture and difference in the global cultural economy', *Theory, Culture and Society*, 7, 295–310.

Arnold, M. (1863) 'The bishop and the philosopher', *Macmillan's Magazine*, VII, 241–56.

Arrighi, G. (1978) *The Geometry of Imperialism*, London: New Left Books.

Ashcroft, B. (2001) *Post-colonial Transformation*, London and New York: Routledge.

Ashcroft, B., Griffiths, G. and Tiffin, H. (1989) *The Empire Writes Back: Theory and Practice in Postcolonial Literatures*, London: Routledge.

Ashcroft, B., Griffiths, G. and Tiffin, H. (eds) (1995) *The Post-colonial Studies Reader*, London: Routledge.

Ashcroft, B., Griffiths, G. and Tiffin, H. (eds) (1998) *Key Concepts in Post-Colonial Studies*, London: Routledge.

Atkins, K. E. (1993) *The Moon is Dead! Give Us our Money!*, London: James Currey.

Back, L. (1995) 'X amount of Sat Siri Akal! Apache Indian, reggae music and the cultural intermezzo', *New Formations*, 27, 128–47.

Back, L. (1996) *New Ethnicities and Urban Culture: Racisms and Multiculture in Young Lives*, London: UCL Press.

Bainbridge, B. (1996) *The Birthday Boys*, London: Penguin.

Ballhatchet, K. (1980) *Race, Sex and Class Under the Raj: Imperial Attitudes and Policies and their Critics*, London: Weidenfeld & Nicolson.

Bank, A. (1999) 'Losing faith in the civilizing mission: the premature decline of humanitarian liberalism at the Cape, 1840–60', in Daunton, M. and Halpern, R. (eds) *Empire and Others: British Encounters with Indigenous Peoples, 1600–1850*, London: UCL Press, 364–83.

Bannister, S. (1830) *Humane Policy; or Justice to the Aborigines of New Settlements*, London: Dawsons.

Barata, O. (1985) 'A sociedade de geografia e a expansão da cultura portuguesa', *Boletim da Sociedade da Geografia de Lisboa*, Separata do Boletim, January–June, Series 103, No. 1–6, 5–32.

Barlow, G. (1921) *The Story of Madras*, London: Humphrey Milford.

Barnett, C. (1995) 'Awakening the dead – who needs the history of geography?', *Transactions of the Institute of British Geographers*, 20, 4, 417–19.

Barnett, C. (1998) 'Impure and worldly geography: the Africanist discourse of the Royal Geographical Society, 1831–1873', *Transactions of the Institute of British Geographers*, 23, 2, 239–51.

Barrett, R. (1907) *Ellice Hopkins: A Memoir*, London.

Barriga, P. (1997) 'Ocidente e Oriente: os dois lados da história', *EXPO '98: Informação*, 47, 11.

Bartlett, R. (1994) *The Making of Europe: Conquest, Colonization and Cultural Change, 950–1350*, Harmondsworth: Penguin Books.

Bauman, Z. (1997) *Postmodernity and its Discontents*, Cambridge: Polity Press.

Bayly, C. A. (1999) 'The British and indigenous peoples, 1760–1860: power, perception and identity', in Daunton, M. and Halpern, R. (eds) *Empire and Others: British Encounters with Indigenous Peoples, 1600–1850*, London: UCL Press, 19–41.

Beasley, M. H. and Gibbons, S. J. (1993) *Taking Their Place: A Documentary History of Women and Journalism*, Washington, DC: The American University Press.

Beck, U. (1999) *World Risk Society*, Cambridge: Polity Press.

Bell, D. and Valentine, G. (1995) *Mapping Desire: Geographies of Sexualities*, London: Routledge.

Beveridge, W. (1942) *Social Insurance and Allied Services*, Cmd 6404, London: HMSO.

Bhabha, H. (1990) *Nation and Narration*, London: Routledge.

Bhabha, H. (1994) *The Location of Culture*, London and New York: Routledge.

Bhachu, P. (1993) 'Identities constructed and reconstructed: representations of Asian women in Britain', in Buijs, G. (ed.) *Migrant Women: Crossing Boundaries and Changing Identities*, Oxford: Berg, 99–117.

Bhachu, P. (forthcoming) '"It's hip to be Asian": fashion and design in global commodity markets', in Jackson, P., Crang, P. and Dwyer, C. (eds) *Transnational Spaces*, London: Routledge.

Bhatia, B. M. (1965) 'Growth and composition of middle class in South India in the nineteenth century', *Indian Economic and Social History Review*, II, 4, 381–8.

Blaut, J. M. (1975) 'Imperialism: the Marxist theory and its evolution', *Antipode* 7, 1–19.

Blaut, J. M. (1992) 'A theory of cultural racism', *Antipode*, 24, 289–99.

Bloom, L. (1993) *Gender on Ice*, Minneapolis: University of Minnesota Press.

Blunkett, D (2001) 'Blunkett calls for honest and open debate on citizenship and community', transcript of speech given to community leaders in Balsall Heath, Birmingham,

11 December 2001, Downing Street Press Office (available online at http://www.pm.gov.uk/news.asp?newsID=3255).

Blunt, A. (1994) *Travel, Gender and Imperialism: Mary Kingsley and West Africa*, New York: Guilford.

Blunt, A. (1999) 'Imperial geographies of home: British domesticity in India, 1886–1925', *Transactions of the Institute of British Geographers*, 24, 4, 421–40.

Blunt, A. and Wills, J. (2000) *Dissident Geographies: An Introduction to Radical Ideas and Practice*, Harlow: Prentice-Hall.

Bolt, C. (1971) *Victorian Attitudes to Race*, Toronto: University of Toronto Press.

Bonnett, A. (1996a) 'Anti-racism and the critique of "white" identities', *New Community*, 22, 1, 97–110.

Bonnett, A. (1996b) '"White studies": the problems and projects of a new "research agenda"', *Theory, Culture and Society*, 13, 2, 145–55.

Bonnett, A. (1997) 'Geography, "race", and whiteness: invisible traditions and current challenges', *Area*, 29, 3, 193–9.

Bonnett, A. (1998a) 'How the British working class became white: the symbolic (re)formation of racialized capitalism', *Journal of Historical Sociology*, 11, 3, 316–40.

Bonnett, A. (1998b) 'Who was white? The disappearance of non-European white identities and the formation of European racial whiteness', *Ethnic and Racial Studies*, 21, 6, 1029–55.

Bonnett, A. (2000) *White Identities: Historical and International Perspectives*, London: Routledge.

Boraine, A. (2000) *A Country Unmasked: South Africa's Truth and Reconciliation Commission*, Oxford: Oxford University Press.

Bowker, J. M. (1864) *Speeches, Letters and Selection from Important Papers*, Grahamstown: Godlonton & Richards.

Boyce Davis, C. (1994) *Black Women, Writing and Identity: Migrations of the Subject*, London and New York: Routledge.

Brah, A. (1979) 'Inter-generational and inter-ethnic perceptions: a comparative study of South Asian and English adolescents in Southall', unpublished PhD thesis, University of Bristol.

Brah, A. (1993) '"Race" and "culture" in the gendering of labour markets: South Asian young Muslim women and the labour market', *New Community*, 19, 3, 441–58.

Brah, A. (1996) *Cartographies of Diaspora*, London: Routledge.

Brantlinger, P. (1986) 'Victorians and Africans: the genealogy of the myth of the dark continent', in Gates, H. L. (ed.) *Race, Writing and Difference*, Chicago: University of Chicago Press, 185–222.

Brechin, G. (1999) *Imperial San Francisco: Urban Power, Earthly Ruin*, Berkeley, CA: University of California Press.

Brewe, A. (1980) *Marxist Theories of Imperialism*, London: Routledge & Kegan Paul.

British Parliamentary Papers: Report from the Select Committee on Aborigines (British Settlements) (1837/1968), reprinted Shannon: Irish University Press.

Buck-Morss, S. (1989) *The Dialectics of Seeing*, Cambridge, MA: MIT Press.

Burton, A. (1994) *Burdens of History: British Feminists, Indian Women and Imperial Culture, 1865–1915*, Chapel Hill, North Carolina: The University of North Carolina Press.

Burton, A. (1998) *At the Heart of Empire: Indians and the Colonial Encounter in Late-Victorian Britain*, Berkeley CA: University of California Press.

Burton, A. (2000) 'Who needs the nation? interrogating "British" history', in Hall, C. (ed.) *Cultures of Empire: A Reader: Colonizers in Britain and the Empire in the Nineteenth and Twentieth Centuries*, Manchester: Manchester University Press, 137–53.

Burton, I. (1875) *The Inner Life of Syria, Palestine, and the Holy Land*, London: Henry S. King.

Burton, R. F. (1885–6) *Plain and Literal Translation of the Arabian Nights' Entertainments, or the Book of a Thousand Nights and a Night*, Benares: Kama Shastra Society.

Burton-Taylor, J. (1998) 'Sorry not such a hard word for Australian public', *ATSIC News* May, 11.

Butler, J. (1879) *Social Purity: An Address*, London.

Butler, J. (1887) *The Revival and Extension of the Abolitionist Cause*, Winchester.

Butler, J. (1997) *The Psychic Life of Power: Theories in Subjection*, Stanford, CA: Stanford University Press.

Callaway, H. (1987) *Gender, Culture and Empire: European Women in Colonial Nigeria*, Basingstoke: Macmillan.

Callinicos, A., Rees, J., Harman, C. and Haynes, M. (eds) (1994) *Marxism and the New Imperialism*, London: Bookmarks.

Carlyle, T. (1843) *Past and Present*, London: Dent, reprinted 1960.

Carlyle, T. (1899) *Shooting Niagara: and After?* in Critical and Miscellaneous Essays: Collected and Republished, vol. 5, London: Chapman and Hall.

Carmichael, S. and Hamilton, C. (1967) *Black Power: The Politics of Liberation in America*, New York: Random House.

Carnegie Corporation, *Annual Reports* 1980–1996.

Carvalho, A. (1998) 'Os vários rostos do herói obscuro: sete retratos diferentes do mesmo modelo: Vasco da Gama continua sem perfil certo', *Diário de Noticias*, 20 May 1998. Copy also available at http://www.instituto-camoes.pt/arquivos/gamaheroi.html.

Castle, G. (ed.) (2001) *Postcolonial Discourses: An Anthology*, Oxford: Blackwell.

Cell, J. W. (1982) *The Highest Stage of White Supremacy*, Cambridge: Cambridge University Press.

Centre for Contemporary Cultural Studies (CCCS) (1982) *The Empire Strikes Back: Race and Racism in 70s Britain*, London: Hutchinson.

Chakrabarty, D. (1992a) 'Postcoloniality and the artifice of history: who speaks for Indian pasts?', *Representations*, 37, 1–24.

Chakrabarty, D. (1992b) 'Of garbage, modernity and citizen's gaze', *Economic and Political Weekly*, XXXVI, 541–6.

Chakrabarty, D. (1999) 'Adda, Calcutta: dwelling in Modernity', *Public Culture*, 11, 109–45.

Chakrabarty, D. (2000) *Provincializing Europe: Postcolonial Thought and Historical Difference*, Princeton, NJ: Princeton University Press.

Chakrabarty, D. (2001) 'Reconciliation and its historiography: some preliminary thoughts', *UTS Review*, 7, 1, 6–16.

Chambers, I. (1993) *Migrancy, Culture, Identity*, London: Routledge.

Chandavarkar, R. (1994) *The Origins of Industrial Capitalism in India: Business Strategies and the Working Classes in Bombay, 1900–1940*, Cambridge: Cambridge University Press.

Cherry-Garrard, A. (1939) *The Worst Journey in the World*, London: Chatto & Windus.

Chissano, J. (1998) 'Mensagem do Presidente Joaquim Chissano', *Boletim Informativo EXPO '98 Moçambique*, 4, 2.

Chomsky, N. (1991) *Deterring Democracy*, London: Verso.

Chomsky, N. (1993) *Year 501: The Conquest Continues*, Boston, MA: South End Press.

Chun, A. (2000) 'Introduction: (post)colonialism and its discontents, or the future of practice', *Cultural Studies*, 14, 379–84.

Churchill, W. and LaDuke, W. (1992) 'Native North America: the political economy of radioactive colonialism', in Jaimes, M. (ed.) *The State of Native America: Genocide, Colonization and Resistance*, Boston, MA: South End Press, 241–66.

Clark, I. D. (1994) *Sharing History: A Sense for All Australians of a Shared Ownership of their History*, Council for Aboriginal Reconciliation Key Issue Paper, No. 4, Canberra: Australian Government Publishing Service.

Clarke, R. (1848) *The Regulations of the Government of Fort St. George at the End of 1847*, London: J&H Cox.

Clayton, D. (2000) *Islands of Truth*, Vancouver: University of British Columbia Press.

Clayton, D. (forthcoming) 'Critical imperial and colonial geographies,' in Anderson, K. *et al.* (eds) *International Handbook of Cultural Geography*, London: Sage.

Clifford, J. (1992) 'Travelling cultures,' in Grossberg, L., Nelson, C. and Treichler, P. (eds) *Cultural Studies*, London: Routledge, 96–116.

Cohen, R. (1995) 'Rethinking "Babylon": iconoclastic conceptions of the diasporic experience', *New Community*, 21, 5–18.

Colenso, J. W. (1862) *The Pentateuch and the Book of Joshua Critically Examined*, vol. 1, London: Longman, Green.

Colley, L. (1992) *Britons: Forging the Nation*, 1707–1837, London: Pimlico.

Comaroff, J. and Comaroff, J. (1991) *Of Revelation and Revolution: Christianity, Colonialism and Consciousness in South Africa*, Chicago: University of Chicago Press.

Comaroff, J. and Comaroff, J. (1995) *Of Revelation and Revolution: The Dialectic of Modernity on a South African Frontier*, Chicago: University of Chicago Press.

Commissão Nacional para a Comemoração dos Descobrimentos Portugueses (CNCDP) (2000) 'Latest activities of the Commission', (www.cncdp.pt/), Accessed 22 March 2000.

Commonwealth of Australia (1991) *Royal Commission into Aboriginal Deaths in Custody*, Canberra: Commonwealth of Australia.

Commonwealth of Australia (1997) *Bringing Them Home: Report of the National Inquiry into the Separation of Children from their Families*, Canberra: Commonwealth of Australia.

Community Cohesion Review Team (CCRT) (2001) *Community Cohesion: Report of the Independent Review Team* ('The Cantle Report'), London: The Home Office.

Community Relations Commission (CRC) (1976) *Between Two Cultures: A Study of Relationships between Generations in the Asian Community in Britain Today*, London: CRC.

Conquest, R. (1962) *The Last Empire*, London: Ampersand.

Cooper, F. and Stoler, A. L. (eds) (1997) *Tensions of Empire: Colonial Cultures in a Bourgeois World*, Berkeley and London: University of California Press.

Corbridge, S. (1993) 'Colonialism, postcolonialism and the political geography of the Third World,' in Taylor, P. J. (ed.) *Political Geography of the Twentieth Century*, London: Belhaven Press.

Cornish, W. R. (1874) *Report on the Census of the Madras Presidency*, vol. 1, Madras: Government Gazette Press.

Costa, A. (1998) 'Foreword', in Commissariat of the Lisbon World Exposition/Parque Expo '98 *Official Guide to the Lisbon World Exposition*, Lisbon: Area Promark/Parque Expo.

Costantinou, C. (1996) *On the Way to Diplomacy*, Minneapolis: University of Minnesota Press.

Council for Aboriginal Reconciliation (1993) *Addressing the Key Issues for Reconciliation: Overview of Key Issues Papers 1–8*, Canberra: Australian Government Publishing Service.

Council for Aboriginal Reconciliation (1994) *Walking Together: The First Steps. Report of the Council for Aboriginal Reconciliation to Federal Parliament 1991–4*, Canberra: Australian Government Publishing Service.

Council for Aboriginal Reconciliation (1999) *Draft Document for Reconciliation: A Draft for Discussion by the Australian People*, Canberra: Australian Government Publishing Service.

Council for Aboriginal Reconciliation (2000) *Document Towards Reconciliation*, in Council for Aboriginal Reconciliation *Corroboree 2000*, Canberra: Australian Government Publishing Service.

Couto, M. (1999) 'A celebration in waiting', *Index on Censorship*, 28, 1, 64–6.

Crush, J. (1994) 'Post-colonialism, decolonization and geography', in Godlewska, A. and Smith, N. (eds) *Geography and Empire*, Oxford: Blackwell.

Crush, J. (ed.) (1995) *Power of Development*, London: Routledge.

Cuambe, D. (1998) 'Ao marcar presença na ultima exposição do seculo: Moçambique presta contributo no debate sobre oceanos', *Savana*, 23 May.

Dart, R. (n.d.) 'The structure of the bushmen', WURD (Wits University Archives, Raymond Dart papers).

Daunton, M. and Halpern, R. (eds) (1999) *Empire and Others: British Encounters with Indigenous Peoples 1600–1850*, London: UCL Press.

Davenport, T. H. R. (1978) *South Africa: A Modern History* (2nd edition), Johannesburg: Macmillan.

Davidoff, L. and Hall, C. (1987) *Family Fortunes: Men and Women of the English Middle-class, 1780–1850*, London: Routledge.

Davies, R. (1996) *Secret Sins: Sex, Violence and Society in Carmarthenshire, 1870–1920*, Cardiff: University of Wales Press.

Debenham, F. (1982) *The Quiet Land*, Denton: Erskine Press.

de Castro, A. (1956) 'Discurso proferido na inaugurção da Exposição do Mundo Português, 23 de Junho da 1940', in *Mundo Português: Imagens de uma Exposição Histórica*, Lisbon: SNI.

Deleuze, G. and Guattari, F. (1988) *A Thousand Plateaus: Capitalism and Schizophrenia*, London: Athlone Press.

Demeritt, D. (1994) 'The nature of metaphors in cultural geography and environmental history', *Progress in Human Geography*, 18, 2, 163–85.

DFID (1997) *Eliminating World Poverty: A Challenge for the 21st Century*, White Paper on International Development, Cm 3789, London: HMSO.

DFID (2000) *Eliminating World Poverty: Making Globalisation Work for the Poor*, White Paper on International Development, Cm 5006, London: HMSO.

Diário do Governo (1933) Decreto-Lei No. 22: 987, Ministério das Colónias, Lisbon, 1580–1.

Diário de Noticias (1 September 1998) 'Slovakia: Vasco da Gama invites', *EXPO '98 Information*, 6.

Dirlik, A. (1994) 'The postcolonial aura – third world criticism in the age of global capitalism,' *Critical Inquiry*, 20, 328–56.

Dixson, M. (1976) *The Real Matilda: Women and Identity in Australia, 1788 to the Present*, Ringwood, Victoria: Penguin Books.

Dodd, V. (2001) 'Blunkett's blame game', *The Guardian*, 11 December, 13.

Dodgshon, R. A. (1999) 'Human geography at the end of time? Some thoughts on the notion of time-space compression', *Environment and Planning D: Society and Space*, 17, 607–20.

Donaldson, L. (1993) *Decolonising Feminisms: Race, Gender and Empire-Building*, London: Routledge.

Dossal, M. (1989) 'Limits of colonial urban planning: a study of mid-nineteenth century Bombay', *International Journal of Urban and Regional Research*, 13, 19–31.

Doty, L. (1996) *Imperial Encounters: The Politics of Representation in North–South Relations*, Minneapolis: University of Minnesota Press.

Drakakis-Smith, D. and Williams, S. W. (eds) (1983) *Internal Colonialism: Essays Around a Theme*, London: Developing Areas Research Group of the Institute of British Geographers.

Drinnon, R. (1980) *Facing West: The Metaphysics of Indian-Hating and Empire-Building*, New York: New American Library.

Driver, F. (1993) *Power and Pauperism: The Workhouse System, 1834–84*, Cambridge: Cambridge University Press.

Driver, F. (1995) 'Geographical traditions: rethinking the history of geography', *Transactions of the Institute of British Geographers*, 20, 4, 403–5.

Driver, F. (2001) *Geography Militant: Cultures of Exploration and Empire*, Oxford: Blackwell.

Driver, F. and Gilbert, D. (eds) (1999) *Imperial Cities: Landscape, Display and Identity*, Manchester: Manchester University Press.

Dubow, S. (1995) *Scientific Racism in Modern South Africa*, Cambridge: Cambridge University Press.

Duncan, J. (1990) *The City as Text: The Politics of Landscape Interpretation in the Kandyan Kingdom*, Cambridge: Cambridge University Press.

Duncan, J. and Gregory, D. (eds) (1999) *Writes of Passage: Reading Travel Writing*, London: Routledge.

Dunkerley, J. (1988) *Power in the Isthmus: A Political History of Modern Central America*, London: Verso.

Dwyer, C (1997) 'Constructions and contestations of Islam: questions of identity for young British Muslim women', unpublished PhD thesis, University of London.

Dwyer, C. (1999a) 'Contradictions of community: questions of identity for young British Muslim women', *Environment and Planning A*, 31, 53–68.

Dwyer, C. (1999b) 'Veiled meanings: young British Muslim women and the negotiation of differences', *Gender, Place and Culture*, 6, 1, 5–26.

Dwyer, C. (1999c) 'Negotiations of femininity and identity for young British Muslim women', in Laurie, N., Dwyer, C., Holloway, S. and Smith, F. (eds) *Geographies of New Femininities*, London: Longman, 135–52.

Dwyer, C. (2000) 'Negotiating diasporic identities: young British South Asian Muslim women', *Women's Studies International Forum*, 23, 4, 475–86.

Dyer, A. S. (1886) *Slavery under the British Flag: Iniquities of British Rule in India and in our Crown Colonies and Dependencies*, London: Sentinel.

Dyer, H. S. (1900) *Pandita Ramabai: The Story of her Life*, London: Morgan & Scott.

Dyer, R. (1988) 'White', *Screen*, 29, 4, 44–64.

Dyer, R. (1997) *White*, London: Routledge.

Eade, J. (1997) 'Identity, nation and religion: educated young Bangladeshi Muslims in London's East End', in Eade, J. (ed.) *Living the Global City*, London: Routledge, 146–62.

Elphick, R. and Giliomee, H. (1989) *The Shaping of South African Society, 1652–1840*, Cape Town: Maskew-Miller-Longman.

Elsner, J. and Rubies, J-P, (eds) (1999) *Voyages and Visions: Towards a Cultural History of Travel*, London: Reaktion Books.

Engels, D. (1983) 'The Age of Consent Act of 1891: colonial ideology in Bengal', *South Asia Research*, 3, 107–34.

Escobar, A. (2001) 'Culture sits in places: reflections on globalism and subaltern strategies of localization', *Political Geography*, 20, 139–74.

Evans, E. (1933) *South with Scott*, London: Collins.

Evans, E. J. (1996) *The Forging of the Modern State: Early Industrial Britain, 1783–1870*, London: Longman.

Everett, G. (1985) 'Frank Leslie (Henry Carter)', *Dictionary of Literary Biography: American Newspaper Journalists, 1690–1872*, vol. 43, Detroit: Gale Research, 291–303.

EXPO '98 Informação (1998) 'Filatelia: Vasco da Gama Volta e Viajar', January, 41, 13.

Exposição Colonial Portuguesa (1934) *Roteiro – Resumo elucidativo do visitante da primeira exposição colonial Portuguesa*, Lisbon: Leitão.

Fawcett, M. G. and Turner, E. M. (1927) *Josephine Butler: Her Work and Principles*, London.

Feary, R. B. (1999) *Cartographies of Desire: Captivity, Race, and Sex in the Shaping of an American Nation*, Norman, OK: University of Oklahoma Press.

Featherstone, M. (1990) 'Global culture: an introduction', in Featherstone, M. (ed.) *Global Culture: Nationalism, Globalization and Modernity*, London: Sage.

Ferreira, A. P. (1996) 'Home bound: the construct of femininity in the Estado Novo', *Portuguese Studies*, 12, 133–44.

Ferreira, A. M. (1998) 'How the exposition came about', *EXPO '98: Official Guide*, Lisbon: EXPO, 23–5.

Figueiredo, A. de (1999) 'The shallow grave of empire', *Index on Censorship*, 28, 1, 42–7.

Fisk, R. (1994) 'Sound of murder on a British housing estate', *The Independent*, 1 September, 7.

Foster, W. (1902) *Founding of Fort St. George, Madras*, London: Eyre & Spottiswoode.

Foucault, M. (1991) 'Politics and the study of discourse', in Burchell, G., Gordon, C. and Miller, P. (eds) *The Foucault Effect: Studies in Governmentality*, Chicago: University of Chicago Press, 51–72.

Frow, J. (1998) 'A politics of stolen time', *Meanjin*, 57, 2, 351–67.

Furedi, F. (1994) *The New Ideology of Imperialism: Renewing the Moral Imperative*, London: Pluto Press.

Gabriel, J. (1994) *Racism, Culture, Markets*, London: Routledge.

Gabriel, J. (1996) 'What do you do when minority means you? *Falling down* and the construction of whiteness', *Screen*, 37, 2, 129–51.

Gaita, R. (2000) 'Guilt, shame and collective responsibility', in Grattan, M. (ed.) *Reconciliation: Essays on Australian Reconciliation*, Melbourne: Black Inc., 275–87.

Galvão, H. (1934) *Album Comemorativo da Primeira Exposição Colonial Portuguesa*, Porto: Litografia Nacional.

Gandhi, L. (1998) *Postcolonial Theory: A Critical Introduction*, New York: Columbia University Press.

Garrett, P. K. (1997) 'Prodigal daughters and pilgrims in petticoats: Grace Greenwood and the tradition of American women's travel writing', PhD dissertation, Louisiana State University and Agricultural and Mechanical College.

Garrity, M. (1980) 'The US colonial empire is as close as the nearest reservation', in Sklar, H. (ed.) *Trilateralism: The Trilateral Commission and Elite Planning for World Management*, Boston, MA: South End Press, 238–68.

Gelder, K. and Jacobs, J. M. (1998) *Uncanny Australia: Sacredness and Identity in a Post-colonial Nation*, Melbourne: Melbourne University Press.

George, S. and Sabelli, F. (1994) *The World Bank's Secular Empire*, Harmondsworth: Penguin Books.

Georgi-Findlay, B. (1996) *The Frontiers of Women's Writing: Women's Narratives and the Rhetoric of Westward Expansion*, Tucson: University of Arizona Press.

Gibson-Graham, J. K. (1998) 'Queer(y)ing globalization', in Pile, S. and Nast, H. (eds) *Places Through the Body*, London: Routledge, 23–41.

Gillespie, M. (1995) *Television, Ethnicity and Cultural Change*, London: Routledge.

Gilroy, P. (1987) *There Ain't No Black in the Union Jack*, London: Routledge.

Gilroy, P. (1992) 'The end of anti-racism', in Donald, J. and Rattansi, A. (eds) *'Race', Culture and Difference*, London: Sage, 49–61.

Gilroy, P. (1993a) *The Black Atlantic: Modernity and Double Consciousness*, London: Verso.

Gilroy, P. (1993b) *Small Acts*, London: Serpent's Tail.

Gooding-Williams, R. (1993) *Reading Rodney King/Reading Urban Uprising*, London: Routledge.

Gordon, R. (1992) *The Bushman Myth: The Making of a Namibian Underclass*, Boulder, CO: Westview Press.

Gordon, R. (2000) '"Bain's Bushmen": scenes at the Empire Exhibition, 1936', in Lindfors, B. (ed.) *Africans on Stage*, Bloomington: Indiana University Press, 267–89.

Goss, I. (1996) 'Postcolonialism: subverting whose empire?', *Third World Quarterly*, 17, 239–50.

Gowan P. (1999) *The Global Gamble: Washington's Faustian Bid for World Dominance*, London: Verso.

Gowans, G. (2001) 'Gender, imperialism and domesticity: British women repatriated from India, 1940–47', *Gender, Place and Culture*, 8, 3, 255–69.

Gran, T. (1984) *The Norwegian with Scott*, London: HMSO Publications.

Greenhalgh, P. (1989) 'Education, entertainment and politics: lessons from the Great International Exhibitions', in Vergo, P. (ed.) *The New Museology*, London: Reaktion.

Greenwood, G. [Sara Jane Clarke Lippincott] (1872) *New Life in New Lands: Notes of Travel*, New York: J. B. Ford and Company.

Gregory, D. (1994) *Geographical Imaginations*, Oxford: Blackwell.

Gregory, D. (1995) 'Imaginative geographies', *Progress in Human Geography*, 19, 447–85.

Gregory, D. (1998) 'Power, knowledge and geography', *Geographische Zeitschrift*, 86, 70–93.

Gregory, D. (2000) 'Post-colonialism', in Johnston, R. J., Gregory, D., Pratt, G. and Watts, M. (eds) *The Dictionary of Human Geography*, Oxford: Blackwell, 611–15.

Grisbrook, C. H. (1846) *Letter Pending on the Kafir Question*, Grahamstown: Godlonton.

Gristwood, A. (1999) 'Commemorating empire in twentieth-century Seville', Driver, F. and Gilbert, D. (eds) *Imperial Cities: Landscapes, Display and Identity*, Manchester: Manchester University Press.

Gutteres, A. (1998) 'Foreword', in Commissariat of the Lisbon World Exposition/Parque Expo '98, *Official Guide to the Lisbon World Exposition*, Lisbon: Area Promark/Parque Expo 9.

Guy, J. (1997) 'Class, imperialism and literary criticism: William Ngidi, John Colenso and Matthew Arnold', *Journal of Southern African Studies*, 23, 219–41.

Haber, J. G. (1991) *Forgiveness*, London: Rowman and Littlefield Publishers, Inc.

Habermas, J. (1989) *The Structural Transformation of the Public Sphere: An Inquiry into a Category of Bourgeois Society*, Cambridge: Polity Press.

Hall, C. (1992) *White, Male and Middle-class: Explorations in Feminism and History*, Cambridge: Verso.

Hall, C. (1994) 'Rethinking imperial histories: The Reform Act of 1867', *New Left Review*, 208, 3–29.

Hall, C. (1996) 'Histories, empires and the post-colonial moment', in Chambers, I. and Curti, L. (eds) *The Post-Colonial Question: Common Skies, Divided Horizons*, London: Routledge, 65–77.

Hall, C. (1999) 'William Knibb and the constitution of the new black subject', in Daunton, M. and Halpern, R. (eds) *Empire and Others: British Encounters with Indigenous Peoples, 1600–1850*, London: UCL Press, 303–24.

Hall, C. (ed.) (2000) *Cultures of Empire: A Reader*, Manchester: Manchester University Press.

Hall, C., McClelland, K. and Rendall, J. (2000) *Defining the Victorian Nation: Class, Race and the Reform Act of 1867*, Cambridge: Cambridge University Press.

Hall, S. (1990) 'Cultural identity and diaspora', in Rutherford, J. (ed.) *Identity: Community, Culture, Difference*, London: Lawrence and Wishart, 222–38.

Hall, S. (1992a) 'The question of cultural identity', in Hall, S., Held, D. and McGrew, A. (eds) *Modernity and its Futures*, Cambridge: Polity, 273–325.

Hall, S. (1992b) 'New ethnicities', in Rattansi, A. and Donald, J. (eds) *Race, Culture, Difference*, London: Sage, 252–9.

Hall, S. (1995) 'Negotiating Caribbean identities', *New Left Review*, 209, 3–14.

Hall, S. (1996a) 'When was the "postcolonial"? Thinking at the limit', in Chambers, I. and Curti, L. (eds) *The Post-Colonial Question: Common Skies, Divided Horizons*, London and New York: Routledge, 242–60.

Hall, S. (1996b) 'Introduction: who needs identity?', in Hall, S. and du Gay, P. (eds) *Questions of Cultural Identity*, London: Sage, 1–17.

Hall, S. *et al.* (1978) *Policing the Crisis: the State, and Law and Order*, London: Macmillan.

Halperin, S. (1997) *In the Mirror of the Third World: Capitalist Development in Modern Europe*, Ithaca, NY: Cornell University Press.

Hamilton, C. (1998) *Terrific Majesty: Shaka Zulu and the Limits of Historical Imagination*, Cape Town: David Philip.

Hamilton, W. B. (1986) 'Witness: an intimate portrait of South Africa', *The Washington Post Magazine*, 8 June.

Hannerz, U. (1996) *Transnational Connections*, London: Routledge.

Haraway, D. (1991) *Primate Visions: Gender, Race and Nature in the World of Modern Science*, London: Routledge.

Hardt, M. and Negri, A. (2000) *Empire*, Cambridge, MA: Harvard University Press.

Harris, O. (1995) 'The coming of the white people: reflections on the mythologisation of history in Latin America', *Bulletin of Latin American Research*, 14, 9–24.

Harris, R. C. (1977) 'The simplification of Europe overseas', *Annals of the Association of American Geographers*, 67, 469–83.

Harvey, P. (1995) 'Nations on display: technology and culture in EXPO '92', *Science as Culture*, 5, 22, 85–105.

Haskell, T. L. (1985) 'Capitalism and the origins of the humanitarian sensibility, Part 1', *American Historical Review*, 90, 339–61.

Haymes, S. (1995) *Race, Culture, and the City: A Pedagogy for Black Urban Struggle*, Albany, NY: State University of New York Press.

Haynes, K. (1993) 'Capitalism and the periodization of international relations: colonialism, imperialism, ultraimperialism and postimperialism', *Radical History Review*, 57, 21–32.

Hebdige, D. (1991) *Subculture: The Meaning of Style*, London: Routledge.

Hechter, M. (1975) *Internal Colonialism: The Celtic Fringe in British National Development, 1536–1966*, London: Edward Arnold.

Heimsath, C. H. (1962) 'The origin and enactment of the Indian Age of Consent Bill, 1891', *Journal of Asian Studies*, 21, 4, 491–504.

Holt, T. (1992) *The Problem of Freedom: Race, Labor, and Politics in Jamaica and Britain, 1832–1938*, Baltimore: Johns Hopkins University Press.

Home, R. (1997) *Of Planting and Planning: The Making of British Colonial Cities*, London: E & F.N. Spon.

hooks, b. (1990) 'Choosing the margin as a space of radical openness', in hooks, b. *Yearning: Race, Gender and Cultural Politics*, Boston: South End Press, 145–53.

hooks, b. (1992) *Black Looks: Race and Representation*, London: Turnaround.

Hopkins, E. (1904) *The National Purity Crusade: Its Origin and Results*, London.

Hossain, H. (1979) 'The alienation of weavers: impact of the conflict between the revenue and commercial interests of the East India Company, 1750–1800', *Indian Economic and Social History Review*, XVI, 323–45.

Howe, S. (2000) *Ireland and Empire: Colonial Legacies in Irish History and Culture*, Oxford: Oxford University Press.

Howell, P. (2000) 'Prostitution and racialised sexuality: the regulation of prostitution in Britain and the British Empire before the Contagious Diseases Acts', *Environment and Planning D, Society and Space*, 18, 321–40.

Hudson, B. (1977) 'The new geography and the new imperialism, 1870–1918', *Antipode*, 9, 12–19.

Hughes, G. (1998) 'Picking over the remains', in Hughes, G. and Lewis, G. (eds) *Unsettling Welfare*, London: Routledge.

Hulme, P. (1995) 'Including America', *Ariel*, 26, 1, 116–23.

Hunt, A. (1985) *This Side of Heaven: A History of Methodism in South Australia*, Adelaide: Lutheran Publishing House.

Huntford, R. (1985) *The Last Place on Earth*, London: Pan.

Hyam, R. (1990) *Empire and Sexuality: The British Experience*, Manchester: Manchester University Press.

Iliffe, J. (1987) *The African Poor: A History*, Cambridge: Cambridge University Press.

Ingold, T. (1993) 'The temporality of the landscape', *World Archaeology*, 25, 2, 152–71.

Ingold, T. (1995) 'Building, dwelling, living: how people and animals make themselves at home in the world', in Strathern, M. (ed.) *Shifting Contexts: Transformations in Anthropological Knowledge*, London: Routledge.

Iriye, A. (1997) *Cultural Internationalism and World Order*, Baltimore: Johns Hopkins University Press.

Jackson, P. (1994) 'Black male: advertising and the cultural politics of masculinity', *Gender, Place and Culture*, 1, 1, 49–59.

Jackson, P (1998) 'Constructions of "whiteness" in the geographical imagination', *Area*, 30, 2, 99–106.

Jackson, W.C. (1797) *Madras Gazette*, Fort St. George, vol. 3, no. 108.

Jacobs, J. M. (1996) *Edge of Empire: Postcolonialism and the City*, London: Routledge.

Jacobs, J. M. (1997) 'Resisting reconciliation: the secret geographies of (post)colonial Australia', in Pile, S. and Keith, M. (eds) *Geographies of Resistance*, London and New York: Routledge, 203–18.

Jacobson, J. (1997) 'Religion and ethnicity: dual and alternative sources of identity among young British Pakistanis', *Ethnic and Racial Studies*, 20, 2, 238–56.

Jaggi, M. (1996) 'Return to Zanzibar', *Guardian*, 17 October, 11.

Jansen, J. (ed.) (1991) *Knowledge and Power in South Africa*, Johannesburg: Skotaville.

Jeyifo, B. (1990) 'The nature of things: arrested decolonization and critical theory', *Research in African Literatures*, 21, 33–47.

Johnston, R. J., Gregory, D., Pratt, G. and Watts, M. (eds) (2000) *The Dictionary of Human Geography* (4th edition), Oxford: Blackwell.

Jones, J. P., Nast, H. and Roberts, S. (eds) (1997) *Thresholds in Feminist Geography: Difference, Methodology, Representation*, Lanham, MD: Rowman and Littlefield.

Jones, R. and Phillips, R. (2001) 'Temporal limits to geographical theory?', paper presented at the International Conference of Historical Geographers, Québec City. August.

Jordanova, L. (1989) 'Objects of knowledge: a historical perspective on museums', in Virgo, P. (ed.) *The New Museology*, London: Reaktion.

Kabbani, R. (1986) *Europe's Myths of Orient: Devise and Rule*, London: Macmillan.

Kaldor, M. (1978) *The Disintegrating West*, London: Allen Lane.

Kaplan, A. (1993) 'Left alone with America: the absence of empire in the study of American culture,' in Kaplan, A. and Pease, D. E. (eds) *Cultures of United States Imperialism*, Durham, NC: Duke University Press, 3–21.

Kaplan, A. and Pease, D. E. (eds) (1993) *Cultures of United States Imperialism*, Durham, NC: Duke University Press.

Kautsky, K. (1970) 'Presentation of Kautsky: ultra-imperialism', *New Left Review*, 59, 41–6.

Kaviraj, S. (1997) 'Filth and the public sphere: concepts and practices about space in Calcutta', *Public Culture*, 10, 1, 83–113.

Kay, C. (1989) *Latin American Theories of Development and Underdevelopment*, London: Routledge.

Kayatekin, S. A. and Ruccio, D. F. (1998) 'Global fragments: subjectivity and class politics in discourses of globalization', *Economy and Society*, 27, 74–96.

Kay Guelke, J. and Morin, K. M. (2001) 'Gender, nature, empire: women naturalists in 19th century British travel literature,' *Transactions of the Institute of British Geographers*, 26, 306–26.

Kiek, E. S. (1927) *An Apostle in Australia: The Life and Reminiscences of Joseph Coles Kirby*, London.

King, A. D. (1990) *Global Cities: Post-imperialism and the Internationalisation of London*, London: Routledge.

King, A. D. (1997) 'Rewriting colonial space', *Progress in Human Geography*, 21, 591–6.

King, R. (ed.) (2000) *Postcolonial America*, Urbana, IL: University of Illinois Press.

Kirby, J. C. (1882) *Three Lectures Concerning the Social Evil: Its Causes, Effects and Remedies*, Port Adelaide.

Kirk, T. (1972) 'Self-government and self-defence in South Africa: the inter-relations between British and Cape politics, 1846–1854', unpublished DPhil thesis, Oxford University.

Knott, K. and Khokher, S. (1993) 'Religion and ethnic identity among young Muslim women in Bradford', *New Community*, 19, 4, 593–610.

Kosambi, M. (1991) 'Girl brides and socio-legal change: Age of Consent controversy', *Economic and Political Weekly*, 26, 1857–68.

Kosambi, M. (1993) *At the Intersection of Gender Reform and Religious Belief: Pandita Ramabai's Contribution and the Age of Consent Controversy*, Bombay: Research Centre for Women's Studies.

Kureishi, H. (1989) 'London and Karachi', in Samuel, R. (ed.) *Patriotism: The Making and Unmaking of British National Identity*. vol 2: *Minorities and Outsiders*, 271–87. London: Routledge.

Lagemann, E. (1989) *The Politics of Knowledge: The Carnegie Corporation, Philanthropy and Public Policy*, Middletown: Wesleyan University Press.

Lanchester, H. V. (1916) *Town Planning in Madras: A Review of the Conditions and Requirements of City Improvement and Development in Madras Presidency*. Madras.

Landau, J. M. (1995) *Pan-Turkism: From Irredentism to Coooperation* (2nd edn.) London: Hurst.

Lane, C. (ed.) (1998) *The Psychoanalysis of Race*, New York: Columbia University Press.

Laqueur, T. W. (1989) 'Bodies, details, and the humanitarian narrative', in Hunt, L. (ed.) *The New Cultural History*, Berkeley and London: University of California Press, 176–204.

Lash, S., Szerszynski, B. and Wynne, B. (1996) *Risk, Environment and Modernity: Towards a New Ecology*, London: Sage.

Leslie, F. (1877) *California: A Pleasure Trip from Gotham to the Golden Gate (April, May, June, 1877)*, New York: G.W. Carleton & Co.

Lester, A. (1998) 'Reformulating identities: British settlers in early nineteenth century South Africa', *Transactions of the Institute of British Geographers*, 23, 515–31.

Lester, A. (2001) *Imperial Networks: Creating Identities in Nineteenth Century South Africa and Britain*, London: Routledge.

Lester, A. (2002a) 'Colonial settlers and the metropole: racial discourse in the early nineteenth century Cape Colony, Australia and New Zealand', *Landscape Research*, 27, 1, 39–49

Lester, A. (2002b) 'Obtaining the "Due observance of justice": the geographies of colonial humanitarianism', *Environment and Planning D: Society and Space*, 20, 277–93.

Levine, P. (1994) 'Venereal disease, prostitution and the politics of empire: the case of British India', *Journal of the History of Sexuality*, 4, 4, 579–602.

Lewandowski, S. J. (1975) 'Urban growth and municipal development in the colonial city of Madras, 1860–1900', *Journal of Asian Studies*, XXXIV, 341–60.

Lewandowski, S. J. (1977) 'Changing form and function in the ceremonial and the colonial port city in India: an historical analysis of Madurai and Madras', *Modern Asian Studies*, 11, 183–212.

Lewis, M. (1997) 'Sexually transmitted diseases in Australia from the late eighteenth to the late twentieth century', in Lewis, M., Bamber, S. and Waugh, M. (eds) *Sex, Disease and Society: A Comparative History of Sexually Transmitted Diseases and HIV/AIDS in Asia and the Pacific*, Westport, CT: Greenwood Press, 249–76.

Lewis, P. (1994) *Islamic Britain*, London: I.B. Tauris.

Lewis, R. (1996) *Gendering Orientalism: Race, Femininity and Representation*, London: Routledge.

Lieven, O. (1995) 'The Russian empire and the Soviet Union as imperial polities', *Journal of Contemporary History*, 30, 607–36.

Lima, F. (1998) 'Portugal adquire passaporte para a "Europa sénior"', *Savana*, 22 May.

Limerick, P. (1987) *The Legacy of Conquest: The Unbroken Past of the American West*, New York: W.W. Norton & Co.

Lindfors, B. (ed.) (1999) *Africans on Stage: Studies in Ethnographic Show Business*, Bloomington: Indiana University Press.

Lipietz, A. (1987) *Mirages and Miracles: The Crises of Global Fordism*, London: Verso.

Livingstone, D. N. (1991) 'The moral discourse of climate: historical considerations on race, place and virtue', *Journal of Historical Geography*, 17, 413–34.

Lloyd, D. (2000) 'Colonial trauma/postcolonial recovery?', *Interventions: International Journal of Postcolonial Studies*, 2, 2, 212–28.

Loomba, A. (1998) *Colonialism/Postcolonialism*, London: Routledge.

Lopez, B. (1986) *Arctic Dreams*, London: Macmillan.

Lorimer, D. A. (1978) *Colour, Class and the Victorians: English Attitudes to the Negro in the Mid-Nineteenth Century*, London: Leicester University Press.

Love, H. D. (1913) *Vestiges of Old Madras, 1640–1800*, vols. I–III, London: John Murray.

Low, G. Ching-Liang (1996) *White Skins/Black Masks: Representation and Colonialism*, London: Routledge.

Ludden, D. (1978) 'Who really ruled Madras Presidency?', *Indian Economic and Social History Review*, XV, no. 4, 517–19.

Macedo, M. J. (1996) 'O Pavilhão de Portugal na Expo 98: Portugueses: "Construtores dos Oceanos": o passado e o futuro', *História*, 27, December, 13–6.

McClintock, A. (1992) 'Postcolonialism and the angel of progress: pitfalls of the term "post-colonialism"', *Social Text*, 31/32, 84–98.

McClintock, A. (1995) *Imperial Leather: Race, Gender and Sexuality in the Colonial Contest*, London: Routledge.

McConville, C. (1985) 'Chinatown', in Davison, G., Dunstan, D. and McConville, C. (eds) *The Outcasts of Melbourne: Essays in Social History*, Sydney: Allen and Unwin, 58–68.

McEwan, C. (2002) 'Postcolonialism', in Desai, V. and Potter, R. (eds) *The Companion to Development Studies*, London: Arnold, 127–31.

McGrath, A. (1984) 'Aboriginal women and their relations with white men in the Northern Territory, 1910–40', in Daniels, K. (ed.) *So Much Hard Work: Women and Prostitution in Australian History*, Sydney: Fontana, 233–97.

McGuigan, J. (1996) *Culture and the Public Sphere*, London: Routledge.

MacKenzie, J. M. (1986) (ed.) *Imperialism and Popular Culture*, Manchester: Manchester University Press.

MacKenzie, J. M. (1988) *Propaganda and Empire: The Manipulation of British Public Opinion, 1880–1960*, Manchester: Manchester University Press.

McNeece, L. S. (1995) 'Tahar Ben Jelloun's postmodern folly? The writer through the looking glass', in Gurnah, A. (ed.) *Essays of African Writing*, 2, Oxford: Heinemann, 37–57.

Macpherson, W. (1999) *The Stephen Lawrence Inquiry: Report*, Cm 4262-I, London: The Home Office.

Madras (1793) *(The) Almanac for the Year*, Madras: Duckworth.

Madueira, L. (1995) 'The discreet seductiveness of the crumbling empire – sex, violence and colonialism in the fiction of António Lobo Anthunes', *Luso-Brazilian Review*, 32, 1, 17–29.

Mandel, E. (1975) *Late Capitalism*, London: New Left Books.

Manzoor, S. (2001) 'Home truths', *The Guardian*, 28 November.

Marini, R. M. (1972) 'Brazilian sub-imperialism', *Monthly Review*, 23, 14–24.

Marks, S. and Trapido, S. (1987) *The Politics of Race, Class and Nationalism in Twentieth Century South Africa*, London: Longman.

Mason, M. (1995) *The Making of Victorian Sexuality*, Oxford: Oxford University Press.

Masselos, J. (1991) 'Appropriating urban spaces: social constructs of Bombay in the time of the Raj', *South Asia*, IV, 1, 33–63.

Massey, D (1994) 'A global sense of place', in *Space, Place and Gender*, Cambridge: Polity Press.

Massey, D. (1995) 'Places and their pasts', *History Workshop Journal*, 39, 182–92.

May, J. (1996a) 'A little taste of something more exotic', *Geography*, 81, 1, 57–64.

May, J. (1996b) 'Globalization and the politics of place: place and identity in an inner London neighbourhood', *Transactions of the Institute of British Geographers*, 21, 1, 194–215.

Mayne, J. C. (1982) *Fever, Squalor and Vice: Sensation and Social Policy in Victorian Sydney*, Brisbane: University of Queensland Press.

Mbembe, A. (2001) *On the Postcolony*, Berkeley, CA: University of California Press.

Meinig, D. W. (1998) *The Shaping of America: A Geographical Perspective on 500 Years of History*, Vol. 3, *Transcontinental America, 1850–1915*, New Haven, CT: Yale University Press.

Melman, B. (1992) *Women's Orients: English Women and the Middle East, 1718–1918*, Basingstoke: Macmillan.

Mercer, K. (1990) 'Welcome to the jungle: identity and diversity in postmodern politics', in Rutherford, J. (ed.) *Identity: Community, Culture, Difference*, London: Lawrence & Wishart.

Mignolo, W. D. (1996) 'Posoccidentalismo: las epistemologias fronterizas y el dilema de los estudios (Latinoamericas) de areas', *Revista Iberoamerica*, 62, 679–96.

Mignolo, W. D. (2000) *Local Histories/Global Designs: Coloniality, Subaltern Knowledges and Border Thinking*, Princeton, NJ: Princeton University Press.

Mitchell, R. D. and Groves, P. A. (eds) (1990) *North America: The Historical Geography of a Changing Continent*, Savage, MD: Rowman & Littlefield.

Mitchell, T. (1988) *Colonizing Egypt*, Cambridge: Cambridge University Press.

Miyoshi, M. (1993) 'A borderless world? From colonialism to transnationalism and the decline of the nation-state', *Critical Inquiry*, 19, 726–51.

Modood, T. (1988) '"Black", racial equality and Asian identity', *New Community*, 14, 3, 397–404.

Mohan, G., Brown, E., Milward B. and Zack Williams A. B. (2000) *Structural Adjustment: Theory, Practice and Impacts*, London: Routledge.

Moon, M. and Davidson, C. N. (eds) (1995) *Subjects and Citizens: Nation, Race, and Gender from Oroonoko to Anita Hill*, Durham, NC: Duke University Press.

Moore, G. and Beier, U. (eds) (1968) *Modern Poetry from Africa*, Harmondsworth: Penguin Books.

Moore-Gilbert, B. (1997) *Postcolonial Theory: Contexts, Practices, Politics*, London: Verso.

Moran, A. (1998) 'Aboriginal reconciliation: transformations in settler nationalisms', *Melbourne Journal of Politics*, 25, 101–31.

Morin, K. M. (1998) 'British women travellers and constructions of racial difference across the nineteenth-century American West', *Transactions of the Institute of British Geographers*, 23, 311–30.

Morin, K. M. (1999) 'Peak practices: Englishwomen's "heroic" adventures in the nineteenth-century American West', *Annals of the Association of American Geographers*, 89, 3, 489–514.

Morin, K. M. and Berg, L. D. (2001) 'Gendering resistance: British colonial narratives of wartime New Zealand', *Journal of Historical Geography*, 27, 2, 196–222.

Morin, K. M. and Kay Guelke, J. (1998) 'Strategies of representation, relationship, and resistance: British women travellers and Mormon plural wives, ca. 1870–1890', *Annals of the Association of American Geographers*, 88, 3, 436–62.

Mosley, P., Harrigan, J. and Bye, J. (1991) *Aid and Power: The World Bank and Policy-based Lending*, volumes 1 and 2, London: Routledge.

Mostert, N. (1992) *Frontiers*, London: Jonathan Cape.

Moura, V. M. (1992) 'Foreword', in Commissariado de Portugal para a Exposição Universal de Sevilla, *Portugal e os Descobrimentos: O encontro das Civilizações*, Seville: Embaixada de Portugal.

Moura, V. M. (1997) *Letras do Fado Vulgar*, Lisbon: Quetzal.

Mukherjee, A. (1990) 'Whose postcolonialism and whose postmodernism?', *World Literature Written in English*, 30, 1–9.

Mulgan, R. (1998) 'Citizenship and legitimacy in post-colonial Australia', in Peterson, N. and Saunders, W. (eds) *Citizenship and Indigenous Australians: Changing Conceptions and Possibilities*, Melbourne: Cambridge University Press, 179–95.

Myers, G. A. (2001) 'Introductory human geography textbook representations of Africa', *The Professional Geographer*, 53, 4, 522–32.

Nairn, T. (1977) *The Break Up of Britain*, London: New Left Books.

National Vigilance Association (1935) *A Brief Record of 50 Years' Work of the National Vigilance Association*, London: National Vigilance Association.

Neild, S. M. (1979) 'Colonial urbanism: the development of Madras City in the eighteenth and nineteenth centuries', *Modern Asian Studies*, 13, 217–46.

Nietzsche, F. (1989) *On the Genealogy of Morals and Ecce Homo*, trans. Kaufmann, W and Hollingdale, R. J., New York: Vintage Books.

Ogborn, M. (1993) 'Law and discipline in 19th century state formation: the Contagious Diseases Acts of 1864, 1866 and 1869', *Journal of Historical Sociology*, 6, 1, 25–57.

O'Donoghue, L. (2000) 'Dream on, Mr. Howard', *The Age*, 25 January.

Oldfield, J. R. (1998) *Popular Politics and British Anti-Slavery: The Mobilisation of Public Opinion Against the Slave Trade, 1787–1807*, London: Cass.

O'Meara, D. (1996) *Forty Lost Years. The Apartheid State and the Politics of the National Party, 1948–1994*, Johannesburg: Ravan.

Ong, A. (1999) *Flexible Citizenship: The Cultural Logics of Transnationality*, Durham NC: Duke University Press.

Osborne, P. (1995) *The Politics of Time: Modernity and the Avant-Garde*, London: Verso.

O'Tuathail, G. (1992) 'Foreign policy and the hyperreal: the Reagan administration and the scripting of South Africa', in Barnes, T. and Duncan, J. (eds) *Writing Worlds: Discourse, Text and Metaphor in the Representation of Landscape*, London: Routledge, 155–75.

Overton, J. (1987) 'The colonial state and spatial differentiation: Kenya, 1895–1920', *Journal of Historical Geography*, 13, 3, 267–82.

Parekh, B. (2000) *The Future of Multi-Ethnic Britain: The Parekh Report*, London: Profile Books.

Parry, B. (1987) 'Problems in current theories of colonial discourse', *Oxford Literary Review*, 9, 27–57.

Parthasarathy, R. (1989) *Journalism in India from the Earliest Times to the Present Day*, New Delhi: Sterling.

Pascoe, P. (1990) *Relations of Rescue: The Search for Female Moral Authority in the American West, 1874–1939*, New York: Oxford University Press.

Paul, R. W. (1963) *Mining Frontiers of the Far West, 1848–1880*, New York: Holt, Rinehart and Winston.

Pavilhão da Europa (1998) 'Vasco da Gama re-visits the EU after 501 years', European Union Pavilion, Lisbon.

Peary, R. (1917) *The Secrets of Polar Travel*, New York: The Century Co.

Pease, D. E. (ed.) (1994) *National Identities and Post-Americanist Narratives*, Durham, NC: Duke University Press.

Perera, V. (1992) *Unfinished Conquest: The Guatemalan Tragedy*, Berkeley, CA: University of California Press.

Phillips, R. (1997) *Mapping Men and Empire: A Geography of Adventure*, London: Routledge.

Phillips, R. (1999a) 'Writing travel and mapping sexuality', in Duncan, J. and Gregory, D. (eds) *Writes of Passage: Reading Travel Writing*, London: Routledge.

Phillips R. (1999b) 'Sexual politics of authorship: rereading the travels and translations of Richard and Isabel Burton', *Gender, Place and Culture*, 6, 3, 241–57.

Phillips, R. (2000) 'Imagined geography and sexuality politics', in Phillips, R., Watt, D. and Shuttleton, D. (eds) *De-centring Sexualities: Politics and Representations Beyond the Metropolis* London: Routledge, 102–24.

Phillips, R. (2002, in press) 'Imperialism and the regulation of sexuality: colonial legislation on Contagious Diseases and Ages of Consent', *Journal of Historical Geography*, 28, 3.

Phillips, R. and Watt, D. (2000) 'Introduction', in Phillips, R., Watt, D. and Shuttleton, D. (eds) *De-centring Sexualities: Politics and Representations Beyond the Metropolis*, London: Routledge, 1–18.

Phillips, W. (1981) *Defending a Christian Country: Churchmen and Society in New South Wales in the 1880s and After*, Brisbane: University of Queensland Press.

Pieterse, J. N. and Parekh, B. (1995) 'Shifting imaginaries: decolonization, internal decolonization and postcoloniality', in Pieterse, J. N. and Parekh, B. (eds) *The Decolonization of Imagination: Culture, Knowledge and Power*, London: Zed Books, 1–19.

Piterberg, F. (2001) 'Erasures', *New Left Review* Second Series, 10, 31–46.

Ponting, H. G. (1921) *The Great White South*, London: Hazell, Watson & Viney Ltd.

Porter, A. (1999) 'North American experience and British missionary encounters in Africa and the Pacific, c. 1800–50', in Daunton, M. and Halpern, R. (eds) *Empire and Others: British Encounters with Indigenous Peoples, 1600–1850*, London: UCL Press, 345–63.

Povinelli, E. A. (1998) 'The state of shame: Australian multiculturalism and the crisis of indigenous citizenship', *Critical Inquiry*, 24, 575–610.

Power, M. (1998) 'The dissemination of development', *Environment and Planning D: Society and Space*, 16, 557–98.

Pratt, M. B. (1984) 'Identity: skin blood heart', in Bulkin, E., Pratt, M. B. and Smith, B. (eds) *Yours in Struggle: Three Feminist Perspectives on Anti-Semitism and Racism*, New York: Long Haul Press, 9–63.

Pratt, M. L. (1992) *Imperial Eyes: Travel Literature and Transculturation*, London: Routledge.

Pratt, M. L. (2001) 'Review of *Writes of Passage: Reading Travel Writing*, J. Duncan and D. Gregory (eds)', *Journal of Historical Geography*, 27, 2, 279–81.

Pred, A. (1995) *Recognizing European Modernities: A Montage of the Present*, London: Routledge.

Pyne, S. J. (1988) *The Ice: A Journey to Antarctica*, Iowa City: University of Iowa Press.

Raman, K. V. (1957) *The Early History of the Madras Region*, Madras: Amudha Nilayam Publishers.

Ranking, J. L (1869) *Report on Civil Sanitation in the Presidency of Madras*, Madras: Government of India.

Rattansi, A. (1997) 'Postcolonialism and its discontents', *Economy and Society*, 26, 480–500.

Read, P. (1998) 'Whose citizens? Whose country?', in Peterson, N. and Saunders, W. (eds) *Citizenship and Indigenous Australians: Changing Conceptions and Possibilities*, Melbourne: Cambridge University Press, 169–78.

Read, P. (2000) *Belonging: Australians, Place and Aboriginal Ownership*, Cambridge: Cambridge University Press.

Reinhardt, R. (1967) *Out West on the Overland Train: Across-the-Continent Excursion with Leslie's Magazine in 1877 and the Overland Trip in 1967*, Palo Alto, CA: American West Publishing Company.

Revill, G. (1993) 'Reading Rosehill: community, identity, and inner-city Derby', in Keith, M. and Pile, S. (eds) *Place and the Politics of Identity*, London: Routledge.

Rich, A. (1986) 'Notes towards a politics of location', in *Blood, Bread and Poetry: Selected Prose, 1979–1985*, London: Virago, 210–32.

Rico, M. (1999) 'Una investigación sobre la guerra de Guatemala culpa al Ejército de genocidio planificado', *El País* (Madrid) 26 February, 3.

Riffenburgh, B. (1993) *The Myth of the Explorer*, Oxford: Oxford University Press.

Robbins, W. G. (1994) *Colony and Empire: The Capitalist Transformation of the American West*, Lawrence: University Press of Kansas.

Robins, K. (1991) 'Tradition and translation: national culture in its global context', in Corner, J. and Harvey, S. (eds) *Enterprise and Heritage: Crosscurrents of National Culture*, London: Routledge.

Robinson, J. (1996) *The Power of Apartheid*, Oxford: Heinemann.

Robinson, J. (1998) '(Im)mobilising space – dreaming (of) change', in Judin, H. and Vladislavic, I. (eds) *blank_____: Architecture, Apartheid and After* Rotterdam: NAi Publishers.

Robinson, J. (1999) 'Cities as spaces of interaction: African participation in Johannesburg's 1936 Empire Exhibition', manuscript available from the author.

Roche, P. A. (1975) 'Caste and the British merchant government in Madras, 1639–1749', *Indian Economic and Social History Review*, XII, 381–407.

Rodinson, M. (1973) *Israel, a Colonial-Settler State?*, New York: Monad Press.

Rogerson, C. (1980) 'Internal colonialism, transnationalization and spatial inequality', *South African Geographical Journal*, 62, 101–20.

Rowe, J. C. (2000) *Literary Culture and U.S. Imperialism: From the Revolution to World War II*, New York: Oxford University Press.

Rowthorn, K. (1975) 'Imperialism in the 1970s – unity or rivalry?', in Radice, H. (ed.) *International Firms and Modern Imperialism*, Harmondsworth: Penguin Books, 158–80.

Rushdie, S. (1991) *Imaginary Homelands*, London: Granta.

Rutherford, J (1990) 'A place called home: identity and the cultural politics of difference', in Rutherford, J. (ed.) *Identity: Community, Culture, Difference*, London: Lawrence and Wishart.

Ryan, J. R. (2002) 'History and philosophy of geography 1999–2000', *Progress in Human Geography*, 26, 1, 84–97.

Ryan, M. (1994) *War and Peace in Ireland: Britain and the IRA in the New World Order*, London: Pluto Press.

Ryan, S. (1996) *The Cartographic Eye: How Explorers Saw Australia*, Cambridge: Cambridge University Press.

Said, E. (1978) *Orientalism*, New York: Vintage.

Said, E. (1979) *The Question of Palestine*, New York: Times Books.

Said, E. (1983) *The World, the Text and the Critic*, Cambridge, MA: Harvard University Press.

Said, E. (1993) *Culture and Imperialism*, London: Vintage.

Said, E. (1999) *Out of Place*, London: Granta.

Said, E. (2000) 'Invention, memory and place', *Critical Inquiry*, 26, 175–92.

Samad, Y. (1993) 'Imagining a British Muslim identification', paper presented at Muslims in Europe: Generation to Generation Conference, St Catherine's College, Oxford, 5–7 April.

Sampaio, J. (1998) 'Foreword' in Commissariat of the Lisbon World Exposition/Parque Expo '98 (1998) *Official Guide to the Lisbon World Exposition*, Lisbon: Area Promark/Parque Expo, 7.

Saraiva, M. (1990) 'O error colonialista', *Boletim da Sociedade de Geografia de Lisboa*, 108, 1–6, 91–103.

Sassen, S. (1991) *The Global City: New York, London, Tokyo*, Princeton, NJ: Princeton University Press.

Sautman, B. (2000) 'Is Xinjiang an internal colony?', *Inner Asia*, 2, 239–71.

Saville, J. (1994) *The Consolidation of the Capitalist State, 1800–1850*, London: Pluto Press.

Schwarz, B. (1999) 'Afterword: postcolonial times: the visible and the invisible', in Driver, F. and Gilbert, D. (eds) *Imperial Cities*, Manchester: Manchester University Press, 268–72.

Schwartz, S. (ed.) (1994) *Implicit Understandings*, Cambridge: Cambridge University Press.

Scott, R. F. (1905) *The Voyage of the Discovery*, London: Smith Elder.

Scott, R. F. (1913) *Scott's Last Expedition*, London: Smith Elder.

Scott, W. (1824) *Report on the Epidemic Cholera As it has Appeared in the Territories Subject to the Presidency of Fort St. George*. Madras: Asylum Press.

Selvon, S. (1995, orig. 1956) *The Lonely Londoners*, London: Longman.

Seton-Watson, H. (1961) *The New Imperialism*, London: The Bodley Head.

Sharma, S., Hutnyk, J. and Sharma, A. (1996) *Dis-Orienting Rhythms: The Politics of the New Asian Dance Music*, London: Zed Books.

Sharpe, J. (2000) 'Is the United States postcolonial?', in King, R. (ed.) *Postcolonial America*, Urbana, IL: University of Illinois Press, 103–21.

Shaw, A. (1988) *A Pakistani Community in Britain*, Oxford: Blackwell.

Shaw, R. and Stewart, C. (eds) (1994) *Syncretism/Anti-Syncretism*, London: Routledge.

Shohat, E. and Stam R. (1994) *Unthinking Eurocentrism: Multiculturalism and the New World Order*, London: Routledge.

Sidaway, J. D. (1997) 'The (re)making of the western "geographical tradition": some missing links', *Area*, 91, 72–80.

Sidaway, J. D. (1999a) 'American power and the Portuguese empire', in Slater, D. and Taylor, P. J. (eds) *The American Century: Consent and Coercion in the Projection of American Power*, Oxford: Blackwell, 195–209.

Sidaway, J. D. (1999b) 'Iberian geopolitics', in Atkinson, D. and Dodds, K. (eds) *Geopolitical Traditions: Critical Histories of Geopolitical Thought*, London: Routledge.

Sidaway, J. D. (2002) *Imagined Regional Communities: Integration and Sovereignty in the Global South*, London: Routledge.

Sidaway, J. D. and Pryke, M. D. (2000) 'The strange geographies of emerging markets', *Transactions of the Institute of British Geographers*, 25, 187–201.

Simon, D. (1991) 'The ties that bind: decolonization and neocolonialism in southern Africa', in Dixon, C. J. and Heffernan, M. (eds) *Colonialism and Development in the Contemporary World*, London: Mansell, 21–45.

Simon, D. (1998) 'Rethinking (post)modernism, postcolonialism and posttraditionalism: South-North perspectives', *Environment and Planning D: Society and Space*, 16, 219–45.

Singh, A. and Schmidt, P. (2000) *Postcolonial Theory and the United States: Race, Ethnicity, and Literature*, Jackson: University Press of Mississippi.

Singh, S. J. (1914) *B. M. Malabari: Rambles with the Pilgrim Reformer*, London: G. Bell.

Sinha, M. (1995) *Colonial Masculinity: The 'Manly Englishman' and the 'Effeminate Bengali' in the Late Nineteenth Century*, Manchester: Manchester University Press.

Sklar, R. L. (1976) 'Postimperialism: a class analysis of multinational corporate expansion', *Comparative Politics*, 9, 75–92.

Slater, D. (1998) 'Post-colonial questions for global times', *Review of International Political Economy*, 5, 647–78.

Slater, D. and Bell, M. (2002) 'Aid and the geopolitics of the postcolonial: critical reflections on New Labour's Overseas Development Strategy', *Development and Change*, 33, 335–6.

Sleman, S. (1991) 'Modernism's last post', in Adam, I. and Tiffin, H. (eds) *Past the Last Post: Theorizing Post-colonialism and Post-modernism*, Hemel Hempstead: Harvester Wheatsheaf, 1–11.

Smith, A. M. (1994) *New Right Discourses on Race and Sexuality: Britain, 1968–1990*, Cambridge: Cambridge University Press.

Smith, G. (1994) 'Political theory and human geography', in Gregory, D., Martin, R. and Smith, G. (eds) *Human Geography: Society, Space and Social Science*, Basingstoke: Macmillan, 54–77.

Smith, N. (1994) 'Geography, empire and social theory', *Progress in Human Geography*, 18, 491–500.

Sorry Books (1998) Collection held at the Australian Institute of Aboriginal and Torres Strait Islander Studies, Canberra.

Spivak, G. C. (1988) 'Can the subaltern speak?', in Nelson, C. and Grossberg, L. (eds) *Marxism and the Interpretation of Culture*, Urbana, IL: University of Illinois Press, 271–313.

Spivak, G. C. (1990) *The Postcolonial Critic: Interviews, Strategies, Dialogues*. New York: Routledge.

Spufford, F. (1996) *I May Be Some Time: Ice and the English Imagination*, London: Faber & Faber.

Stepan, N. (1982) *The Idea of Race in Science: Great Britain, 1800–1960*, London: Macmillan.

Stern, M. (1877, rpt. 1972) 'Introduction', Mrs. Frank Leslie, *California: A Pleasure Trip from Gotham to the Golden Gate, April, May, June 1877*, New York: Nieuwkoop, B. De Graaf.

Stern, M. (1953) *Purple Passage: The Life of Mrs. Frank Leslie*, Norman, OK: University of Oklahoma Press.

Stoler, A. L. (1989) 'Rethinking colonial categories: European communities and the boundaries of rule', *Comparative Studies in Society and History*, 1, 134–61.

Stoler, A. L. (1991) 'Carnal knowledge and imperial power: gender, race and morality in colonial Asia', in di Leonardo, M. (ed.) *Gender at the Crossroads of Knowledge: Feminist Anthropology in the Postmodern Era*, Oxford: Oxford University Press, 51–101.

Stoler, A. L. (1995) *Race and the Education of Desire: Foucault's* History of Sexuality *and the Colonial Order of Things*, Durham, NC: Duke University Press.

Stoler, A. L. and Cooper, F. (1997) 'Between metropole and colony: rethinking a research agenda', in Cooper, F. and Stoler, A. L. (eds) *Tensions of Empire: Colonial Cultures in a Bourgeois World*, Berkeley and London: University of California Press, 1–58.

Subrahmanyam, S. (1993) *The Portuguese Empire in Asia 1500–1700: A Political and Economic History*, London: Longman.

Subrahmanyam, S. (1997) *The Career and Legend of Vasco da Gama*, Cambridge: Cambridge University Press.

Sylvester, C. (1999) 'Development studies and postcolonial studies: disparate tales of the "Third World"', *Third World Quarterly*, 20, 703–21.

Szporluk, R. (1994) 'After empire: what?', *Daedalus*, 123, 21–39.

Talboys, J. (1878) *Early Records of British India: A History of the English Settlements in India*, Calcutta: Wheeler.

Tapscott, C. (1995) 'Changing discourses of development in South Africa', in Crush, J. (ed.) *Power of Development*, London: Routledge, 176–91.

Taussig, M. (1992) 'Culture of terror – space of death: Roger Casement's Putumayo Report and the explanation of torture', in Dirks, N. B. (ed.) *Colonialism and Culture*, Ann Arbor, MI: University of Michigan Press, 135–74.

Tavuchis, N. (1991) *Mea culpa: A Sociology of Apology and Reconciliation*, Stanford, CA: Stanford University Press.

Taylor, C. B. (1883) *Speech on the Second Reading of a Bill for the Repeal of the Contagious Diseases Acts, 1866–69*, London: Effingham Wilson.

The Reconciliation Convention, (1997) *Channel Nine News*, 15 May.

Thomas, N. (1994) *Colonialism's Culture: Anthropology, Travel and Government*, Cambridge: Polity Press.

Thompson, F. (1988) *The Rise of Respectable Society: A Social History of Victorian Britain, 1830–1900*, London: Fontana.

Thomson, D. (1977) *Scott's Men*, London: Allen Lane.

Thorne, S. (1999) *Congregational Missions and the Making of an Imperial Culture in Nineteenth Century England*, Stanford, CA: Stanford University Press.

Thrift, N. and Leyshon, A. (1994) 'A phantom state? The de-traditionalization of money, the international financial system and international financial centres', *Political Geography*, 13, 299–327.

Tompkins, J. (1992) *West of Everything: The Inner Life of Westerns*, New York: Oxford University Press.

Trouillot, M-R. (2000) 'Abortive rituals: historical apologies in the global era', *Interventions: International Journal of Postcolonial Studies*, 2, 2, 171–86.

Turley, D. (1991) *The Culture of English Antislavery, 1780–1860*, London: Routledge.

Valverde, M. (1991) *The Age of Light, Soap and Water: Moral Reform in English Canada, 1885–1925*, Toronto: McClelland & Stuart.

Van Heyningen, E. B. (1984) 'The social evil in the Cape Colony 1868–1902: prostitution and the Contagious Diseases Acts', *Journal of Southern African Studies*, 10, 2, 170–97.

Vanly, I. S. (1993) 'Kurdistan in Iraq', in Chaliand, G. (ed.) *People Without a Country: The Kurds and Kurdistan*, London: Zed Books, 139–93.

Verax (pseud.) (1895) *The Social Evil in South Calcutta*, Calcutta: Calcutta Central Press.

Vigne, R. (1998) '"Die Man Wat Die Groot Trek Veroorsaak het": Glenelg's personal contribution to the cancellation of D'Urban's dispossession of the Rarabe in 1835', *Kleio*, XXX, 23–45.

Visão (1998) *Guia Expo '98, Edição Especial*, May–September, Lisbon.

Viswanathan, G. (1989) *Masks of Conquest: Literary Study and British Rule in India*, New York: Columbia University Press.

Viswanathan, G. (1998) *Outside the Fold: Conversion, Modernity, and Belief*, Princeton, NJ: Princeton University Press.

Vitorino, A. (1997) 'Reconciliar o País com o projecto', *EXPO '98 Informação*, February, 5.

Walkowitz, J. R. (1980) *Prostitution and Victorian Society: Women, Class and the State*, Cambridge: Cambridge University Press.

Ward, J. M. (1976) *Colonial Self-Government: The British Experience, 1759–1856*, Toronto: University of Toronto Press.

Ware, V. (1992) *Beyond the Pale: White Women, Racism and History*, London: Verso.

Warren, J. F. (1993) *Ah Ku and Karayuki-san: Prostitution in Singapore, 1870–1940*, Oxford: Oxford University Press.

Watson, J. L. (1977) *Between Two Cultures: Migrants and Minorities in Britain*, Oxford: Blackwell.

Wentzel, W. (1982) *Poverty and Development in South Africa, 1890–1980*, Working Paper 46, Southern African Labour and Development Research Unit, Cape Town: University of Cape Town.

Werbner, R. P. (1998) *Memory and the Postcolony: African Anthropology and the Critique of Power*. London: Zed Books.

Wheeler, D. (1993) *Historical Dictionary of Portugal*, London: Scarecrow Press.

Wheeler, D. (1998) 'Letter to the membership: from Vasco da Gama, 1498, to EXPO 1998, A tale of two Lisbon World fairs', *Portuguese Studies Review*, 6, 2, 5–10.

Wheeler, S. (1996) *Terra Incognita*, London: Verso.

White, L. (1990) *The Comforts of Home: Prostitution in Colonial Nairobi*, Chicago: University of Chicago Press.

White, R. (1991) *'It's Your Misfortune and None of My Own': A New History of the American West*, Norman, OK: University of Oklahoma Press.

Williams, A. (1997) 'The postcolonial flâneur and other fellow-travellers: conceits for a narrative of redemption', *Third World Quarterly*, 18, 821–42.

Williams, F. (1993) 'Gender, race and class in British welfare policy', in Cochrane, A. and Clarke, D. (eds) *Comparing Welfare States: Britain in International Context*, London: Sage.

Williams, P. and Chrisman, L. (1993) 'Colonial discourse and post-colonial theory: an introduction', in *Colonial Discourse and Post-colonial Theory: A Reader*, Hemel Hempstead: Harvester Wheatsheaf, 1–20.

Williams, R. (1985) *The Country and the City*, London: Hogarth Press.

Williams, S. W. (1977) 'Internal colonialism, core-periphery contrasts and devolution: an integrative comment', *Area*, 9, 272–8.

Wilson, E. (1972) *Diary of the Terra Nova Expedition*, London: Blandford Press.

Wilson, F. (1983) 'The second Carnegie Inquiry into poverty and development', *Social Work*, 19.

Wilson, F. (1986) *South Africa: The Cordoned Heart*, Cape Town: The Gallery Press.

Wilson, F. and Ramphele, M. (1989) *Uprooting Poverty: The South African Challenge*, Cape Town: David Philip.

Witoszek, N. (1997) 'The anti-Romantic Romantics: nature, knowledge and identity in nineteenth-century Norway', in Teich, M., Porter, R. & Gustafsson, B. (eds) *Nature and Society in Historical Context*, Cambridge: Cambridge University Press.

Woolley, J. [A Pupil of] (1873) *Vice and its Victims in Sydney*, Sydney.

Yeoh, B. S. A. (1996) *Contesting Space: Power Relations and the Urban Built Environment in Colonial Singapore*, Kuala Lumpur: Oxford University Press.

Young, R. (1990) *White Mythologies: Writing History and the West*, London: Routledge.

Young, R. (1994) *Colonial Desire: Hybridity in Theory, Culture and Race*, London: Routledge.

Young, R. (2001) *Postcolonialism: An Historical Introduction*, Oxford: Blackwell.

Yuval-Davis, N. (1997) *Gender and Nation*, London: Sage.

Zirker, D. (1994) 'Brazilian foreign policy and subimperialism during the political transition of the 1980s: a review and reapplication of Marini's theory', *Latin American Perspectives*, 80, 21, 115–31.

NOTES ON CONTRIBUTORS

Morag Bell is Professor of Geography at Loughborough University. Her research interests are in cultural geographies of British imperialism and its legacies. Her recent work draws on postcolonial critiques to examine the role of international philanthropy in the exercise of Western cultural power. She has published widely and received research funding from a range of sources including the British Academy, the ESRC and the Wellcome Trust for the History of Medicine.

Alison Blunt is Lecturer in Geography at Queen Mary, University of London. Her research interests include geographies of home, identity and mixed descent, focusing on the Anglo-Indian community in India, Australia and Britain, and cultures of imperial travel and domesticity. Her books include *Travel, Gender, and Imperialism: Mary Kingsley and West Africa* (Guildford, 1994); edited with Gillian Rose, *Writing Women and Space: Colonial and Postcolonial Geographies* (Guildford, 1994); and, with Jane Wills, *Dissident Geographies: an Introduction to Radical Ideas and Practice* (Prentice Hall, 2000).

Claire Dwyer is Lecturer in social and cultural geography at University College London with particular interests in the cultural politics of multiculturalism, feminist geography and qualitative methodologies. Her research focuses on debates about Muslim state-funded schools; identities of young British Muslim women and the building of mosques. She is currently working on the transnationalities of British-Asian commodity culture.

Haydie Gooder is a postgraduate in the School of Anthropology, Geography and Environmental Studies at the University of Melbourne. She is currently completing a PhD on the 'sorry people', those settler Australians involved in various expressions of sympathy for indigenous Australian causes. She is also involved, with Jane M. Jacobs and Marcia Langton, in an Australian Research Council project auditing reconciliation events across Australia.

Jane M. Jacobs teaches Geography at the University of Edinburgh, and previously taught in the School of Anthropology, Geography and Environmental Studies at the University of Melbourne. Her recent books include *Edge of Empire: Postcolonialism and the City* (Routledge, 1996); with Ken Gelder, *Uncanny Australia: Sacredness and Identity in a Postcolonial Nation* (Melbourne University Press, 1998); and, edited with Ruth Fincher, *Cities of Difference* (Guilford, 1998).

M. Satish Kumar is Lecturer at the School of Geography, Queen's University, Belfast, and previously worked as Associate Professor in Human Geography at Jawaharlal Nehru University, New Delhi and as Commonwealth Fellow at the

University of Cambridge. His research is on the development geography of South Asia and urbanization, and he has a forthcoming book entitled *Urbanising the Developing World: From Colonial to a Postcolonial Context* (Pluto).

Alan Lester is Senior Lecturer in Human Geography at the School of Cultural and Community Studies, University of Sussex. His research focuses on the differential construction of, and contestation between, British colonial discourses in the nineteenth century. Much of his work has centred on the Cape Colony and the broader historical geographies of South Africa, but he is currently engaged in a project of examining connections between settler communities and humanitarians across a more extensive imperial terrain. He is author of *Imperial Networks: Creating Identities in Nineteenth-Century South Africa and Britain* (Routledge, 2001).

Cheryl McEwan is Lecturer in Human Geography at the University of Birmingham. Her research interests span cultural, feminist and postcolonial geographies. Her current research is concerned with gender and citizenship in postapartheid South Africa, as well as broader issues of globalization, culture, citizenship and identities in transnational spaces. She also has a longstanding interest in the history and philosophy of geography, particularly in relation to feminism and postcolonialism. She is author of *Gendes, Geography and Empire* (Ashgate, 2000).

Mark McGuinness is Lecturer in Cultural Geography at Bath Spa University College. His research and teaching interests are an attempt to connect writings in cultural geography, cultural studies. He is currently working on a research project exploring the imaginative geographies of white working-class British migration into apartheid-era South Africa.

Karen M. Morin is Assistant Professor in the Department of Geography, Bucknell University, USA. She is a feminist historical geographer who primarily studies travel writing and gender relations in the context of nineteenth-century American and British imperialisms. She is currently working on a number of projects that link postcolonialism to the historical geography of the USA.

Richard Phillips is Lecturer in Geography at the European Studies Research Institute at the University of Salford. His publications include *Mapping Men and Empire: A Geography of Adventure* (Routledge, 1997) and, edited with Diane Watt and David Shuttleton, *De-centring Sexualities: Politics and Representations Beyond the Metropolis* (Routledge, 2000). He is currently writing a book on sexuality politics in the British Empire.

Marcus Power is Lecturer at the School of Geography, University of Leeds. His research focuses principally on Lusophone Africa and explores a range of interconnected issues relating to geo-politics, development and postcolonialism. These include the cultural politics of 'development' in African societies, the aftermath of state-socialism in the 'Global South' and the legacies of colonialism in Portugal and in former Portuguese colonies in Africa.

Jenny Robinson is Lecturer in Geography at the Open University, having previously worked at the LSE and the University of Natal, Durban. Her research centres on the relationship between power and space, specifically in cities and mostly in relation to South African politics. She has also written on issues in feminist politics, including questions of difference and methodology, and more recently on the implications of Julia Kristeva's psychoanalytic writing for feminist theorizations of space. Her current research is focused on the politics of urban development and the resources available for imagining urban futures in cities of poor countries.

James D. Sidaway is Associate Professor of Geography at the National University of Singapore. His current research focuses on transnational regional communities, reconfigurations of boundaries and sovereignties and the sociology of geographical knowledges. He is author of *Imagined Regional Communities: Integration and Sovereignty in the Global South* (Routledge, 2002).

John Wylie is Lecturer in the Department of Geography at the University of Sheffield. His research focuses upon historical and contemporary cultures of travel and exploration. He is currently interested in phenomenological approaches to issues of landscape, perception and embodiment, and how these may configure relations between the self and nature.

INDEX